PROFESSIONAL

HTML5 Mobile Game Development

Pascal Rettig

WILEY

John Wiley & Sons, Inc.

Professional HTML5 Mobile Game Development

Published by
John Wiley & Sons, Inc.
10475 Crosspoint Boulevard
Indianapolis, IN 46256
www.wiley.com

Copyright © 2012 by Pascal Rettig

Published by John Wiley & Sons, Inc., Indianapolis, Indiana

Published simultaneously in Canada

ISBN: 978-1-118-30132-6
ISBN: 978-1-118-30133-3 (ebk)
ISBN: 978-1-118-42144-4 (ebk)
ISBN: 978-1-118-43394-2 (ebk)

Manufactured in the United States of America

10 9 8 7 6 5 4 3 2 1

For general information on our other products and services please contact our Customer Care Department within the United States at (877) 762-2974, outside the United States at (317) 572-3993 or fax (317) 572-4002.

Wiley publishes in a variety of print and electronic formats and by print-on-demand. Some material included with standard print versions of this book may not be included in e-books or in print-on-demand. If this book refers to media such as a CD or DVD that is not included in the version you purchased, you may download this material at http://booksupport.wiley.com. For more information about Wiley products, visit www.wiley.com.

Library of Congress Control Number: 2012942105

This book is dedicated to my wife, business partner, best friend, and all-around support system, Martha.
Thank You.

CREDITS

EXECUTIVE EDITOR
Carol Long

PROJECT EDITOR
Jennifer Lynn

TECHNICAL EDITOR
Chris Ullman

PRODUCTION EDITOR
Christine Mugnolo

COPY EDITOR
San Dee Phillips

EDITORIAL MANAGER
Mary Beth Wakefield

FREELANCER EDITORIAL MANAGER
Rosemarie Graham

ASSOCIATE DIRECTOR OF MARKETING
David Mayhew

MARKETING MANAGER
Ashley Zurcher

BUSINESS MANAGER
Amy Knies

PRODUCTION MANAGER
Tim Tate

VICE PRESIDENT AND EXECUTIVE GROUP PUBLISHER
Richard Swadley

VICE PRESIDENT AND EXECUTIVE PUBLISHER
Neil Edde

ASSOCIATE PUBLISHER
Jim Minatel

PROJECT COORDINATOR, COVER
Katie Crocker

COMPOSITOR
Jeff Lytle, Happenstance Type-O-Rama

PROOFREADER
Nancy Carrasco

INDEXER
Johnna VanHoose Dinse

COVER DESIGNER
Ryan Sneed

COVER IMAGE
© Daniel Schweinert / iStockPhoto

ABOUT THE AUTHOR

PASCAL RETTIG is a lifelong programmer who got his start programming by writing BASIC games on the Apple II at the ripe age of 7. Pascal has a Bachelor of Science and a Master of Engineering in computer science and electrical engineering from the Massachusetts Institute of Technology '02 and has been hacking and building stuff on the web since 1995. Pascal built the HTML5 game-based language learning system GamesForLanguage.com in 2011 and is currently a partner at the interactive web agency Cykod. He organizes one of the country's oldest monthly HTML5 Game Development meetups in Boston each month and runs the HTML5 Game Development news site html5gamedevelopment.org.

ABOUT THE TECHNICAL EDITOR

CHRIS ULLMAN is a senior software developer at MIG, specializing in .NET, and a technical editor/author, who has spent many years stewing in web-related technologies, like a teabag left too long in the pot. Coming from a computer science background, he gravitated toward MS solutions during the summer of ASP (1997). He cut his teeth on Wrox Press ASP guides, and since then he has edited or contributed to more than 30 books, most notably as lead author for Wrox's bestselling *Beginning ASP/ASP.NET 1.x/2* series. These days he lives out on the moors of Cornwall and spends his non-computing time running, writing music, and attempting with his wife, Kate, to curb the enthusiasm of three very boisterous children.

ACKNOWLEDGMENTS

I'D LIKE TO THANK MY WIFE, Martha, who not only had to put up with me spending every moment of free time I had writing this book (while working on two startups) but also was gracious enough to design all the custom game art used in this book, ensuring that readers aren't stuck with the dreaded curse of programmer art.

I'd also like to thank my family for supporting me in this endeavor and continuing to accept me as a family member despite my best efforts to lock myself away for the duration.

I'd like to particularly thank my editors, Carol Long, Jennifer Lynn, and San Dee Phillips, for helping a newbie author through the process of turning some pages of code into a cohesive book; and technical reviewer Chris Ullman, who did his best to ensure this book made it to print as error-free as possible.

Lastly, I'd like to thank the Boston HTML5 Game Development community. Boston has an incredible technology community, and being around such motivated, smart people keeps me learning, energized, and constantly hacking away at new projects.

CONTENTS

INTRODUCTION

THE GAMING WORLD AND THE WEB have been on a collision course with each other since social games began bringing gaming to the masses and helped make what was once a subculture a mainstream, mass-market phenomenon. Throw mobile into the mix and suddenly you have a massive phenomenon that is going to become more important as more devices get into people's hands.

For example, one story making its way around the web as of this writing is that game developer Rovio, creator of the *Angry Birds* franchise, is estimated to be worth approximately 8 billion dollars, almost the same as venerable phone maker Nokia. These days people spend more time on their phones and tablets than ever before, and games (in addition to social networks) account for a significant portion of that time. Smartphones and tablets are significantly displacing dedicated mobile gaming devices from Nintendo and Sony. With HTML5, game developers now have technology that has the capability to reach more people than ever imaginable from a single codebase.

HTML5 mobile game development is currently a new technology that people aren't sure what to make of yet, much like smartphone games were in 2008 when the Apple App Store launched. However, there are some serious heavyweights pushing for the success of HTML5 gaming. Facebook, which launched its App Center in May 2012, has made HTML5-based Web Apps first-class citizens on mobile and is looking for ways to monetize on mobile and get out from underneath the thumb of the 30% fee Apple takes for in-app purchases in its app store. Carriers such as AT&T similarly view web apps as a way to recapture revenue lost to Google and Apple.

All is not rosy in the HTML5 game development picture, however. Different devices have different capabilities, levels of performance, and screen resolutions, and navigating the dangerous waters of mobile HTML5 game development requires some careful sailing. That's where this book comes in. Its goal is to provide a pragmatic roadmap to build mobile games in HTML5, covering both the possibilities and limitations of the medium. If HTML5 game development on the desktop is still in its infancy, mobile HTML5 game development is still embryonic. The possibilities to do great things are within reach, but the first smash success in the medium is still to be seen.

Getting into a technology at an early stage can provide significant benefits. One of the wonderful things in working in new technologies is that the noise level is minimal, and less is required to generate a splash than in other established mediums. HTML5 games, especially mobile ones, have budgets that are tiny fractions of the millions of dollars that standard PC and console games have, and yet they have the opportunity to create a smash hit in an instant due to the viral nature of the web. Mobile HTML5 games have even more potential for explosive growth because they can be shared instantly with a link rather than requiring the recipients to download an app that might not be available for their device from an app store.

This book is a journey through the world of possibilities that the exciting realm of HTML5 mobile game development presents and I hope you'll jump aboard.

WHO THIS BOOK IS FOR

This book is for anyone who wants to build interactive games in a browser using standards-based, plug-in-free technology. It has a focus on mobile game development because this is where HTML5 has an advantage versus competing web technologies such as Flash, but the games you build will be playable on desktop browsers as well.

Developing games for mobile HTML5 requires cross-disciplinary skills over a range of different mediums. To do it right you must have a basic grasp of the JavaScript language because you'll be pushing JavaScript to its limits to build games in the browser. This book does not try to teach you JavaScript from the ground up, but instead relies on a basic understanding of the language to cover ground quickly.

If you don't use JavaScript on a daily basis, you may find some spots of code hard to follow. All is not lost however—if you want to get up to speed on JavaScript quickly, Douglas Crockford's seminal work on JavaScript called *JavaScript: The Good Parts*" (O'Reilly, 2008) is only 180 pages and can familiarize you with the language and can be used as a reference when techniques you might not be familiar with are mentioned in this book.

If you are a desktop game developer more familiar with C++ than JavaScript, you can follow along with the text, but again because JavaScript (despite its C-like syntax) has more in common with Lisp than C++, you may want to review the Crockford book as well. JavaScript's weak typing, mutable method bindings, and closure support may cause some confusion.

ActionScript developers coming from building games in Flash should feel right at home. The only major stumbling block is that HTML5 Game development is more disjointed than Flash. Make sure you pay close attention to Chapter 7, "Learning About Your HTML5 Game Development Environment," because that chapter shows you how to inspect and debug JavaScript, so you don't feel lost when something goes wrong in your game. Browsers have powerful script-debuggers built in, so you shouldn't miss the Flash IDE too much.

WHAT THIS BOOK COVERS

This book covers creating games using HTML5 that run on HTML5-capable smartphones such as iOS devices and Android. Windows phone 7.5, which supports Canvas, is also targeted in some instances, but because its Canvas performance is restrictive and doesn't support the standards-based multitouch events, support for the Windows phone is limited in some cases.

You can get the most out of this book if you target mobile Safari on iOS 5.0 and up and Chrome for Android on Android 4.0 and up because these devices both have fast JavaScript engines and hardware-accelerated Canvas support. Many of the games run on older versions of Android, but performance will be limited.

HOW THIS BOOK IS STRUCTURED

This book is comprised of seven sections, each with a special purpose to teach you about mobile HTML5 game development.

Part I, "Diving In," teaches you over the course of three chapters how to build a mobile HTML5 game from scratch that runs on any device that supports canvas. It shows the nitty-gritty of what's required to get a game up and running quickly without pulling in any external libraries.

Part II, "Mobile HTML5," takes a step back and covers in detail the state of HTML5 on mobile devices along with a couple of libraries—jQuery and Underscore.js—that you use to build games in the rest of the book.

Part III, "JavaScript Game Dev Basics," first walks you through how to inspect and debug your game and how to run JavaScript from the command line using Node.js. It then goes through the process to build a reusable HTML5 game engine from the ground up, showing how you can structure and organize your code into coherent modules.

Part IV, "Building Games with CSS3 and SVG," takes a detour from canvas to show you how to use two other technologies—CSS3 and Scalable Vector Graphics (SVG)—to build games on mobile devices. Chapter 14, "Building Games with SVG and Physics," also introduces the popular JavaScript Physics engine Box2D.

Part V, "HTML5 Canvas," first covers the canvas tag in detail and then proceeds to build a touch-friendly 2-D platformer and a level editor for that platformer to build levels.

Part VI, "Multiplayer Gaming," shows how you can create games that can provide a meaningful interaction among players, asynchronously and in real-time using WebSockets.

Part VII, "Mobile Enhancements," examines how to use some of the additional HTML5-family of APIs to enhance your game, covering geolocation and device orientation as well as covering the state of HTML5 sound on mobile devices.

Part VIII, "Game Engines and App Stores," surveys the landscape of game engines available for HTML5—both commercial and open-source—and helps you decide which engine is appropriate. It also covers emerging technologies that enable you to publish hardware-accelerated HTML5 games into the native mobile App stores.

WHAT YOU NEED TO USE THIS BOOK

The samples in this book run on modern desktop browsers in Windows, OS X, or Linux. The term *modern desktop browsers* refers to Internet Explorer versions 9 and up, and up-to-date versions of Safari, Firefox, or Chrome.

If you want to run the samples on a mobile device, for best results you need an iOS device running iOS 5.0 or greater or an Android device running Android 4.0 or newer. Many of the examples work on Android 2.2 and above, but performance may be limited.

If you run on a Mac, you can run a number of the examples via the iOS simulator that can be installed with XCode. Android simulators are unfortunately too slow currently to be a good test bed for running HTML5 games.

CONVENTIONS

To help you get the most from the text and keep track of what's happening, we've used a number of conventions throughout the book.

> **WARNING** *Boxes like this one hold important, not-to-be-forgotten information that is directly relevant to the surrounding text.*

> **NOTE** *Notes, Tips, hints, and tricks are offest and placed in italics like this.*

SIDEBAR

Asides to the current discussion are offset like this.

As for styles in the text:

➤ We *highlight* new terms and important words when we introduce them.

➤ We show keyboard strokes like this: Ctrl+A.

➤ We show filenames, URLs, and code within the text like so: `persistence.properties`.

➤ We present code in two different ways:

```
We use a monofont type with no highlighting for most code examples.
We use boldface to emphasize code that is particularly important in the
present context.
```

SOURCE CODE

As you work through the examples in this book, you may choose either to type in all the code manually or to use the source code files that accompany the book. All the source code used in this book is available for download at www.wrox.com. At the site, simply locate the book's title (either by using the Search box or by using one of the title lists) and click the Download Code link on the book's detail page to obtain all the source code for the book.

> **NOTE** *Because many books have similar titles, you may find it easiest to search by the ISBN; this book's ISBN is 978-1-118-30132-6.*

After you download the code, decompress it with your favorite compression tool. Alternatively, you can go to the main Wrox code download page at www.wrox.com/dynamic/books/download.aspx to see the code available for this book and all other Wrox books.

ERRATA

We make every effort to ensure that there are no errors in the text or in the code. However, no one is perfect, and mistakes do occur. If you find an error in one of our books, like a spelling mistake or faulty piece of code, we would be grateful for your feedback. By sending in errata you may save another reader hours of frustration and at the same time you can help us provide even higher quality information.

To find the errata page for this book, go to www.wrox.com and locate the title using the Search box or one of the title lists. Then, on the book details page, click the Book Errata link. On this page, you can view all errata that has been submitted for this book and posted by Wrox editors. A complete book list, including links to each book's errata, is also available at www.wrox.com/misc-pages/booklist.shtml.

> **NOTE** *A complete book list including links to errata is also available at* www.wrox.com/misc-pages/booklist.shtml.

If you don't spot "your" error on the Book Errata page, click on the Errata Form link and complete the form to send us the error you have found. We'll check the information and, if appropriate, post a message to the book's errata page and fix the problem in subsequent editions of the book.

P2P.WROX.COM

For author and peer discussion, join the P2P forums at p2p.wrox.com. The forums are a web-based system for you to post messages relating to Wrox books and related technologies and interact with other readers and technology users. The forums offer a subscription feature to e-mail you topics of interest of your choosing when new posts are made to the forums. Wrox authors, editors, other industry experts, and your fellow readers are present on these forums.

At p2p.wrox.com you can find a number of different forums to help you not only as you read this book, but also as you develop your own applications. To join the forums, just follow these steps:

1. Go to p2p.wrox.com and click the Register link.

2. Read the terms of use and click Agree.

3. Complete the required information to join, as well as any optional information you want to provide, and click Submit.

4. You will receive an e-mail with information describing how to verify your account and complete the joining process.

> **NOTE** *You can read messages in the forums without joining P2P, but to post your own messages, you must join.*

After you join, you can post new messages and respond to messages other users post. You can read messages at any time on the web. If you would like to have new messages from a particular forum e-mailed to you, click the Subscribe to This Forum icon by the forum name in the forum listing.

For more information about how to use the Wrox P2P, read the P2P FAQs for answers to questions about how the forum software works as well as many common questions specific to P2P and Wrox books. To read the FAQs, click the FAQ link on any P2P page.

PART I
Diving In

Flying Before You Walk

WHAT'S IN THIS CHAPTER?

➤ Creating the HTML5 for a game

➤ Loading images and drawing on canvas

➤ Setting up your game's structure

➤ Creating an animated background

➤ Listening for user input

WROX.COM CODE DOWNLOADS FOR THIS CHAPTER

The wrox.com code downloads for this chapter are found at www.wrox.com/remtitle .cgi?isbn=9781118301326 on the Download Code tab. The code is in the chapter 01 download and individually named according to the names throughout the chapter.

INTRODUCTION

Games have long been a medium that pushes technology to its limits. This book continues that proud tradition by taking the core technologies of the web—HTML, CSS, and JavaScript—and pushing them to the edges of their capabilities and performance. HTML5 as a game medium has come a long way capability-wise in a short amount of time, and many people believe in-browser gaming will be one of the primary distribution mechanisms for games in the coming years.

Even though it's not an environment originally designed for creating games, HTML5 is actually a nice, high-level environment for doing just that. So, in lieu of trying to abstract away all the boilerplate by building an engine immediately, you can get right to the good stuff: a one-off game built from the ground up on HTML5—a top-down 2-D space shooter called *Alien Invasion*.

BUILDING A COMPLETE GAME IN 500 LINES

To drive home the point of how easy it is to build games in HTML5, the final game you build in the first three chapters contains fewer than 500 lines of code, all without using any libraries.

Understanding the Game

Alien Invasion is a top-down 2-D shooter game built in the spirit of the game *1942* (but in space) or a simplified version of *Galaga*. The player controls a ship, shown at the bottom of the screen, flying the ship vertically through an endless space field while defending Earth against an incoming hoard of aliens.

When played on a mobile device, control is via left and right arrows shown on the bottom left of the screen, and a Fire button on the right. When played on the desktop, the user can use the keyboard's arrow keys to fly and the spacebar to fire.

To compensate for all the different screen sizes of mobile devices, the game resizes the play area to always play at the size of the device. On the desktop it plays in a rectangular area in the middle of the browser page.

Structuring the Game

Nearly every game of this type consists of a few of the same pieces: some asset loading, a title screen, sprites, user input, collision detection, and a game loop to tie it all together.

The game uses as few formal structures as possible. Instead of building explicit classes, you take advantage of JavaScript's dynamic typing (more on this in the section "Building Object-Oriented JavaScript"). Languages such as C, C++, and Java are called "strongly typed" because you need to be very explicit about the type of parameters that you pass around to method. This means you need to explicitly define base classes and interfaces when you want to pass different types of objects to the same method. JavaScript is weakly (or dynamically) typed because the language doesn't enforce the types of parameters. This means you define your objects more loosely, adding methods to each object as needed, without building a bunch of base classes or interfaces.

Image asset handling is dead simple. You load a single image, called a *sprite sheet*, that contains all your game's sprite images in a single PNG and execute a callback after that image loads. The game also has a single method for drawing a sprite onto your canvas.

The title screen renders a sprite for the main title and shows the same animated starfield from the main game moving in the background.

The game loop is also simple. You have an object that you can treat as the current scene, and you can tell that scene to update itself and then to draw itself. This is a simple abstraction that works for both title and end game screens as well as the main part of the game.

User input can use a few event listeners for keyboard input and a few "zones" on your canvas to detect touch input. You can use the HTML standard method `addEventListener` to support both of these.

Lastly, for collision detection, you punt the hard stuff and just loop over the bounding boxes of each of the objects to detect a collision. This is a slow and naive way to implement collision detection, but it's simple to implement and works reasonably well as long as the number of sprites you check against is small.

The Final Game

To get a sense of where the game is headed, check out Figure 1-1, and visit `http://cykod.github.com/AlienInvasion/` on both a desktop browser and whatever mobile device you have handy. The game should run on any smartphone that supports HTML5 canvas; however, canvas performance on Android versions before Ice Cream Sandwich is poor.

Now, it's time to get started.

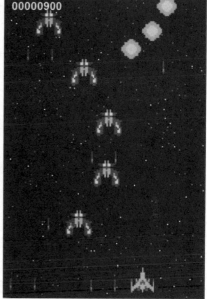

FIGURE 1-1: The final game.

ADDING THE BOILERPLATE HTML AND CSS

The main boilerplate for an HTML5 file is minimal. You get a valid HTML file with a `<canvas>` element inside of a `container` centered on the page, as shown in Listing 1-1.

LISTING 1-1: Boilerplate game HTML

```html
<!DOCTYPE HTML>
<html lang="en">
<head>
  <meta charset="UTF-8"/>
<title>Alien Invasion</title>
  <link rel="stylesheet" href="base.css" type="text/css" />
</head>
<body>
  <div id='container'>
    <canvas id='game' width='320' height='480'></canvas>
  </div>
  <script src='game.js'></script>
</body>
</html>
```

The only external files so far are the `base.css` file, an external style sheet, and a nonexistent `game.js` file that will contain the JavaScript code for the game. Drop the HTML from Listing 1-1 into a new directory, and call it **index.html**.

In `base.css` you need two separate sections. The first is a CSS reset. CSS resets make sure all elements look the same in all browsers and any per-element styling and padding is removed. To do this, the reset sets the size of all elements to 100% (16 pixels for fonts) and removes all padding, borders, and margins. The reset used is the well-known Eric Meyer reset: `http://meyerweb.com/eric/tools/css/reset/`.

You can simply copy the CSS code verbatim to the top of `base.css`.

Next, you need to add two additional styles to the CSS file, as shown in Listing 1-2.

LISTING 1-2: Base canvas and container styles

```css
/* Center the container */
#container {
  padding-top:50px;
  margin:0 auto;
  width:480px;
}
/* Give canvas a background */
canvas {
  background-color: black;
}
```

The first container style gives the container a little padding at the top of the page and centers its content in the middle of the page. The second style gives the canvas element a black background.

GETTING STARTED WITH CANVAS

You hopefully noticed a `canvas` tag in the middle of the HTML on the page (as shown in Listing 1-2):

```html
<canvas id='game' width='320' height='480'></canvas>
```

This is where all the action for the game takes place—so much exciting stuff you can do in such an unassuming tag.

The tag has an `id` for easy reference along with a `width` and `height`. Unlike most HTML elements, you generally never want to add a CSS `width` and `height` onto canvas elements. Those styles visually resize your canvas but do not affect the pixel dimensions of the canvas, which is controlled by the `width` and `height` on the element. Most of the time you should leave these alone.

Accessing the Context

Before you can do any drawing onto canvas, you need to fetch the context from the `canvas` element. The context is the object that you actually make API calls against (not the `canvas` element itself.) For 2-D canvas games, you can pull out the 2-D context, as shown in Listing 1-3.

LISTING 1-3: Accessing the rendering context

```javascript
var canvas = document.getElementById('game');

var ctx = canvas.getContext && canvas.getContext('2d');
if(!ctx) {
    // No 2d context available, let the user know
    alert('Please upgrade your browser');
```

```
  } else {
    startGame();
  }
  function startGame() {
   // Let's get to work
  }
```

First, grab the element from the document. These initial chapters use built-in browser methods for all DOM (Document Object Model) interaction; later you are introduced to how to do the same things more concisely using jQuery.

Next, call `getContext` on the `canvas` element. A double-ampersand (`&&`) short circuit operator protects you from calling a nonexistent method. This is used in the next `if` statement in case the visiting browser doesn't support the `canvas` element. You always want to "fail loudly" in this case, so the players correctly blame their browser instead of your code. "Failing loudly" means that instead of "failing silently" with a white screen and an error hiding on the JavaScript console, the game explicitly pops up with a message that tells the user that something went wrong.

There is a 3-D WebGL-powered rendering context available on desktop browsers (excluding Internet Explorer), but it is called `glcanval` and is available only on mobile Nokia devices at the time of this writing. WebGL is another standard, separate from HTML5, that allows you to use hardware-accelerated 3-D graphics in the browser.

Add the code from Listing 1-3 to a file named `game.js`. You now can start playing with the `canvas` element.

Drawing on Canvas

This initial tutorial doesn't use any of the vector-based drawing routines, but for the sake of getting something up on the screen quickly, you can draw a rectangle on the page. Modify the `startGame()` method of your `game.js` file to read as follows:

```
function startGame() {
    ctx.fillStyle = "#FFFF00";
    ctx.fillRect(50,100,380,400);
}
```

To draw a filled rectangle, you use the `fillRect` method on the `ctx` object, but first you need to set a fill style. You can pass in standard CSS color representations as strings to `fillStyle`, including hexadecimal colors, RGB triples, or RGBA quads.

To layer a semitransparent rectangle on top of the existing one, add the following:

```
function startGame() {
    ctx.fillStyle = "#FFFF00";
    ctx.fillRect(50,100,380,400);
    // Second, semi-transparent blue rectangle
    ctx.fillStyle = "rgba(0,0,128,0.5);";
    ctx.fillRect(0,50,380,400);
}
```

If you add the preceding code and reload your `index.html` file, you see a nice, big blue rectangle smack dab in the middle of your black canvas.

Drawing Images

Alien Invasion is an old-school, top-down 2-D shooter game with retro-looking bitmap graphics. Luckily canvas provides an easy method called `drawImage` that comes in a couple of flavors, depending upon whether you want to draw an entire image or just a portion of an image.

The only complication is that, to draw those graphics, the game needs to load the image first. This isn't a huge deal because browsers are handy at loading images; however, they load them asynchronously, so you need to wait for a callback to let you know that the image is ready to go.

Make sure you have copied the `sprites.png` file over from the book assets for Chapter 1 into an `images/` directory underneath your current game, and then add the code from Listing 1-4 to the bottom of your `startGame` function.

LISTING 1-4: Drawing images with canvas (canvas/game.js)

```
function startGame() {
  ctx.fillStyle = "#FFFF00";
  ctx.fillRect(50,100,380,400);

  // Second, semi-transparent blue rectangle
  ctx.fillStyle = "rgba(0,0,128,0.8);";
  ctx.fillRect(25,50,380,400);

  var img = new Image();
  img.onload = function() {
    ctx.drawImage(img,100,100);
  }
  img.src = 'images/sprites.png';
}
```

If you reload the page, you should now see the sprite sheet layered on top of your rectangles. See `canvas/game.js` in the chapter code for the complete code. You can see the code first waits for the `onload` callback before trying to draw the image onto the context and then sets the `src` after setting up the callback. The order is important because Internet Explorer does not trigger the `onload` callback if the image is cached if you reverse the order of the two lines. You can see the results—admittedly not pretty—in Figure 1-2.

This first example uses the simplest `drawImage` method—one that takes an image and an *x* and *y* coordinate and then draws the entire image on the canvas.

Modify the `drawImage` line to read as follows:

```
var img = new Image();
img.onload = function() {
  ctx.drawImage(img,100,100,200,200);
}
img.src = 'images/sprites.png';
```

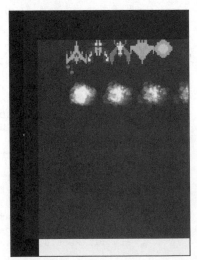

FIGURE 1-2: The spritesheet and drawn rectangles.

The image has now shrunk down to the size of the extra parameters that you passed in which are the destination width and height. This is a second form of `drawImage` that enables you to scale images up or down to any dimensions.

The last form of `drawImage`, however, is the one that you'll use the most often with bitmapped games. It is also the most complicated and takes a total of nine parameters:

```
drawImage(image, sx, sy, sWidth, sHeight, dx, dy, dWidth, dHeight)
```

This form enables you to specify a source rectangle in the image using parameters `sx`, `sy`, `sWidth`, and `sHeight` and a destination rectangle on the canvas using parameters `dx`, `dy`, `dWidth`, and `dHeight`. As you've probably figured out, to pull out an individual frame from one of the sprites in the sprite sheet, this is the format you want to use. Now give it a shot by changing the call to `drawImage` to:

```
var img = new Image();
img.onload = function() {
  ctx.drawImage(img,18,0,18,25,100,100,18,25);
}
img.src = 'images/sprites.png';
```

If you reload the page, you see there's now a single instance of the player ship on the canvas. So far so good. In the next section, you start to build out the structure for an actual game.

IMMEDIATE VERSUS RETAINED MODE

Canvas is a tool for creating games in what's commonly referred to as *Immediate mode*. When you use canvas, all you are doing is drawing pixels onto the page. Canvas doesn't know anything about your spaceships or missiles that fly around. All it cares about are pixels, and most canvas games clear the canvas completely between frames and redraw everything at an updated position.

Contrast this with using the DOM to create a game. Using the DOM would be equivalent to creating a game in Retained mode, as the browser keeps track of the "scene graph" for you. This scene graph keeps track of the position and hierarchy of objects. Instead of starting from scratch in each frame, you need to adjust only the elements that have changed and the browser takes care of rendering everything correctly. Which is better? Well, it depends on your game. See the discussion in Chapter 12, "Building Games in CSS3," to learn when to use which method.

CREATING YOUR GAME'S STRUCTURE

The code built so far has been a good way to exercise the canvas capabilities you'll be using, but it will need to be reorganized to turn it into a useful structure for a game. Now take a step back to look at some of the patterns you want to use putting together the game.

Building Object-Oriented JavaScript

JavaScript is an object-oriented (OO) language. As such, most elements in JavaScript are objects including strings, arrays, functions and, well, objects are objects in the OO sense.

But this doesn't mean that JavaScript has all the trappings of *object-oriented programming* (OOP) that you might expect. First, it doesn't have a classical inheritance model. Second, it doesn't have a standard constructor mechanism, relying instead on either constructor functions or object literals.

Instead of classical inheritance, JavaScript implements *prototypical inheritance,* meaning you can create an object that represents the prototype, or blueprint, for a set of descendant objects that all share the same base functionality

CLASSICAL VERSUS PROTOTYPICAL INHERITANCE

Most popular object-oriented languages used today, including Java and C++, rely on classical inheritance, which means object behavior is defined by creating explicit classes and instantiating objects from those classes. JavaScript has a much more fluid method of defining classes based on the idea of prototypes, which means you create an actual object that behaves the way you want and then create child objects off of that.

Because methods are just regular JavaScript objects, many times developers also simply copy attributes from other objects to fake Java-style interfaces or multiple inheritance. This flexibility shouldn't necessarily be viewed as a problem; rather, it means that developers have a lot of flexibility for how to create objects and can pick the best method for the specific use case.

Alien Invasion uses constructor functions combined with prototypical inheritance where it makes sense. Using object prototypes can make object creation up to 50 times faster and provides memory savings, but it is also more restricting because you can't use closures to access and protect data. *Closures* are a feature of JavaScript that allows you to keep variables in a method around for later use even when a method has finished execution.

Chapter 9, "Bootstrapping the Quintus Engine: Part I," discusses object-creation patterns in more detail, but for now just realize that the use of different methods is intentional.

Taking Advantage of Duck Typing

There's a famous saying that if it walks like a duck and talks like a duck, then it must be a duck. When programming in strongly-typed languages, there's no doubt whether it's a duck—it must be an instance of the "Duck" class, or if you program in Java, implement the iDuck interface.

In JavaScript, a dynamically-typed language, parameters, and references are not type-checked, meaning you can pass any type of object as a parameter to any function, and that function happily treats that object like the type of whatever object it was expecting until something blows up.

This flexibility can be both a good and a bad thing. It's a bad thing when you end up with cryptic error messages or errors during run time. It's a good thing when you use that flexibility to keep a shallow inheritance tree but can still share code. The idea of using objects based on their external interface rather than their type is called *duck typing*.

Alien Invasion uses this idea in a couple of places: game screens and sprites. The game treats anything that responds to method calls of step() and draw() as valid game screen objects or valid sprites. Using duck typing for game screens enables *Alien Invasion* to treat title screens and in-game screens as the same type of object, making it easy to switch between levels and title screens. Similarly, using duck typing for sprites means that the game can be flexible with what can be added to a game board, including the player, enemies, projectiles, and HUD elements. HUD, which is short for Heads Up Display, is the term commonly used for elements that sit on top of the game, such as number of lives left and the player's score.

Creating the Three Principle Objects

The game needs three principle, mostly persistent objects: a Game object tying everything together; a SpriteSheet object for loading and drawing sprites; and a GameBoard object for displaying, updating, and handling the collision of sprite elements. The game also needs a gaggle of different sprites such as the player, enemies, missiles, and HUD objects, such as the score and number of remaining lives, but those are introduced individually later.

LOADING THE SPRITESHEET

You have already seen most of the code necessary to load a sprite sheet and display sprites on the page. All that remains is to extract the functionality into a package. One enhancement puts in a map of sprite names to their locations to make it easier to draw the sprites on the screen. A second enhancement encapsulates the onload callback functionality to hide the details from any calling classes.

Listing 1-5 shows the entire class.

LISTING 1-5: The SpriteSheet class

```
var SpriteSheet = new function() {
  this.map = { };
  this.load = function(spriteData,callback) {
    this.map = spriteData;
    this.image = new Image();
    this.image.onload = callback;
    this.image.src = 'images/sprites.png';
  };
  this.draw = function(ctx,sprite,x,y,frame) {
    var s = this.map[sprite];
    if(!frame) frame = 0;
    ctx.drawImage(this.image,
                  s.sx + frame * s.w,
                  s.sy,
                  s.w, s.h,
                  x,   y,
                  s.w, s.h);
  };
}
```

Although the class is short and has only two methods, it does have a number of things to note. First, because there can be only one SpriteSheet object, the object is created with

```
new function() { ... }
```

This puts the constructor function and the new operator on the same line, ensuring that only one instance of this class is ever created.

Next, two parameters pass into the constructor. The first parameter, spriteData, passes in sprite data linking the rectangles of sprites to names. The second parameter, callback, passes as a callback to the image onload method.

The second method, draw, is the main workhorse of the class because it does the actual drawing of sprites onto a context. It takes as parameters the context, the string specifying the name of a sprite from the spriteData map, an *x* and *y* location to draw the sprite, and an optional *frame* for sprites with multiple frames.

The draw method uses those parameters to look up the spriteData in the map to get the source location of the sprite as well as the width and height. (For this simple SpriteSheet class, every frame of the sprite is expected to be the same size and on the same line.) It uses that information to figure out the parameters to the more complicated drawImage method, discussed in the "Drawing Images" section earlier in this chapter.

Although this code is designed to be a one-off and only useful for this specific game, you still need to separate the game data, such as the sprite data and levels, from the game engine to make it easier to test and build in pieces.

Add in the SpriteSheet to the top of a new file called engine.js file and replace the startGame function in game.js with the following code:

```
function startGame() {
  SpriteSheet.load({
    ship: { sx: 0, sy: 0, w: 18, h: 35, frames: 3 }
  },function() {
    SpriteSheet.draw(ctx,"ship",0,0);
    SpriteSheet.draw(ctx,"ship",100,50);
    SpriteSheet.draw(ctx,"ship",150,100,1);
  });
}
```

Here the StartGame function calls SpriteSheet.load and passes in the details for a couple of sprites. Next, in the callback function (after the images/sprites.png file loads) to test out the drawing function, it draws three sprites on the canvas.

Modify the bottom of your index.html file to load engine.js first and then game.js:

```
<body>
  <div id='container'>
    <canvas id='game' width='480' height='600'></canvas>
  </div>
  <script src='engine.js'></script>
  <script src='game.js'></script>
</body>
```

Check out sprite_sheet/index.html in the chapter code for the preceding example in a working form.

Now that the game can draw sprites on the page, you can set up the main game object to orchestrate everything else.

CREATING THE GAME OBJECT

The main game object is a one-off object called, perhaps not surprisingly, Game. Its main purpose is to initialize the game engine for *Alien Invasion* and run the game loop as well as provide a mechanism for changing the main scene that displays.

Because *Alien Invasion* doesn't have an input subsystem, the Game class is also responsible for setting up listeners for keyboard and touch input. To start, only keyboard input is handled; touch input is added in the next chapter.

Now that the game starts to take shape, a few additional considerations are necessary. Instead of just executing code willy-nilly when it is evaluated, it generally makes sense to wait for the page to finish downloading before initializing the game. The Game class takes this into consideration and listens for a "load" event from the window before booting up the game.

The code for the Game class will be added at the top of engine.js.

Implementing the Game Object

Now walk through the 40+ lines of code that make up the Game object a section at a time. (See the full listing at the top of game_class/engine.js in the chapter code.) The class starts off much like the SpriteSheet, as a one-time class instance:

```
var Game = new function() {
```

Next is the initialization routine, called with the ID of the canvas element to fill, the sprite data that is passed to the SpriteSheet, and the callback when the game is ready to start.

```
// Game Initialization
  this.initialize = function(canvasElementId,sprite_data,callback) {

    this.canvas = document.getElementById(canvasElementId);
    this.width = this.canvas.width;
    this.height= this.canvas.height;

    // Set up the rendering context
    this.ctx = this.canvas.getContext && this.canvas.getContext('2d');

    if(!this.ctx) { return alert("Please upgrade your browser to play"); }

    // Set up input
    this.setupInput();

    // Start the game loop
    this.loop();

    // Load the sprite sheet and pass forward the callback.
    SpriteSheet.load(sprite_data,callback);
  };
```

Much of this code should be familiar from earlier in the chapter. The parts where you grab the `canvas` element and check for a `2d` context are straightforward. Next is a call to `setupInput()`, which is discussed next. Finally, the game loop starts, and the data for the sprite sheet passes through to `SpriteSheet.load`.

The next section sets up input:

```
// Handle Input
var KEY_CODES = { 37:'left', 39:'right', 32 :'fire' };
this.keys = {};
this.setupInput = function() {
  window.addEventListener('keydown',function(e) {
    if(KEY_CODES[event.keyCode]) {
     Game.keys[KEY_CODES[event.keyCode]] = true;
     e.preventDefault();
    }
  },false);
  window.addEventListener('keyup',function(e) {
    if(KEY_CODES[event.keyCode]) {
     Game.keys[KEY_CODES[event.keyCode]] = false;
     e.preventDefault();
    }
  },false);
}
```

The main point of this block is to add event listeners for `keydown` and `keyup` events for those keys that you care about: specifically the left arrow, the right arrow, and the spacebar. For those events, the listeners translate a numeric Keycode to a friendlier identifier and update a hash called `Game.keys` to represent the current state of the user input. The player uses the `Game.keys` hash to control the ship. For keys used by the game, the event handlers also call `e.preventDefault()`, which prevents the browser from performing any default behavior in response to the key presses. (For the arrow keys and the spacebar, the browser would normally try to scroll the page.)

One more point about the preceding event handler code: It uses the W3C event model `addEventListener` method. This code is supported in current versions of the Chrome, Safari, and Firefox browsers, but only Internet Explorer (IE) versions 9 and above. This is not a huge deal because canvas isn't supported pre-IE9 in any case, but if you want to add compatibility for older browsers, it's something you need to be careful with. (The engine built starting in Chapter 9, "Bootstrapping the Quintus Engine Part I," uses jQuery's on method to enable easy browser-independent event attachment.)

The last section of the `Game` class is relatively short:

```
// Game Loop
var boards = [];
this.loop = function() {
  var dt = 30/1000;
  for(var i=0, len = boards.length;i<len;i++) {
    if(boards[i]) {
      boards[i].step(dt);
      boards[i] && boards[i].draw(Game.ctx);
    }
  }
  setTimeout(Game.loop,30);
```

```
    };

    // Change an active game board
    this.setBoard = function(num,board) { boards[num] = board; };
};
```

The `boards` are the pieces of the game updated and drawn onto the canvas. An example of a board might be a background or a title screen. (In the next chapter, you create a special board for handling sprites.) The `Game.loop` function loops through all the boards, checks if there is a board at that index, and if so, calls that board's `step` method with the approximate number of seconds that have passed, followed by calling the board's `draw` method, passing in the rendering context. For the `draw` call, the step call may have removed the board, so checking again that the board exists with `boards[i] &&` keeps the code from blowing up. Finally, `setTimeout` is used in the loop function to ensure that the loop runs again in 30 milliseconds. Using `setTimout` instead of `setInterval` ensures that timer events don't back up if the game slows down, which could lead to strange warp-like behavior. Because `setTimeout` doesn't retain the context of the called function, `Game.loop` needs to explicitly refer to the `Game` object instead of using the `this` keyword.

TIMER METHODS

There's more to JavaScript timers for game development than just `setTimeout` or `setInterval`. Chapter 9 discusses the `requestAnimationFrame` method that enables the browser to sync calls to your game with screen updates. Also, hard coding the amount of time that has passed to a fixed number is generally a bad idea as the timer may be called at different intervals depending on browser performance, but it should be okay for this simple type of game.

Because boards drop from index 0 to the highest index, background boards (such as the starfield in the next section) should be added to lower indexes, whereas elements added at the end, such as the score and HUDs, should be drawn last.

Finally, the only method on the `Game` object that is called regularly during the game, `Game.setBoard`, is defined. All this method does is set one of the game boards used in the `loop` method. It is used to switch active `GameBoards`, which are used for title screens as well as the main section of the game.

Refactoring the Game Code

As you build games in the browser, you'll want to keep attention on the structure of what you're building. JavaScript is a very flexible language, and without some discipline in how your game is structured, things can fall apart quickly. A common pattern in this book will be to show you how to use an API or technique quickly and simply and then take some time to structure that code into a library or module.

The initial code for displaying a sprite on the screen in `game.js` is going to be replaced with code that does the same but is structured in a way to be usable in a more complicated game.

Update `game.js` to use the `Game` class. Remove anything you have in `game.js` and add the code shown in Listing 1-6.

LISTING 1-6: A refactored game.js method (game_class/game.js)

```
var sprites = {
 ship: { sx: 0, sy: 0, w: 18, h: 35, frames: 3 }
};
var startGame = function() {
    SpriteSheet.draw(Game.ctx,"ship",100,100,1);
}
window.addEventListener("load", function() {
  Game.initialize("game",sprites,startGame);
});
```

All this code does is set up the available sprites, create a dummy `startGame` function that draws a ship on the canvas to make sure everything is working correctly, and then listen for the load event on the window object to call the `Game.initialize` function with the appropriate arguments.

Reload your `index.html` file (or run the code example `game_class/index.html`) to see a lonesome ship hanging out near the canvas element.

ADDING A SCROLLING BACKGROUND

Are you crying out for something more interesting than boilerplate setup code? Here's the good news: From here on it gets much more interesting. Start by adding an animated starfield onto the page to give the game some space-like qualities.

You can create a scrolling starfield in a few ways, but in this case you need to be a little careful with the number of objects that get drawn on the screen because drawing too many sprites per frame slows down the game on mobile devices. One way around this is to create an offscreen canvas buffer, draw a bunch of random stars on that buffer, and then simply draw that starfield moving slowly down the canvas. You'll be limited to a few different layers of moving stars, but this effect should be good enough for a retro shooter.

> ### THE VAGARIES OF HTML5 PERFORMANCE
>
> The performance question isn't straightforward. One of the truisms of HTML5 is that you never know what method has better performance without trying it out. When deciding which way to implement a feature, your best bet is to go right to the source: Test it out! You can see the performance for different numbers of stars and ways to draw starfields at `http://jsperf.com/prerendered-starfield`. `JSPerf.com` is a great place to test your intuition. To see the results of the starfield test, scroll down the page and hit "Run Tests" to see the performance of the different runs. In this case, the answer isn't so cut and dry. Most desktops do better drawing individual stars, whereas iOS mobiles do better drawing the offscreen buffer, at the time of this writing at least. As canvas will get better hardware acceleration across the board in the near future, it seems like a safe bet that the fillrate limited offscreen buffer (as described in this section) will be substantially faster in the months and years to come.

Now break down a few of the necessary pieces before looking at the class as a whole. (You can skip to the end of the section to see the full class if you want to peek ahead.)

The `StarField` class needs to do three main things. The first is to create an offscreen canvas. This is actually quite easy because canvas is just a regular DOM element with two attributes, `width` and `height`, and can be created the same way as any other DOM elements:

```
var stars = document.createElement("canvas");
stars.width = Game.width;
stars.height = Game.height;
var starCtx = stars.getContext("2d");
```

Because the stars field needs to be the same size as the game's canvas, you can set the size by pulling out the `width` and `height` properties that were set in the `Game.initialize` method.

After you create the canvas, you can start drawing stars (or rectangles) onto it. The easiest way to do this is to call `fillRect` once for each star that needs to be drawn. A `for` loop combined with using `Math.random()` to generate a random *x* and *y* location gets the job done:

```
starCtx.fillStyle = "#FFF";
starCtx.globalAlpha = opacity;
for(var i=0;i<numStars;i++) {
    starCtx.fillRect(Math.floor(Math.random()*stars.width),
                     Math.floor(Math.random()*stars.height),
                     2,
                     2);
}
```

The only piece that hasn't been mentioned is the `globalAlpha` property. This property sets the level of opacity for the canvas element. Because there are multiple layers of stars moving at different speeds, a nice effect is to have the slower stars be slightly less bright than the faster moving ones to simulate their being farther away.

Next is the `draw` method. The `Starfield` needs to draw the entire canvas element containing the stars onto the game's canvas; however, because it will scroll constantly, it needs to be drawn twice: once for the top half and once for the bottom half. The method uses the starfield's offset, a number between zero and the height of the game to first draw whatever part of the starfield has been shifted off the bottom of the game back at the top, and then draws the bottom part.

```
this.draw = function(ctx) {
    var intOffset = Math.floor(offset);
    var remaining = stars.height - intOffset;
    if(intOffset > 0) {
      ctx.drawImage(stars,
              0, remaining,
              stars.width, intOffset,
              0, 0,
              stars.width, intOffset);
    }
    if(remaining > 0) {
      ctx.drawImage(stars,
              0, 0,
              stars.width, remaining,
              0, intOffset,
```

```
            stars.width, remaining);
    }
  }
```

The code looks slightly confusing because it uses the nine-parameter version of `drawImage` to draw the slices, but it's actually just slicing the starfield into a top half and a bottom half, and drawing the top half at the bottom of the game canvas and the bottom half at the top of the canvas.

Listing 1-7 shows the Starfield class in its entirety, which should go into the `game.js` file.

LISTING 1-7: The Starfield (starfield/game.js)

```javascript
var Starfield = function(speed,opacity,numStars,clear) {

  // Set up the offscreen canvas
  var stars = document.createElement("canvas");
  stars.width = Game.width;
  stars.height = Game.height;

  var starCtx = stars.getContext("2d");
  var offset = 0;

  // If the clear option is set,
  // make the background black instead of transparent
  if(clear) {
    starCtx.fillStyle = "#000";
    starCtx.fillRect(0,0,stars.width,stars.height);
  }
  // Now draw a bunch of random 2 pixel
  // rectangles onto the offscreen canvas
  starCtx.fillStyle = "#FFF";
  starCtx.globalAlpha = opacity;
  for(var i=0;i<numStars;i++) {
    starCtx.fillRect(Math.floor(Math.random()*stars.width),
                     Math.floor(Math.random()*stars.height),
                     2,
                     2);
  }
  // This method is called every frame
  // to draw the starfield onto the canvas
  this.draw = function(ctx) {
    var intOffset = Math.floor(offset);
    var remaining = stars.height - intOffset;
    // Draw the top half of the starfield
    if(intOffset > 0) {
      ctx.drawImage(stars,
               0, remaining,
               stars.width, intOffset,
               0, 0,
               stars.width, intOffset);
    }
    // Draw the bottom half of the starfield
    if(remaining > 0) {
      ctx.drawImage(stars,
```

```
                    0, 0,
                    stars.width, remaining,
                    0, intOffset,
                    stars.width, remaining);
        }
    }
    // This method is called to update
    // the starfield
    this.step = function(dt) {
        offset += dt * speed;
        offset = offset % stars.height;
    }
}
```

Only two parts haven't been discussed. The `step` function at the bottom gets called with the fraction of a second that has elapsed since the last call to step. All it needs to do is update the `offset` variable based on the elapsed time and the speed, and then use the modulus (%) operator to make sure the offset is between zero and the height of the `Starfield`.

There's also a conditional to check if the `clear` parameter is set. This parameter is used to fill the first layer of stars with a black fill. (Later layers need to be transparent so that they overlay over each other correctly.) This prevents the need to explicitly clear the canvas between frames and saves some processing time.

To see the starfield in action, you need to modify your `startGame` function in `game.js` to add some starfields. Modify it to add three starfields of varying opacity by setting it to the following:

```
var startGame = function() {
    Game.setBoard(0,new Starfield(20,0.4,100,true))
    Game.setBoard(1,new Starfield(50,0.6,100))
    Game.setBoard(2,new Starfield(100,1.0,50));
}
```

Only the first starfield has the clear parameter set to `true`. Each starfield has a higher speed combined with a higher opacity than the last. This gives an effect of stars at different distances speeding by.

PUTTING IN A TITLE SCREEN

An animated starfield, although nice, isn't a game. To start to build out the same elements of the game, one of the first requirements for a game is to display a title screen showing the users what they can play.

The title screen for *Alien Invasion* isn't going to be anything special—just a text title and a subtitle. So a generic `GameScreen` class with a title and subtitle centered on the screen is enough to get the job done.

Drawing Text on Canvas

Drawing text on the canvas is straightforward and allows you to use any font loaded on the page. This flexibility means you can use any of the standard web-safe fonts as well as any fonts that have been loaded via `@font-face` onto the page.

The declarations for @font-face take some care because depending on the browsers that need to be supported, four different file formats need to be available. Luckily, if you aren't going to install the files locally, but rather serve them off an online service such as the free Google web fonts, all that's needed is a single linked style sheet. (You can browse the fonts available for free use at Google web fonts at (www.google.com/webfonts.)

For *Alien Invasion*, the font Bangers gives the game a nice retro "Invasion of the Body Snatchers" feel. Add the following line to your HTML (not your JavaScript) below the base.css link tag:

```
<head>
  <meta charset="UTF-8"/>
  <title>Alien Invasion</title>
  <link rel="stylesheet" href="base.css" type="text/css" />
  <link href='http://fonts.googleapis.com/css?family=Bangers'
   rel='stylesheet' type='text/css'>
</head>
```

Next, the game needs a TitleScreen class to display some text centered on the screen. To do this you must use a new canvas method that hasn't been discussed yet, fillText, and two new canvas properties, font and textAlign.

The current font used is set by passing a CSS style to context.font, for example:

```
ctx.font = "bold 25px Arial";
```

This declaration would set the current font used by both measureText and fillText to 25 pixels high, make it bold, and use the Arial font family.

To make sure the text is centered on a specific location horizontally, you'll need to set the context .textAlign property to center.

```
ctx.textAlign = "center";
```

After you calculate the location for the text and set the font style appropriately, you can use fillText to draw solid text onto the canvas:

```
fillText(string, x, y);
```

fillText takes the string to draw and an *x* and *y* location for the top-left corner.

Armed with these text-drawing methods, you now have the tools to draw a title screen that shows a title and a subtitle and calls an optional callback when the user presses the fire key.

Listing 1-8 shows the code to get that done. Add the TitleScreen class to the bottom of your engine.js file.

LISTING 1-8: The TitleScreen (titlescreen/engine.js)

```
var TitleScreen = function TitleScreen(title,subtitle,callback) {
  this.step = function(dt) {
    if(Game.keys['fire'] && callback) callback();
  };
```

```
    this.draw = function(ctx) {
      ctx.fillStyle = "#FFFFFF";
      ctx.textAlign = "center";

      ctx.font = "bold 40px bangers";
      ctx.fillText(title,Game.width/2,Game.height/2);

      ctx.font = "bold 20px bangers";
      ctx.fillText(subtitle,Game.width/2,Game.height/2 + 40);

    };
```

Similar to the `Starfield` object, `TitleScreen` defines a `step` and a `draw` method. The `step` method has only one task: to check if the fire key is pressed, and if so, call the callback that was passed in.

The `draw` does the majority of the actual work. First, it sets a `fillStyle` (white) that will be used on both the title and subtitle. Next, it sets the font for the title. You can horizontally center the title on the page by moving *x* to half the width of the canvas. Next is a call to `fillText` with this calculated *x* location and half the height of the canvas.

To draw the subtitle, the same calculation is repeated with a new font, and then the vertical position is offset by 40 pixels to place it below the title.

You now need to add the title screen onto the page as a new board above the background starfields. Modify your `startGame` method as shown, and add in a new callback called `playGame`:

```
var startGame = function() {
  Game.setBoard(0,new Starfield(20,0.4,100,true))
  Game.setBoard(1,new Starfield(50,0.6,100))
  Game.setBoard(2,new Starfield(100,1.0,50));
  Game.setBoard(3,new TitleScreen("Alien Invasion",
                                  "Press space to start playing",
                                  playGame));
}

var playGame = function() {
  Game.setBoard(3,new TitleScreen("Alien Invasion", "Game Started..."));
}
```

If you reload the browser, you should see a title screen, and after you press the spacebar, the title screen should update the subtitle to say "Game Started." The `playGame` function will be replaced with code to actually start to play the game in the next section.

ADDING A PROTAGONIST

The first step to turn *Alien Invasion* into an actual, playable game is to add a player-controlled ship. This is the first sprite that you add to the game. In the next chapter, you create a GameBoard class to manage the many sprites that are on the page at once during normal gameplay, but for now a single sprite is enough to start.

Creating the PlayerShip Object

The first step is to get a ship created and drawn on the page. Open up game.js and add the player ship class to the bottom:

```
var PlayerShip = function() {
    this.w =  SpriteSheet.map['ship'].w;
    this.h =  SpriteSheet.map['ship'].h;
    this.x = Game.width/2 - this.w / 2;
    this.y = Game.height - 10 - this.h;
    this.vx = 0;
    this.step = function(dt) {
      // TODO - added the next section
    }
    this.draw = function(ctx) {
      SpriteSheet.draw(ctx,'ship',this.x,this.y,1);
    }
}
```

Much like a game screen, a sprite has the same two external methods: step and draw. Keeping the interface consistent allows sprites and game screens to be mostly interchangeable. In initializing the sprite, a few more variables are set that give the sprite a position on the page and a height and a width. (The next chapter uses the position and height and width to do simple bounding box collision detection.)

The width and height of the sprite are pulled from the sprite sheet. Although you could hard-code the width and height here, using the dimensions from the sprite sheet mean there is only one location that needs to be changed if the dimensions need to be changed.

Next, modify the playGame function to read as follows:

```
var playGame = function() {
  Game.setBoard(3,new PlayerShip());
}
```

If you reload the index.html file and press the spacebar, you can see the player ship hanging out at the bottom of the page.

Handling User Input

The next task is to accept user input to allow the player to move the ship back and forth across the game. This is handled in the step function inside of PlayerShip.

The step function has three main parts. The first is to check for user input to update the ship's movement direction; the second is to update the x coordinate based on the direction; and finally the function needs to check that the updated x position is within the bounds of the screen. Replace the TODO comment in the preceding step method with the following code:

```
this.step = function(dt) {
  this.maxVel = 200;
  this.step = function(dt) {
    if(Game.keys['left']) { this.vx = -this.maxVel; }
    else if(Game.keys['right']) { this.vx = this.maxVel; }
```

```
      else { this.vx = 0; }

      this.x += this.vx * dt;

      if(this.x < 0) { this.x = 0; }
      else if(this.x > Game.width - this.w) {
        this.x = Game.width - this.w;
      }
    }
  }
}
```

The first part of the method checks the `Game.keys` map to see if the user is currently pressing the left or the right arrow keys, and if so sets the velocity to the correct positive or negative value. The second part of the code simply updates the *x* position with the current velocity multiplied by the fraction of a second since the last update. Finally, the method checks to see if the x position is either off the left side of the screen (less than zero) or off the right side of the screen (greater than the width of the screen minus the width of the ship). If either of those conditions is `true`, the value of *x* is modified to be within that range.

SUMMARY

You now know how to get the framework of an HTML5 game up-and-running, including loading a sprite sheet, drawing on canvas, adding in a parallax background, and taking in user input. At this point, you can fire up the `player/index.html` file and fly your ship left and right using the arrow keys. Congratulations! You're well on your way to having your first HTML5 game up-and-running. The next chapter builds on these initial pieces of code to add in enemies, levels, and the rest. Chapter 3, "Enhancing The Game," finishes this initial game by adding in mobile support.

Making It a Game

WHAT'S IN THIS CHAPTER?

➤ Exploring scene management

➤ Adding projectiles and enemies

➤ Using collision detection

➤ Creating explosions

WROX.COM CODE DOWNLOADS FOR THIS CHAPTER

The wrox.com code downloads for this chapter are found at www.wrox.com/remtitle .cgi?isbn=9781118301326 on the Download Code tab. The code is in the chapter 02 download and individually named according to the names throughout the chapter.

INTRODUCTION

In Chapter 1, "Flying Before You Walk," you put together the framework of your first HTML5 mobile game and got a spaceship flying around the screen. Until this point what's been built so far is more a toy than a game. To make it a game, you need to add some enemies and set up the various elements of the game so that they can interact with each other.

CREATING THE GAMEBOARD OBJECT

The first step to turning *Alien Invasion* into a game is to add a mechanism that handles a bunch of sprites on the page at the same time. The current Game object can handle a stack of boards, but those boards all act independently of each other. Also, although the Game object provides a mechanism to swap boards in and out, it doesn't make it easy to add an arbitrary number of sprites onto the page. Enter the GameBoard object.

Understanding the GameBoard

The purpose of the GameBoard object is much like the game board in a game of checkers. It provides a spot to drop all the pieces and dictates their movement. In this section you break down some of the responsibilities of this object. The responsibilities of the GameBoard can be broken down into four distinct categories:

➤ It is responsible for keeping a list of objects and handling adding sprites to and removing sprites from that list.

➤ It also needs to handle looping over that list of objects.

➤ It needs to respond the same way as previous boards. It needs to have a step and a draw function that calls the appropriate functions on each of the objects in the object list.

➤ It needs to handle checking of collisions between objects.

The next few sections walk through each of the parts of the GameBoard object, which will behave like a simple scene graph. Scene graphs are discussed in detail in Chapter 12, "Building Games with CSS3." The GameBoard class will be added to the bottom of the engine.js file.

Adding and Removing Objects

The first and most important responsibility of the GameBoard class is to keep track of the objects in play. The easiest way to keep track of a list of objects is simply to use an array, in this case an array called objects.

The GameBoard class will be described piecemeal, but the whole thing goes at the bottom of the engine.js file:

```
var GameBoard = function() {
  var board = this;
  // The current list of objects
  this.objects = [];
  this.cnt = [];
```

This array is where objects that show up in the game are added to and removed from.

Next, the class needs the capability to add objects. This is simple enough. Pushing objects onto the end of the objects' list gets most of the job done:

```
// Add a new object to the object list
this.add = function(obj) {
  obj.board=this;
  this.objects.push(obj);
  this.cnt[obj.type] = (this.cnt[obj.type] || 0) + 1;
  return obj;
};
```

For an object to interact with other objects, however, it needs access to the board it's a part of. For this reason when GameBoard.add is called, the board sets a property called board on the object. The object can now access the board to add additional objects, such as projectiles or explosions, or remove itself when it dies.

The board also must keep a count of the number of objects of different types that are active at a given time, so the second-to-last line of the function initializes the count to zero if necessary using a boolean OR and then increments that count by 1. Objects won't be assigned types until later in this chapter, so this is a little bit of forward-looking code.

Next is removal. This process is slightly more complicated than it first might seem because objects may want to remove themselves or other objects in the middle of a step while the GameBoard loops over the list of objects. A naive implementation would try to update GameBoard.objects but because the GameBoard would be in the middle of looping over all the objects, changing them mid-loop would cause problems with the looping code.

One option is to make a copy of the list of objects at the beginning of each frame, but this could get costly to do each frame. The best solution is to first mark objects for removal in a separate array and then actually remove them from the object list after every object has had its turn. Following is the solution GameBoard uses:

```
// Mark an object for removal
this.remove = function(obj) {
  var wasStillAlive = this.removed.indexOf(obj) != -1;
  if(wasStillAlive) { this.removed.push(obj);  }
  return wasStillAlive;
};

// Reset the list of removed objects
this.resetRemoved = function() { this.removed = []; }

// Remove objects marked for removal from the list
this.finalizeRemoved = function() {
  for(var i=0,len=this.removed.length;i<len;i++) {
    var idx = this.objects.indexOf(this.removed[i]);
    if(idx != -1) {
      this.cnt[this.removed[i].type]--;
      this.objects.splice(idx,1);
    }
  }
}
```

At the beginning of each step, resetRemoved is called to reset the list of objects to be removed. The remove method first checks if an object has already been removed and then adds it to the list of objects to remove only if it's not already there. It then returns true if the object was added or false if the object was already dead. After every object has its turn, finalizeRemoved is called. This method finds the removed objects in the objects list using Array.indexOf and then uses the Array .splice method to cut those objects out of the list. When an object is removed from the list, it is effectively dead because it no longer has its step and draw methods called.

Iterating over the List of Objects

Because much of what GameBoard does is iterate over a list of objects, it stands to reason that a couple of helper methods to make that easier would come in handy. Two main methods are needed. First, a simple iterate method that calls the same function on every object in the object list is useful for the step and draw methods. Second, a detect method that returns the first object for which a passed-in function returns `true` makes collision detection easier. Both of these methods are listed here:

First up is `iterate`:

```
// Call the same method on all current objects
this.iterate = function(funcName) {
    var args = Array.prototype.slice.call(arguments,1);
    for(var i=0,len=this.objects.length;i<len;i++) {
      var obj = this.objects[i];
      obj[funcName].apply(obj,args)
    }
};
```

Although the meat of the function is just a loop over `this.objects`, the method does have a couple of interesting JavaScript features.

The first line of the method is a well-known JavaScript hack. The `arguments` object, which is available in every method call, contains a list of the arguments passed into that method and is used by methods that accept varying numbers of arguments. `arguments` acts in many ways like an array, but it's not an actual array. This is a shame because in this case you'd like to get all the arguments out except for the first, which is the `funcName`, so that they can be passed on to the function to be called on every object. `arguments` doesn't have the slice method, but because JavaScript enables you to take methods and apply them to whatever object you like using `call` or `apply`, the line

```
var args = Array.prototype.slice.call(arguments,1);
```

can do just that and turn the `arguments` object into a proper array starting at the second element. Inside of the loop the code looks up the method in the object's properties using the square bracket operator and then calls `apply` to call that method with whatever the passed in arguments are.

Next is the detect method, which will be used later for collision detection. Its job is to run the same function on all of a board's objects and return the first object that the function returns `true` for. In the abstract this doesn't seem all that useful, but if you need to do collision detection or find a specific object based on certain parameters, the detect method is useful.

```
// Find the first object for which func is true
  this.detect = function(func) {
    for(var i = 0,val=null, len=this.objects.length; i < len; i++) {
      if(func.call(this.objects[i])) return this.objects[i];
    }
    return false;
  };
```

`detect` consists of a loop over the objects and a call to the passed-in function with the object passed in as the `this` context. If that function returns `true`, then the object is returned; otherwise, the functions returns `false` after it runs out of objects to compare against.

Defining the Board Methods

Next are the standard board functions, `step` and `draw`. Using the methods already defined, these functions have trivial definitions:

```
// Call step on all objects and then delete
// any objects that have been marked for removal
```

```
this.step = function(dt) {
  this.resetRemoved();
  this.iterate('step',dt);
  this.finalizeRemoved();
};

// Draw all the objects
this.draw= function(ctx) {
  this.iterate('draw',ctx);
};
```

Both step and draw use the iterate method to call a specifically named function on each object in the list, with step also making sure to reset and finalize the list of removed items.

Handling Collisions

The last bit of functionality in the purview of GameBoard is the handling of collisions. *Alien Invasion* uses a simplified collision model that reduces each of the sprites on the board to a simple rectangular bounding box. If the bounding boxes of two different objects overlap, then those two sprites are deemed to be colliding. Because each sprite has an *x* and a *y* position in addition to a width and a height, this box is easy to calculate.

> **NOTE** *A bounding box is the smallest rectangle that encompasses the entirety of an object. Using bounding boxes to do collision detection instead of polygons or exact pixel data is faster to calculate, but is much less accurate.*

GameBoard uses two functions to handle collision detection. The first, overlap, simply checks for the overlap between two objects' bounding boxes and returns true if they intersect. The easiest way to do this detection is clever. Rather than check whether one object is in the other, you simply need to check if one object couldn't be in the other and negate the result.

```
this.overlap = function(o1,o2) {
  return !((o1.y+o1.h-1<o2.y) || (o1.y>o2.y+o2.h-1) ||
           (o1.x+o1.w-1<o2.x) || (o1.x>o2.x+o2.w-1));
};
```

What's going on here is that the bottom edge of object one is checked against the bottom edge of object two to see if object one is to the right of object two. Next, the top edge of object one is checked against the bottom edge of object two and so on through each of the corresponding edges. If any of these are true, you know object one doesn't overlap object two. By simply negating the result of this detection, you can tell if the two objects overlap.

With a function in your pocket to determine overlap, it becomes easy to check one object against all the other objects in the list.

```
this.collide = function(obj,type) {
  return this.detect(function() {
    if(obj != this) {
      var col = (!type || this.type & type) && board.overlap(obj,this)
      return col ? this : false;
```

```
      }
    });
  };
```

`Collide` uses the `detect` function to match the passed-in object against all the other objects and returns the first object for which overlap returns `true`. The only complication is the support for an optional type parameter. The idea behind this is that different types of objects want to collide with only certain objects. Enemies, for example, don't want to collide with themselves, but they do want to collide with the player and the player's missiles. By doing a bitwise AND operation, collisions against objects of multiple types can be performed without the loss of speed that an array or hash lookup would require. One caveat is that each of the different types must be a power of two to prevent overlap of different types.

For example, if types were defined as the following:

```
var OBJECT_PLAYER = 1,
    OBJECT_PLAYER_PROJECTILE = 2,
    OBJECT_ENEMY = 4,
    OBJECT_ENEMY_PROJECTILE = 8;
```

an enemy could check if it collides with a player or a player's missile by doing a bitwise OR of the two types together:

```
board.collide(enemy, OBJECT_PLAYER | OBJECT_PLAYER_PROJECTILE)
```

Objects can also be assigned multiple types, and the `collide` function would still work as planned.

With that, the `GameBoard` class is complete. See `gameboard/engine.js` for the full version of the object in the code for this chapter.

Adding GameBoard into the Game

With the `GameBoard` class complete, the next step is to add it into the game. A quick modification of the `playGame` function from `game.js` does the trick:

```
var playGame = function() {
  var board = new GameBoard();
  board.add(new PlayerShip());
  Game.setBoard(3,board);
}
```

Reload the `index.html` file, and you should see exactly the same behavior as at the end of Chapter 1. All that's been done is to have the `GameBoard` take over managing the ship sprite. This is less than impressive because so far the game isn't putting the `GameBoard` class to good use because it just has a single sprite in it. This is remedied in the next section.

FIRING MISSILES

Now it's time to give the player something to do besides just fly left and right across the screen. You are going to bind the spacebar to fire off a pair of projectiles.

Adding a Bullet Sprite

The first step to giving the player some destructive capacity is to create a blueprint for the player missile object. This object is added to the game at the player's location whenever the player presses the fire key.

The `PlayerShip` object didn't use the object prototype to create methods because in general there is only one player in the game at a time so it's unnecessary to optimize for object creation speed or memory footprint. To contrast, there are going to be a lot of `PlayerMissiles` added to the game over the course of a level, so making sure they are quick to create and small from a memory usage standpoint is a good idea. (The JavaScript garbage collector can cause noticeable hiccups in game performance, so making its job easier is in your best interest.) Because of the frequency with which `PlayerMissile` objects are going to be created, using object prototypes makes a lot of sense. Functions created on an object's prototype need to be created and stored in memory only once.

Add the following highlighted text to the top of `game.js` to put in the sprite definition for the missile (don't forget the comma on the previous line):

```
var sprites = {
  ship: { sx: 0, sy: 0, w: 37, h: 42, frames: 1 },
  missile: { sx: 0, sy: 30, w: 2, h: 10, frames: 1 }
};
```

Next add the full `PlayerMissile` object (see Listing 2-1) to the bottom of `game.js`:

LISTING 2-1: The PlayerMissile Object

```
var PlayerMissile = function(x,y) {
  this.w = SpriteSheet.map['missile'].w;
  this.h = SpriteSheet.map['missile'].h;
  // Center the missile on x
  this.x = x - this.w/2;
  // Use the passed in y as the bottom of the missile
  this.y = y - this.h;
  this.vy = -700;
};

PlayerMissile.prototype.step = function(dt)  {
  this.y += this.vy * dt;
  if(this.y < -this.h) { this.board.remove(this); }
};

PlayerMissile.prototype.draw = function(ctx)  {
  SpriteSheet.draw(ctx,'missile',this.x,this.y);
};
```

The initial version of the `PlayerMissile` class clocks in at a mere 14 lines and much of it is boilerplate you've seen before. The constructor function simply sets up a number of properties on the sprite, pulling the width and height from the `SpriteSheet`. Because the player fires missiles vertically upward from a turret location, the constructor uses the passed-in y location for the location of the bottom of the missile by subtracting the height of the missile to determine its starting y location. It also centers the missile on the passed-in x location by subtracting half the width of the sprite.

As discussed previously, the step and draw methods are created on the prototype to be efficient. Because the player's missile moves only vertically up the screen, the step function needs to adjust only the y property and check if the missile has moved completely off the screen in the y direction. If the missile has moved more than its height off the screen (that is, `this.y < -this.h`), it removes itself from the board.

Finally, the `draw` method just draws the missile sprite at the missile's x and y locations using the `SpriteSheet` object.

Connecting Missiles to the Player

To actually get a missile onto the screen, the `PlayerShip` needs to be updated to respond to the fire key and add a pair of missiles onto the screen for each of its two turrets. You also need to add in a reloading period to limit the speed at which missiles are fired.

To put in this limit, you must add a new property called `reload`, which represents the remaining time before the next pair of missiles can be fired. You also must add another property called `reloadTime`, which represents the full reloading time. Add the following two initialization lines to the top of the `PlayerShip` constructor method:

```
var PlayerShip = function() {
    this.w =  SpriteSheet.map['ship'].w;
    this.h =  SpriteSheet.map['ship'].h;
    this.x = Game.width / 2 - this.w / 2;
    this.y = Game.height - 10 - this.h;
    this.vx = 0;
    this.reloadTime = 0.25;  // Quarter second reload
    this.reload = this.reloadTime;
```

`reload` is set to `reloadTime` to prevent the player from immediately firing a missile when they press fire to start the game.

Next, modify the step method to read as follows:

```
this.step = function(dt) {
  if(Game.keys['left']) { this.vx = -this.maxVel; }
  else if(Game.keys['right']) { this.vx = this.maxVel; }
  else { this.vx = 0; }
  this.x += this.vx * dt;

  if(this.x < 0) { this.x = 0; }
  else if(this.x > Game.width - this.w) {
    this.x = Game.width - this.w
  }

  this.reload-=dt;
  if(Game.keys['fire'] && this.reload < 0) {
    Game.keys['fire'] = false;
```

```
    this.reload = this.reloadTime;
    this.board.add(new PlayerMissile(this.x,this.y+this.h/2));
    this.board.add(new PlayerMissile(this.x+this.w,this.y+this.h/2));
  }
}
```

This code adds two new player missiles on the left and right sides of the ship if the player presses the fire key and is not in the process of reloading. Firing a missile simply consists of adding it to the board at the right location. The `reload` property is also reset to `reloadTime` to add in a delay between missiles being fired. To ensure the player needs to press and release the spacebar to fire and can't just hold it down, the key is set to `false`. (This doesn't quite have the intended effect because `keydown` events are fired on repeat.)

Reload the game (or fire up `http://mh5gd.com/ch2/missiles/`) and test out firing some missiles. You can adjust `reloadTime` to see the effect it has on the speed missiles are fired.

ADDING ENEMIES

A space shooter isn't any fun without enemies, so next you will add some enemies into the game by creating an `Enemy` sprite class. Although there will be multiple types of enemies, they are all represented by the same class and differentiated only by different templates for their image and movement.

Calculating Enemy Movement

You define the movement for enemies with an equation that contains a few pluggable parameters that enable enemies to exhibit relatively complex behavior without a lot of code. The equation sets the velocity of an enemy at a given time since it was added to the board:

$$vx = A + B * sin(C * t + D)$$

$$vy = E + F * sin(G * t + H)$$

All the letters A through H represent constant numbers. Don't let these equations intimidate you. All they say is that the velocity of an enemy is based on a constant value plus a value that repeats cyclically. (Using a sine enables the cyclical value.) Using an equation such as this allows the game to add enemies that twirl around the screen in interesting patterns and adds some dynamism to the game that a bunch of enemies flying in a straight line wouldn't. Sines and cosines are used often in game development for animation because they provide a mechanism for smooth movement transitions. See Table 2.1 for a description of the effect each parameter A–H has on the movement of an enemy.

> **NOTE** *Parabolas created with quadratic equations (a + bx + cx*x) are also useful for this but don't provide periodic behavior, so they aren't quite as useful in this situation.*

TABLE 2-1: Parameter Descriptions

PARAMETER	DESCRIPTION
A	Constant horizontal velocity
B	Strength of horizontal sinusoidal velocity
C	Period of horizontal sinusoidal velocity
D	Time shift of horizontal sinusoidal velocity
E	Constant vertical velocity
F	Strength of vertical sinusoidal velocity
G	Period of vertical sinusoidal velocity

A number of different combinations of values produce different behaviors. If B and F are set to zero, then the enemy flies straight because the sinusoidal component in both directions is zero. If F and A are set to zero, then the enemy flies with a constant *y* velocity but moves back and forth smoothly in the *x* direction.

You create a variety of different enemies in the section "Setting Up the Enemies" by setting different variations of parameters.

In a production game, if you don't want to worry about handling the math yourself, you could consider using a tweening engine such as TweenJS (www.createjs.com/TweenJS), which can handle smoothly moving objects from one position to another in a number of interesting manners.

Constructing the Enemy Object

You can create enemies from a blueprint that sets the sprite image used, the initial starting location, and the values for the movement of constants A–H. The constructor also enables an override object to be passed in to override the default blueprint settings.

Much like `PlayerMissile`, the `Enemy` object adds methods onto the prototype to speed object creation and reduce the memory footprint.

This initial version of `Enemy` looks much like the previous two sprite classes that have been built (`PlayerShip` and `PlayerMissile`), with a constructor function shown in in Listing 2-2 that initializes some state; a `step` method that updates the position and checks if the sprite is out of bounds; and a `draw` function that renders the sprite. Because of the need to copy over from the blueprint and any override parameters and set up the velocity equation parameters, the constructor function is a little more complicated than previous ones.

JavaScript doesn't have a built-in method to easily copy attributes over from another object, so you need to roll your own loop over the attributes to do it. To prevent the need for the blueprint to set each of the parameters A–H, each of those are also be initialized to zero.

LISTING 2-2: The Enemy Constructor

```
var Enemy = function(blueprint,override) {
  var baseParameters =  { A: 0, B: 0, C: 0, D: 0,
                          E: 0, F: 0, G: 0, H: 0 }
  // Set all the base parameters to 0
  for (var prop in baseParameters) {
    this[prop] = baseParameters[prop];
  }
  // Copy of all the attributes from the blueprint
  for (prop in blueprint) {
    this[prop] = blueprint[prop];
  }
  // Copy of all the attributes from the override, if present
  if(override) {
    for (prop in override) {
      this[prop] = override[prop];
    }
  }
  this.w = SpriteSheet.map[this.sprite].w;
  this.h = SpriteSheet.map[this.sprite].h;
  this.t = 0;
}
```

The constructor first copies three sets of objects into the `this` object: the base parameters, the blueprint, and the override. Because the enemy can have different sprites depending on the blueprint, the `width` and the `height` are set afterward based on the `sprite` property of the object. Finally, a `t` parameter is initialized to 0 to keep track of how long this sprite has been alive.

If the repetition in this code bothers you, don't worry! You clean it up in the section "Refactoring the Sprite Classes" later in this chapter.

Stepping and Drawing the Enemy Object

The `step` function (see Listing 2-3) for the enemy should update the velocity based on the aforementioned equation. The `this.t` property needs to be incremented by `dt` to keep track of how long the sprite has been alive. Next, the equation from earlier in this chapter can be plugged directly into the step function to calculate the *x* and *y* velocity. From the *x* and *y* velocity, the *x* and *y* location are updated. Finally, the sprite needs to check if it's gone off the board to the right or the left, in which case the enemy can remove itself from the page.

LISTING 2-3: The Enemy Step and Draw Methods

```
Enemy.prototype.step = function(dt) {
  this.t += dt;
  this.vx = this.A + this.B * Math.sin(this.C * this.t + this.D);
  this.vy = this.E + this.F * Math.sin(this.G * this.t + this.H);
  this.x += this.vx * dt;
  this.y += this.vy * dt;
  if(this.y > Game.height ||
     this.x < -this.w ||
     this.x > Game.width) {
```

continues

LISTING 2-3 *(continued)*

```
        this.board.remove(this);
    }
}

Enemy.prototype.draw = function(ctx) {
    SpriteSheet.draw(ctx,this.sprite,this.x,this.y);
}
```

The draw function is a near duplicate of the `PlayerMissile` object; the only difference is that it must look up which sprite to draw in a property called `sprite`.

Adding Enemies on the Board

Now you add some initial enemy sprites to the top of `game.js` along with a simple enemy blueprint for one enemy that can fly down the page:

```
var sprites = {
  ship: { sx: 0, sy: 0, w: 37, h: 42, frames: 1 },
  missile: { sx: 0, sy: 30, w: 2, h: 10, frames: 1 },
  enemy_purple: { sx: 37, sy: 0, w: 42, h: 43, frames: 1 },
  enemy_bee: { sx: 79, sy: 0, w: 37, h: 43, frames: 1 },
  enemy_ship: { sx: 116, sy: 0, w: 42, h: 43, frames: 1 },
  enemy_circle: { sx: 158, sy: 0, w: 32, h: 33, frames: 1 }
};

var enemies = {
  basic: { x: 100, y: -50, sprite: 'enemy_purple', B: 100, C: 2 , E: 100 }
};
```

Next, modify `playGame` to add a pair of enemies to the top of the page:

```
var playGame = function() {
  var board = new GameBoard();
  board.add(new Enemy(enemies.basic));
  board.add(new Enemy(enemies.basic, { x: 200 }));
  board.add(new PlayerShip());
  Game.setBoard(3,board);
}
```

Using the `enemies` object as a blueprint for the enemy makes adding an enemy onto the page as simple as calling `new Enemy()` with that blueprint. To make the second enemy appear to the right of the first, an override object is passed in setting x to `200`.

Reload the file, and when the game starts, you should have a couple of bad guys snake their way down the screen and then disappear off the bottom. You can also take a look at `http://mh5gd. com/ch2/enemies` to see the effect this code has. These enemies aren't doing any collision detection, so they won't interact with the player.

The basic enemy has only three of the enemy movement parameters defined: B (horizontal sinusoidal movement), C (horizontal sinusoidal period), and E (vertical fixed movement). Play with these parameters to affect the movement. Increasing C, for example, increases the frequency with which the enemies bounce back and forth.

REFACTORING THE SPRITE CLASSES

At this point the game has three different sprite classes that all share a lot of the same boilerplate code. This means it's time to apply the Rule of Three.

As described by Wikipedia, the rule is:

> *Rule of three is a code refactoring rule of thumb to decide when a replicated piece of code should be replaced by a new procedure. It states that the code can be copied once, but that when the same code is replicated three times, it should be extracted into a new procedure. The rule was introduced by Martin Fowler in Refactoring and attributed to Don Roberts.*

> http://en.wikipedia.org/wiki/Rule_of_three_(computer_programming)

Even though *Alien Invasion* is a one-off game engine that isn't intended to be turned into a general-purpose engine, it still pays to put in a little bit of time to refactor the code when it makes sense to clean up any rampant duplication and make the game easier to fix and extend.

No one writes perfect code the first time, especially when prototyping and trying out new features. When that code works, however, failing to refactor and clean up code during development leads to *technical debt*. The more technical debt you have on a project, the more painful it is to make changes and add new features. Refactoring can clean up technical debt by removing unused code, reducing code duplication, and cleaning up abstractions, all things that don't make your game better necessarily but make your life as a game developer better.

In *Alien Invasion*, the main culprits of duplication in these three sprite classes are the boilerplate setup code and the `draw` method, which is the same across all three methods. It's time to extract those into a base object called `Sprite`, which can handle initialization given a set of setup parameters as well as a sprite to use. Inside the `Enemy` constructor, the three loops to copy one object into another is also a good opportunity for refactoring.

If you haven't done a lot of prototypical inheritance in JavaScript, the syntax may look strange. Because JavaScript doesn't have the idea of classes, instead of defining a class that represents the inherited properties, you create a prototype object where JavaScript will look when a parameter isn't defined on the actual object.

Creating a Generic Sprite Class

In this section you create the `Sprite` object that all other sprites inherit from. Open up `engine.js` and add the following code shown in Listing 2-4:

LISTING 2-4: A Generic Sprite Object

```
var Sprite = function() { }

Sprite.prototype.setup = function(sprite,props) {
  this.sprite = sprite;
  this.merge(props);
```

continues

LISTING 2-4 *(continued)*

```
   this.frame = this.frame || 0;
   this.w =  SpriteSheet.map[sprite].w;
   this.h =  SpriteSheet.map[sprite].h;
}

Sprite.prototype.merge = function(props) {
  if(props) {
    for (var prop in props) {
      this[prop] = props[prop];
    }
  }
}
Sprite.prototype.draw = function(ctx) {
   SpriteSheet.draw(ctx,this.sprite,this.x,this.y,this.frame);
}
```

This code goes into `engine.js` because it's generic engine code versus game-specific code. The constructor function is empty because each sprite has its own constructor function, and the `Sprite` object is created only once for each of the descendant sprite object definitions. Constructor functions in JavaScript don't work the same as constructors in other OO languages such as C++. To get around this, you need a separate setup function to be called explicitly in the descendant objects.

This setup method takes in the name of the sprite in the `SpriteSheet` and a properties object. The sprite is saved in the object, and then properties are copied over into the `Sprite`. The width and height are also set here as well.

Because copying over properties into an object is such a common need, `Sprite` also defines a `merge` method that does just that. This method is used in the `setup` method.

Finally, the `draw` method, which is nearly identical in every sprite so far, can be defined once here and then will be available in every other sprite.

Refactoring PlayerShip

Armed with the `Sprite` class, the `PlayerShip` object can be refactored to simplify setup. The new code is marked in bold in Listing 2-5:

LISTING 2-5: A Refactored PlayerShip

```
var PlayerShip = function() {
  this.setup('ship', { vx: 0, frame: 1, reloadTime: 0.25, maxVel: 200 });

  this.reload = this.reloadTime;
  this.x = Game.width/2 - this.w / 2;
  this.y = Game.height - 10 - this.h;

  this.step = function(dt) {
    if(Game.keys['left']) { this.vx = -this.maxVel; }
    else if(Game.keys['right']) { this.vx = this.maxVel; }
    else { this.vx = 0; }
```

```
      this.x += this.vx * dt;
      if(this.x < 0) { this.x = 0; }
      else if(this.x > Game.width - this.w) {
        this.x = Game.width - this.w
      }
      this.reload-=dt;
      if(Game.keys['fire'] && this.reload < 0) {
        this.reload = this.reloadTime;
        this.board.add(new PlayerMissile(this.x,this.y+this.h/2));
        this.board.add(new PlayerMissile(this.x+this.w,this.y+this.h/2));
      }
    }
  }

  PlayerShip.prototype = new Sprite();
```

At the top of the constructor function, the setup method is called, wiping out some boilerplate code. A few of the properties are set when setup is called, but a few are set afterward because they depend on the values of the other properties such as the object's width and height, which isn't available until after setup is called. Next, the draw method is removed because it is handled by Sprite.

Finally, the code to actually set up PlayerShip's prototype comes after the PlayerShip constructor function is defined.

Refactoring PlayerMissile

The PlayerMissile object was already compact, but refactoring helps make it even shorter. See Listing 2-6.

LISTING 2-6: Refactored PlayerMissile

```
var PlayerMissile = function(x,y) {
  this.setup('missile',{ vy: -700 });
  this.x = x - this.w/2;
  this.y = y - this.h;
};


PlayerMissile.prototype = new Sprite();

PlayerMissile.prototype.step = function(dt)  {
  this.y += this.vy * dt;
  if(this.y < -this.h) { this.board.remove(this); }
};
```

The constructor method still needs to explicitly set the x and y location because these are dependent on the width and height of the sprite (which aren't available until after setup is called). The step method is unaffected by the refactoring, and the draw method can be removed as it's handled by Sprite.

Refactoring Enemy

The Enemy object benefits the most from the refactoring, particularly in the constructor method. Instead of using a number of loops to copy parameters into the object, a few calls to merge simplify the method down to three lines. See Listing 2-7.

LISTING 2-7: Refactored Enemy Object (Partial Code)

```
var Enemy = function(blueprint,override) {
  this.merge(this.baseParameters);
  this.setup(blueprint.sprite,blueprint);
  this.merge(override);
}
Enemy.prototype = new Sprite();
Enemy.prototype.baseParameters = { A: 0, B: 0, C: 0, D: 0,
                                   E: 0, F: 0, G: 0, H: 0,
                                   t: 0 };
```

The `step` method is unaffected (and so isn't shown in Listing 2-7) and the draw method can be removed. Notice that `merge` is called explicitly to merge in the set of `baseParameters` and the `override` parameters. The predefined `baseParameters` object is also pulled out of the constructor and put into the prototype. Although not a huge optimization, it prevents the need for the static `baseParameters` object to be re-created each time a new `Enemy` is created just for the sake of being copied over into the object. Because `baseParameters` isn't going to be modified, one copy of the object will do.

HANDLING COLLISIONS

Alien Invasion is slowly coming together. It now has a player, missiles, and enemies flying around the screen. Unfortunately, none of these pieces are interacting by blowing each other up as is expected in a save-the-planet-from-destruction shooter game.

The good news is that the majority of the hard work for handling collisions has already been done. The `GameBoard` object already knows how to take two objects and figure out if they are overlapping as well as determine if one object is colliding with any others of a specific type. All that's necessary now is to add the appropriate calls to those collision functions.

For collisions, Alien Invasion can use two mechanisms. The first is to do proactive checks in every object's `step` function against any objects it has an interaction with. The second would be to have a general collision phase where objects trigger collision events when they hit each other. The former is simpler to implement, whereas the latter offers better overall performance and can be better optimized. *Alien Invasion* is going to go the simpler route, but the platformer game built in Chapter 18, "Creating a 2-D Platformer," uses the more complicated mechanism.

Adding Object Types

To ensure that objects collide only with objects that it makes sense for them to collide with, objects need to be assigned types. This was discussed at the beginning of the chapter but has not yet been implemented in the game. The first step is to determine the different object types the game has and add some constants to keep from having to use magic numbers in the code.

Add the code from Listing 2-8 to the top of game.js to define five different types of objects.

LISTING 2-8: Object Types

```
var OBJECT_PLAYER = 1,
    OBJECT_PLAYER_PROJECTILE = 2,
    OBJECT_ENEMY = 4,
    OBJECT_ENEMY_PROJECTILE = 8,
    OBJECT_POWERUP = 16;
```

> **NOTE** *Each of these types shown in Listing 2-8 is a power of two, which is an efficiency optimization to enable the use of bitwise logic as discussed earlier.*

Next, add three lines to game.js setting the type of each Sprite at an appropriate spot after each Sprite's prototype assignment code:

```
PlayerShip.prototype = new Sprite();
PlayerShip.prototype.type = OBJECT_PLAYER;

...

PlayerMissile.prototype = new Sprite();
PlayerMissile.prototype.type = OBJECT_PLAYER_PROJECTILE;

...

Enemy.prototype = new Sprite();
Enemy.prototype.type = OBJECT_ENEMY;
```

Each object now has a type that can be used for collision detection.

Colliding Missiles with Enemies

To prevent duplicated effort, instead of objects checking for collisions with every type of object they might hit, objects check only against objects that they actually "want" to hit. This means that PlayerMissile objects check if they are colliding with Enemy objects, but Enemy objects won't check if they are colliding with PlayerMissile objects. Doing so keeps the number of calculations down a little bit.

Now that objects can be hit, they need to have a method to deal with what should happen when they are hit. To begin with, add a method to Sprite that removes an object whenever it gets hit. This method can be overridden down the road by the various inherited objects.

Add the following function to the bottom of engine.js below the rest of the Sprite object definition:

```
Sprite.prototype.hit = function(damage) {
  this.board.remove(this);
}
```

This initial version of the hit method just removes the object from the board, regardless of the amount of damage done.

Add a damage value to the `PlayerMissile` constructor function:

```
var PlayerMissile = function(x,y) {
  this.setup('missile',{ vy: -700, damage: 10 });
  this.x = x - this.w/2;
  this.y = y - this.h;
};
```

Next, open up `game.js`, and edit the `PlayerMissile` step method to check for collisions:

```
PlayerMissile.prototype.step = function(dt)  {
  this.y += this.vy * dt;
  var collision = this.board.collide(this,OBJECT_ENEMY);
  if(collision) {
    collision.hit(this.damage);
    this.board.remove(this);
  } else if(this.y < -this.h) {
      this.board.remove(this);
  }
};
```

The missile checks to see if it's colliding with any `OBJECT_ENEMY` type objects and then calls the `hit` method on whatever object it collides with. It then removes itself from the board because its job is done.

Fire up the game, and you should be able to shoot down the two enemies flying down the screen.

Colliding Enemies with the Player

To make it a fair fight, enemies need to have the ability to take down the player as well when they make contact.

Adding essentially the same chunk of code to the `Enemy` step method allows the `Enemy` to take out the player. Modify the step method to read as follows:

```
Enemy.prototype.step = function(dt) {
  this.t += dt;
  this.vx = this.A + this.B * Math.sin(this.C * this.t + this.D);
  this.vy = this.E + this.F * Math.sin(this.G * this.t + this.H);
  this.x += this.vx * dt;
  this.y += this.vy * dt;

  var collision = this.board.collide(this,OBJECT_PLAYER);
  if(collision) {
    collision.hit(this.damage);
    this.board.remove(this);
  }

  if(this.y > Game.height ||
      this.x < -this.w ||
      this.x > Game.width) {
      this.board.remove(this);
  }
}
```

This code is identical to the code added to the `PlayerMissile` object except that it calls `collide` with an `OBJECT_PLAYER` object type.

After making those changes, fire up the game and let your player be taken out by one of the ships.

Making It Go Boom

So far the collisions have the correct effect; however, there's something to be said for a more dramatic effect to liven things up. The `sprites.png` file has a nice explosion animation in there for just that reason. The explosion image was generated using the explosion generator on `http://www.positech.co.uk/`.

Add the sprite definition to the top of `game.js` for the explosion:

```
var sprites = {
  ship: { sx: 0, sy: 0, w: 37, h: 42, frames: 1 },
  missile: { sx: 0, sy: 30, w: 2, h: 10, frames: 1 },
  enemy_purple: { sx: 37, sy: 0, w: 42, h: 43, frames: 1 },
  enemy_bee: { sx: 79, sy: 0, w: 37, h: 43, frames: 1 },
  enemy_ship: { sx: 116, sy: 0, w: 42, h: 43, frames: 1 },
  enemy_circle: { sx: 158, sy: 0, w: 32, h: 33, frames: 1 },
  explosion: { sx: 0, sy: 64, w: 64, h: 64, frames: 12 }
};
```

Now add some `health` to the blueprint for a basic enemy:

```
var enemies = {
  basic: { x: 100, y: -50, sprite: 'enemy_purple',
           B: 100, C: 4, E: 100, health: 20 }
};
```

Next, you need to override the default `hit` method from `Sprite` for the `Enemy` object. This method needs to reduce the health of the `Enemy`, so check if the `Enemy` has run out of health; if so add an explosion to the `GameBoard` at the center of the `Enemy`, as shown in Listing 2-9.

LISTING 2-9: Enemy Hit Method

```
Enemy.prototype.hit = function(damage) {
  this.health -= damage;
  if(this.health <=0) {
    if(this.board.remove(this)) {
      this.board.add(new Explosion(this.x + this.w/2,
                                   this.y + this.h/2));
    }
  }
}
```

Finally, the `Explosion` class needs to be built. The class is a basic sprite that when added onto the page just flips itself through its frames and then removes itself from the board. See Listing 2-10.

LISTING 2-10: The Explosion Object

```
var Explosion = function(centerX,centerY) {
  this.setup('explosion', { frame: 0 });
  this.x = centerX - this.w/2;
  this.y = centerY - this.h/2;
  this.subFrame = 0;
};

Explosion.prototype = new Sprite();

Explosion.prototype.step = function(dt) {
  this.frame = Math.floor(this.subFrame++ / 3);
  if(this.subFrame >= 36) {
    this.board.remove(this);
  }
};
```

The `Explosion` constructor method takes the passed in `centerX` and `centerY` position and adjusts the *x* and *y* location by moving the sprite half of its width to the left and half the height up. The `step` method doesn't need to worry about moving the explosion each frame; it just needs to update the `subFrame` property to cycle through each of the frames of the explosion animation. Each frame of the explosion animation plays for three game frames to make it last a little bit longer. When all 36 `subFrames` of the explosion have played through (12 actual frames), the `Explosion` removes itself from the board.

Reload the game, and try to take out the enemies flying down the screen. It should take two missiles to take out an enemy now, but that enemy should explode in a nice fiery blast.

REPRESENTING LEVELS

Alien Invasion now has all the mechanics necessary to play the game. The only missing component is to put together some level data and a mechanism for adding enemy ships onto the screen.

Before getting into the levels, add a few more enemy types to give some variety to the page.

Setting Up the Enemies

You could create an endless number of variations of enemy movement, but for this game you'll set up five different types of enemy behavior using the various enemy sprite types as a start. You can play with the definitions and add more if you like. You could make a number of other variations, but this set of five is a good start. Replace the `enemies` definition at the top of `game.js` with Listing 2-11.

LISTING 2-11: Enemy Definitions

```
var enemies = {
  straight: { x: 0,   y: -50, sprite: 'enemy_ship', health: 10,
              E: 100 },
```

```
    ltr:      { x: 0,    y: -100, sprite: 'enemy_purple', health: 10,
                B: 200, C: 1, E: 200   },
    circle:   { x: 400,   y: -50, sprite: 'enemy_circle', health: 10,
                A: 0,   B: -200, C: 1, E: 20, F: 200, G: 1, H: Math.PI/2 },
    wiggle:   { x: 100, y: -50, sprite: 'enemy_bee', health: 20,
                B: 100, C: 4, E: 100 },
    step:     { x: 0,    y: -50, sprite: 'enemy_circle', health: 10,
                B: 300, C: 1.5, E: 60 }
};
```

With just a variation on the movement parameters, the enemies have wildly differing movement styles. The straight enemy has only vertical velocity parameter E, so it moves downward at a constant rate.

The ltr enemy (short for left-to-right) has a constant vertical velocity, but then a sinusoidal horizontal velocity (parameters B and C) gives it a smooth sweeping motion from left to right.

The circle has primarily sinusoidal motion in both directions, but adds a time shift in the Y direction with parameter H to give a circular motion to the enemy.

The wiggle and the step enemies have the same parameters set, just to different amounts. With a smaller B value and larger C and E values, the wiggle enemy just snakes down the screen, while the step enemy, with a larger B and a smaller C and E, makes its way down the page slowly by sliding back and forth across the whole screen.

Setting Up Level Data

Knowing that levels in *Alien Invasion* will be populated with strings of enemies of the same type, the next step is to figure out a good mechanism for encoding the level data in a compact manner. When that has been figured out, you can work backward and figure out what the level object needs to do to spawn those enemies onto the page. Working from how you want to use a piece of code back to the implementation is a good way to end up with code that is easy to work with. It may take a little bit more work on the implementation, but you'll be happier in the long run.

One initial impulse you might have would be to encode the starting location of each enemy and each enemy type in an array. Because a level might have a hundred or more enemies, this would get laborious quickly. A better option is to encode each string of enemies as a single entry with a start time, end time, and per-enemy delay. This way each string of enemies is succinctly encoded into the level data, and you can take one look at the definition and get a good understanding of what's going on.

Add the level data for level 1 to the top of game.js by inserting Listing 2-12.

LISTING 2-12: Level Data

```
var level1 = [
 // Start,    End, Gap,   Type,    Override
  [ 0,       4000, 500, 'step' ],
  [ 6000,   13000, 800, 'ltr' ],
  [ 12000,  16000, 400, 'circle' ],
  [ 18200,  20000, 500, 'straight', { x: 150 } ],
  [ 18200,  20000, 500, 'straight', { x: 100 } ],
```

continues

LISTING 2-12 *(continued)*

```
    [ 18400,   20000, 500, 'straight', { x: 200 } ],
    [ 22000,   25000, 400, 'wiggle', { x: 300 }],
    [ 22000,   25000, 400, 'wiggle', { x: 200 }]
  ];
```

Each line gives a start time in milliseconds, an end time in milliseconds, and a gap in milliseconds between each enemy followed by the enemy type and any override parameters.

Loading and Finishing a Level

Defining how the `level` class is going to consume level data is half the battle; the other half is deciding on how the `Level` object will be used by the `PlayGame` method to start the game. The easiest solution is to simply create another sprite-like object that is added to the game board and spawns enemies at the correct time intervals. When the `Level` is out of enemies, it can make a callback to indicate success.

Again working backward, you write the way the `Level` object should be used before tackling the actual implementation. Replace the existing `playGame` method with the one shown in Listing 2-13, and add new `winGame` and `loseGame` methods as well.

LISTING 2-13: Modified Game Initialization Methods

```
var playGame = function() {
  var board = new GameBoard();
  board.add(new PlayerShip());
  board.add(new Level(level1,winGame));
  Game.setBoard(3,board);
}
var winGame = function() {
  Game.setBoard(3,new TitleScreen("You win!",
                                  "Press fire to play again",
                                  playGame));
}
var loseGame = function() {
  Game.setBoard(3,new TitleScreen("You lose!",
                                  "Press fire to play again",
                                  playGame));
}
```

Adding the level becomes as trivial as adding a new `Level` sprite to the board and passing in the level data `level1` and the success callback `winGame`.

The `winGame` method just reuses the `TitleScreen` object to show a success message and a message letting the player know they can replay the game.

The `loseGame` method works the same way as the `winGame` method but with a less congratulatory message. Lose game so far isn't called yet anywhere, but this can be remedied by adding a custom hit method to the `PlayShip` object. Add the following definition to `game.js` under the rest of the `PlayerShip` methods (make sure to add it underneath where the prototype is set):

```
PlayerShip.prototype.hit = function(damage) {
  if(this.board.remove(this)) {
    loseGame();
  }
}
```

The `PlayerShip` doesn't get an explosion when it dies; this is just for simplicity's sake. However, you could add one in and add a callback to the end of the explosion step to show the `loseGame` screen only after the `PlayerShip` has finished blowing up.

Implementing the Level Object

All that's left now is the implementation of the `Level` object. This object's duties have already been defined by how the level data and `playGame` and `winGame` methods were set up. The `Level` object has only two methods: the constructor function, which makes a copy of the level data for its own use (and modification) and the `step` method, which loops through the level data and adds enemies onto the board as necessary.

Add the constructor function shown in Listing 2-14 to the bottom of `engine.js`.

LISTING 2-14: Level Object Constructor

```
var Level = function(levelData,callback) {
  this.levelData = [];
  for(var i =0; i<levelData.length; i++) {
    this.levelData.push(Object.create(levelData[i]));
  }
  this.t = 0;
  this.callback = callback;
}
```

The one major responsibility of the constructor function is to make a deep copy of the passed-in level data. Cloning the data is necessary because the method is going to modify the level data as the level progresses. Because objects are passed by reference in JavaScript, this would prevent the level from being reused if the player were to play the level a second time.

The cloning is slightly more complicated than it seems because JavaScript doesn't have a built-in mechanism for deep cloning a list of objects inside an `Array`. To get around this, each entry in the level data is looped over and the built-in `Object.create` method is called to create a new object with the existing data as the prototype. That new object is then pushed onto a new `Array`.

Next is the meat of the `Level` object, the `step` method. Even though `Level` isn't a normal `Sprite`, it's going to pretend it is and behave like one by responding to the step and draw methods. The `step` method in Listing 2-15 has the responsibility to keep track of the current time and dropping enemies onto the page in sequence.

LISTING 2-15: Level Step Method

```
Level.prototype.step = function(dt) {
  var idx = 0, remove = [], curShip = null;

  // Update the current time offset
  this.t += dt * 1000;

  //  Example levelData
  //   Start, End,  Gap, Type,   Override
  // [[ 0,    4000, 500, 'step', { x: 100 } ]
  while((curShip = this.levelData[idx]) &&
        (curShip[0] < this.t + 2000)) {
    // Check if past the end time
    if(this.t > curShip[1]) {
      // If so, remove the entry
      remove.push(curShip);
    } else if(curShip[0] < this.t) {
      // Get the enemy definition blueprint
      var enemy = enemies[curShip[3]],
          override = curShip[4];

      // Add a new enemy with the blueprint and override
      this.board.add(new Enemy(enemy,override));

      // Increment the start time by the gap
      curShip[0] += curShip[2];
    }
    idx++;
  }
  // Remove any objects from the levelData that have passed
  for(var i=0,len=remove.length;i<len;i++) {
    var idx = this.levelData.indexOf(remove[i]);
    if(idx != -1) this.levelData.splice(idx,1);
  }

  // If there are no more enemies on the board or in
  // levelData, this level is done
  if(this.levelData.length == 0 && this.board.cnt[OBJECT_ENEMY] == 0) {
    if(this.callback) this.callback();
  }
}

// Dummy method, doesn't draw anything
Level.prototype.draw = function(ctx) { }
```

This is a complex method. The method is broken into three main sections:

➤ The first section uses a `while` statement to loop over the beginning of the `levelData` array until it gets past any active ships. (This prevents the need to loop over every element in the array.) For each row in the level data, it checks if it is passed the end value (the second element of the array). If so, it adds that element to a list of elements to be removed from the `levelData` array. If not, it pulls out the enemy blueprint and the override and adds a new enemy onto the board. It then increments the start value (the first element of the array) by the length of between-enemy gap. Modifying the start time allows the `step` method to handle adding a string of enemies on the page without any additional logic.

➤ The second section of the `step` method should look familiar from the `GameBoard` object. All it is does is look at all the entries in `levelData` that have been added to the remove list and splices them out of the array, much like the `finalizeRemoved` method in `GameBoard` did.

➤ The final section consists of a conditional that checks if there are no more upcoming enemies in `levelData` and if the number of enemies on the board is zero. If both of those conditions are true, then the level is considered over, and the callback, if one is set, is called. This allows the level to know when it has been completed.

Finally, the `Level` object needs a `draw` method so that it can play nicely with `GameBoard`, but that method is just a stub that doesn't actually do anything.

Fire up the game with all the `Level` pieces in, and you should see the game and enemies in all their glory.

SUMMARY

Congratulations! You took the stub of a game—a lonely spaceship flying around empty space—and turned it into a playable game with waves of enemies and win and failure screens.

You may have noticed a slight issue so far, though—it's not mobile. The next chapter remedies this when you add touch controls and support for resizing. A few finishing touches, such as scoring, can turn *Alien Invasion* into a polished, playable mobile game that works on the desktop as well.

3

Finishing Up and Going Mobile

WHAT'S IN THIS CHAPTER?

➤ Exploring scene management

➤ Adding projectiles and enemies

➤ Using collision detection

➤ Creating explosions

WROX.COM CODE DOWNLOADS FOR THIS CHAPTER

The wrox.com code downloads for this chapter are found at www.wrox.com/remtitle
.cgi?isbn=9781118301326 on the Download Code tab. The code is in the chapter 03
download and individually named according to the names throughout the chapter.

INTRODUCTION

One of the much-touted advantages of HTML5 is its support on mobile devices, something
that, despite the name of the book, has been ignored in the game so far. This is remedied in
this chapter. Adding mobile support to *Alien Invasion* means recognizing when the game is
played on a touch device and responding correctly. In this case it means adding in touch controls and resizing the game to fit the device.

ADDING TOUCH CONTROLS

Since the introduction of the iPhone in 2007, the direction of input mobile devices has been
clear: The touchscreen has won. To make *Alien Invasion* playable on mobile and table devices,
it must be playable with only the screen as an input device.

Drawing Controls

To make mobile gameplay possible, the common solution is to add visible touch controls to the screen. These controls can consist of three square buttons at the bottom of the page: a left arrow to move the ship left, a right arrow to move the ship right, and an "A" button to fire.

To add in the controls, a new game board at a higher position than anything else is added in. Because it will be rendered after everything else, the controls always sit nicely on top of the page.

The game needs to handle different screen resolutions. To this end, instead of drawing fixed size input squares (which could end up being too large or too small depending on the device), the game adjusts the size of the squares based on the width of the game. Based on some informal testing, dividing the width of the game into five regions works well enough. Buttons are large enough to be hit easily but don't take up too much screen real estate.

The first step is to add the controls onto the page. Open up `engine.js` and add the following object (as shown in Listing 3-1) to the bottom.

LISTING 3-1: TouchControls for Alien Invasion

```
var TouchControls = function() {
  var gutterWidth = 10;
  var unitWidth = Game.width/5;
  var blockWidth = unitWidth-gutterWidth;

  this.drawSquare = function(ctx,x,y,txt,on) {
    ctx.globalAlpha = on ? 0.9 : 0.6;
    ctx.fillStyle =  "#CCC";
    ctx.fillRect(x,y,blockWidth,blockWidth);

    ctx.fillStyle = "#FFF";
    ctx.textAlign = "center";
    ctx.globalAlpha = 1.0;
    ctx.font = "bold " + (3*unitWidth/4) + "px arial";

    ctx.fillText(txt,
                 x+blockWidth/2,
                 y+3*blockWidth/4+5);
  };


  this.draw = function(ctx) {
    ctx.save();
    var yLoc = Game.height - unitWidth;

    this.drawSquare(ctx,gutterWidth,yLoc,
                    "\u25C0", Game.keys['left']);

    this.drawSquare(ctx,unitWidth + gutterWidth,yLoc,
                    "\u25B6",Game.keys['right']);

    this.drawSquare(ctx,4*unitWidth,yLoc,"A",Game.keys['fire']);
    ctx.restore();
```

```
        };

        this.step = function(dt) { };
    };
```

This object sets up some values based on the width of the game that will be used to draw objects. Each block is set up to be 1/5th of the width minus a 10-pixel gutter to separate the buttons.

For each frame, the object's draw method is called. This method calls an internal method, drawSquare, which draws a single rectangle with some text on it at the specified location. Instead of drawing triangles, the code uses the Unicode UTF-8 symbols for the left and right arrows. The characters \u25C0 and \u25B6 represent left and right triangles.

> **NOTE** *Unicode characters can be expressed in JavaScript by prefixing backslash u (\u) in front of the UTF-8 code for that letter or symbol.*

The draw method uses the save and restore methods on the 2-D canvas context to prevent the changes to opacity and font from affecting any other canvas calls.

The drawSquare method does most of the actual work. It takes in an *x* and *y* location, the text to draw on the button, and determines whether the button is currently held down; then it draws a filled rectangle and text to create the button. The button state is used to set the opacity using the globalAlpha property for the background of the button so that players can see when they press down the button.

To actually have this board appear, it needs to be added to the Game object on initialization. Modify the Game.initialize in the engine.js method by adding the setBoard call as well as a couple of properties onto Game that are used by TouchControls:

```
    // Game Initialization
    this.initialize = function(canvasElementId,sprite_data,callback) {
      ...
      this.setupInput();
      this.setBoard(4,new TouchControls());
      this.loop();
      SpriteSheet.load(sprite_data,callback);
    };

    // Game Initialization
    this.initialize = function(canvasElementId,sprite_data,callback) {
      this.canvas = document.getElementById(canvasElementId);
      this.width = this.canvas.width;
      this.height= this.canvas.height;

      this.ctx = this.canvas.getContext && this.canvas.getContext('2d');
      if(!this.ctx) { return alert("Please upgrade your browser to play"); }

      this.setupInput();

      this.loop();

      SpriteSheet.load(sprite_data,callback);
    };
```

Touch controls aren't yet enabled to control the player, but if you use the keyboard, you should see the buttons light up in response to the controls as if they were pressed.

Responding to Touch Events

To make these boxes work with touch events, the game needs to be set up to listen for a new set of browser events: `touchstart`, `touchmove`, and `touchend`. You've most likely come across browser events before, such as the well-known `click` event. These new events are available on non-Windows touch devices only and are special in that they contain not only the details about the event, but also about any other touches currently on the device. The details for these additional events are held in three arrays inside of the event object, described in Table 3-1.

TABLE 3-1: Touch Event Properties

EVENT PROPERTY	DESCRIPTION
`event.touches`	All the touches currently on the devices
`event.targetTouches`	All the touches on the same DOM object as the event
`event.changedTouches`	All the touches changed in this event

The game uses both the `targetTouches` array and the `changedTouches` array to good effect.

The `targetTouches` is used for the two buttons on the left that control movement. You want the user to be able to press and hold down either button to move left and right. As such, each time there is a touch event, the game sees if there are any touches currently hitting either of those two buttons and marks the button as down if that is the case, even if the touch that triggered the event isn't on either button.

For firing, as a design choice, the game requires the player to press the Fire button each time they want to fire a missile. (Holding down the fire key doesn't count.) For that reason, the game counts the fire key as down only if the user actually pressed that key in the last step.

Add the code in Listing 3-2 to the `TouchControls` class before the ending curly brace:

LISTING 3-2: **TouchControls touch tracking**

```
var TouchControls = function() {
  ...

  this.step = function(dt) { };

  this.trackTouch = function(e) {
    var touch, x;
    e.preventDefault();
    Game.keys['left'] = false;
    Game.keys['right'] = false;
    for(var i=0;i<e.targetTouches.length;i++) {
```

```
        touch = e.targetTouches[i];
        x = touch.pageX / Game.canvasMultiplier - Game.canvas.offsetLeft;
        if(x < unitWidth) {
          Game.keys['left'] = true;
        }
        if(x > unitWidth && x < 2*unitWidth) {
          Game.keys['right'] = true;
        }
      }
      if(e.type == 'touchstart' || e.type == 'touchend') {
        for(i=0;i<e.changedTouches.length;i++) {
          touch = e.changedTouches[i];
          x = touch.pageX / Game.canvasMultiplier - Game.canvas.offsetLeft;
          if(x > 4 * unitWidth) {
            Game.keys['fire'] = (e.type == 'touchstart');
          }
        }
      }
    }
  };

  Game.canvas.addEventListener('touchstart',this.trackTouch,true);
  Game.canvas.addEventListener('touchmove',this.trackTouch,true);
  Game.canvas.addEventListener('touchend',this.trackTouch,true);
  Game.playerOffset = unitWidth + 20;
};
```

In the preceding description, the controls have been referred to as "buttons" because that is the way they are drawn. But if you examine the hit detection code, you notice they are actually targeted as columns. Only the *x* location of the hit is used to determine if a user is pressing a button. This is a behavior used in a number of mobile app store games, and it works well because players can be less exact when trying to press the buttons and can place their hands vertically on the device where they feel comfortable.

This code adds in a method called `trackTouch` to `TouchControls` that acts as the universal handler for any touch events. The first thing `trackTouch` does is call `e.preventDefault()`. This gets rid of any existing behavior that might be associated with that event, including scrolling, clicking, zooming, and so on. Doing this prevents the page from exhibiting any default behavior when the user interacts with the canvas element. (At least on iOS it does. As of this writing, on Android you can still trigger scroll and zoom via multitouch. Hopefully that will be fixed soon.)

Next, the `trackTouch` method sets both the left and right keys to `false`. It does this because either or both of these keys will be set back to `true` if there is a touch noted on the button. Performing the detection this way allows users to slide their finger between the two buttons to move back and forth or swap fingers without the game missing a beat. For any touches, the game sees if they are located in the first two units on the left of the canvas and if so maps those to the left and right movement buttons.

For firing missiles, only the `changedTouches` are looked at. This is, as mentioned before, because the player is forced to press the Fire button repeatedly to fire missiles in rapid succession. The game checks if any of the touches are in the last section on the right and if so sets the fire key to `true` or `false` depending on whether the event is a `touchstart` or a `touchend`, respectively.

Finally a variable called `playerOffset` is set to the `unitWidth` + 20. The point of this is to have the player move up on the screen if touch controls are present, but sit on the bottom of the screen if the game is played on a desktop browser.

For this to have an effect, the `PlayerShip` needs to be initialized with a new y location. Modify the bolded line of `PlayerShip` in `game.js`:

```
var PlayerShip = function() {
   this.setup('ship', { vx: 0, reloadTime: 0.25, maxVel: 200 });
   this.reload = this.reloadTime;
   this.x = Game.width/2 - this.w / 2;
   this.y = Game.height - Game.playerOffset - this.h;
   ...
```

The player will now be set up off the bottom of the screen as is appropriate for the device to prevent the control buttons from obscuring gameplay.

Testing on Mobile

To test this game on an actual mobile device, you need to run the game on a web server, either by setting one up on your development machine or by deploying the code to a web host. Both of these methods are a bit outside the scope of this book.

> **NOTE** *You can find lots of hosting companies on the web of varying quality. DreamHost (`http://dreamhost.com`) is usually an acceptable choice if you are just starting.*

In the long run, you need to test your games without having to deploy them. This enables you to make changes and quickly test them without any intermediate steps to slow down the process. If you use Windows, you can most likely install IIS, depending on your version of Windows, but IIS configuration can be involved and, unless you're comfortable with window configuration tasks, you may want to use one of the following options. If you use a Mac, you can access Web Sharing from the Sharing section of System Preferences. On Linux you can install Apache.

If getting a fully configured web server seems daunting, you can check out WAMP at `http://www.wampserver.com/en/`. WAMP is a project designed to give you a zero-configuration Apache server on Windows. Web sharing on OS X and native packaging of Apache on Linux is usually a better option for the other platforms. For simple needs you can also try mongoose at `http://code.google.com/p/mongoose/`, a web server that you execute from the directory you want to serve.

Assuming you are on a network with Wi-Fi, and your development machine and your mobile device are on the same network, you should now access your development machines from your mobile device when you have a web server set up and configured and your files are in the proper location. (This depends on the server and configuration.)

Look up the IP address for your machine on the local network. This is most likely different from the Public IP address that machines on the web see because most Wi-Fi networks are behind a router. To find your IP address on Windows, the easiest way is to bring up the Command Prompt program (usually in Accessories) and type **ipconfig**.

You should see a number that looks like xxx.xxx.xxx.xxx (usually something like `192.168.0.50`) in addition to some other cruft. You may see a couple of other IP addresses that end in 1, such as 192.168.0.1. This is the gateway address and not the address of your computer.

On a Mac or Linux, bring up Terminal and type **ifconfig**.

On Linux you may need to type `sudo ifconfig`. Again you should see a number that looks like an IP address among a bunch of other lines of information.

Armed with that IP address and the path underneath the document root (the directory where your web server serves files from) of your game, you should now bring up your game on a mobile device by typing in the IP address followed by the path. You can also run the version of the game to this point at `http://mh5gd.com/ch3/touch/`.

If you fire the game up on a mobile device, you immediately notice a problem: While the game is playable, it's small by default, and the canvas element is overriding the touch events, which means zooming in is difficult. (You can zoom by pinching on the whitespace around the canvas.) This is remedied in the next section.

MAXIMIZING THE GAME

Screen real estate on mobile devices is valuable especially for mobile games. The last thing you want to do is waste some of that real estate by not having maximized the game.

Setting the Viewport

The first step is to tell the browser that you don't want to let users zoom in and out of the page. This is done by setting a viewport `<meta>` tag in the HTML. The viewport tag began its life as an iOS-only feature but has since spread to Android as well. Add the following to the `<head>` of your HTML document.

```
<meta name="viewport" content="width=device-width, user-scalable=0,
minimum-scale=1.0, maximum-scale=1.0"/>
```

This tag tells the browser to set the width of the page to the actual device's pixel width and not to let the user zoom in and out. Chapter 6, "Being a Good Mobile Citizen," discusses this tag in depth.

If you reload the page, you notice the game is zoomed in a bit but still doesn't correctly fit on the page.

Resizing the Canvas

To fix the size issue and set the game up on the page so it fits as well as possible, there are a few extra steps that need to be taken. This is more difficult than it may seem due to various mobile peculiarities. Chapter 6 covers this topic in depth, but following is the basic pseudo-code:

```
Check if browser has support for touch events

Exit early if screen is larger than a max size or no touch support

Check if the user is in landscape mode,
```

```
    if so, ask them to rotate the browser

Resize container to be larger than the page
to allow removal of address bar

Scroll window slightly to force removal of address bar.

Set the container size to match the window size

Check if you're on a larger device (like a tablet)
    if so, set the view size to be twice
    the pixel size for performance
If not,
    set canvas to match the size of the window.

Finally, set the canvas to absolute position
in the top left of the window
```

Moving on to the actual code, add the method from Listing 3-3 to the bottom of the definition of the Game object in engine.js before the return statement:

LISTING 3-3: setupMobile

```javascript
this.setupMobile = function() {

  var container = document.getElementById("container"),
      hasTouch =  !!('ontouchstart' in window),
      w = window.innerWidth, h = window.innerHeight;

  if(hasTouch) { mobile = true; }

  if(screen.width >= 1280 || !hasTouch) { return false; }

  if(w > h) {
    alert("Please rotate the device and then click OK");
    w = window.innerWidth; h = window.innerHeight;
  }

  container.style.height = h*2 + "px";
  window.scrollTo(0,1);
  h = window.innerHeight + 2;

  container.style.height = h + "px";
  container.style.width = w + "px";
  container.style.padding = 0;

  if(h >= this.canvas.height * 1.75 ||
     swx >= this.canvas.height * 1.75) {
    this.canvasMultiplier = 2;
    this.canvas.width = w / 2;
    this.canvas.height = h / 2;
```

```
            this.canvas.style.width = w + "px";
            this.canvas.style.height = h + "px";
        } else {
            this.canvas.width = w;
            this.canvas.height = h;
        }
        this.canvas.style.position='absolute';
        this.canvas.style.left="0px";
        this.canvas.style.top="0px";
    };
```

The `innerWidth` and `innerHeight` need to be checked multiple times. This is because the size of the window changes over the course of the method call after the user rotates the device and after the `window.scrollTo` method is called to remove the address bar.

The other trick is that the CSS size of the `canvas` element can be set independently from its pixel size (specified with the `width` and `height` attributes on the tag.) This enables you to scale the visual size of the element up without having to push lots more pixels. The downside to this is that pixels will be effectively four times as large, making the game look slightly pixelated. In the case of a retro-shooter such as *Alien Invasion*, this isn't a huge deal, but it's something to note.

The `setupMobile` now must be called from `Game.initialize`. In addition, the game should add touch controls onto the page if only they are supported by the device. Modify the method to read

```
    // Game Initialization
    this.initialize = function(canvasElementId,sprite_data,callback) {
        this.canvas = document.getElementById(canvasElementId);

        this.playerOffset = 10;
        this.canvasMultiplier= 1;
        this.setupMobile();

        this.width = this.canvas.width;
        this.height= this.canvas.height;

        this.ctx = this.canvas.getContext &&
                    this.canvas.getContext('2d');

        if(!this.ctx) {
            return alert("Please upgrade your browser to play");
        }
        this.setupInput();
        if(this.mobile) {
            this.setBoard(4,new TouchControls());
        }

        this.loop();

    SpriteSheet.load(sprite_data,callback);
    };
```

With a check for `this.mobile`, the game will add only the visual touch controls and bind to touch events if the device supports it.

Adding to the iOS Home Screen

There's a last set of meta tags needed to reach HTML5-gaming nirvana: full-screen play. This code works only on an iOS device, iPad, iPhone, or iPod Touch.

Add the following two <meta> tags to the <head> below the viewport declaration:

```
<meta name="apple-mobile-web-app-capable" content="yes">
<meta name="apple-mobile-web-app-status-bar-style" content=
"black">
```

Now reload the game, and then click the button to add it to your home screen. With the exception of a small sliver of status bar at the top of the page, your game can now run full screen. (See Chapter 6 for a full explanation of these tags.) You can also run the version of the game to this point at http://mh5gd.com/ch3/resize.

ADDING A SCORE

There's still one obvious piece to the game that is clearly missing: a point system for users to brag about to their friends. This is something that you can remedy quickly by adding a new game board to the game.

Add the contents of Listing 3-4 to the bottom of engine.js.

LISTING 3-4: GamePoints

```
var GamePoints = function() {
  Game.points = 0;
  var pointsLength = 8;
  this.draw = function(ctx) {
    ctx.save();

    ctx.font = "bold 18px arial";
    ctx.fillStyle= "#FFFFFF";

    var txt = "" + Game.points;

    var i = pointsLength - txt.length, zeros = "";
    while(i-- > 0) { zeros += "0"; }

    ctx.fillText(zeros + txt,10,20);

    ctx.restore();
  }
  this.step = function(dt) { }
}
```

This object has one purpose in its life: to draw the score in the top left of the game. The current score for the game is stored directly on the Game object in a property named points. Every time a new `GamePoints` object is created, the game assumes a new game is beginning and resets the score to 0.

For every frame, the game grabs the current score and pads it with leading zeros so that it's always `pointsLength` digits long. It then calls `fillText` to draw the points onto the screen.

To get the points onto the page, a `GamePoints` object needs to be created. Open up `game.js` and add the initializer to the fifth board:

```
var playGame = function() {
  var board = new GameBoard();
  board.add(new PlayerShip());
  board.add(new Level(level1,winGame));
  Game.setBoard(3,board);
  Game.setBoard(5,new GamePoints(0));
};
```

Board 5 was chosen because Board 4 was just used by the `TouchControls` in the last section.

If you were to reload the game, you'd now see the points in the top left of the page, but they are sadly stuck at zero. Because the player should get points every time an enemy is killed, the easiest thing to do is add some logic to the `Enemy.hit` method.

Modify that method in `game.js` to read:

```
Enemy.prototype.hit = function(damage) {

  this.health -= damage;

  if(this.health <=0) {
    if(this.board.remove(this)) {
      Game.points += this.points || 100;
      this.board.add(new Explosion(this.x + this.w/2,
                                   this.y + this.h/2));
    }
  }
};
```

The points are increased on a per-enemy basis, but if the enemy doesn't have a point property set, it defaults to 100. You can modify the `enemies` blueprint to make the point amounts vary by enemy type.

Reload the game, and you should be able rack up a score. You can also run the version of the game to this point at `http://mh5gd.com/ch3/score`.

MAKING IT A FAIR FIGHT

Alien Invasion is now down to its last enhancement, giving the enemies a little bit of fire power to fight back.

Cribbing from `PlayerMissile`, the game needs an object, `EnemyMissile`, to represent the enemy projectiles being fired. Add the code in Listing 3-5 to the bottom of `game.js` to create `EnemyMissile`.

LISTING 3-5: The EnemyMissile object

```
var EnemyMissile = function(x,y) {
  this.setup('enemy_missile',{ vy: 200, damage: 10 });
  this.x = x - this.w/2;
  this.y = y;
};

EnemyMissile.prototype = new Sprite();
EnemyMissile.prototype.type = OBJECT_ENEMY_PROJECTILE;

EnemyMissile.prototype.step = function(dt)  {
  this.y += this.vy * dt;
  var collision = this.board.collide(this,OBJECT_PLAYER)
  if(collision) {
    collision.hit(this.damage);
    this.board.remove(this);
  } else if(this.y > Game.height) {
      this.board.remove(this);
  }
};
```

`EnemyMissile` is much like the evil twin to `PlayerMisisle`. It has a different vertical direction, a different type, a different type to collide against, and a different check for when it's off the board. The functionality is all the same; it's just doing it in reverse.

To get `EnemyMissile` objects onto the page, the `Enemy` step function needs to fire some off at some random interval. As an added complication, some enemies can fire two missiles at a time, much like the player, and some can fire just one, straight down the center.

The sprite `enemy_missile` also needs to be defined, so add this entry to the `sprites` list at the top of `game.js`:

```
var sprites = {
  ship: { sx: 0, sy: 0, w: 37, h: 42, frames: 1 },
  missile: { sx: 0, sy: 30, w: 2, h: 10, frames: 1 },
  enemy_purple: { sx: 37, sy: 0, w: 42, h: 43, frames: 1 },
  enemy_bee: { sx: 79, sy: 0, w: 37, h: 43, frames: 1 },
  enemy_ship: { sx: 116, sy: 0, w: 42, h: 43, frames: 1 },
  enemy_circle: { sx: 158, sy: 0, w: 32, h: 33, frames: 1 },
  explosion: { sx: 0, sy: 64, w: 64, h: 64, frames: 12 },
  enemy_missile: { sx: 9, sy: 42, w: 3, h: 20, frame: 1 }
};
```

Modify the `Enemy` object as highlighted here to add in missile firing capabilities:

```
Enemy.prototype = new Sprite();
Enemy.prototype.type = OBJECT_ENEMY;

Enemy.prototype.baseParameters =
            { A: 0, B: 0, C: 0, D: 0,
              E: 0, F: 0, G: 0, H: 0,
              t: 0, firePercentage: 0.01,
```

```
                    reloadTime: 0.75, reload: 0 };

Enemy.prototype.step = function(dt) {
  this.t += dt;

  this.vx = this.A +
            this.B * Math.sin(this.C * this.t + this.D);
  this.vy = this.E +
            this.F * Math.sin(this.G * this.t + this.H);

  this.x += this.vx * dt;
  this.y += this.vy * dt;

  var collision = this.board.collide(this,OBJECT_PLAYER);
  if(collision) {
    collision.hit(this.damage);
    this.board.remove(this);
  }

  if(this.reload <= 0 &&
     Math.random() < this.firePercentage) {
    this.reload = this.reloadTime;
    if(this.missiles == 2) {
      this.board.add(
        new EnemyMissile(this.x+this.w-2,this.y+this.h/2)
      );
      this.board.add(
        new EnemyMissile(this.x+2,this.y+this.h/2)
      );
    } else {
      this.board.add(
        new EnemyMissile(this.x+this.w/2,this.y+this.h)
      );
    }

  }
  this.reload-=dt;

  if(this.y > Game.height ||
     this.x < -this.w ||
     this.x > Game.width) {
       this.board.remove(this);
  }
};
```

The first change affects baseParameters. A couple of additional defaults need to be added to the enemy to control the likelihood of firing and the speed at which the enemy can fire: firePercentage and reloadTime, respectively. firePercentage is a number against which a random number is checked. If the random number is less than firePercentage, the enemy fires one or more missiles. Because this method is called each step frame, firePercentage needs to be a relatively small number to prevent the enemies from firing constantly.

Next is reloadTime and reload, which work exactly like their PlayerShip counterparts, preventing missiles from being fired in rapid succession.

The code to actually fire missiles also matches the code from the player, except that based on the number of missiles the `Enemy` has been configured with (1 or 2), the code needs to check whether to send one missile firing from the center of the enemy or two missiles firing from the left and the right side of the `Enemy`. Much like `PlayerShip`, the `Enemy` needs be prevented from firing missiles in rapid succession. To prevent this, the reload time is checked, and only after the `Enemy` reloads its weapons does it check against a randomly generated number to see if it should `fire`.

If you load up the game, you should have enemies firing missiles as expected; however, all the enemies will be firing just one missile at the same frequency.

To adjust the frequency of firing, you need to modify the enemy blueprints at the top of `game.js`. Modify the `enemies` array to have the `ltr` and `wiggle` enemies each fire two missiles at a time (matching their sprite image) and reduce the `firePercentage` of the `straight` and `wiggle` enemies to `0.001` to prevent them from firing too many missiles at once, as shown here:

```
var enemies = {
  straight: { x: 0,   y: -50, sprite: 'enemy_ship', health: 10,
              E: 100, firePercentage: 0.001 },
  ltr:   { x: 0,    y: -100, sprite: 'enemy_purple', health: 10,
              B: 75, C: 1, E: 100, missiles: 2  },
  circle: { x: 250,   y: -50, sprite: 'enemy_circle', health: 10,
              A: 0,   B: -100, C: 1, E: 20,
              F: 100, G: 1, H: Math.PI/2 },
  wiggle: { x: 100, y: -50, sprite: 'enemy_bee', health: 20,
              B: 50, C: 4, E: 100, firePercentage: 0.001,
              missiles: 2 },
  step:   { x: 0,    y: -50, sprite: 'enemy_circle', health: 10,
              B: 150, C: 1.2, E: 75 }
};
```

With that, reload the game, and you should have a playable game with active enemies. You can also play the game at `http://mh5gd.com/ch3/fair/`.

SUMMARY

It's been a whirlwind in the first three chapters, having gone from making the first few marks onto the canvas to building a fully functional mobile space shooter. As a demo game, *Alien Invasion* isn't bad, but as a full-fledged space shooter there's still lots that could be done: high scores, ship animations, sounds, longer and varied levels, new enemies, and boss fights. The good news is that the code on Github at `https://github.com/cykod/AlienInvasion` can be forked and enhanced. If you've been following along, you've stepped through every line of the game and should know it inside and out. Check the readme file for what others have done.

PART II
Mobile HTML5

HTML5 for Mobile

WHAT'S IN THIS CHAPTER?

➤ Getting acquainted with the history behind HTML5

➤ Understanding feature detection and progressive enhancement

➤ Using HTML5 for gaming

➤ Using HTML5 for mobile

➤ Understanding the state of mobile browsers

WROX.COM CODE DOWNLOADS FOR THIS CHAPTER

The wrox.com code downloads for this chapter are found at www.wrox.com/remtitle .cgi?isbn=9781118301326 on the Download Code tab. The code is in the chapter 04 download and individually named according to the names throughout the chapter.

INTRODUCTION

HTML5 is a wonderful technology that, by the time it's fully implemented in all browsers in 2020, is going to pick up your dry cleaning, tidy up your apartment, walk your dog, and bring about world peace. Actually, it will do none of those things, but from some of the hype lauded onto the standard, you might think it would. There is one thing HTML5 is guaranteed to do: make the world a more interesting place.

CAPTURING A BRIEF HISTORY OF HTML5

Technically, HTML5 is the next standard in a long line of standards being worked on and promoted by the World Wide Web consortium. The World Wide Web Consortium (online at www.w3.org), known as the W3C, is the primary standards body responsible for standardizing the web so that different content producers and browsers makers can build technology, including HTML5, that interoperates correctly.

Understanding How HTML5 Grew Up "Different"

HTML5 began life a little differently from its predecessors and didn't start its life as the brainchild of the W3C. Rather, HTML5 was birthed in many ways as a rebellion to the standard the W3C was pushing at the time: XHTML 2.0.

XHTML 2.0 had a lot of things going for it and, if it had really taken off, would have made the web a more consistent place instead of the Wild West of bad markup that exists today. But it suffered from a fatal flaw that made it practically a nonstarter: It wasn't backward compatible. That meant that if you had a perfectly valid HTML 4 site, you would have to throw that site out and start from scratch to make it XHTML 2.0-compliant. In addition, jumping back to 2004, the speed at which the W3C was innovating the web was slow as molasses, with the last update to the HTML 4 standard, HTML 4.01, having been released four years previously in 2000.

In response to disappointment over the XHTML 2.0 standard, an offshoot known as the Web Hypertext Application Technology Working Group (WHATWG) formed in 2004. The WHATWG was made up of members from Apple, Mozilla, and Opera, and it immediately began to work on a new standard. Fast forward to 2007 and the standard the WHATWG had been working on over the previous three years and which had been gaining some significant momentum is proposed to the W3C as the starting point for a new standard called HTML5, to be developed concurrently with XHTML 2.

The W3C relented and started working on HTML5, pushing out the first working draft at the beginning of 2008. Furthermore, it abandoned XHTML 2.0 in 2009 when it let the charter of the working group that was developing the spec expire, an acceptance of the reality of the time that XHTML was a dead standard.

Looking Toward HTML6? HTML7? Nope, Just HTML5

In January 2011, the editor of the HTML5 spec at the WHATWG, Ian Hickson, announced that the working group was going to treat the HTML5 spec as a "living document" that would continue to be updated and worked on indefinitely. The W3C was still going to release an official snapshot of HTML5, but the document itself will continue to be updated as new technical recommendations come in.

What does that mean for developers? On the good side, there's lots of cool stuff coming down the pipeline that will take it from idea to single browser implementation to being well supported and in the specification—in a fraction of the time that it used to take. As a developer you're going to get lots of goodies, which makes it a fun time to be building stuff. On the down side, there's a lot of stuff coming down the pipeline, such as direct access to video cameras and support for joypads, but browser fragmentation is again a big issue, as well as just keeping up with everything going on.

Going to the Spec

One of the great things about the HTML5 spec is that it's readable. Even though it's a document aimed at browser implementers, it's nonetheless an incredibly useful document for web developers and worth checking out whenever you need to figure something out authoritatively. A lot of times, the spec can answer your question more efficiently than the normal practice of Googling for the answer. If you haven't been there already, take a quick visit to the permanent home of the HTML spec, "Living Standard," which is permanently housed at www.whatwg.org/html.

The next time you look something up, such as the parameters to a variation of drawImage, spend a bit of time getting comfortable with the format and organization of the spec, because it provides the easiest way to look up specific features of HTML5. Only when there's a nonstandard implementation or not yet a spec for a feature should you start elsewhere.

Differentiating the HTML5 Family and HTML5

Since the term HTML5 entered the public's consciousness, generally agreed to be around April 2010 when Steve Jobs wrote his infamous "Thoughts on Flash" letter (www.apple.com/hotnews/thoughts-on-flash), "HTML5" has been used as an umbrella term for a number of different standards. Some of those standards were part of HTML5 at some point and have since been broken out, whereas others have always been their own standard.

Some of the standards that are often included when someone says "HTML5" are as follows:

➤ SVG

➤ CSS3

➤ WebGL

➤ Web Workers

➤ Web Storage

➤ Web SQL Database

➤ Web Sockets

➤ Geolocation

➤ Microdata

➤ Device API

➤ File API

The use of the umbrella term *HTML5* to include all these is technically wrong, but it's also rather convenient. HTML5 is the buzzword people know and understand. To most developers it just means building something natively in the browser without plug-ins, and I think that's ok.

This book is clear when referring to a specific part of the HTML5 specification or another specification, but most of the time it refers to the family of technologies that HTML5 has come to encompass.

USING HTML5 THE RIGHT WAY

As explained in the last section, through a fortuitous confluence of circumstances, for the first time in the history of the web, web developers have an official W3C-approved specification (okay, it's a "working draft" right now) that syncs up with the realities and desires of day-to-day development. For web developers that had been starved for so long by the stagnation of the web, the current renaissance of activity truly feels like being suddenly handed a large piece of cake after having had to dig around for scraps of bread.

The number of goodies added to the web developer's toolbox in the past few years is staggering. Even Microsoft, traditionally mired in a bog in proprietary technology, has jumped in and is making a serious push toward supporting standards-based web development without proprietary plug-ins.

Having Your Cake and Eating It, Too

HTML5 is truly a browser-driven spec in that the browser makers are the ones who are pushing the standard forward. This means that a lot of features that start out in one browser or multiple browsers with incompatible implementations are eventually unified as the browser makers come to an agreement on details and implementation.

The most obvious example of this evolution from initial implementation to standard is with CSS3 vendor prefixes. (As noted earlier, technically CSS3 is not part of HTML5.) When new CSS3 features leap onto the scene, you generally must write a number of lines that may differ only slightly by vendor prefix. For example, in 2010, to add a drop shadow onto a container, you would have had to write the following:

```
-moz-box-shadow:5px 5px 10px #000;;
-webkit-box-shadow:5px 5px 10px #000;;
-ms-box-shadow:5px 5px 10px #000;;
-o-box-shadow:5px 5px 10px #000;;
 box-shadow:5px 5px 10px #000;;
```

That includes four vendor-specific versions and then a forward-looking standards-based version. Fast forward to 2011, and it becomes possible to simply write this:

```
box-shadow:5px 5px 10px #000;
```

Although keeping track of the rate of change is daunting, as a developer you get the best of both worlds: shiny tools you can use immediately (albeit carefully, especially when standards aren't yet finalized) combined with standardization coming over months instead of years.

Sniffing Browsers

In the bad old days of web development, you might see the following littered throughout the `<head>` of an HTML document:

> **WARNING** *The following code is an example of what* not *to do, so please don't use either of these examples.*

```
<!--[if IE 6]>
 <link rel='stylesheet' href='ie6.css' type='text/css'/>
<![endif]-->
<!--[if IE 7]>
 <link rel='stylesheet' href='ie7.css' type='text/css'/>
<![endif]-->
```

Alternatively, you might also at some point have written this:

```
function isIE() {
 if(navigator.userAgent.match(/MSIE (\d+\.\d+);/i)) {
   isVersion = new Number(RegExp.$1);
   return true;
 } else {
   return false;
 }
}

if (isIE()) {
 if(ieVersion == 6) { /* IE6 only Code */ }
 else if(ieVersion == 7) { /* IE7 only Code */ }
}
```

The first of these snippets is known as *conditional comments* (an Internet Explorer-only [IE-only] feature), whereas the second is known as *UA sniffing* because it tries to decipher the browser being used from the string of information provided by the browser, called the `userAgent`.

Although using these snippets to determine how your application should act might have been a workable solution in 2007, when accommodating three browser versions—IE6, IE7, and Firefox 2— would have accounted for nearly 95% of the market, the current round of browser wars have shaken things up dramatically, as shown in Figure 4-1, which uses data provided by `statcounter.com`.

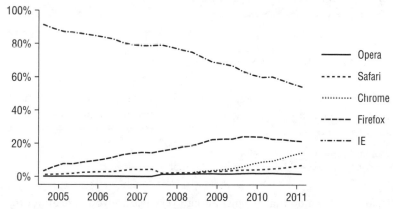

FIGURE 4-1: Desktop browser usage.

As of this writing, IE on the desktop has slipped to just more than 50% of the browser share and is split between four different versions: IE6, IE7, IE8, and IE9, with IE10's release just around the corner. Chrome is on the rise, now in the double digits; and Firefox, although declining a bit, is still more than 20%. Safari has been slowly and steadily on the rise and may hit double digits in 2012 if

Apple continues to roll. With the exception of IE, most users of other browsers are most likely to use a current version or one of the previous two releases due to the way the browsers are now actively pushing auto-updates. IE has also rolled out auto-updates, but users of older operating systems are limited to the browser they can use (IE6 for Windows 2000, IE8 for Windows XP, and IE9 for Windows Vista).

Auto-update notwithstanding, taking into consideration still-in-use previous versions of all the browsers, you're looking at more than 15 combinations of desktop browsers and versions that need to be supported. To make things worse, this book isn't talking primarily about desktop browsers, is it? On mobile devices the dominant browser players in the United States are iOS and Android, with Firefox, Windows Phone 7 (WP7), Opera, Symbian, and Blackberry also in the running. Add in a boatload of different devices and screen sizes, the rise of the tablets, and fragmentation across Android, and your head should start to spin.

You could probably start writing conditional comments and doing browser sniffing right now and never stop because new devices are released all the time.

Determining Capabilities, Not Browsers

It's not all doom and gloom, however. With the right approach, you can develop for both the now and the future. The most important aspect of this approach is the idea of testing the capabilities of browsers rather than trying to identify the browser itself.

An initial naive way to check for support (which was common in pre-HTML5 days) would be to scour the Internet to figure out which browsers support, for example, the `Canvas` tag and then match versions. You might try something like the following code:

> **WARNING** *The following code is again an example of what* not *to do.*

```
var canvasSupported = (isIE() && ieVersion >= 9) ||
                      (isFirefox() && ffVersion >= 1.5) ||
                      (isOpera() && oVersion >= 9) ||
                      ... And so on ..
```

As you probably figured out, this is a bad idea. It suffers from needing to keep up-to-date on all the different types of browsers that people use and knowing what's supported in which. It's a recipe for disaster. Life would be good if you could just write

```
function isCanvasSupported() {
    // Directly check if the browser knows about the canvas element
}
```

Actually you can do just that, and you can do that for just about every feature you care about in HTML5.

The most common method is to try to create an element and check if it supports a certain method. Or if the functionality is not per DOM-element, you can just check if the browser has a necessary method. Following is an example of each:

```
function isCanvasSupported(){
    // First create a <canvas> element
```

```
        var elem = document.createElement('canvas');

        // Next make sure it supports getContext and can return a 2D context
        return !!(elem.getContext && elem.getContext('2d'));
    }

    function isGeolocationSupported() {
        // Check if the geolocation object is defined
        return navigator.geolocation;
    }
```

Now, before you go off and check the spec and write functions for each of the features you want to support, the good people behind Modernizr (`ww.modernizr.com`) have done all the hard work for you, all for the cost of loading one script that is less than 7 kb when served compressed. If you want to pull the file size down further, you can add only the checks you need to your custom download.

Modernizr enables you to reduce feature detection checks to the following:

```
    if(Modernizr.canvas) {
        // Do something with canvas
    }
```

Modernizr provides more than 40 checks for support for next-generation features and is adding checks often, so it should be your go-to resource.

Enhancing Progressively

Now that you have the ability to know exactly what features are supported in the browser your code runs in, how do you best use that information? The answer is, "It depends."

In some situations, the lack of support for a specific feature is a nonstarter. If your game depends on canvas, for example, lack of canvas support means the game isn't going to run. In other situations, lack of a feature might reduce the user's experience, but it shouldn't prevent the user from accessing your game.

> **PROGRESSIVE ENHANCEMENT IN THE REAL WORLD**
>
> My company built a game for `GamesForLanguage.com` called *SpaceWords*, which lets multiple players use their smartphones as controls for the game. If the browser supports orientation events, the game uses those events as the movement input, allowing players to control their ship by rotating their phone. If the smartphone doesn't support those events, the game uses touch events. Finally, if the phone doesn't support touch events, the game uses normal `MouseDown` events.

In each case, access to more functionality means you could bring a better experience to the player without leaving those on less-capable devices out of the game entirely. *Progressive enhancement* is the buzzword for starting out with a base level of functionality and including additional features for only those that support it.

In the best of situations, you can use the same code for both the minimal support and the enhanced features, and only include additional code for the enhanced experience. As most developers do their development and testing on the most capable devices, this means you have a better chance of having working code on the less-capable devices than if you use completely different codebases for the two.

Polyfilling in the Gaps

The last section discussed how the lack of support for a specific feature can be a nonstarter for some situations. This isn't exactly true because sometimes you can find a polyfill to fill in the gaps.

A *polyfill* is a chunk of code that backports features to browsers that don't support the feature natively. For mobile, this may not be an issue because the mobile stack is generally good as long as you are on a recent smartphone.

The support diminishes, however, the minute you step out of the iOS, Android, and WP7 space into Blackberrys and feature phones. In those situations polyfills, such as those for local storage and CSS3 features, become very useful.

The advantage of detecting features instead of browsers comes to the forefront again because a true polyfill exposes the same interface as the native feature. This means that you can often add a polyfill script to the head of your document and add enhanced functionality to older browsers for free.

CSS3 Pie (`http://css3pie.com/`), for example, provides a polyfill that adds CSS3 decorations like rounded corners, gradients, and drop shadows to older versions of IE.

Not surprisingly, given its focus, Modernizr provides a great list of the polyfills on its wiki: `https://github.com/Modernizr/Modernizr/wiki/HTML5-Cross-Browser-Polyfills`.

CONSIDERING HTML5 FROM A GAME PERSPECTIVE

In this chapter you've heard a lot about HTML5 but not much about how HTML5 can help you build games on mobile devices. This section discusses the main ways to build games with HTML5, and the next section covers mobile-friendly features that can make your games more interesting. Now look briefly at the three main ways you can build games from an HTML5 perspective. (Each of these is covered in much more detail in later chapters, and Chapter 12, "Building Games with CSS3" explains which method to pick for your specific game.)

Canvas

`Canvas`, which is discussed in detail in Chapter 15, "Learning Canvas," and used throughout the book, is in many ways the most interesting feature game-wise of the actual HTML5 standard. It gives developers access to a fast frame buffer where you can draw images and graphics.

Most discussions of `Canvas` in this book mean 2-D canvas because that is the only canvas context that's currently well supported on mobile devices. But there will be a discussion about the Webgl context briefly as well as support for 3-D canvas, which is poised to appear on mobile devices (or may already be there by the time this book gets in your hands). Figure 4-2 shows the canvas plat-former built in Chapter 18, "Creating a 2D Platformer."

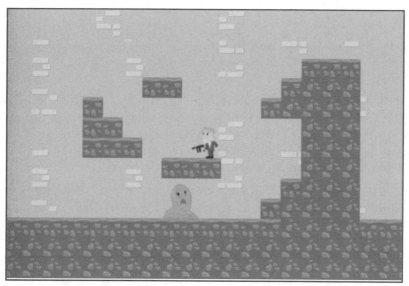

FIGURE 4-2: A mobile 2D platformer.

CSS3/DOM

As you see in Chapter 12, "Building Games with CSS3," CSS3 adds a lot of power to traditional HTML DOM elements and can definitely be considered a viable technology to build a game on. For games with touch interfaces (that is, mobile), it may be quicker to use CSS3 and the DOM because the browser handles a lot of the hit detection and interaction for you. In addition, support for hardware-accelerated transforms and animation on mobile WebKit gives a performance boost over canvas in many situations. Figure 4-3 Shows the CSS3 RPG built in Chapter 13, "Crafting a CSS3 RPG."

FIGURE 4-3: A CSS3 RPG.

SVG

The black sheep of the family, SVG has actually been hanging out doing its thing since 2004. However, with the release of IE9 in April 2011, as the first release of IE to support it natively, people are coming around slowly to its benefits and potential uses.

Scalable Vector Graphics (SVG) provides a way to draw resolution-independent graphics. Much like Flash, SVG stores the instructions to draw elements rather than the resultant pixels that make up those elements. This means that, provided it's used correctly, SVG creates small file sizes good for mobile devices. It also generates its own scene graph—much like the standard DOM—and is well supported on WebKit mobile and useful in touch games.

In many ways SVG combines the best of both worlds between `Canvas` and CSS3. The major problem is that performance is lacking, so if you are building an action game, SVG is probably not an option. Figure 4-4 shows the SVG game built in Chapter 14, "Building Games with SVG and Physics."

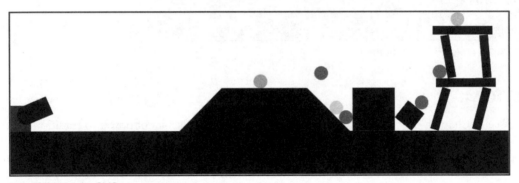

FIGURE 4-4: An SVG cannon game.

CONSIDERING HTML5 FROM A MOBILE PERSPECTIVE

One of the phrases that you hear a lot these days is "mobile first." This phrase means considering mobile devices as your primary target and considering support for additional browsers later on. This might not seem obvious with mobile browsers, as of 2012, barely in the double digits of overall usage, but it's more than just a numbers game. Considering mobile devices first means you start with a number of significant constraints and work out from there.

Mobile devices have small screens and screens of different sizes and aspect ratios. They have limited processing power and bandwidth and often have limited storage. All these constraints force you, as a developer, to optimize your web app—make it more adaptable; make it load faster and be more performant. Not surprisingly, these are all things that can bring a better experience to users with desktop browsers as well. Web developers have been a bit lazy, viewing their projects on 30-inch monitors connected to fat Internet pipes and running on four-core multithreaded processors. Most likely a good portion of your target demographic for casual web games doesn't share the same hardware specifications. Considering the mobile usage of your site as a primary consideration can help you move away from that attitude.

Understanding the New APIs

The family of specifications tied together as "HTML5" is a large family, and some pieces you couldn't care less about from a game perspective. Are advances in semantic, tags such as the `<aside>`, and support for microdata actually going to help you build a great game? Probably not. But there are a lot of exciting Application Programming Interfaces (APIs) that you should care about, the most interesting of which from a game perspective are shown in Table 4-1.

TABLE 4-1: New HTML5 APIs

API NAME	DESCRIPTION
Touch	Most mobile devices support touch events that act much like their mouse counterparts but with the addition of touch tracking and multitouch, meaning you can track more than one touch at a time, which is important for action games where you need to have onscreen controls.
Orientation and Acceleration	Supports detecting changes to orientation and acceleration events when a user physically moves their phone around.
Application Cache	Allows you to cache the assets needed for your game offline, meaning you can configure your game to launch without any Internet access.
Offline Storage	Provides ability to store the game state locally. It means you don't need to save everything constantly to the server and can let your players pick up right where they left off, without needing access to a server.
Geolocation	Has the ability to detect the physical location of a player in the real world.

What's Coming: WebAPI

Although the APIs available provide access to a number of the features on mobile devices, some significant gaps still exist as of this writing. The Mozilla WebAPI project aims to fill those gaps with access to hardware and operating system resources that would normally be available for only native apps. Cool stuff like access to the camera, file system, and vibrator motor could make for interesting features to build a game around. The progress of WebAPI is documented on the Mozilla wiki at `https://wiki.mozilla.org/WebAPI`.

SURVEYING THE MOBILE BROWSER LANDSCAPE

Before the advent of the iPhone and Mobile Safari in 2007, web browsing on your phone was in a sad state of affairs, with only Opera offering a mobile browsing experience that didn't view mobile browsing as a limited, menu-driven experience. In the years since, mobile browsers have become more capable, and the JavaScript engines on those browsers have become better by leaps and bounds.

What was unimaginable five years ago, that you could play the same web games on your phone as on your desktop browser, is slowly approaching reality with every new HTML5 game that pops on to the scene. Although the hardware is important, much like the situation on the desktop, the browser that runs on your target device is the most important arbiter of the features available.

WebKit: The Market Dominator

The good news is that unlike the desktop, the two dominant smartphone platforms—iOS and Android—have excellent mobile browsers. Even better, they both share the WebKit engine, which means that you can expect a comparable set of features and rendering engine between the two. WebKit isn't the only mobile HTML5 browser in town, but WebKit browsers do make up more than 80% of mobile U.S. traffic as of December 2011, according to www.statcounter.com.

WebKit began its life as the KHTML rendering engine and KDE JavaScript engine (KJS) inside the open-source Konquerer web browser. Apple adopted (and forked) KHTML and KJS and rebranded them as WebCore and JavaScriptCore under the umbrella of WebKit.

Since KHTML and KJS (and thus WebCore and JavaScriptCore) were originally released under GNU's Lesser General Public License (LGPL), companies releasing products off of them, including Apple, were required to release the source code of those changes to WebKit back to the open source community. This means that because the project has remained open source, many mobile device manufacturers, including Google, Nokia, Blackberry, Amazon, and HP have used it as the basis for their mobile browsers and have been releasing their changes back to the community, accelerating the quality of mobile browsing all around.

As mentioned previously, the two dominant smartphone platforms with HTML5 capable browsers—iOS and Android—both use a WebKit-based browser as the default device browser. Android, however, doesn't use JavaScriptCore but instead uses Google's V8 JavaScript engine to execute JavaScript.

WebKit is also used in Safari, Apple's default browser, as well as Google Chrome. As such, when doing mobile development, your best bet is to use Chrome or Safari to get results closer to the majority of the mobile market than if you were to use Firefox or IE. As the developer tools in Chrome are best in class, consider using Chrome as your primary development browser.

Although it may seem like having 80% of the market behind a world-class browser engine is a dream come true for developers, the truth is that not all WebKit browsers are made alike. Quirksmode.org did a comparison of the differences between the various mobile WebKit versions and declared:

> *There is no "WebKit on mobile!"*

You can view the full report on the Quirksmode.org website at www.quirksmode.org/webkit_mobile.html.

Opera: Still Plugging Along

Opera was an early entrant to the mobile space with Opera Mobile in 2000. Opera Mini, released in 2005, was one of the first useful browsers on mobile devices that used an intermediate server to process and compress requests to speed up delivery to the low-bandwidth and low-horsepower devices of the day. Opera has since lost its dominant market position in the United States. Worldwide, Opera still holds a 24.5% market share across all its products, making it the world's most popular mobile browser. However, that may not last long.

Firefox: Mozilla's Mobile Offering

Mozilla's mobile browser for Android, Fennec (Apple prohibits installing another browser on the iPhone or iPod), is close to the cutting edge. It supports a good chunk of wanted HTML5 functionality, including some features such as multitouch and orientation support that are missing on Android and on some default WebKit-based browsers.

However you may feel about Firefox's development path on the desktop, Mozilla provides a valuable role in the community as the ombudsperson of the Internet, making sure that the concerns of your average netizen don't get drowned out under the cacophony of corporate interests that dominate the Net. Having a product on mobile devices ensures that next-generation devices aren't left without Mozilla representation.

WP7 Internet Explorer 9

Although Windows Phone 7 generally received good reviews when it was released, it has yet to take significant market share. The 7.5 release shares a rendering engine with the desktop IE9, Trident 5.0, and supports SVG, HTML5, and CSS3 along with JIT compiling to boost JavaScript performance. Much like the desktop, however, IE sometimes marches to its own drummer, so if you want to support IE9 (as you should), you should at least bring your app up on an emulator early in the process and test on the real hardware early and often.

Tablets

With all the discussion of phones, don't forget about tablets: a rapidly growing market segment sitting squarely between traditional mobile and the desktop. Tablets have their own issues. They are generally underpowered compared to desktops but have higher screen resolutions than phones, meaning games need to push lots of pixels without necessarily having the hardware to back it up. The good news is that WebKit again dominates the browser space on the most popular iOS and Android tablet devices. The same rules apply: test support for different capabilities and device screen sizes.

Android provides a particular challenge because the emulator is slow compared to iOS's emulator; so effectively testing the incredibly wide range of Android devices is difficult.

SUMMARY

Mobile browsing is still evolving, both from a technology perspective and from a user perspective. The mobile browser space is still evolving at a speed comparable to (if not faster than) the desktop space. Any specifics about which HTML5 features are supported on which mobile browsers may be obsolete by the time this book makes it to the bookshelves. Luckily, you know not to bind yourself to specific browsers but rather to the self-proclaimed capabilities of those browsers.

Never rely on the information in charts for what features you enable per device for your game; always go right to the source and check capabilities (either directly or with Modernizr). The only time you should check grids of browser capabilities is to get a sense of what features you should spend time adding to your game and what portion of browsers implement those features. For a good overview, visit sites such as `http://mobilehtml5.org`, but your best bet is always to try the browsers themselves.

5

Learning Some Helpful Libraries

WROX.COM CODE DOWNLOADS FOR THIS CHAPTER

The `wrox.com` code downloads for this chapter are found at www.wrox.com/remtitle .cgi?isbn=9781118301326 on the Download Code tab. The code is in the chapter 05 download and individually named according to the names throughout the chapter.

INTRODUCTION

The most significant barrier, in the pre-Ajax days, to JavaScript becoming a viable platform for interactive cross-browser application development was the subtle differences between the various browsers. Inconsistent implementations of assorted features across the various browsers (with Internet Explorer being particularly guilty) meant that to interact with a web page, developers needed to know the ins and outs of each browser and modify their code to handle the different incompatible implementations. Combine this difficulty with the verboseness of manipulating elements on the page and making asynchronous web calls, and it's no surprise people viewed JavaScript as a toy compared to what people were doing in Java and Flash. That view began to change as libraries, which made the developer experience more consistent and the JavaScript code more concise, began to gain widespread use.

LEARNING JAVASCRIPT LIBRARIES

jQuery has become the most popular JavaScript library by leaps and bounds, and is used on more than 40% of all websites in the world (see `http://w3techs.com/technologies/overview/javascript_library/all`). It has gained its popularity for two main reasons: It's good at its job and it's namespace friendly, meaning that you never need to worry about jQuery getting in the way of your other code. You learn jQuery in this chapter and use it throughout the book.

You also learn another smaller library called Underscore.js. Whereas jQuery is concerned primarily with the manipulation of DOM elements and making Ajax calls, Underscore.js provides a number of utility functions that make JavaScript a more developer-friendly language, specifically targeted at functional programming. A self-proclaimed utility-belt for JavaScript, Underscore calls itself " ... the tie to go along with jQuery's tux." It uses many of the same idioms as jQuery and is also namespace-friendly.

> ### DO YOU EVEN NEED A LIBRARY?
>
> Technically, you could get by without any sort of JavaScript library. None of what you're going to use jQuery or Underscore for is impossible to do with JavaScript directly. It just happens to be a lot less painful. Using JavaScript, you would end up with longer, less understandable code and need to write a lot more branching statements to handle different browser implementations.

STARTING WITH JQUERY

If you are already comfortable with jQuery, you may be tempted to skip this section. However, at least take a quick glance because this section covers jQuery from a game-specific angle.

Adding jQuery to Your Page

The jQuery library consists of a single JavaScript file. To load jQuery on your page, you need to load this file via a `<script>` tag. You have two options for doing this. You can download jQuery directly, or you can load it via a Content Delivery Network (CDN).

Loading jQuery directly means that you have complete control over the file and the page. This is both a good and a bad thing. jQuery is a large library, and if it's not served properly (minified and compressed), it can be a beast. jQuery 1.7 clocked in at nearly 250 kb; if served compressed and minified, however, jQuery is only 33 kb. If you are serving it directly off your web server you need to make sure you are serving a minified version with its cache headers set correctly, so the code isn't sent on subsequent reloads. (See the next chapter for more details on cache headers.)

Another advantage of using a CDN is that most CDNs have edge-locations around the world, meaning wherever in the world your game players are located, they will be near a CDN server location with a fast connection to the Internet. This isn't something that you can always guarantee when serving files off a standard web server.

One last advantage of using a CDN is that, given the ubiquity of jQuery, there's a good chance that visitors already have a CDN version of jQuery cached in their browser, meaning 0 bytes need to be sent.

To serve jQuery off the Google CDN, all you need is to add a single <script> tag to the page:

```
<script
src='http://ajax.googleapis.com/ajax/libs/jquery/1.7.1/
    jquery.min.js'>
</script>
```

The jQuery website (http://docs.jquery.com/Downloading_jQuery#CDN_Hosted_jQuery) has a number of options but the one hosted by Google is by far the most popular. To serve it locally, you need to download the file from http://jquery.com and stick it somewhere you can access it:

```
<script src='js/jquery.min.js'></script>
```

As for where in your page the <script> tag should be added, it's up to you. The only restriction is that it should be before the first reference of the jQuery object. Most websites that use jQuery for enhancing the page recommend putting it at the bottom of the page before the </body> tag. For games this is less important because nothing is going to be visible on the page until jQuery and the rest of the JavaScript is loaded.

Understanding the $

All JavaScript loaded into a page shares a global namespace. This means that if you have a top-level variable defined in one JavaScript file, it could be accessed and overwritten in a subsequently loaded JavaScript file.

Sometimes this is a good thing. When writing a game, for example, it's nice to partition your code into various files and still have it all work together. When writing a library, however, it would be nice if you didn't need to worry about every method in your library conflicting with methods in your game. You might, for example, want to add a hide() method to your game objects without having it conflict with the hide() method provided by your DOM manipulation library.

jQuery solves this problem by wrapping everything it does into a single object called the jQuery object. So if you want to hide an element on the page that has an ID of "my-object-id" (and didn't know any other jQuery), you could write:

```
var elem = document.getElementById("my-object-id");
jQuery(elem).hide();
```

jQuery has a couple of additional tricks up its sleeve. First, you can use the $ object instead of typing the full word jQuery. The following code is equivalent to what you wrote previously:

```
var elem = document.getElementById("my-object-id");
$(elem).hide();
```

You're still missing the most powerful part of jQuery, though, and that is CSS selectors. As opposed to passing an actual DOM object to jQuery, you can just pass a string that represents a CSS selector, and jQuery matches one or more objects that match that selector. So you could get the preceding code down to one line:

```
$("#my-object-id").hide();
```

If you remember your CSS, prefixing something with a pound sign (#) means you're targeting an ID property.

jQuery also supports more complicated selectors, so you could, for example, write:

```
$("#my-form > input[type=checkbox]:checked").hide();
```

This would hide all the currently checked check boxes directly inside of an element with an ID of `my-form`.

Manipulating the DOM

Much of what jQuery is good at is "manipulating the DOM." This phrase means modifying the structure and content of a web page. The term DOM stands for Document Object Model, which is the programmatic interface to the web page.

The jQuery `hide()` method is only one of the many functions jQuery provides for manipulating the DOM. A few of the methods (`attr`, `css`, `animate`, `val`, `html`, and `text`) have two forms: a "getter" form and a "setter" form. The getter form often takes no arguments or a single string argument and returns a value; a setter form usually takes one or two arguments, a property and a value, or an object literal to set multiple values at once. Following are some examples using the different forms:

```
// Return the href of the first link on the page
var myHref= $("a").attr('href');

// Set the href for all links on the page
$("a").attr("href","http://www.google.com");

// Set the href and target for all links on the page
$("a").attr({ href: "http://www.google.com",
              target: "_blank" });

// Return the HTML in the first paragraph element
var myHTML = $("p").html();

// Set the HTML on all paragraph elements
var myHTML = $("p").html("Lorem ipsum dolor sic amet");
```

The getter versions return only the appropriate value of the first element that matches the set, whereas the setter value sets all matching elements.

The following list shows some of the most common jQuery methods you can use and their descriptions.

➤ `$(selector).show()` /`$(selector).hide()`: Show and hide matched elements on the page.

➤ `$(selector).addClass(name)` /`$(selector).removeClass(name)`: Add or remove a CSS class from an element.

➤ `$(selector).empty()`: Clear any content in an element.

➤ `$(selector).val(newValue)` /`$(selector).val()`: Set or return the value of an input element.

➤ `$(selector).attr(attributeName)` / `$(selector).attr(attributeName, value)` / `$(selector).attr(attributeHash)`: Retrieve or set an arbitrary attribute on an object.

➤ `$(selector).css(propertyName)` / `$(selector).css(propertyName,value)` / `$(selector).css(propertyHash)`: Retrieve or set an arbitrary CSS style on a DOM object.

➤ `$(selector).animate(propertyHash)`: Change a CSS style over time.

➤ `$(selector).fadeIn()` / `$(selector).fadeOut()`: Fade an element into view or fade it out of view.

➤ `$(selector).append(content)` / `$(content).appendTo(selector)`: Add some content to the bottom of a container.

➤ `$(selector).html()` / `$(selector).html(newHtml)`: Get or set the HTML in an element directly.

GET COMFORTABLE READING THE DOCUMENTATION

This section has touched on only a few of the methods available. You need to become comfortable with the jQuery documentation site at `http://api.jquery .com` because the easier it is for you to find your way around the documentation, the easier of a time you can have building dynamic interfaces on the web.

You revisit a lot of these jQuery methods in Chapter 12, "Building Games with CSS3," when you build a role-playing game (RPG) using DOM elements.

USING A JQUERY ALTERNATIVE SUCH AS ZEPTO.JS.

jQuery's greatest strength is that it unifies the programmer experience across all different browsers from IE6 forward. Its greatest strength, however, also leads to two great weaknesses: It's large and can be slow. Zepto.js is a library that was created by JavaScript wizard Thomas Fuchs to provide a jQuery like syntax without the bloat of jQuery.

For the most part, Zepto.js is a drop-in replacement focused on modern browsers other than Internet Explorer (IE). Because it has a razor-sharp focus on supporting WebKit-based and Firefox browsers, the current minified JavaScript code is under 6 kb and works great on almost all mobile devices (WP7 being the exception). Zepto.js does not work on IE, including IE9, so if you target desktop browsers for your game as well, jQuery is still the better option.

If you want to keep your loading and your file size down, and still get the convenience of jQuery, look at Zepto.js at `http://zeptojs.com/`.

Creating Callbacks

One of the most significant features of JavaScript that developers from other languages often have trouble with is the idea of functions as first-class objects. Although most other languages support callback mechanisms, the ubiquity of callbacks and the passing around of functions as parameters make JavaScript a bit different.

As you know, functions in JavaScript are created with the `function()` keyword. Functions can have names, for example:

```
function sayPhrase() { ... }
```

Or they can be anonymous:

```
function() { ... }
```

What good are anonymous functions? Well, as mentioned, they can be passed in parameters and treated like normal objects. If you want to save your anonymous function for later, you could write:

```
var sayPhrase = function() { ... }
```

Doing so also drives home the point that functions can be treated like normal objects and can be assigned to variables like any other value. (This book mostly shows this later form to make it apparent that functions get passed around just like any other object.)

To call `sayPhrase` you need to append parentheses to the name, but if you don't want to call the function and instead just want to pass it to another function as a callback, leave the parentheses off.

```
sayPhrase(); // Call sayPhrase

// Pass sayPhrase as a callback to another function
otherFunction(sayPhrase);
```

When you understand functions as first-class objects in jQuery, there's a second subtlety related to calling functions. JavaScript, as you know, is an object-oriented (OO) language, albeit not a typical one. Objects are data structures that combine data with methods for interacting with that data.

A standard, object-based method call in JavaScript looks like the following:

```
bobObj.sayPhrase();
```

In the preceding code, `bobObj` is an object with a method called `sayPhrase`. Like most OO languages, you have a special keyword you can use to refer to the current object. Unlike most other languages, however, the current object (generally called the *context*) is much more malleable in JavaScript than in other languages. For example:

```
var bobObj = {
   phrase: "Yay!",
   sayPhrase: function() { alert(this.phrase); }
   };

// Will pop up an alert with "Yay!"
bobObj.sayPhrase();

// Will pop up an alert with "undefined" after 100ms
setTimeout(bobObj.sayPhrase, 100);
```

In the first example, everything works as expected. The `this` keyword is bound to the object you expect, `bobObj`. In the second example, however, the context of the function `sayPhrase` is lost because it is used as in a callback. There are a couple of ways around this. This first is not to use the `this` keyword but to refer to the object directly:

```
bobObj = {
    phrase: "Yay!",
    sayPhrase: function() { alert(bobObj.phrase); }
    };
// Works correctly
setTimeout(bobObj.sayPhrase, 100);
```

This method is okay for one-off objects, but it is much more common to have many instances of an object, so referring to the object explicitly isn't possible. (This issue can also be skirted with a design-pattern implemented during object creation as discussed in Chapter 9, "Bootstrapping the Quintus Engine: Part I.")

A second way around this is to use the jQuery `proxy` function to permanently bind the context:

```
bobObj = {
    phrase: "Yay!",
    sayPhrase: function() { alert(this.phrase); }
    };
// Create a proxied function
var proxiedFunc = $.proxy(bobObj.sayPhrase, bobObj);
// Will pop up an alert with "Yay!" after 100ms
setTimeout(proxiedFunc, 100);
```

Any time `proxiedFunc` is called from now on, the `this` keyword will be bound to `bobObj`.

Underscore.js (discussed later in this chapter) also has a handy method that does the same thing. Using underscore, the `setTimeout` could be rewritten as

```
var proxiedFunc = _.bind(bobObj.sayPhrase, bobObj)
setTimeout(proxiedFunc);
```

Understanding the subtleties of callbacks is important in HTML5 game development because callbacks are used frequently. Making certain you know how to pass functions and knowing the context of `this` at any given time is essential.

Binding Events

One common use for callbacks is for binding event handlers. jQuery, as of version 1.7, provides a unified methodology for attaching events in using `$(selector).on`. Because it does so much, `$(selector).on` has a complicated definition with a number of optional arguments. The most common form is:

```
jQuery.on( events [, selector] [, data], handler )
```

Only two of the parameters are required: `events` and `handler`. The `events` parameter is a string of comma-separated event names, but most commonly there will be only one name. Following is the simplest example of calling `$(selector).on` for binding a click event to a link with an ID of start-button:

```
$("a#start-button").on("click",function(event) {
  alert('Starting Game!');
});
```

Notice the standard selector `$("a#start-button")` followed by the event to be bound, `"click"`, and then the callback.

> ### THE SPECIAL CASE OF DOCUMENT READY
>
> Ensuring that your code runs at the proper time takes some care. If you try to run JavaScript that refers to DOM elements that haven't been loaded yet, you'll be in trouble. Often you'll want to wait to run your JavaScript until the whole page has loaded. This is before the `window.onload` event, which triggers after all assets and images have loaded. You can use the standard event syntax to wait for this event: `$(document).on("ready",function() { ... });` but because it's so common, jQuery provides a shortcut of just passing a function to the jQuery operator: `$(function() { ... })`.

In some cases you need to prevent the event handler from taking the default action. In the preceding example, you might not want the page to go to the `href` destination of the link you just clicked by default. In that case, you need to tell the event that you don't want the default behavior to take place. You do this by calling `preventDefault` on the event object passed in as a parameter:

```
$("a#start-button").on("click",function(event) {
 event.preventDefault();
 alert('Starting Game!');
});
```

`event.preventDefault` is used most often for HTML elements with some default action, such as links, inputs elements and forms, or with keyboard events where you don't want the page scrolling around.

If later you want to turn off any click events that you have bound to `start-button`, you can call `$(selector).off` as shown here:

```
$("a#start-button").off("click");
```

This call turns off all click handlers on the button. If you want to turn off a specific handler, you need to pass that handler as the second argument.

To follow up on the discussion of context in callbacks from the last section, jQuery intentionally changes the `this` object in event callbacks to be the DOM element that triggered the event. This behavior is something you must plan for if you need access to the context from outside of the callback.

If you want to hide the Start button after it is clicked, for example, you could write the following:

```
$("a#start-button").on("click",function(event) {
 event.preventDefault();
 alert('Starting Game!');
 $(this).hide();
});
```

You need to wrap the `this` object in the jQuery object selector using `$(this)`.

JavaScript also has the capability to do event delegation, which means that you can bind an element to events on its children. This can be useful for mobile game development because mobile games often contain a multitude of elements that are frequently added and removed from the page that needs to be interacted with via touch events.

Binding events to each of these elements individually would be both time-consuming and slow. If instead you were to use event delegation, you could bind only to the container element but still receive all the events as needed.

To give a concrete example of the usefulness of this, you create a simple game called *Block Clicker*, the code for which is shown in Listing 5-1. The goal of the game is to click as many blocks that appear on the page before time runs out. If the player clicks 15 of the 20 blocks, they win; otherwise, they lose.

LISTING 5-1: binding.html—A simple shape clicking game

```
var width=$(window).width(), height=$(window).height(),
    countdown = 20, countup = 0;

var nextElement = function() {
  if(countdown == 0) {
    gameOver();
    return;
  }
  var x=Math.random()*(width - 50),
      y=Math.random()*(height - 50);
  $("<div>").css({
      position:'absolute',
      left: x,    top: y,
      width: 50, height: 50,
      backgroundColor: 'red'
    }).appendTo("#container");
  countdown--;
}

var gameOver = function() {
  // Stop additional nextElement calls from firing
  clearInterval(timer);
  if(countup > 15) {
    alert("You won!");
  } else {
    alert("You lost!");
  }
}
var timer = setInterval(nextElement,500);
$("#container").on('mousedown','div',function(e) {
    countup++;
    $(this).fadeOut();
});
```

The first thing this code does is get the dimensions of the window using jQuery; then it defines a couple of variables to store the number of blocks left to display and the number the user has clicked.

It then defines a `nextElement` function that is called each time a block is to be added to the page. This function first checks if the game is over by looking at the `countdown` variable and calls the gameOver method if it is. If the game is not over, a random *x* and *y* position is generated and a new 50-by-50-pixel red square block is created, styled, and positioned on the screen.

The gameOver function first clears the interval timer, so that no more elements are added onto the page, and then pops up an alert message either telling the player that they won or lost.

Next is a call to setInverval to ensure a new block is created every 500 milliseconds.

Finally, with one call to $(selector).on, the game captures all the mousedown events on all the <div>s inside the #container element, even for elements that have not yet been created. When the player clicks a <div>, the countup variable is increased, and the element is faded out. In this case the mousedown event is used instead of a click event because the click event requires the mouse to be released over the same element as it is clicked on, which slows down the game.

> **NOTE** *Users can cheat in the* Block Clicker *game by clicking the fading element quickly in succession. Can you think of a way to prevent this?*

Making Ajax Calls

So far, only one aspect of jQuery has been discussed in detail, DOM manipulation, but the library has some more useful tricks. jQuery also provides a simple and consistent interface for making AJAX call back to a web server. Using AJAX allows your game to push and pull data to and from a web server without requiring a full page reload. One thing to remember when making Ajax calls is that they are, by definition, asynchronous. This means that you can't be sure when they are going to be finished.

Calling Remote Servers

jQuery provides one method to rule them all when it comes to making Ajax calls, called $.Ajax. If you look at the documentation for $.Ajax at http://api.jquery.com/jQuery.ajax/, you can notice that the method takes more than 30 different options to configure various parts of the request being made.

This level of configurability can be overwhelming when you just want to send or grab some data. Luckily jQuery provides a few shorthand methods. For example, say you want to load a JSON file of level data; you could simply write:

```
$.getJSON("level1.js",function(levelData) {
    // Do something with your levelData
});
```

Behind the scenes, jQuery handles creating an XMLHttpRequest object (the browser object that actually performs the call), registers the onreadystatechange callback, and checks that the appropriate status is returned before parsing the returned data and calling your callback with the levelData. If none of that previous sentence made any sense, don't worry about it; the main point is that the details of handling AJAX calls directly is fairly involved, so the nice wrapper jQuery provides around those calls means you can focus on your game instead of the transport mechanism.

`$.getJSON` can also be used to make JSONp requests, which is a workaround for the same domain limitation that normally hampers AJAX calls. To use JSONp simply add a `callback=?` parameter to the requested URL (provided the remote server supports JSONp).

`$.getJSON` is only one of the helper methods available. Some of the other ones you can use are as follows. Only the common forms of the methods are shown here:

➤ `$.get(url,[ data, ], successCallback(data) )`: Makes a get request (as you probably expected) and returns the data. You can use this method when you load HTML or other data formats (like a text file) that you want to process before dumping on the page.

➤ `$(selector).load(url)`: A convenient method that loads the response of an AJAX get request into whatever elements were matched by the selector. Use it to quickly load content from a server (such as a top-ten list or a credits page) directly onto the page.

➤ `$.getScript(url)`: Makes a get request but evaluates the response as JavaScript, which is useful when you want the server to directly generate JavaScript that is executed by the client. `$.getScript` is also useful because it can load data from any domain, whereas any other AJAX call besides getJSON requires that you target the same domain.

➤ `$.post(url, [data, ], success(data))`: Makes a post request (with optional data) to a URL. Posts are generally done to send large amounts of data to the server and are useful for submitting form data.

For more details on all the Ajax methods available in jQuery, check out the full documentation online at `http://api.jquery.com/category/ajax/`.

Using Deferreds

One of the problems with the asynchronous part of AJAX is that when you try to do multiple things at a time but can't be sure which one is going to get done first, the logic required can get a little hairy, requiring a number of state variables or a bunch of nested callbacks. Luckily, as of jQuery 1.5, all jQuery Ajax methods return an object known as a `Deferred` that, and when used correctly, it can greatly simplify your callback code.

Say you want to load three separate JSON data files and then do something when you are done. With `Deferreds` you could write:

```
$.when($.getJSON('level1.json'),
       $.getJSON('enemies.json'),
       $.getJSON('player.json'))
    .then(function(level,enemies,player) {
       // We know all three files have loaded
    }).fail(function() {
       // One or more files failed to load
    });
```

You don't need to worry about success or failure of each individual call or the order they respond in. You instead get to wrap them up in a nice package and get a callback when all the remote calls are done. (`Deffereds` are documented at `http://api.jquery.com/category/deferred-object/`.)

USING UNDERSCORE.JS

Although jQuery provides a number of utility methods that can make your life easier when writing JavaScript, the main focus of jQuery is to modify the DOM and provide simplified Ajax support. It doesn't provide a lot of utility methods for other purposes. (jQuery does provide some, though; see `http://api.jquery.com/category/utilities/` for some examples.)

Luckily, there's a library called the Underscore.js that was created for just that purpose. Underscore is a small library (under 4 kb minified and gzipped) that provides approximately 60 methods that can make your JavaScript easier to understand and more compact.

Accessing Underscore

Underscore.js is included in your project as a single JavaScript file, much like jQuery. Also similar to jQuery, the author made the decision not to pollute the existing JavaScript namespace but rather to wrap all the methods inside of a single function identified, not surprisingly, by the underscore character, "_".

You can call underscore methods in two ways either in a functional or an object-oriented style. Following is an example of each:

```
_.isString(myVar);
_(myVar).isString();
```

The functional method calls the function directly on the underscore object, whereas the OO method first calls the underscore on the target (much like jQuery does with selectors) and then calls the method on the resulting object.

Working with Collections

The bulk of the methods in Underscore.js are targeted at working with collections, whether they are arrays or objects. Because much of what you do in game development is the manipulations of lists of objects such as sprites, these methods come in handy. Say you have an array of objects called `sprites` and you want to call the `update()` method on each of them in turn. You could write a `for` loop:

```
for(var i=0,len=sprites.length;i<len;i++) {
  sprites[i].update();
}
```

Alternatively with Underscore.js, this becomes

```
_(sprites).invoke('update');
```

The latter method is both shorter and clearer about the intention of the code. The only downside is that there is some overhead involved in calling an Underscore method instead of just writing your own loop. In most cases, however, this overhead is negligible, and the advantage of smaller, more compact code is worth the trade-off.

Some of the most common and helpful methods are documented in the following list.

- ➤ `_.each(list, callback, [context])`: Calls back each element of the list as an argument to the callback. It uses the native `forEach` in the browsers that support it. Notice `_.each` takes an additional "context" object that is bound to `this` inside the callback.

- ➤ `_.map(list, callback, [context])`: Similar to `_.each`, except it takes the return values from the callback method and returns a new array.

- ➤ `_.find(list, callback, [context])`: Returns the first item in the list for which the callback function returns `true`. It's useful for finding an element in a list based on some arbitrary criteria function.

- ➤ `_.filter(list, callback, [context])`: Similar to `_.find` except that it returns an array of all the items for which the callback returns `true`.

- ➤ `_.without(array, [*values])`: Returns a new array without any instances of values removed; useful, for example, for removing dead sprites from a list.

- ➤ `_.uniq(array, [isSorted], [iterator])`: `_.uniq` returns a copy of an array with any duplicate elements removed. If the array happens to be in a sorted state, pass `true` to `isSorted` to improve performance.

Taken together, these methods make working with lists of objects much more concise.

Using Utility Functions

Underscore also provides a number of general utility functions that can make your life easier.

- ➤ `_.bindAll(object, [*methodNames])`: Modifies any calls to `methodNames` on `object` so that the context is always `object`. This means you can pass methods to jQuery event handlers, for example, without needing to worry about the context of `this`.

- ➤ `_.keys(object)` / `_.values(object)`: Returns all of an object's keys or values.

- ➤ `_.extend(destination, *sources)`: Copies all the properties from a list of source objects over to the destination, overwriting any existing properties.

- ➤ `_.is[ObjectType]`: Underscore.js provides a good number of methods of the form `_.is[ObjectType]` to check the type of a passed-in object. This is useful because JavaScript doesn't provide built-in type checking methods. The methods Underscore provides are `_.isEqual`, `_.isEmpty`, `_.isElement`, `_.isArray`, `_.isFunction`, `_.isString`, `_isNumber`, `_.isBoolean`, `_.isNaN`, `_.isNull`, and `_.isUndefined`. All the `_.is[ObjectType]` methods are relatively self-explanatory: They each check the type of the object passed in and return `true` or `false`. They provide a succinct way to do type checking on JavaScript objects, which is useful for checking arguments and faking polymorphism by having methods behave differently depending on what is passed into them.

- ➤ `_.uniqueId([prefix])`: Generates a globally unique identifier for client-side DOM elements or models. This is useful because you often want to add unique ID attributes to elements you add to the page.

These utility methods, particularly _.extend are used frequently in the book.

Chaining Underscore Method Calls

Because Underscore does such nice things on collections, it would be nice if the syntax for dealing with multiple calls to Underscore methods in a row were cleaner.

Following is an example of the problem. If you want to pull out the maximum *y* value of all the sprites of the *enemy* category, you could write

```
_(_(_(sprites)
    .filter(function(s) { return s.category == "enemy"; }))
    .pluck('y'))
    .max();
```

If you can follow all those nested _(..) calls, good luck; it's not something that is particularly readable. For just this reason, Underscore provides a mechanism called *chaining*.

```
_.chain(sprites)
    .filter(function(s) { return s.category == "enemy"; })
    .pluck('y')
    .max().value();
```

When you want to chain a number of underscore functions in a row, call _.chain(), and then when you are done, call .value().

SUMMARY

Two useful JavaScript libraries—jQuery and Underscore—can help you write more compact code, devoid of per-browser checks and boilerplate code, that is easier to understand and maintain.

Although not using a library is certainly an option (*Alien Invasion*, after all, was built without libraries), the cost of adding both jQuery and Underscore is less than 40 kb, or approximately the size of a small JPG. Take advantage of the hard work that people have put in before you to make cross-browser development easier.

Being a Good Mobile Citizen

WHAT'S IN THIS CHAPTER?

➤ Maximizing game size

➤ Taking advantage of iOS features

➤ Dealing with limited bandwidth

➤ Using the Application Cache

WROX.COM CODE DOWNLOADS FOR THIS CHAPTER

The wrox.com code downloads for this chapter are found at www.wrox.com/remtitle
.cgi?isbn=9781118301326 on the Download Code tab. The code is in the chapter 06
download and individually named according to the names throughout the chapter.

INTRODUCTION

You can overcome many of the challenges for developing on mobile with a little bit of pre-
planning and knowledge of the limitations of the target platform. Where things get difficult
is when desktop games are shoehorned into mobile devices without a lot of forethought or
respect for the restrictions that mobile brings to the table. This chapter prepares you for
the peculiarities you need to know to successfully develop and release an HTML5 game
on mobile.

RESPONDING TO DEVICE CAPABILITIES

One of the major challenges of game development on mobile devices is how to maximize screen real estate on small devices while supporting the great variety of screen resolutions and aspect ratios of these devices. Unlike single platform mobile devices such as the Apple App store, the DS, or the PSP, mobile HTML5 games not only need to deal with a plethora of different devices, each with their own resolution and aspect ratio, but also with the possibility that the play can be either in landscape or portrait mode.

Maximizing Real Estate

When a player plays your game on a tiny screen, such as those on mobile devices, one of the best things you can do is make sure the game takes up the full height and width of the available screen real estate.

ADDING A LAUNCHER

If the game is supposed to be embedded within other content on the page, you may want to add a "launcher" step to your game where you wait for an action from the user before you start loading the game.

Desktops, however, have different considerations. In general, you want to put a limit on the size of the game versus the size of screen. For example, maxing out the screen on a 24" desktop monitor is most likely too slow for the current generation of browsers and hardware and will also make your artwork too pixelated for bitmap-based games. The other alternative is to dramatically increase the viewable area of the game on the desktop, but this can cause additional problems. You also generally want your game to play similarly whether it's played on the desktop or a mobile device.

The solution most engines have come up with is to maximize the game to a certain size when it's on a mobile device but leave it in a container of fixed size when users play your game on the desktop.

Ideally, you should develop your game in such a way that the exact dimensions and aspect ratio don't matter. This is easier said than done, depending on the genre. For a platformer or a role-playing game (RPG), you should build your game in such a way that the amount of the level visible on the screen shifts depending on the screen size and dimensions. Things are more difficult when you have a fixed play area that needs to be fully onscreen at all times. In this case you need to ensure you maximize the size of the playable area while keeping the aspect ratio constant.

Using a fixed aspect ratio can lead to some less-than-ideal situations because many devices have vastly differing aspect ratios for landscape and portrait mode. In general if you need to keep your game area to a fixed aspect ratio, you can optimize only for one view—either portrait or landscape—and then either ask the user to rotate the device (you don't have the ability to lock screen rotation in HTML5) or accept that your game lives in a smaller box than is ideal.

Resizing Canvas to Fit

In this section, you look at some code that handles the screen adjustment for you. In each case you start with some boilerplate HTML and a <canvas> element that's 480 pixels by 480 pixels centered on the page:

```
<!DOCTYPE HTML>
<html lang="en">
<head>
  <meta charset="UTF-8"/>
  <title>Page Resize</title>
  <link rel="stylesheet" href="lib/base.css" type="text/css" />
  <script src='lib/jquery.min.js'></script>
</head>
<body>
  <div id='container'>
    <canvas id='game' width='480' height='480'></canvas>
  </div>
</body>
</html>
```

Other than the library jQuery, the only external resource listed is the style sheet called base.css. As in the previous chapter, the base.css style sheet consists only of the Meyer reset and a couple of game-specific styles. Below the reset, add the following two styles:

```
#container {
  padding-top:50px;
  margin:0 auto;
  width:480px;
}
canvas {
  background-color:green;
}
```

If you open this on a desktop browser, you notice a nice green <canvas> element centered on the page.

Next, add the following code before the closing </body> tag:

```
<script>
// Wait for the document.ready callback
$(function() {
  var maxWidth = 480;
  var maxHeight = 440;
  var handleResize = function() {
    // Get the window width and height
    var w = window.innerWidth ||
            window.document.documentElement.clientWidth ||
            window.document.body.clientWidth;
    var h = window.innerHeight ||
            window.document.documentElement.clientHeight ||
            window.document.body.clientHeight;
    if(w < maxWidth) {
      $("#container").css('width','auto');
      $("#game").css({position: 'absolute',
                      top: 0, left: 0, zIndex: 10000 })
```

```
                     .attr({width: w, height: Math.min(h,maxHeight) });
        }
    }
    handleResize();
});
</script>
```

This snippet of code, which runs on document ready, will be based on the width of the window, either leaving the Canvas sitting in the middle of the page or changing the positioning of the Canvas to an absolute position at the full size of the browser. You can see the code by running `resize.html` in the chapter code.

This is unfortunately one circumstance in which jQuery doesn't have a solution that works for all browsers. The code to determine the scrollbar-less height and width of the client window is different depending on the browser. Internet Explorer (IE) is again the culprit here, so if you want to ignore versions of IE before version 9, the height and width calculation code can be shortened down to the following:

```
// Get the window width and height
var w = window.innerWidth, h = window.innerHeight;
```

In Canvas-based games this is normally fine; for DOM-based games that might support older versions of IE, you want the full string. Because this example uses `<canvas>`, the rest of the examples in this chapter use the shorter string.

DEALING WITH BROWSER RESIZING, SCROLLING, AND ZOOMING

Just because players bring up your game in a browser at a certain size doesn't mean it's going to stay that way. Users may resize their desktop browser or may rotate their mobile device to get a better view. Most mobile devices that support HTML5 also enable users to pinch to zoom in and out of the page. You must consider all these actions when you develop a game on mobile.

Handling Resizing

Even if you don't intend to resize your game when played on the desktop, you should consider adjusting the game to fit the screen on mobile as the player will most likely rotate the device to get a better view of the game.

Listing 6-1 shows what code that adjusts the size of the Canvas element each time the browser is resized would look like. Because there isn't a game attached to this example, the code that calls the game code to let it know that it's been resized has been commented out. This is the `// Game .resize(newDim);` line. You can see this example by running `resize.html` in the chapter code.

LISTING 6-1: resize.html—A self-resizing Canvas

```
<script>
// Wait for the document.ready callback
$(function() {
```

```
        var maxWidth = 480;
        var maxHeight = 440;
        var initialWidth = $("#game").attr('width');
        var initialHeight = $("#game").attr('height');
        var handleResize = function() {
          // Get the window width and height
          var w = window.innerWidth, h = window.innerHeight,
             newDim;
          if(w <= maxWidth) {
           newDim = { width: Math.min(w,maxWidth),
                     height: Math.min(h,maxHeight) };
           $("#game").css({position:'absolute', left:0, top:0 });
           $("#container").css('width','auto');
          } else {
           newDim = { width: initialWidth,
                     height: initialHeight };
           $("#game").css('position','relative');
           $("#container").css('width',maxWidth);
          }
          $("#game").attr(newDim)
          // Let the game know the page has resized.
          // Game.resize(newDim);
        }
        $(window).bind('resize',handleResize);
        handleResize();
      });
    </script>
```

The updated code now has an `else` condition to allow it to swap between either the full page or the centered state. To do this, the code stores the initial width and height of the Canvas and, if the width is larger than the predetermined max width, changes the element back to relative positioning and its original size. You can try this out by resizing your browser window up and down.

A binding to the window's resize event makes sure the `handleResize()` method is called every time the browser is resized.

You need to consider one more facet with resizing. Because the game has already been initialized with a specific size, it must resize itself mid-game. How easy this is to do depends on the game you create, but it's something you need to think about from the start to either make a decision to support or not support. What resizing involves is very game dependent. A platformer might just show more or less of the surrounding area while a card game would need to zoom the entire view in and out.

Preventing Scrolling and Zooming

To make up for limited screen sizes, surfing the web on a mobile browser involves a lot of scrolling. For websites that aren't set up with a mobile version, it also generally involves pinching to zoom in and out. Allowing either of these actions during normal gameplay would be disastrous.

If you load up `resize.html` from the previous section on a mobile device and slide your fingers over the Canvas area, you notice the entire page performs as you might expect a web page to: It scrolls. If you double-click the green Canvas area, it zooms in.

The workaround to prevent this from happening is simple: Bind to the `touchMove` event and call `event.preventDefault()`. Add the following to the bottom of the resize code from the last section (still in the jQuery `document.ready` section):

```
$(document).on("touchmove",function(event) {
    event.preventDefault();
});
```

Now reload the page and try again. The page should stop in its tracks if you try to scroll around. If you don't want to be quite as greedy (for example, you've been tasked with creating one of those interactive ads polluting sidebars everywhere), you could limit the handler to only your Canvas object:

```
$("#game").on("touchmove",function(event) {
    event.preventDefault();
});
```

This code enables the player to manipulate the rest of the page, zoom in on your game, and then play it without fear of scrolling or zooming.

IN-GAME SCROLLING AND ZOOMING

What if you want players to scroll, pinch, and zoom? In most situations you want to re-create that behavior in-game instead of using the browser's built-in behavior. Touch events, described in detail in Chapter 10, "Bootstrapping the Quintus Engine: Part II," provide a mechanism for tracking multitouch that enables you to track higher-level behaviors such as pinching to zoom.

Setting the Viewport

Preventing zooming and scrolling is good, but if you load the device on an iPhone, one of the first things you notice is that none of the browser resizing seems to work. The green Canvas stays zoomed out.

The reason for this is that unless you tell the browser explicitly how big to make the page, it starts zoomed out as if you were viewing a normal web page. To fix this you need to add a special meta tag to the head to set the viewport (the visible area of the page). In games, the most common viewport setting is to set the viewport to 100% device resolution and prevent the user from scaling at all. Add the following meta tag to the head of your document:

```
<meta name="viewport" content="width=device-width, initial-scale=1.0,
maximum-scale=1.0, user-scalable=no">
```

Reload the page on your mobile device to see the green Canvas zoomed in to take up the full page. Although the viewport began as an iOS-only feature, it is now supported on Android and Mozilla's Fennec mobile browser as well.

> **LIES, DAMN LIES, AND PIXELS**
>
> In the good old days, pre-iPhone4, a web developer could count on a pixel being a pixel. With the introduction of the iPhone 4's Retina display, suddenly that was no longer true. Because thousands of websites were developed to the exact width of 320 pixels of the iPhone in portrait mode and would look foolish if shrunk down to a quarter of their normal size, Apple introduced the idea of CSS pixels. The iPhone 4 and later still pretend to have resolutions of 320×480, but they actually have double that resolution. To take advantage of that resolution, you can jump through some hoops that will be discussed in Chapter 15, "Learning Canvas, the Hero of HTML5," during the in-depth discussion of Canvas. For now, most devices have trouble pushing pixels at a speed to make game developers happy at 320×480, so this isn't necessarily something that you need to take advantage of immediately.

Removing the Address Bar

You can use one more trick to get a bit more real estate on the page, and that's to remove the address bar on iOS devices. Do this using the trick of scrolling the page slightly after it is loaded:

```
window.scrollTo(0,1);
```

This works only if the content of the page is longer than the full size of the page. To make things more difficult, removing the address bar also affects the reported innerHeight of the page.

This presents a little bit of a problem because you want to resize the Canvas to the full size of the page, but the size of the page may change after you've done the full resize. To get around this, you can simply set the height of the container element to a value known to be larger than the final height without the address bar. Then scroll the window and recalculate the innerHeight. Change the top of the handleResize method to read as follows:

```
var touchDevice = !!('ontouchstart' in document);

var handleResize = function() {
  var w = window.innerWidth, h = window.innerHeight, newDim;

  // Make sure the content is bigger than the page.
  if(w <= maxWidth && touchDevice) {
    $("#container").css({height: h * 2});
  }
  window.scrollTo(0,1);

  // Get the height again, scrollTo may have changed the innerHeight
  h = window.innerHeight;
```

You want to do this container resize trick only on browsers that support touch events because other ones (such as normal desktop browsers) scroll normally. Adding a bunch of additional empty space just adds unnecessary scrollbars that make the page scroll around. For this reason, the variable touchDevice is set to either true or false depending on whether the document object supports the ontouchstart event.

Finally there's one more subtlety to deal with regarding resizing. iOS doesn't currently fire a resize event when the device changes orientation from vertical to horizontal (portrait to landscape), so to handle the resize in that situation, you need a different event to bind to: `orientationchange`. You can use the `touchDevice` check from earlier to decide which event to listen to. Replace the preceding resize event above `handleResize` with the following:

```
var resizeEvent = touchDevice ? 'orientationchange' : 'resize';
$(window).on(resizeEvent,handleResize);
```

The code now determines whether to listen to `resize` or to `orientationchange` events.

Listing 6-2 shows the full code with all the mobile-specific adjustments described earlier for reference:

LISTING 6-2: addressbar.html—A resizing Canvas with mobile adjustments

```
<script>
// Wait for document ready callback
$(function() {
  var maxWidth = 480;
  var maxHeight = 480;
var initialWidth = $("#game").attr('width');
  var initialHeight = $("#game").attr('height');
  var touchDevice = 'ontouchstart' in document;
  var handleResize = function() {
    var w = window.innerWidth, h = window.innerHeight, newDim;
    // Make sure the content is bigger than the page.
    if(w <= maxWidth && touchDevice) {
      $("#container").css({height: h * 2});
    }
    window.scrollTo(0,1);
    // Get the height again, scrollTo may have changed the innerHeight
    h = window.innerHeight;
    if(w <= maxWidth) {
     newDim = { width: Math.min(w,maxWidth),
               height: Math.min(h,maxHeight) };
      $("#game").css({position:'absolute', left:0, top:0 });
      $("#container").css("width","auto");
    } else {
      newDim = { width: initialWidth,
                height: initialHeight };
      $("#game").css('position','relative');
      $("#container").css('width', maxWidth);
    }
    $("#game").attr(newDim)
    // Let the game know the page has resized.
    // Game.resize(newDim);
  };
    var resizeEvent = touchDevice ? 'orientationchange' : 'resize';
    $(window).on(resizeEvent,handleResize);

    $(document).on("touchmove",function(event) {
      event.preventDefault();
    });
```

```
    handleResize();
  });
</script>
```

Leaving this code sitting bare on document ready isn't going to be a viable solution for long. The preceding code will be incorporated into the mobile engine Quintus built in Chapter 9, "Bootstrapping the Quintus Engine: Part I."

CONFIGURING YOUR APP FOR THE iOS HOME SCREEN

You need to add a few more pieces to your game to let people save it to their home screen. The first is to add a meta tag indicating your game is "web-app-capable." Users can save your game to the home screen regardless of whether your app marks itself as web-app-capable, but if you explicitly mark it as such, your app automatically loads in full-screen mode without the address bar or the button bar at the bottom of the page.

Making Your Game Web App Capable

To make your game web-app-capable, you need to add the following meta tag to the `<head>` of your document:

```
<meta name="apple-mobile-web-app-capable" content="yes">
```

A second meta tag can make your app look more like a regular app when it launches. Mobile Safari uses a light gray status bar by default, but you can switch it to the standard black status bar by adding another meta tag:

```
<meta name="apple-mobile-web app-status-bar-style" content="black" />
```

Your options for the content of this meta tag are `"default"` that means to leave it gray; `"black"` that as described previously makes it the standard black status bar used by apps that leave the status bar on; and `"black-translucent"` that pushes your content up to the top of the page but leaves the status bar as semi-transparent over your content. For most cases, `"black"` is the best option unless you want a full 480×320 pixel area to play with, in which case you can use `"black-translucent"`.

Adding a Startup Image

Apple gives you an additional option to improve the launch experience when your app is on the home screen. This is the startup image that displays while the device gets your app up and running. You can add a `<link>` tag to your `<head>` to specify this. First, create a 320×460 pixel image in portrait orientation, and then add a meta tag linking to that image:

```
<link rel="apple-touch-startup-image" href="/path/to/320x460-startup-image.png">
```

If you want to support more than just than a low-res iPhone version, you can add a complete set of startup images for the iPhone and iPhone 4+ Retina display along with the iPad in portrait and landscape mode by adding the appropriate media query to each of the links:

```
<!-- 320x460 for iPhone before iPhone 4 and iPod Touch -->
<link rel="apple-touch-startup-image" media="(max-device-width: 480px) and
 not (-webkit-min-device-pixel-ratio: 2)" href="/path/to/320x460-startup-
```

```
image.png" />

<!-- 640x920 for Retina display on iPhone 4 and above-->
<link rel="apple-touch-startup-image" media="(max-device-width: 480px) and
 (-webkit-min-device-pixel-ratio: 2)" href="/path/to/640x920-startup-
image.png" />

<!-- 768x1004 for iPad in Portrait mode -->
<link rel="apple-touch-startup-image" media="(max-device-width: 1024px) and
 (orientation: portrait)" href="/path/to/768x1004-startup-image.png" />

<!-- 1024x748 for iPad in Landscape mode. Image should be rotated 90
degrees clockwise. -->
<link rel="apple-touch-startup-image" media="(max-device-width: 1024px) and
 (orientation: landscape)" href="/path/to/1024x748-startup-image.png" />
```

> **WARNING** *Make sure you use the exact image sizes and rotations as described in the preceding comments.*

If you don't specify a startup image, by default, the user sees an image of the last state that your game was in when it was last closed.

Configuring Home Icons

The devil, as some say, is in the details. The last touch you can add to your game to make it appear just like a real native app is to add a `<link>` tag specifying a custom home screen icon. At its simplest, you can add this icon by specifying a `<link>` tag with an `"apple-touch-icon"` relation that points to a 57 × 57 pixel PNG image:

```
<link rel="apple-touch-icon" href="/path/to/57x57-icon-image.png" />
```

This image shouldn't have any of the standard iOS icon embellishments, but rather should just be a square icon image. iOS can add the rounded corners and the gloss finish if you use this version of the meta tag.

Using this version, though, can leave Android users with a subpar experience, however, because Android won't add the additional enhancements to the image. To fix this, you can use a "precomposed" icon that has already been tricked-out in glossy style by specifying:

```
<link rel="apple-touch-icon-precomposed" href="/path/to/57x57-precomposed-
icon-image.png" />
```

To accommodate the iPad and the iPhones with a Retina display, adding a triumvirate of icons with the sizes set explicitly does the trick:

```
<!-- 72x72 for iPad -->
<link rel="apple-touch-icon-precomposed" sizes="72x72"
href="/path/to/72x72-icon-image.png" />

<!-- 114x114 for Retina Display on iPhone 4 and up -->
<link rel="apple-touch-icon-precomposed" sizes="114x114"
```

```
href="/path/to/114x114-icon-image.png" />

<!-- 57x57 for iPhone pre iPhone 4 and iPod Touch, Android 2.1+ -->
<link rel="apple-touch-icon-precomposed" sizes="57x57"
href="/path/to/57x57-icon-image.png" />
```

Much like the `favicon.ico` file, iOS can search for a files with some variation of `"apple-touch-icon.png"` in the root of your site and use those automatically, but you should explicitly let the device know what icons are available.

TAKING MOBILE PERFORMANCE INTO CONSIDERATION

Desktop browsers have reached the point in which building any type of simple game using HTML5 is an achievable objective. You don't need to jump through many hoops to get a 2-D platformer or top-down shooter game running smoothly.

On mobile, performance is a different story. You need to consider performance from the beginning if you want to give users a smooth experience. To get a sense of the performance limitations of desktop, now look at the comparison between MacBook pro, iPhone, and iPad for various simple rendering tests (see Figure 6-1).

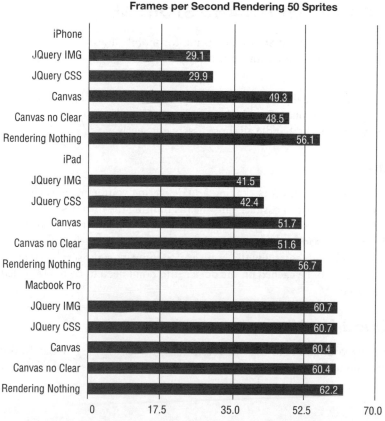

FIGURE 6-1: Comparison of HTML5 rendering methods on mobile.

You can run the tests by going to `http://cykod.github.com/mobile-html5-tests`. The tests consist of creating various numbers of image sprites and moving them vertically down a 320 × 320 board. The graph in Figure 6-1 shows the results for rendering 50 sprites. The tests run through five ways to do the rendering. The first uses `<img>` tag-based sprites. The second uses CSS `background-image`-based sprites. The third uses CSS sprites but uses `-webkit-transform` instead of just setting the left and top. The fourth and fifth ways both use Canvas, with the fifth foregoing the full-Canvas clear.

On the desktop, it doesn't matter how you render the sprites or how many you render; the frame rate hovers around 60 frames per second. On mobile it's a different story. The frame rate drops immediately on both the iPad2 and the iPhone4 using IMG or CSS sprites. The iPad2, with it's more powerful processor, can hang on to its frame rate for a bit longer using Canvas sprites, but in both cases the frames-per-second decreases noticeably when rendering 100 image-based, moving sprites.

Although 100 sprites might seem like a lot, if you consider projectiles, particle effects, background tiles, and other animations, it's not an unreasonable number for a simple game. What these results mean is that at the moment, decisions about your game need to be made with an understanding of the mobile platform. That's the bad news. The good news is that performance improves all the time, and other options exist for deploying onto mobile devices than just using Mobile Safari.

ADAPTING TO LIMITED BANDWIDTH AND STORAGE

Given the predominance of Wi-Fi in the United States, designing for mobile doesn't necessarily mean your players will be on 3G when they play your game, but it does make it a possibility that you need to take into consideration.

If you create an RPG with hundreds of megabytes of assets, you need an incremental loading system that doesn't try to download everything at once. Even if the user is on 4G or Wi-Fi, the mobile browser won't have the cache space or the memory to handle all those assets efficiently.

Optimizing for Mobile

What does optimizing for mobile mean? It means packaging and delivering your game in such a way as to let the player into the game as quickly as possible. This means limiting the libraries you use, minifying your JavaScript and CSS assets, and using spritesheets to limit the number of separate requests the device must make to download images. It also means setting up your web server to serve assets compressed to reduce the bandwidth costs. Finally, it means configuring your server to serve the proper cache headers to ensure assets can be cached on the device and don't need to be downloaded every time the player plays the game.

Good for Mobile Is Good for All

The good news is that optimizing your game for mobile doesn't only affect mobile devices. Making your game load faster and play smooth can result in a better all-around experience on desktop as well as mobile.

Many times, given the speed of desktop browsers these days, it doesn't seem worth following best practices because the benefit seems incremental. This is a stance that is actually more damaging to your game than might first appear. Chances are, as a game and web developer, you have a relatively new machine connected to the Internet via a fast connection. Potential players of your game around the country and around the world are unlikely to all be that lucky.

Some players may be on a dial-up service (which supports speeds a good deal slower than 3G) and looking to play on computers that should have been retired ages ago. Because the web is a casual gaming space, you must accommodate a much wider range of hardware. Using mobile as a baseline is a good start to ensure you make the necessary optimizations.

Minifying Your JavaScript

The majority of the size of your HTML5 games will most likely consist of JavaScript and image files. The JavaScript files should be written with plenty of helpful comments to go along with nice indenting, descriptive variable and function names, and generous spacing.

Just because you write your files that way, though, doesn't mean you need to serve them to your player that way. A number of compressors are available that can take your JavaScript, strip out the comments and whitespace, and then transform the parts down to greatly reduce the resulting size of the file. jQuery 1.7.1, for example, runs almost 250 K in size before being minified down to approximately 93 K.

To aid in minifying down your code, you can do a couple of things. The first is to wrap your code in an anonymous function to get it out of the global scope. You often see code written something like this:

```
(function(window) {
  // Bunch of stuff defined.
  window.exportedFunction = function() { .. }
})(window);
```

Here, all the code is wrapped up in an anonymous function and explicitly sets any of its exports on the passed-in window class. This makes it explicit as to which variables are global. There are variations on this pattern, but the crux of it is that the global namespace isn't filled with lots of junk.

The second thing you can do to minify your code is to make sure to use the "var" keyword to create local variables that don't need to be available outside of the wrapping function. Using local variables this way allows the minifiers to automatically rename these variables down to short names such as *a* and *b*, which allows for even better compression of the files.

A number of JavaScript minifiers are available. Three of the most popular are Yahoo's YUI compressor (http://developer.yahoo.com/yui/compressor/), Google's Closure compiler (http://code.google.com/closure/compiler/), and Uglify.js (https://github.com/mishoo/UglifyJS). This book uses Uglify.js because it's popular and written in JavaScript.

To run Uglify.js, you need some sort of command-line JavaScript environment. Chapter 9 discusses getting Node.js, a command-line and server-side framework for running JavaScript, up and running. In the meantime you can play with the output of Uglify.js by passing some code through the online version at http://marijnhaverbeke.nl/uglifyjs.

Setting Correct Headers

One of the worst things you can do is force a player to redownload large asset files that haven't changed when they visit your game the second time. Setting expiration headers far into the future means you tell the browser it can cache whatever assets it likes.

What files does it make sense to allow the browser to cache? Almost any asset file, including images, audio, level data, and so on should be cacheable if it's not generated dynamically on the server.

At its simplest, if you use Apache, you can add a directive to set expiration way out in the future:

```
<Directory /path/to/asset/files>
   ExpiresDefault "access plus 10 years"
</Director>
```

This directive requires that you have the `mod_expires` Apache module installed.

You need to ensure that you can update your game assets if you make changes to your game, however. One way to ensure that you are always serving up-to-date assets when caching is turned on is to append the last modified time in seconds (known as the *mtime*) of the file to the URL, as follows:

```
<script src='js/game.js?1326075236'></script>
```

If your HTML file is served dynamically, this is easy to do. If it's served via a static file, you can hard code a modified date using a build script.

For assets loaded dynamically, use a similar method. In general, keeping a global version number that gets automatically appended to any loaded assets is the simplest method for small games.

Lastly, make sure you turn caching off during development. There is nothing more infuriating than trying to hunt down a bug that you have already fixed but the browser is serving an old version of your code.

Making sure that your assets serve the right cache headers is only half the battle. The second half is to ensure that assets that benefit from compression are served gzipped to browsers that support it (which, at this time, is every browser you should be concerned about playing an HTML5 game on, even including the venerable IE6).

If you use Apache, this is handled by the `mod_deflate` module. Ensure `mod_deflate` is enabled, and then add the following to your virtual host or to an .htaccess file:

```
AddOutputFilterByType DEFLATE application/javascript application/
x-javascript text/html text/plain text/xml text/css
```

Your JavaScript, HTML, CSS, plain text, and XML files can now be served compressed over the wire.

Serving from a CDN

To really make your assets fly, your best bet is to actually forgo serving them yourself and serve them directly from a content delivery network, also known as a *CDN*. CDNs are designed to serve files fast from edge-locations spread throughout the country and the globe. Serving files from a nearby location means that requests will be answered faster (there's less round-trip time for packets getting passed back and forth,) but the biggest advantage is usually simply that CDNs are optimized for serving files quickly, so they have the infrastructure and fat Internet pipes to do so.

Amazon.com's Cloudfront is one of the most popular CDNs and is relatively easy to get started with and inexpensive until you rack up significant bandwidth. Cloudfront works with Amazon.com's S3, a cloud storage service. You need to configure Cloudfront to pull from a specific S3 bucket, but from then on, any file you upload to S3 will be available via Cloudfront.

To sign up for S3 and Cloudfront, you need to sign up for an account at http://aws.amazon.com/. From there you can launch the AWS Management console. From the console, go to the S3 tab (it may prompt you to sign up for the service first) and click Create Bucket. Enter a unique bucket name. The bucket name needs to be unique across all S3 buckets, so it may take a little bit of creativity to come up with a name.

Next you need to click the Cloudfront tab and create a new distribution. Click the Create Distribution button, and select the bucket you just created. You can press Continue through the remaining screens until your distribution is ready to go. After you create the distribution, it can take up to five minutes to set up, but you can see the domain name for your distribution in the properties. Any file you upload to your bucket is available under that domain name and served up lightning quick.

You can copy files up manually to S3 using the management console, but there are numerous tools and libraries that can help do this for you as well, such as s3sync: https://github.com/ms4720/s3sync.

Nonimage and script resources (meaning data resources such as .json level data and CSVs) are generally loaded via Ajax, which has a same origin policy. The same origin policy requires that you load assets from the same domain/subdomain, protocol, and port as your main HTML script was loaded from. This isn't a deal-breaker for most assets because images, audio, video, and JavaScript files can load without issue, but it's something to keep in mind.

GOING OFFLINE COMPLETELY WITH APPLICATION CACHE

With everything that's been discussed in this chapter on being a good mobile citizen, there's still one piece that's missing, the Holy Grail of web page apps: allowing users to play your game without any Internet access. Configured correctly, users with your game saved to their home screen can fire up your game while riding on the subway and kill aliens to their heart's content. The secret to adding this capability to your game resides in configuring your game to correctly use the Application Cache, an HTML5 standard defined under Offline Web Applications.

Creating Your Manifest File

The main crux of what's necessary to make your app available offline consists of linking your HTML page to a manifest file by modifying the <html> tag at the beginning of your page as such:

```
<html lang="en" manifest="/manifest.appcache">
   .. Rest of your HTML ..
</html>
```

The name of the manifest file is actually up to you; however, the agreed-upon file suffix is .appcache and the file needs to be served with the mime-type of text/cache-manifest that is generally not preconfigured by Apache. You can add the following to your Apache config or to an `.htaccess` file to ensure the file is served correctly:

```
AddType text/cache-manifest .appcache
```

You generally want to explicitly override the expired header for the `manifest.appcache` file to prevent it from being cached. With `mod_expires` enabled in Apache, you can do this with the following declaration in either a config file or an `.htaccess` file:

```
ExpiresByType text/cache-manifest "access plus 0 minutes"
```

Next, you need to actually write the cache manifest file. This is actually a fairly simple text document that starts with the uppercase words "CACHE MANIFEST" and follows with up to three different sections:

➤ CACHE: For files that should be cached.

➤ NETWORK: For resources that should be available only when online.

➤ FALLBACK: For resources that should have a fallback version used when the device is offline. FALLBACK resources are specified by an online version followed by an offline version.

➤ CACHE and NETWORK each consist of a list of files or paths. (Wildcards are also permitted.)

If you load a page that has been cached while the device is online, the browser makes a request for the manifest file. If the file has changed, all the files download again. If the file hasn't changed (or has been cached normally in the browser), then none of the cached files reload. Because you may often update assets without changing which assets are in your manifest, the most common way to change the manifest file is with a version number in a comment.

Say you have a game that loads from an `index.html` inside the `/myGame` directory and that has static assets in `/myGame/images` and `/myGame/js`. Then say it has a high-score list that loads from `/myGame/high-scores.php` and an advertisement that loads from `/myGame/ads.php`. You might set up a cache manifest file like the following:

```
CACHE MANIFEST
# Version: 1
# Remember to update the version whenever you change a file

CACHE
# Cache the game index.html file and all assets
/myGame/index.html
/myGame/js/*
/myGame/images/*

NETWORK
# Always try to pull the high scores from the network
/myGame/high-scores.php

FALLBACK
# Fallback to a static ad if user is not connected
/myGame/ads.php /myGame/static-ad.html
```

> **NOTE** *The HTML file with the manifest declaration is automatically cached by default and doesn't need to be in the manifest file, but there's no harm in being explicit that it is going to be cached.*

After your players have played your game, the next time they bring up the game, it pulls all the assets from the Application Cache. If the players are online, pressing /myGame/ads.php downloads your real ads (or whatever is in that file,) while pressing the file while offline loads a /myGame/static-ad.html from the Application Cache. If you try to press the high score list at /myGame/high-scores.php, the browser attempts to make the request regardless of whether the device is online.

Checking If the Browser Is Online

You may want your game to behave differently depending on whether you are online. Mobile Safari and the Android browser can use the navigator.onLine flag to check whether the browser thinks it's online, as follows:

```
if(navigator.onLine) {
  // do something when online
} else {
  // Fallback
}
```

This is a little bit of a crutch, though, and life isn't quite that simple. Just because navigator.onLine returns true doesn't mean that you can actually access data over the web. The browser may be on Wi-Fi without an Internet connection or may have such a poor connection that it can't actually download any data. The rule is to always catch any network errors even if the device is under the false impression that it is online.

On desktop, navigator.onLine is broken for this same reason, with the Chrome developers going as far as to mark the bug as "WONT FIX."

Listening for More Advanced Behavior

This section has scratched only the surface of the Application Cache. There are eight different events defined in the HTML5 spec for the Application Cache. A full robust implementation with on-the-fly updating of the cache would need to do a good deal more work to handle all the different situations. The good news is that most of the time all you care about is caching your files for offline use.

A Final Word of Warning

Testing and debugging Application Cache can be a pain, especially when you already have cache headers turned on as suggested. The easiest way to test is to turn off your cache headers, verify the browser is hitting the server for each of the files, add in your manifest, and disable Wi-Fi or Ethernet. You can quickly determine how your game behaves under offline conditions. After you have it worked out in a desktop browser, give reloading the game a shot on a mobile device in Airplane mode to see how you did.

As a secondary word of caution—stay away from enabled cache headers and Application Cache while in development. You can quickly lose your sanity trying to constantly figure out whether your browser uses new or cached resources.

SUMMARY

Whew! Being a good mobile citizen takes a lot of work! Luckily a good deal of the hard work is boilerplate that is set and forgotten about. That statement applies to mobile meta tags, cache headers, and application cache. What the statement doesn't apply to is making sure your game can work within the constraints of the mobile devices you target. That takes some care and planning, and most likely some prototyping to determine how far you can push the current generation hardware.

PART III
JavaScript Game Dev Basics

Learning about Your HTML5 Game Development Environment

WHAT'S IN THIS CHAPTER?

➤ Choosing a development environment

➤ Exploring the Chrome Developer tools

➤ Debugging your JavaScript

➤ Improving and optimizing your game

➤ Debugging for mobile

WROX.COM CODE DOWNLOADS FOR THIS CHAPTER

The wrox.com code downloads for this chapter are found at www.wrox.com/remtitle
.cgi?isbn=9781118301326 on the Download Code tab. The code is in the chapter 07
download and individually named according to the names throughout the chapter.

INTRODUCTION

When paired with a good text editor, over the past decade, browsers have developed into remark-
able development environments for building, debugging, and optimizing web games. To find an
HTML5 IDE, you need to look no further than the browser you use every day to surf the web.

Although nearly all browsers have decent debugging environments, this book specifically covers the Chrome Developer tools. Chrome is available on all platforms (Windows, OS X, and
Linux) and provides an up-to-date WebKit browser, matching in many ways with the WebKit
browser on most mobile devices.

PICKING AN EDITOR

Before you can get your code up and running in a browser, you need to write some code in some sort of an editor. Which text editor or development environment you use is up to you. You can go the IDE-like route and use a full-fledged development environment such as WebStorm, Aptana, Netbeans, or even Visual Studio. Alternatively, many developers get by with just a good text editor. On the PC, Notepad++ is a popular choice. On the Mac, TextMate or MacVim (if you're the adventurous type) are good choices. On Linux, Emacs or gVIM can get the job done. Stay away from Dreamweaver because its job is more focused on writing HTML than JavaScript and can do more harm than good.

EXPLORING THE CHROME DEVELOPER TOOLS

Chrome is available on all platforms, and its developer tools are top-notch. Almost any piece of information you want to view about your page is available as it's running, and you can execute arbitrary JavaScript from the console. Safari has tools that are nearly identical (they share the same codebase); however, Safari isn't available for Linux and isn't nearly as popular as Chrome among developers.

Activating Developer Tools

Unlike Firebug, Chrome developer tools come pre-installed with Chrome and just need to be opened. To access the tools, you can go to the Wrench menu in top-right corner of the browser, select Tools, and then select Developer Tools. On a PC or Linux, you can also press Ctrl+Shift+I to open them. On a Mac, Command+Option+I works.

Inspecting Elements

The first tab on developer tools is Elements (see Figure 7-1) and it enables you to view the current state of the Document Object Model (DOM). This is different from the HTML you see in View Source, which shows you the HTML loaded from the server because JavaScript may have modified the DOM. On the left pane, you can browse around the DOM, opening and closing individual block elements as wanted and modifying attributes by double-clicking them. You can also right-click (Ctrl-click on a Mac) to make further modifications, such as editing the Node as HTML or adding or removing elements.

If you want to inspect a specific DOM element on the page, you can also right-click (Ctrl-click on a Mac) on any DOM element on the page and select Inspect Element. On the left, this shows you the location in the page's HTML of the element you clicked. On the right, it shows all the properties for the element. The most prominent details are the CSS styles, which display from the least specific at the bottom up to the most specific at the top. Styles that have been overridden by more specific styles are crossed out.

You can enable and disable specific styles by clicking the check box to the right of that style. You can also edit an existing style by clicking either the property or the value, or add a new style by clicking the closing curly bracket below the style. Deleting the property name also removes the property from the style entirely.

To view the end result of the application of all the styles, open the Computed Style tab above the Styles tab. This is useful, for example, when you want to figure out pixel-based values, such as the width of an element in pixels when elements are sized in percentages.

Below the Styles is the Metrics tab (see Figure 7-2) that shows the box model representation of the current element.

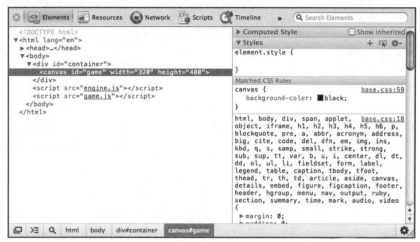

FIGURE 7-1: Inspecting an element.

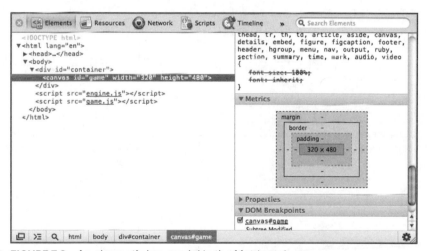

FIGURE 7-2: An element's box model in the Metrics tab.

Beneath the Metrics tab is the Properties tab (refer to the bottom of Figure 7-2), which, if you open it up shows any of the properties that element has as well as the properties that object inherits. You can modify these properties in the same way as CSS styles, by double-clicking the value and editing it. You can also remove a property by removing the property name. Some required properties can't be removed or changed.

Below the Properties tab is the DOM Breakpoints tab. If you have trouble tracking elements added or removed from the page, you can add breakpoints on DOM modification (see Figure 7-3) that pauses JavaScript execution at the appropriate time.

The final tab on the right, Event Listeners, shows the events applied to that DOM element.

Inspecting and modifying elements and viewing styles are less important in Canvas-based games than in normal applications, but if you build games with CSS3 or SVG, you'll appreciate seeing the specific styles applied to each DOM element as well as the hierarchy of styles. You might often run into a situation in which you have trouble applying a style to an object, and seeing which specific selector is overriding it can be useful.

Viewing Page Resources

The second tab, Resources (see Figure 7-4), is used to view all the resources that the page and any embedded frames use. Resources include any HTML, Scripts, Stylesheets, and art assets, but also things, such as Indexed DB usage, Local Storage, Session Storage, Cookies, and Application Cache.

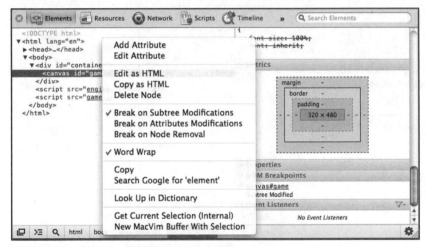

FIGURE 7-3: Adding a DOM breakpoint.

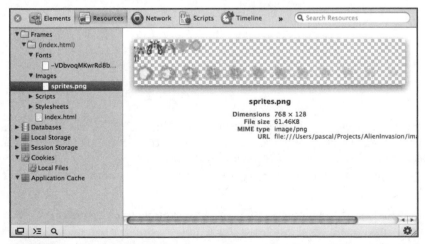

FIGURE 7-4: The Resources tab.

This tab is invaluable, particularly in games when you need to see the current state of Local Storage or Application Cache. You can add, edit, and remove keys and values from Local Storage. Much like the Elements tab, in many of the locations of the Resources tab, you can add, edit, and modify the various entries. Editing is normally done with a double-click, whereas adding is done by pressing the plus at the bottom of the screen or by clicking an empty row. You can remove elements by highlighting them and pressing the X at the bottom of the screen or by right-clicking (Ctrl-clicking on a Mac) and clicking Delete. You cannot modify page assets and application cache using developer tools, but you can easily change everything else for the interface.

The most common use of the tab is to check on Cookies, Local Store, and Application Cache because these elements can be tricky to debug. Viewing the application cache (see Figure 7-5) in particular can help you understand whether your game caches as expected.

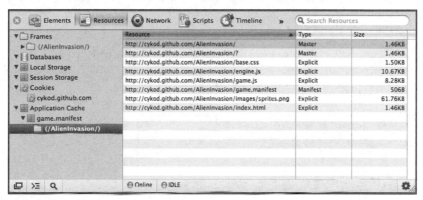

FIGURE 7-5: Viewing the Application cache.

Tracking Network Traffic

Next is the Network tab (see Figure 7-6). This tab, as you most likely expect, tracks all network requests your game makes, which includes downloading HTML, JavaScript, and Assets along with making Ajax requests or setting up WebSockets.

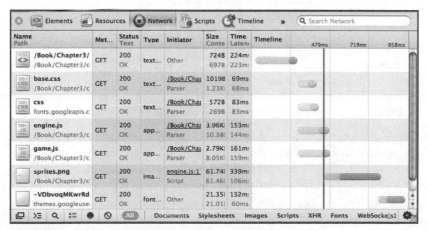

FIGURE 7-6: The Network tab.

Problems with your game can generally be traced to either JavaScript errors or resource loading problems. Resource loading problems, such as putting the wrong path in to a JavaScript file or asset, strike far more often than you might guess and cause headaches because they aren't the first thing you'll try to debug.

Taking a quick peak at the Network tab can help you solve many resource loading problems. It shows you the actual response status of each of the resources you want to load and highlights any problems with the file you load. The tab needs to be open to capture resource usage, so you may need to reload the page to view the requests made.

One common problem is the issue of capitalization. When you test a game locally using a `file://` URL, the capitalization of filenames doesn't matter. If you have a file called `engine.js` and you try to load it in a script file as `Engine.js`, the browser happily loads the file and pretends that nothing is wrong. After you deploy your game on a website, unless your web server is a Windows machine, capitalization matters, and the asset won't load.

Imagine you load your game that works perfectly locally but sits there blankly after you put it on the web. Before trying to track down imaginary browser bugs, open the Network tab. If you see something such as Figure 7-7, you can pinpoint the issue right away.

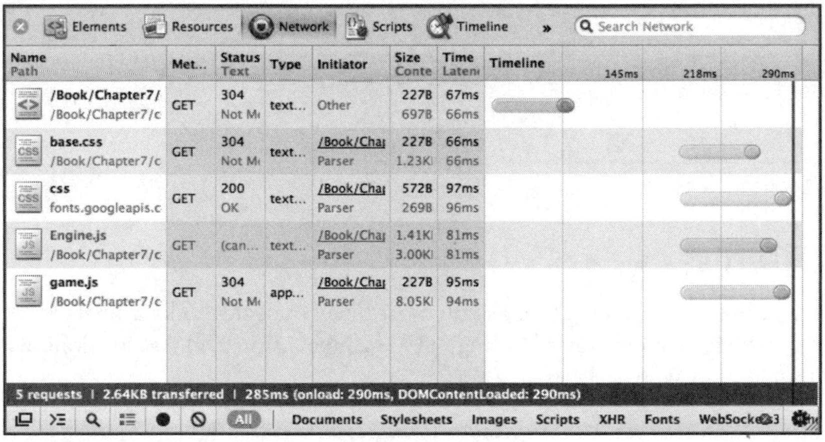

FIGURE 7-7: A resource that failed to download.

The request for the mistakenly capitalized `Engine.js` is invalid. Although this would probably be something you would eventually figure out with other methods, when you get deep into asset requests, taking a quick peek at the Network tab to check on invalid paths can save you a lot of time and frustration when suddenly some sprite isn't showing up on the screen.

A second major use of the Network tab is tracking down slow requests. Getting your game loaded and playable as quickly as possible should always be a goal. Pulling assets from a slow server can cause a marked slowdown in your game. If you refer to Figure 7-6, you can see exactly how long each of the assets loaded by Chapter 3's *Alien Invasion* takes to load. In this case the `sprites.png` file takes the most time. Moving the file to a CDN might help, but because the entire game loads in less than 1 second, there's probably not that much optimization left to do here. In a larger game with lots of assets loading from different servers, you'll have more to optimize.

Clicking an individual request shows you all the details of the request and the server's response. If your code talks back to the server via Ajax calls, the tab becomes even more invaluable because you can trace the parameters and response of the server. Websockets, as of this writing, aren't supported by developer tools to the extent that you can see the data passed back and forth, so you need to log any data you need to see.

DEBUGGING JAVASCRIPT

Because HTML5 games are heavy on JavaScript, you'll often want to inspect your running game when stuff goes wrong or behaves unexpectedly. Luckily, Developer Tools provides a debugging environment that is second to none, allowing you to look at the objects, functions, and values as well as stop your game's execution at a specific point and look at the exact state of the game.

Examining the Console Tab

Your first stop when something goes wrong should be the Console tab. It alerts you to any JavaScript errors that have occurred while running your game. Errors are highlighted in red, and you get a filename and line number where the error occurred (see Figure 7-8).

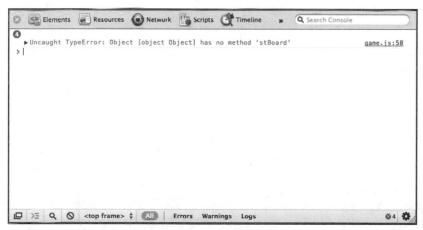

FIGURE 7-8: A JavaScript error in the console.

Clicking the filename on the right takes you to the file where the problem occurred and with the offending line highlighted (see Figure 7-9). You can click the little arrow to the left of the error to open the callback, which shows you all the nested function calls needed to get to the current line.

FIGURE 7-9: A JavaScript error at the spot of the error.

In addition to highlighting errors, you can also use the `console.log` method to log messages and data to the console. If you log a string it shows up as a string in the console with a matching line number called `console.log`. If you log something more complex than a string, the full object appears in the console and can be inspected by clicking the arrow next to the entry.

For example, you can add the following to the `playGame` method from Chapter 3, "Finishing Up and Going Mobile," in `game.js`:

```
var playGame = function() {
  var board = new GameBoard();
  board.add(new PlayerShip());
  board.add(new Level(level1,winGame));
  console.log("Logging board");
  console.log(board);
  Game.setBoard(3,board);
  Game.setBoard(5,new GamePoints(0));
};
```

Your console would look like Figure 7-10 when you start the game. In Figure 7-10, the second entry, the `board`, has been opened by clicking the arrow, enabling you to see all the properties it contains.

> **NOTE** `console.log` *isn't supported on all browsers, and on some older browsers it's available only when developer tools are enabled. It can slow down your game if you call it frequently, so make sure you remove any calls before publishing your game.*

Lastly, and perhaps most important, you can use the console to execute arbitrary JavaScript and examine objects while your game runs.

Anything you type into the console executes when you press Enter/Return, meaning if you add a JavaScript function to your game, you can use it from the console. This is useful for things such as turning on a developer mode, adding health to make your game easier to test, and jumping to arbitrary points in your game. Using *Alien Invasion* as an example, you can test starting the game or showing the "you lose" screen which normally plays after you get hit by an enemy by executing the appropriate method from the console (see Figure 7-11).

FIGURE 7-10: Logging an object to the console.

FIGURE 7-11: Running commands on the console.

Any global variables or objects you enter on the console can turn into clickable objects as if you called `console.log` on them from somewhere in your game. So if you need to look at the state of an object, just enter it on the console, open it, and then click down to the wanted property to see what is occurring.

Exercising the Script Tab

When you want to see the JavaScript that is loaded for your game or you need to dig deeper by running the step debugger on your code, it's time to open the Script tab.

By default, the Script tab shows you the first file with JavaScript in it, but you can open up any file with JavaScript in it by clicking the filename (see Figure 7-12) in the top left of the tab.

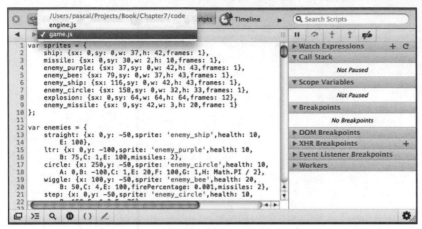

FIGURE 7-12: Selecting a different file from the Script tab.

Debugging is generally done by adding a breakpoint to your code at the spot you are interested in. Breakpoints tell the browser to pause the execution of your game and hand control over to the debugger. You can add breakpoints to a script file by clicking the gutter on the left of the file on the appropriate line. This adds a flag to that line, and the next time that the game hits that line of code, all execution stops (see Figure 7-13).

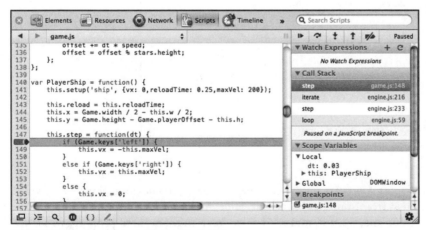

FIGURE 7-13: A breakpoint in the Script tab.

At this point, the tabs on the right fill up with lots of useful information. The first three—Watch Expressions, Call Stack, and Scope Variables—are generally used the most.

Watch Expressions, which are empty by default, is the spot where you can add expressions to be evaluated in the current scope where the browser is stopped. If the value of a specific variable is important to figuring what's happening, you can add it here for easy viewing. You can also add arbitrary expressions, such as calculations. Click the little plus button on the tab header, and enter the expression. Because the expression is evaluated in the current context, you can use the local variable and the `this` object in the expression. Mousing over a watch and pressing the minus sign removes it. For complex values, such as objects and arrays, you can click the little arrow to open the details of the watched element.

The second tab, Call Stack, shows where in the chain of function calls you are currently. Often the problem you debug isn't related to the code that causes the error but rather to the code that called it with invalid parameters. Clicking any of the other methods in the call stack shifts the code view to the spot of the method call.

If, by some misfortune you debug code that has been minimized, you can click the helpful Prettyprint button on the bottom of the window. It's represented by a pair of curly braces. This can format any code in the code window in a sensible way, making it easier to figure out what's occurring.

The last tab, Scope Variables, is like an automatic set of watch variables that shows you all the variables defined in the current scope. Because many times you'll be concerned with the values of variables local to the current method, it saves you the step to add a watch. Unlike watched expressions, however, you can actually change the value of variables by clicking their values, which is handy if you need to change any values to try different values out.

Just looking at your code at one specific line won't generally give you the information you need to debug your game. You most likely want to step through your program in small controlled steps to track down exactly where things are going afoul. To do this, you can use the small row of controls above the tabs on the right (see Figure 7-14).

FIGURE 7-14: The script debugging controls.

The first button either pauses the script execution or restarts it if it is paused. If you've hit a breakpoint script, execution will already be paused and clicking this button restarts it until the next breakpoint is hit. The next button, Step Over the Next Function Call, is used to step line-by-line over your code. The debugger won't jump any deeper into the stack but just executes all the code on a single line and then goes to the next one. The next two buttons, Step into the Next Function Call and Step out of Current Function Call, enable you greater control over how you progress through the code. If you want to step further down the stack, press the first one; if you want to execute code until the current method returns, press the second. Finally, after you figure out what's happening, you can press the last button to toggle enabling and disabling all break points. Turning off breakpoints is useful when you need to play your game for a moment to achieve certain conditions. You can then press this button to toggle breakpoints back on to stop your code exactly where you need to be.

PROFILING AND OPTIMIZING YOUR CODE

HTML5 Canvas performance on the desktop has reached a point on most browsers in which you don't need to pay too much attention to performance when you create a simple 2-D game. (This was not the case in 2010, when Canvas implementations were much slower.) On mobile it's a different story. Anything you can do to optimize your game will most likely pay dividends with a smoother game experience and a wider range of devices with an acceptable frame rate.

Developer tools comes with three different tools to help you eke out those last few bits of performance of your game. Start with the most important one first.

Running Profiles

Profiling your code means tracking the time taken to execute every function call in your game. There are ways to do this in the code by logging the start and end time around each function call, but luckily Developer Tools comes with a dead-simple way to do this at the click of the button without changing your code.

To create a profile of your game's execution, open the Profiles tab in Developer Tools; make sure the Collect JavaScript CPU profile is selected; and then click Start. Play your game for a bit, and then click Stop. You can also click the small Record button (the gray circle).

You get a result that looks something like Figure 7-15, showing a breakdown of each method call in your game, how long the game spent in the method (the self column), and how long the entire method took, including calls to any other methods (the total column.) The majority of the time appears to be spent in a mysterious item called "(program)." This row actually represents the browser and in the case of Canvas games usually represents extra processor cycles not used by your game. If you develop a CSS3 or SVG game, however, you may not actually have that many free cycles (look at the Timelines feature to optimize this) because the browser may do a lot of work handling animations and transitions.

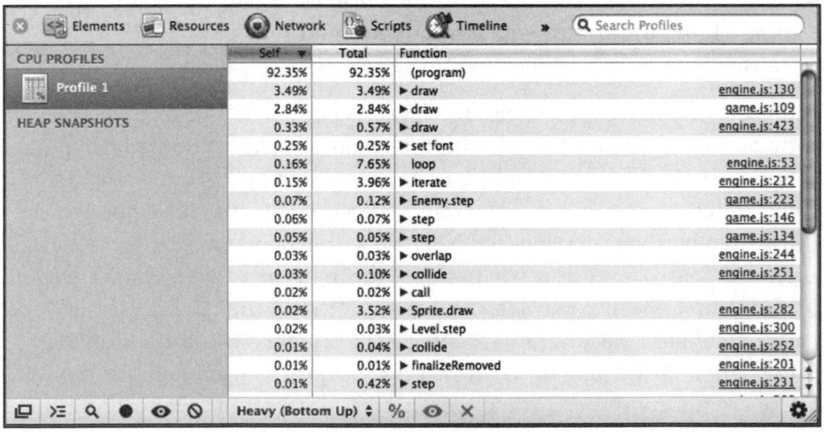

FIGURE 7-15: A profile of *Alien Invasion* in Chrome.

Figure 7-15 shows the breakdown for *Alien Invasion*; you can see the various draw methods take a good deal of the time. Unfortunately this isn't a great spot to optimize because these draw methods are simple and just call the Canvas draw method. What this does mean, however, is that figuring a way to reduce the number of draw calls might be a way to optimize the game.

One area in which you might originally have supposed there would be a good chance to improve performance was the collision method because it's quite basic, but before you spend hours optimizing a routine, make sure it would actually make a difference. The total percentage of time spent in the game is 100%–92.35% [the percentage spent in the "(program)" chunk], which equals 7.65%. The total time spent in collide is only 0.10%. This means that the `collide` method represents only 0.10%/7.65%, or 1.3% (0.013), of total game execution time. You can optimize that method by reducing its execution by 50% (a big optimization), which would result in only a .65% increase in execution speed. This is not something that would necessarily be noticeable to the user and is probably not worth your time to optimize.

When optimizing, you need to recognize where it's worth spending your time optimizing. In this case even though the `collide` method uses a native algorithm and could be optimized easily, it's probably not worth the time. In other situations in which many different objects collide on the screen, it would be a better target.

The other factor is that although most mobile browsers share WebKit roots; Android and iOS have different JavaScript engines. This means that whereas Chrome developer tools may be a good indication of where there are performance problems on Android, it isn't quite as good an indicator for iOS. In this case you may want to fire up Safari on the desktop, launch the developer tools (which are nearly identical to Chrome's because they share the same codebase) and profile there. Figure 7-16 shows the result of running a similar profile benchmark on Safari.

	Self ▼	Total	Average	Calls	Function	
	91.84%	100.00%	91.84%	1	(program)	
	6.01%	6.01%	0.00%	3560	▶ drawImage	
	0.36%	0.36%	0.00%	411	▶ fillText	
	0.31%	0.35%	0.00%	12249	▶ (anonymous function)	engine.js:237
	0.22%	0.49%	0.00%	243	▶ (anonymous function)	engine.js:404
	0.12%	8.14%	0.00%	321	▶ (anonymous function)	engine.js:51
	0.12%	4.39%	0.00%	473	▶ (anonymous function)	engine.js:198
	0.11%	0.46%	0.00%	1299	▶ (anonymous function)	engine.js:207
	0.10%	0.24%	0.00%	84	▶ (anonymous function)	engine.js:143
	0.09%	3.49%	0.00%	1637	▶ (anonymous function)	engine.js:122
	0.09%	2.71%	0.00%	963	▶ (anonymous function)	game.js:109
	0.06%	0.06%	0.00%	963	▶ (anonymous function)	game.js:134
	0.05%	3.55%	0.00%	1637	▶ (anonymous function)	engine.js:266
	0.05%	0.51%	0.00%	1299	▶ (anonymous function)	engine.js:236
	0.04%	0.22%	0.00%	426	▶ (anonymous function)	game.js:215
	0.04%	0.04%	0.00%	321	▶ setTimeout	
	0.04%	0.04%	0.00%	1812	▶ (anonymous function)	engine.js:229

FIGURE 7-16: A profile of *Alien Invasion* in Safari.

The JavaScript engine used in Safari doesn't do as good a job with anonymous functions as Chrome's V8 JavaScript engine, but it does give an added advantage of enabling you to drill down into the time spent in native method calls. If you have trouble with iOS and need to optimize, give your anonymous methods names (`function collideCallback() { .. }` instead of `function() { .. }`) even if you don't need them for later reference.

In Chrome, the Profiles tab also has two other profile snapshots: CSS selector profile and Heap profile. The former isn't likely going to be that useful in HTML5 game development because most lookups are generally by IDs, but the heap snapshot can be useful. If you run into memory problems, you most likely have a memory leak caused by not removing all the references to objects that are no longer used. Taking a heap snapshot shows you the memory size of DOM and JavaScript objects at a specific time.

Play your game for a bit and then take a heap snapshot, and you should detect any anomalies. For example, if you play your game for a while, take a snapshot, and then sort by the number of objects in descending order by clicking the pound sign (#) and notice that you have 2,000 sprite objects hanging around; you most likely aren't getting rid of sprites correctly when they die. Also keep a lookout for objects that balloon to sizes larger than expected because this most likely means they keep more data around than they probably intend.

Two of the other tabs, Timelines and Auditing, can be useful for debugging web-page performance problems, but they don't help terribly much in game optimization, so they aren't covered here.

Actually Optimizing Your Game

With all these tools at your disposal, the next question on your mind is most likely "How do I actually optimize my game?" The answer, as you might expect, is "It depends." It depends on the browser you use and what you want to do.

The first step is to figure out where you might benefit from some optimization. Profiling, as discussed earlier, is a good place to start. Both CPU profile and heap snapshots can help you pinpoint where you might want to target your efforts—the former because it can tell you spots in the code that take a lot of time and the latter because it can give you an idea of what types of objects you create a lot of. Optimizing objects of which there are thousands is a good place to start.

Next, with the code that could use some help, take a look to see if there are either algorithmic changes that could help or syntax changes that might improve performance. JavaScript is a flexible language, and sometimes that flexibility is used to the detriment of performance. Sometimes things that seem like they might be performant actually end up costing CPU cycles. Unlike other languages, such as C, where you can examine the resultant Assembly code to see how the compiler thinks the code should be run, the only way to figure this out in JavaScript is to write a test and test that code across different browsers.

Now take a simple example of three different ways to create objects (see Listing 7-1):

LISTING 7-1: Object creation methods

```
var Obj1 = function() {}
Obj1.prototype.yay = function(x) {};
Obj1.prototype.boo = function(y) {};

var Obj2 = function() {
  this.yay = function(x) {};
  this.boo = function(y) {};
```

```
    }

var Obj3 = function() {
  function yay(x) {};
  function boo(y) {};
  return {
   yay: yay,
   boo: boo
  }
}
```

Each of these three patterns of object creation yield an object that behaves exactly the same, yet the fastest method (`Obj1`, which uses prototypes) is more than 25 times faster than the slowest method (`Obj2`, using anonymous methods assigned to this) in Chrome 18. To run the test, go to `http://jsperf.com/object-creation-tests`.

Now, on a circa 2010 MacBook Pro, the second method still clocks in at 1.7 million objects per second; so unless you create lots and lots of objects, the difference isn't going to be particularly noticeable in your typical game. This speaks to the heart of the problem: Make sure you spend your time optimizing efficiently by first profiling and then testing your intuition.

Sites such as `http://jsperf.com` make it easy to set up a test of whatever it is you want to optimize and enable you to quickly determine if your intuition is correct and if the potential increase in speed is worth the effort.

MOBILE DEBUGGING

Debugging on the desktop is okay, but because this book is about mobile games, there's no substitution for debugging on real hardware. Unfortunately, with the exception of Chrome for Android, there's no built-in way to debug your page.

If you are on Android with version 4.0 (Ice Cream Sandwich) or newer and have Chrome installed on your device and the Android SDK installed on your desktop, you can enable Remote Debugging as described in the Google documentation at `http://code.google.com/chrome/mobile/docs/debugging.html`.

For iOS, things aren't quite as convenient. For simply watching for JavaScript errors, you can turn on the debug console. This is switched on by going to Settings ➪ Safari ➪ Advanced. Any page you load now shows the Safari Debug console at the top. If there are errors, they will be noted, and you can click the tab to see some more details. This is most likely not quite enough when you want to track down some hard-to-debug, platform-specific issue. The good news is there is a tool called Weinre, which is part of Apache's cordova project that adds basic remote-debugging capability: `https://github.com/apache/incubator-cordova-weinre`.

The way Weinre works is by running a Java-based server on a computer that a mobile device can connect to by including the appropriate script tag. When connected, you can access a limited subset of tabs that behave similarly to Developer Tools (see Figure 7-17).

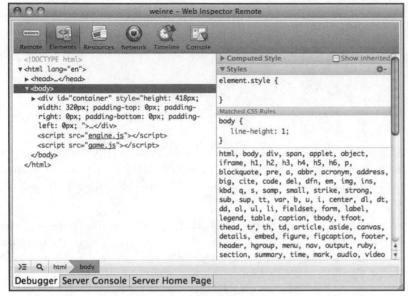

FIGURE 7-17: The Weinre remote inspector.

Because Weinre is just a script you load on the mobile device, you don't have access to a script debugger or the Profiles tab, but you can inspect elements and execute code in a JavaScript console. To start with Weinre, you need to either download the straight Java JAR file, or, if you are on a Mac, you can download the Mac package.

If you have downloaded the JAR file, run it by executing the following command in the directory you have extracted Weinre to:

```
java -jar weinre.jar ~DHboundHost -all-
```

If you have downloaded the OS X package, you need to create a directory called **.weinre** (the leading period is important; don't forget it) in your home directory and open a file called `server.properties` with the following contents:

```
boundHost:    -all-
```

Next, double-click the Weinre app to start it.

In both cases, the `boundHost` option is necessary so your mobile device can access the Weinre server.

> **WARNING** *Running Weinre with* `boundHost` *set to* `-all-` *is a potential security risk; you should do this only when you are on a local, trusted network.*

The normal setup for using Weinre is to set up your development machine as a web server and run the Weinre Java server on it as well. Grab the IP address of your machine on the local network (described in Chapter 6, "Being a Good Mobile Citizen") and then hard code the script tag to your machine into the HTML of your game. For example, if your development machine is set to the IP address 192.168.1.20, and you run Weinre on port 8080 (which is the default), add the following to your game's HTML file:

```
<script src="http://192.168.1.20:8080/target/
target-script-min.js#anonymous"></script>
```

Load your game by selecting the proper location on your machine. Next select the Weinre server location in another browser (in the previous example, this would be http://192.168.1.20:8080); or if you run the Mac application, just click one of the other tabs.

Although Weinre is no substitute for the full debugging environment you have on the desktop, it provides an invaluable tool when you run into problems you need to debug directly on a mobile device.

SUMMARY

Developer tools built into Chrome are useful for debugging and optimizing your game. Knowing how to use the tools in your browser to hone in on exactly where you are running into a problem can make you a productive developer because you'll never be sitting at a blank screen wondering why nothing works. A basic rule of thumb when things aren't working is to start with a look at the Network tab, add the `console.log` statement, and then move onto full step-debugging. On a mobile device your options are more limited, but using tools such as Weinre means you'll have some more information to debug your game.

Running JavaScript on the Command Line

WHAT'S IN THIS CHAPTER?

➤ Installing a server JavaScript environment

➤ Understanding Node.js

➤ Installing and using Node modules

➤ Writing your own Node command-line module

WROX.COM CODE DOWNLOADS FOR THIS CHAPTER

The wrox.com code downloads for this chapter are found at www.wrox.com/remtitle .cgi?isbn=9781118301326 on the Download Code tab. The code is in the chapter 08 download and individually named according to the names throughout the chapter.

INTRODUCTION

JavaScript has always been predominantly used as a browser-based language throughout its history. Although it has had forays into the server side dating back to Netscape's LiveWire in 1996, JavaScript on the server never seemed to gain much traction. This started to change in 2010 following a November 2009 JSConf presentation on Node.js. Suddenly—and almost inexplicably—people were interested in running JavaScript separate from the browser. In the intervening years JavaScript has turned into a perfectly acceptable language to use on the server and the command line. This chapter will show you how to install, run, and write JavaScript from the command line to support your game.

LEARNING ABOUT NODE.JS

Other server-side JavaScript environments are available; however, Node.js (commonly now just referred to as *Node*) is by far the most popular and has the best cross-platform support (Windows, OS X, and Linux). Because of this popularity, Node is the JavaScript environment discussed in this book.

One of the core ideas of Node is that all I/O should be nonblocking. This means any time the server waits on some data or some input, it shouldn't prevent the execution of other code. The way that Node handles this is through the use of *callbacks*, which are executed automatically when the resource that was blocking becomes available. This is often referred to as *evented programming*. It's something that JavaScript programmers are familiar with because it's the way that most user interfaces (including web pages) are programmed: You add an event listener with a callback that gets called when that event is triggered.

The reason it's essential to write nonblocking code in Node is that Node is single-threaded, meaning that there is only a single thread of execution at a given time. If the code stalls for any reason, the entire server stops taking requests. This might seem like a disadvantage, but by being single-threaded, Node can handle a huge number of concurrent requests without massive amounts of memory usage. Being single-threaded also means that Node doesn't need to switch contexts between threads, which provides a performance boost. Combine this with the speed of the underlying JavaScript engine V8 (the engine that powers Chrome), and you can see why people are excited. A language that people decried as a kiddie scripting language for years suddenly is beating server-side language stalwarts such as Python, PHP, and Ruby in benchmarks.

Server-side JavaScript runs outside of the browser. You might want to do this for two primary reasons. The first is to write a server that can handle web requests. The second is to write command-line scripts that can automate certain tasks. This book discusses both uses.

This chapter discusses using Node to write command-line scripts in JavaScript that do stuff such as lint your code and package and minify your JavaScript. Chapter 18, "Creating a 2-D Platformer," and Chapter 19, "Building a Canvas Editor," discuss building game servers using Node, something that an evented single-threaded server does well.

INSTALLING NODE

With the release of Node 0.6, easy installation on Windows became a reality. Previously you needed to install a UNIX-style POSIX environment such as Cygwin to get Node to run. Since 0.6, Node comes with installer packages for Windows and OS X available at `http://nodejs.org`.

You can run the installer package and follow the prompts to get Node up and running, unless you use Windows, in which case you have no other option. The installer isn't the ideal method to install node, as it won't set up a development environment alongside it. Without this development environment, you won't be able to install modules with native C and C++ code. For this reason, you should follow these instructions for your specific platform.

Installing Node on Windows

On Windows, the only current option is to install Node from a package or compile with Visual Studio. You will, unfortunately, have difficulty installing modules that have native source code that needs to be compiled (such as the node-canvas module used in a later section).

As of this writing, there isn't an up-to-date, prebuilt node-canvas Windows library, so to follow along with the tutorial in the next section that uses `node-canvas`, you can download VMWare's VMPlayer software at `www.vmware.com/products/player`. VMPlayer is a free piece of software that enables you to run a virtual Linux computer from inside of Windows. You can download a Linux image from `www.thoughtpolice.co.uk/vmware`.

Find the Ubuntu Desktop image (not the server image) with the largest number (11.10 as of this writing), download it, and run it from VMPlayer. When that machine is up and running inside of VMPlayer, you can launch the command line from Applications ➪ Accessories ➪ Terminal. From there follow the Linux installation instructions. To copy a file into the Linux virtual machine, you can just drag it from your desktop onto the machine and it will add it to the desktop.

Installing Node on OS X

On OS X, you need a build environment to install native modules as well. This means either installing XCode or installing the command-line tools for XCode. If you aren't going to use the XCode IDE, you can get away with just installing the free command-line tools, which are available at no charge from `https://developer.apple.com/downloads`.

You need to create a free developer ID account if you don't already have one to access the page. After you set up your build environment (either XCode or the preceding download), install Homebrew if you don't already have it installed. Homebrew provides an isolated environment for installing a large variety of packages. You can download Homebrew by following the instructions at `http://mxcl .github.com/homebrew`.

After you install Homebrew, you can run the following command from Terminal:

```
brew install node
```

This code installs an up-to-date version of Node so you are up and running with npm, the node package manager.

Installing Node on Linux

On Linux, life is generally simpler and you can use the pre-installed package manager to get up and running if it's provided. On Ubuntu you should run the following:

```
sudo apt-get install node
```

If your package manager doesn't have an up-to-date version, you can download the source package from `http://nodejs.org`, untar it, and then run the standard build and install commands to begin:

```
./configure
make
make install
```

You may need to run the last command as root to install Node globally.

Tracking the Latest Version of Node

Node is a fast-moving project, and if you want to stay on the bleeding edge, you can download the latest version, commonly referred to as HEAD, from the github repository at `https://github.com/joyent/node.git`.

As is usually the case with open-source software, you should be careful using the latest version of Node in a production project. It's generally much safer to stick with a numbered release unless you desperately need a feature or bug fix in the latest version and are working on a larger project that won't release for a while.

INSTALLING AND USING NODE MODULES

After you install Node, you can use any of the hundreds of modules that people have packaged and made available. To do this use npm, the node package manager, which provides an automated way to download and install libraries and utilities. Previously, npm was installed separately from Node, but they are now packaged together. If you don't have npm installed, make sure you run a newer version of Node.

If npm isn't installed, you can still install it by following the instructions at `http://npmjs.org/`. But first check that your Node install is up-to-date.

Installing Modules

By default, npm installs packages locally into a directory called `node_modules` under your current directory. When you build a server-side app, this makes a lot of sense so you can control exactly which versions of libraries are used. When you use Node from the command line, however, you often want to install certain modules globally, so the binaries are available wherever you are.

To install a module globally, use the `--global` option. One module particularly useful is the jshint module. This module, a slightly less opinionated derivative of Douglas Crockford's JSLint tool, parses your JavaScript code and gives you feedback about what parts need to be tuned up.

To install this module, run the following command from the command line:

```
npm install --global jshint
```

This installs the jshint module and makes the binary accessible from the command line.

Hinting Your Code

With the jshint node module installed, you can now run `jshint` from the command line to run a quick syntax check on your code. JSHint can discover errors such as missing semi-colons or odd structures that wouldn't necessarily prevent your code from running, but might lead to tough-to-find bugs down the road.

To run `jshint` on a file, run the command at the command line followed by the name of the file. For example:

```
jshint engine.js
```

JSHint generates a list of descriptive warnings, including line and column numbers, which can help you improve the JavaScript you write.

Uglifying Your Code

When you deploy your game for players to play, you want it to load as quickly as possible. One way to cut down on the load time is to keep the size of what you transfer over the wire as small as possible. Run your JavaScript code through one of the many JavaScript minifiers that have been written to reduce file size.

JavaScript minifiers take your JavaScript, remove the whitespace, and then rewrite and shorten local variables and parameters to significantly reduce the size of the code. Using the *Alien Invasion* game from Chapter 3, "Finishing Up and Going Mobile," running engine.js and game.js through the uglify-js minifier reduces the size of the code from almost 19 K to just more than 11 K, a compression of more than 40%.

To install uglify-js, install the module via npm globally:

```
npm install --global uglify-js
```

The uglify-js binary takes only one file, so if you want to merge multiple files into one (as you should), you'll need to concatenate them separately. On Windows you can run the following:

```
type file1.js file2.js > all.js
uglify-js all.js > all.min.js
```

On OS X and Linux, run the following:

```
cat file1.js file2.js | uglify-js > all.min.js
```

You now have one file—all.min.js—that contains all the code from any files you pass in minified down into a single, easy-to-serve file.

Reducing the number of files you serve can also speed up game load because each separate web request the browser needs to make takes some additional time, especially on mobile devices. For a production game, write a shell script you can run to do this in an automated fashion before you deploy.

CREATING YOUR OWN SCRIPT

Although there have been hundreds of useful node modules written, you'll have specific needs when you build your game in which some simple server-side scripting is useful. There are plenty of options for scripting languages you could use, including Bash, Windows Script, Python, Ruby, or PHP, but because your game is going to be JavaScript and your game libraries are going to be in JavaScript, it make some sense to write command-line scripts in JavaScript as well.

To gain some experience building a node module, this section walks you through building a script for generating spritesheets and some corresponding JSON from a directory of image files. Figure 8-1 shows a sample output image with sprites lined up in a row.

FIGURE 8-1: A generated spritesheet.

The only hiccup in this process is that the module used in this section, node-canvas, doesn't compile easily on Windows because of its native-C dependencies. (To get around this, see the earlier section on getting a virtual Linux machine up and running on Windows.)

Creating a package.json File

To start, create a new directory called `spriter` for the script you want to write; then open a `package.json` file in that directory. The `package.json` is a file npm uses to get information about your module and its dependencies. Fill in the contents of your `package.json` file to match Listing 8-1, replacing your name and e-mail address where appropriate.

LISTING 8-1: Package.json file

```
{
  "name": "Spriter",
  "description": "A Sprite Map generator",
  "author": "Your Name <youremail@domain.com>",
  "version": "0.0.1",
  "dependencies": {
    "canvas" : "0.10.2",
    "futures": "2.3.1"
  },
  "bin": "./bin/spriter",
  "main": "./spriter.js"
}
```

The name, description, author, and version fields should be relatively self-explanatory. If you plan to publish your module to npm, the version field is important as you update you module. The `dependencies` field is a hash of other modules this module depends on and the versions that should be installed. The `bin` field will be used later when the module is linked to allow you to call this script from anywhere at the command line. Finally the `main` parameter indicates which file holds the main script file that handles exports. `bin` and `main` aren't needed now, but they will be needed in subsequent sections.

This code uses a neat server-side Canvas module that gives you a Canvas 2-D API you can use from server-side node code. It has a dependency on a pair of graphics libraries called *cairo* and *pixman* that you need to install. It also uses the futures module, which provides Promises and Deferreds functionality. If you aren't familiar with Promises or Deferreds, don't worry; they will be touched on later in this chapter.

On Linux you can install either the libcairo2-dev (Debian and Ubuntu) or the cairo-devel (Fedora and openSUSE) package. On Ubuntu—or if you run the Ubuntu virtual machine—this means running the following from the command line:

```
sudo apt-get install libcairo2-dev
```

On OS X install cairo via Homebrew with the following:

```
brew install cairo pixman
```

After you install the cairo library, run the following command from your `spriter` directory to install any dependencies:

```
npm install
```

This downloads and installs the Canvas dependency into the `node_modules` subdirectory, and you should start building this node script.

Using Server-Side Canvas

The first thing you need to do is test the server-side Canvas functionality to ensure it's usable. Draw the standard canvas example of two overlapping rectangles.

File I/O is generally done in an asynchronous manner in Node when writing web servers. However, when writing command-line scripts, you can relax the callback pattern some and use the `Sync` versions of methods that do their jobs synchronously.

Node provides a method called `fs.writeFilSync` that takes a filename and a buffer and writes the contents of that buffer to the file. `node-canvas` has a method called `canvas.toBuffer()` that can generate the buffer from the canvas. You can use `canvas.toBuffer()` asynchronously with a callback, but in this case you can use the synchronous version.

Open the `spriter.js` file in your `spriter` directory, and enter the code from Listing 8-2 into it.

LISTING 8-2: Spriter.js boilerplate

```
var fs = require('fs'),
    Canvas = require('canvas'),
    canvas = new Canvas(200,200),
    ctx = canvas.getContext('2d');
ctx.fillStyle = "#CCC";
ctx.fillRect(0,0,100,100);
ctx.fillStyle = "#C00";
ctx.fillRect(50,50,100,100);
fs.writeFileSync("./sprites.png",canvas.toBuffer());
```

The vast majority of this code is standard Canvas code similar to what you would write in the browser. The only parts that are different are the initial require statements and the call to write the file out.

Modules that you install via npm are loaded by calling `require("..")` and then assigning the returned value to a variable for use. The `fs` module is a built-in library that provides basic file system access in Node.

The `canvas` module, which you installed in the last section, provides functionality that mimics the client-side Canvas object. You can create new Canvas objects by calling the following:

```
new Canvas(width,height)
```

In Listing 8.2 you created a canvas that was 200 pixels by 200 pixels and then retrieved the context object the same way you would on the client.

Finally, after a few simple drawing calls, the one-line command to write the canvas out to a .png file is called:

```
fs.writeFileSync("./sprites.png",canvas.toBuffer());
```

This creates a buffer object and then writes the buffer to the file specified in the first parameter.

To test this, you can run the following:

```
node ./spriter.js
```

This should generate a file in the same directory called `sprites.png` with the two overlapping rectangles. If you run into any errors, double-check that you installed the canvas module correctly.

Creating a Reusable Script

To make the `spriter` script usable both by other modules and from the command line, you need to make a few changes to the `spriter.js` file and add the necessary `spriter` script to the `bin` directory.

Node provides an object called `exports` that is returned whenever you `require()` a file. If you aren't returning an object, you can also override what's returned by setting `module.exports` to whatever you want to return. In the case of `spriter`, you need to expose only a single function that creates sprites in a sprite file.

Rewrite the `spriter.js file` to what's contained in Listing 8-3.

LISTING 8-3: An exported spriter.js file

```
var fs = require('fs'),
    Canvas = require('canvas');

function spriter() {
  var canvas = new Canvas(200,200),
      ctx = canvas.getContext('2d');
  ctx.fillStyle = "#CCC";
  ctx.fillRect(0,0,100,100);
  ctx.fillStyle = "#C00";
  ctx.fillRect(50,50,100,100);
  fs.writeFileSync("./sprites.png",canvas.toBuffer());
}

// Make the spriter method available
module.exports = spriter;
```

The functionality is now wrapped up in a function that can be called externally.

Next, open a file called `spriter` (no extension) in a `bin` subdirectory of your module, and add the code in Listing 8-4.

LISTING 8-4: bin/spriter command-line script

```
#!/usr/bin/env node
var spriter = require('../spriter');
spriter();
```

The only purpose of this script is to load the module you just wrote and then call the spriter function.

You need to make the file executable by flipping on the executable bit. Run the following from the command line in your spriter directory:

```
chmod a+x bin/spriter
```

Next, you can use the npm link command to make the bin file available throughout the system while still letting you modify the code. From the spriter directory, run the following:

```
npm link
```

You can now run the spriter command from the command line anywhere in the system and have the (admittedly useless) sprites.png file created. In the next section, you turn spriter into a useful sprite map generator.

WRITING A SPRITE-MAP GENERATOR

With the logistics of putting together a Node module out of the way, next up is actually making that module useful. The purpose of the module is to generate a sprite map PNG and corresponding JSON given a directory of image files. Sprite maps are useful in HTML5 game development because you don't want to load hundreds of separate image files to handle animations, but rather, as you've seen, load one or a small number of spritesheet files that have multiple images on them.

Follow these steps to achieve the goal of the script:

1. Take a directory of image files in numbered sequences (that is, ship01.png, ship02.png, ..., enemy01.png, enemy02.png, ...).

2. Output a sprite map where each row of images corresponds to a numbered list of files.

3. Output a JSON file detailing the pixel locations and number of frames of each sprite that can be loaded into the game engine that will be built in the next few chapters.

The next sections will put together the pieces for this script.

Using Futures

The way to load images with node-canvas is the same as you might load them on the client side: Set the src property and then wait for an onload event. Because this is an asynchronous event, in theory, images may load out of order (or not load at all) and keeping track of all this requires a bit of housekeeping or a vast amount of nested callbacks.

Luckily, there's the Promise pattern, which encapsulates the idea of handling future events in a sequential manner. You saw an example of this in Chapter 5 during the discussion of Deferreds. Node has a number of different modules that provide Promise and Deferred objects (similar to those in jQuery.) One of the best ones is the `Futures` module, which provides a bunch of types of objects to make your life easier. Because it's usable on both Node and the browser, it's definitely a module worth getting familiar with.

The `spriter` script uses the `Join` module from `Futures`, which provides a way to easily load a bunch of asynchronous events and then trigger only when all have completed.

To create a new Join you simply call the following:

```
var join = Join();
```

You can add a new Promise to the object by calling the following:

```
var promiseFunction = join.add();
```

After you add all the promises to the join, you can call the following:

```
join.when(function(args) {
    /* Triggered when all promises have been called */
}
```

For example, the code in Listing 8-5 shows how you could use the Futures module to load two images:

LISTING 8-5: An example using join

```
var join = Join(),
    img1 = new Image(),
    img2 = new Image();
img1.onload = join.add();
img1.src = "images/image1.png";
img2.onload = join.add();
img2.src = "images/image2/png";
join.when(function() {
  // Both images have been loaded
});
```

Little bookkeeping needs to be done to track the potentially out-of-order loading of both images. The only important part is that `join.when` is called after all the images have been added. Listing 8-5 is essentially the code, scaled-up to however many images are in the passed-in directory that the `spriter` script will use.

Working from the Top Down

Now it's time to replace the basic Canvas demo in `spriter.js` with the actual code to generate a sprite map. In this case it's probably easiest to work from the top down, starting with the highest-level method for generating the sprite map and then writing the helper methods necessary to make it work.

From a high-level perspective, the `spriter` needs to load a directory full of images and sort the images into rows by the filenames. Then `spriter` needs to calculate the size of the Canvas it needs to create based on the width of each sprite and the number of images per row and the height of each row. The `spriter` assumes that each image in each row will be the same size. (This is a requirement of the game engine, so it's not an unreasonable assumption.) You then need to actually draw each of the images to canvas and generate the JSON. Finally the `sprites.png` and `sprites.json` files need to be generated.

To start, rewrite the `spriter` method. Open `spriter.js` and replace all the code there with the code in Listing 8-6.

LISTING 8-6: Rewritten spriter method

```
function spriter(directory) {
  var files = fs.readdirSync(directory),
      rowData = {},
      // Load all the images
      join = loadImages(directory,files,rowData);

  // Wait for the all images to load
  join.when(function() {
    // Get the dimensions of the output sprite map
    var dimensions = calculateSize(rowData),
        canvas = new Canvas(dimensions.width, dimensions.height);

    // Draw the images to the canvas and return the JSON data
    var jsonOutput = drawImages(rowData,canvas);

    // Write out both the sprites.png and sprites.json files
    fs.writeFileSync("./sprites.png",canvas.toBuffer());
    fs.writeFileSync("./sprites.json",JSON.stringify(jsonOutput));
    util.print("Wrote sprites.png and sprites.json\n");
  });

  // Make the spriter method available
  module.exports = spriter;
```

Now break down the preceding code. The top of the file now contains a few more Node modules that need to get pulled in, including the aforementioned `futures` module. The code also pulls out some objects to top-level variables (`Canvas.Image` and `Futures.join`) from existing modules for easier access.

Next the `spriter` function takes a directory name that will be passed in from the `bin/spriter` script. It loads all the files in that directory with a quick call to `fs.readdirSync`. Those files are then passed to the as-of-yet-unwritten `loadImages` method, which returns a `join` that triggers when all the images have loaded. `loadImages` also fills in the `rows` object, which is an object that matches sprite names to the list of sprite images that make up that row.

Next, after the `join.when` callback is triggered, the total dimensions of the Canvas are calculated from the rows of images and a canvas object of that size is created by calling an also yet-to-be-written method called `calculateSize`. Finally, the actual drawing to the Canvas is done by the last method that you need to write: `drawImages`.

canvas now contains the rendered sprite map, and the `jsonOutput` variable has the sprite data indicating the position of each sprite, so all that's needed is to write out both files to disk. To convert the `jsonOutput` (which is a JavaScript object) into a string, you can call the built-in JSON `.stringify` method.

If you were writing client-side code, you would need to be careful to wrap all this in closure to prevent namespace pollution, but because Node gives each file its own scope, this isn't necessary.

Loading Images

Now you can attack the `loadImages` method. It takes in the directory, list of files, and a rows data structure that it needs to populate with lists of images.

Its job is to go over each file in the list, add it to the appropriate row, create an `Image` object, and then start the loading of the image, binding the `onload` method to the `Join` object to handle the asynchronous loading as described previously.

The `loadImages` method uses a regular expression to pull out the name and file number from the filename to allow for indexing by row and sorting. Add Listing 8-7 to the bottom of `spriter.js`.

LISTING 8-7: The loadImages method

```
function loadImages(directory,files,rowData) {
  var fileRegex = /^(.*?)([0-9]+)\.[a-zA-Z]{3}$/,
      join = Join();

  for(var i=0;i<files.length;i++) {
    (function(file) {
      var results = file.match(fileRegex),
          img = new Image();

      if(results) {
        var rowName = results[1],
            fileNum = parseInt(results[2],10);

        img.onload = join.add();
        img.onerror = function() {
          util.print("Error loading: " + file + "\n"); process.exit(1);
        }

        img.src = directory.replace(/\/$/,"") + "/" + file;

        rowData[rowName] = rowData[rowName] || [];
        rowData[rowName].push([fileNum,img]);
      }
    })(files[i]);
  }

  return join;

}
```

`loadImages` has a few interesting parts. The first is the regular expression stored in `fileRegex`. This has two capturing groups used to grab the row name and the file number. `spriter` assumes that each file is in the format of `filename0000.ext` where the final `0000` represents the sprite number of the row. This is a common way files are output when generating a list of images.

The first capturing group of the regular expression (capturing groups are saved values created by surrounding a portion of the regular expression with parentheses) is as follows:

```
(.*?)
```

`.*` means match any character, but adding a question mark `?` to the end means make the matcher nongreedy. This means it can match any character up until the matching part.

The second capturing group—`([0-9]+)`—matches any group of numbers, including 1, 001, and 9999.

Calling `String.match(regexp)` either returns `null` if the string doesn't match, or any array of matches if the regular expression matches. The code in Listing 8.7 stores the result of the regular expression match in the `results` variable and pulls the `rowName` and `fileNum` values out of the capturing groups.

The second interesting part of the code is the anonymous function inside of the `for` loop. This pattern, which you have probably come across before, is known as immediately invoked function expression (IIFE). It's useful in JavaScript because it creates its own scope that enables you to save a variable for later use in a callback. In this case, it's used because the `onerror` callback needs to alert the user to which file was a problem.

Without an IIFE, the following `onerror` callback

```
img.onerror = function() {
        util.print("Error loading: " + file + "\n"); process.exit(1);
    }
```

would just print out the last value assigned to the `file` variable, which can lead to massive amounts of confusion. By using an IIFE, the anonymous function creates a closure, which means the `file` variable is saved.

The `onload` method is replaced with the aforementioned call to `join.add()`. The variable `join` is returned from the method because is it used by `spriter` to indicate when all the images are loaded.

The main data structure created by `loadImages` is `rows`. This is passed in as a parameter, but because objects in JavaScript are passed by reference, any changes you make to the `rows` object are available in the calling method. In this case, the `rows` object is populated by a data structure that looks something like the following:

```
{
   'sprite_one': [ [ 2, Image ],
                   [ 1, Image ],
                   ... ],
   'sprite_two': [ [ 1, Image ],
                   [ 2, Image ],
                   ... ]
}
```

Each key of the object matches an array of entries that links a sprite number to the actual Image object. These images may or may not be ordered correctly, depending on how the operating system returns the list of files. (These are not guaranteed to be ordered.)

Calculating the Size of the Canvas

Next is the method to calculate the size of the Canvas. This method's job is to add the height of each row of images, find the size of the largest row, and use that as the width of the resultant sprite map image. The largest row is used because images need to be square in size. Add the code in Listing 8-8 to the bottom of spriter.js.

LISTING 8-8: Calculating the image size in calculateSize

```
var maxSpriteWidth = 1024;

function calculateSize(rowData) {
  var maxWidth = 0,
      totalHeight = 0;

  for(var spriteName in rowData) {
    // Order by ascending number
    var row = rowData[spriteName],
    firstImage = row[0][1],
    width = firstImage.width * row.length,
    rows = 1;

    if(width > maxSpriteWidth) {
      rows = Math.ceil(width / maxSpriteWidth);
      width = maxSpriteWidth;
    }

    maxWidth = Math.max(width,maxWidth);
    totalHeight += firstImage.height * rows;
  }

  return { width: maxWidth, height: totalHeight };
}
```

This fairly simple method loops over the rows, grabs the first image from each row (remember each image in a row is expected to be the same size), and then uses that image's height as the height of the row and the width of the image multiplied by the number of images as the width of the row. It also uses the Math.max to pull out the maximum row width as the final width of the image. Next, it checks if the resultant image is wider than the maximum sprite width; if so it calculates the number of rows for the sprite and sets the width of the final sprite to the maximum width. Finally, it returns an object with the calculated width and height.

Drawing Images on the Server-Side Canvas

All that's left to do, referring back to Listing 8.6, is to write the drawImages method, which takes in the rows data and the created Canvas, draws the images in rows, and then returns the jsonOutput that will be used by your game engine to output.

This is actually simpler than it might seem because drawing an image to Canvas is a single call to `drawImage`. The only thing you need to be careful about is to sort each row of data by its image index to prevent sprites from showing up in the wrong order. Add the code in Listing 8-9 to the bottom of `spriter.js`.

LISTING 8-9: Creating drawImages

```
function drawImages(rowData,canvas) {
    var ctx = canvas.getContext('2d'),
        curY = 0,
        jsonOutput = {};

    for(var spriteName in rowData) {
     // Order by ascending number
      var row = rowData[spriteName].sort(function(a,b) {
                                      return a[0] - b[0];
                                    }),
          firstImage = row[0][1],
          imageWidth = firstImage.width,
          rowHeight = firstImage.height,
          rowWidth = Math.min(imageWidth * row.length, maxSpriteWidth),
          cols = Math.floor(rowWidth / imageWidth),
          rows = Math.ceil(row.length / cols);

      jsonOutput[spriteName] = { sx: 0, sy: curY, cols: cols,
                                 tilew: imageWidth, tileh: rowHeight,
                                 frames: row.length };

      for(var i =0;i<rows;i++) {
        for(var k=0;k<cols;k++) {
          if(row[k+i*cols])   {
            ctx.drawImage(row[k + i*cols ][1],k*imageWidth,curY);
          }
        }
        curY += rowHeight;
      }
    }

    return jsonOutput;

}
```

The `drawImages` method takes in the rows' data and the Canvas and then loops over each row. For each row, it calls the JavaScript `sort` method with a method that sorts images by the first element of the array. It then grabs the first image from each row to calculate the height of the row and the width of each row.

Armed with this information, it can create the `jsonOutput` entry for this row based on the width and height of each frame and the current *y* location on the Canvas (stored in `curY`).

The code then loops over each image in the row, based on the number of rows and columns for that sprite, and draws it at the correct *x* and *y* location, updating `curY` to keep each row of the sprite and each sprite at the correct *y* location.

Updating and Running the Script

With `drawImages` written, `spriter.js` is now complete; however, the script file in `bin/spriter` needs to be updated to pass in the directory passed to it. Modify `bin/spriter` to match the code in Listing 8-10.

LISTING 8-10: An updated script

```
#!/usr/bin/env node
var spriter = require('../spriter');
spriter(process.argv[2]);
```

The only change is the addition of the `process.argv[2]`, which passes in the first argument after the script name to the script.

You can now run the `spriter` command from the command line; passing the name of a directory of images and the script should output two files in the directory you run the script from: `sprites.json` and `sprites.png`.

If this were to be a production-ready script to be made available via npm, you would most likely want to allow more options to be passed in to the script to control the outputted files and regular expression used to match files. All that code is relatively boilerplate code that you can work out yourself from existing modules. Most of the time the scripts you write for yourself are going to be razor-focused on helping you automate your build and deployment process, so handling a hundred and one different options is left as an exercise for you.

After you have your module working, you can create a tarball of that directory and use `npm install`, passing in the name of the tarball to install that module on different computers. See the instructions on npmjs.org for more details at `http://npmjs.org/doc/install.html`.

If you want to publish your module to npm's list of packages so that it can be installed directly by name via `npm install`, look at the documentation for the `npm publish` command at `http://npmjs.org/doc/publish.html`. (You need to create a user account using `npm adduser` first.)

SUMMARY

Now you have Node.js up and running; you've installed a few modules and used the scripts therein to lint and minify your code. You also wrote your own module and script to generate a sprite map and corresponding JSON file that you can use in later chapters to prevent the need to create sprite maps by hand and calculate positions of individual sprites and frames. You revisit Node in Chapter 19, "Building a Canvas Editor," and Chapter 21, "Going Real Time," when you use it as a web server for writing multiplayer games, which is a use case Node excels at.

Bootstrapping the Quintus Engine: Part I

WHAT'S IN THIS CHAPTER?

➤ Designing and creating the Quintus API

➤ Creating an efficient game loop

➤ Adding classical Inheritance to JavaScript

➤ Building an event system

➤ Creating a component system

WROX.COM CODE DOWNLOADS FOR THIS CHAPTER

The `wrox.com` code downloads for this chapter are found at `www.wrox.com/remtitle .cgi?isbn=9781118301326` on the Download Code tab. The code is in the chapter 09 download and individually named according to the names throughout the chapter.

INTRODUCTION

This chapter covers the initial bootstrapping of the Quintus HTML5 Mobile-friendly Game Engine, the reusable, developer-friendly engine used in the rest of the book. This chapter discusses the basic connective tissue of the engine, whereas the next chapter talks about loading and rendering assets and handling user input.

JavaScript is not a language originally intended for game development, but it has come a long way since being primarily used as a language for dynamically checking and unchecking check boxes. JavaScript now fits well as a language for interactive game development.

CREATING A FRAMEWORK FOR A REUSABLE HTML5 ENGINE

Although the game built in Chapters 1 through 3 is perfectly acceptable for a one-off game, the code is fairly brittle and specific to the game itself. In the next few chapters, you put together a more general engine that allows for better code reuse from game to game.

This engine is going to be called *Quintus*. Quintus means "fifth" in Latin (which seemed appropriate) and will be used for the rest of the games built in this book. As mentioned in Chapter 6, "Being a Good Mobile Citizen," the engine has two dependencies: jQuery and Underscore.js. You've seen that you can build a game in HTML5 without any dependencies; doing so, however, means that this book would contain more nongame-related code and spend less time on actual game development.

When building a game in JavaScript, you don't need to reinvent the wheel for traditional patterns used in game development. Although JavaScript has its quirks as a language, it's extremely malleable and can be molded to fit most programming styles you like. This doesn't mean that you can build a performant game any way you want; certain styles of development lend themselves well to JavaScript's asynchronous, single-threaded nature better than others.

Designing the Basic Engine API

The primary guts of the engine are housed in a single file called `quintus.js`. To make the engine do anything useful, additional modules need to be pulled in for functions such as rendering and input. The Quintus engine has a few specific requirements:

1. You need to have multiple instances of the engine running on the same page. This requirement ensures that the engine acts as a self-contained unit and doesn't interfere with itself or other parts of the page.

2. Where possible, the engine should provide sensible defaults for options to prevent the need for a lot of configuration to get something up and running.

3. The engine should be flexible enough to be usable for both simple examples and more complex games as well as allow support for different rendering engines (for example Canvas, CSS, SVG, and potentially WebGL).

Working backward from these requirements, Listing 9-1 shows a simple API for how a basic animated example could be written.

LISTING 9.1: A simple Quintus API example

```
var MyExample = Quintus();
MyExample.load('assetName.png',function() {
  var object = new MyExample.CanvasSprite({
                   asset: 'assetName.png', x: 0, y: 0
               });

  object.update = function(dt) {
    // Code to update the object
  };
```

```
MyExample.gameLoop(function(dt) {
    this.clear();

    object.update(dt);
    object.render(this.ctx);
  });

});
```

This simple example loads a single asset and creates a single object that is updated and drawn on the screen.

Although this might suffice for a limited example, a more full-featured use case would require the addition of stage and scene functionality that automatically handles the updating and rendering of a number of objects. In this case the engine would take over the handling of the game loop. A slightly more full-featured game might look like listing 9.2.

LISTING 9.2: A more complicated API example

```
var MyGame = Quintus()
              .include("Input,Sprites,Scenes")
              .setup();

var spriteType1 = MyGame.CanvasSprite.extend({
   // Overrides for this type of object
});

var spriteType2 = MyGame.CanvasSprite.extend({
   // Overrides for this type of object
});

MyGame.load([ 'asset1.png', 'asset2.png', 'sprites.json'],function() {

  var scene1 = new MyGame.Scene(function(stage) {
    stage.add(new MyGame.SpriteType1({ ... Options .. });
    stage.add(new MyGame.SpriteType2({ ... Options .. });
  });

  MyGame.stageScene(scene1);
});
```

Here the game extends the base Quintus functionality with the `Quintus.Input`, the `Quintus.Sprites`, and the `Quintus.Scenes` extensions and then creates a couple of reusable sprite types. The game loads multiple assets, including a spritesheet, and then when those are loaded it creates a new scene object. Finally, it stages the scene, which starts the scene-based game loop (if it hasn't already been started) and handles the updating and rendering of the scene.

Starting the Engine Code

With a developer-friendly API for the engine defined, open up `quintus.js` and start writing the initial code that acts as a base for all the engine code to follow. Quintus takes a page from jQuery's playbook and uses a single method as a factory method and a container object for extensions to the engine.

To create a new game with Quintus, just call the `Quintus` method and then use and extend that individual object with additional functionality. Because multiple instances of Quintus might exist on a single page, you need to load any extensions to the engine in an individual instance.

To achieve this, you can create a function called `Quintus` that creates, augments, and finally returns a new object. Listing 9.3 shows the initial structure of the engine.

LISTING 9.3: The basic engine structure

```
var Quintus = function(opts) {
  var Q = {};

// Some base options to be filled in later
  Q.options = {
    // TODO: set some sensible defaults
  };
  if(opts) { _(Q.options).extend(opts); }


  Q._normalizeArg = function(arg) {
    if(_.isString(arg)) {
      arg = arg.replace(/\s+/g,'').split(",");
    }
    if(!_.isArray(arg)) {
      arg = [ arg ];
    }
    return arg;
  };

 // Shortcut to extend Quintus with new functionality
 // binding the methods to Q
 Q.extend = function(obj) {
    _(Q).extend(obj);
    return Q;
  };

  // Syntax for including other modules into quintus
  Q.include = function(mod) {
    _.each(Q._normalizeArg(mod),function(m) {
      m = Quintus[m] || m;
      m(Q);
    });
    return Q;
  };

  // TODO: Additional Quintus Code goes here

  return Q;
}
```

This initial code provides the base for the modular architecture that the rest of the engine will be built on. The main thing the code does is create an `options` object and extend that object with any additional passed-in options in `opts`.

Continuing through the code, you can use the _normalizeArg method to take a string of passed-in, comma-separated names and turn them into an array of names with any whitespace stripped out. This convenience method enables you to write, for example, "sword, shield, health" instead of ["sword", "shield", "health"]. If you pass in an array then, that array of elements is used without transformation. _normalizeArg is used in case a list of includes are passed in.

The Q.include and Q.extend methods are used to extend Quintus functionality with additional modules like Sprites and Scenes. To aid in chaining, they also return the Q variable.

Quintus is a method that takes an optional options hash and returns an instance of the engine with a base level of functionality.

ADDING THE GAME LOOP

As you already know, the actual execution of your game from frame to frame is orchestrated by the game loop, which is responsible for updating the game state and then rendering the current frame of the game on the screen. The main rendering and JavaScript engine in your browser both run together in a single thread, which means that you can't use a single tight loop for the game loop as you might in an environment with true multithreading. Instead, as you saw in the first chapter, your game loop must be run with a timer that cedes control from your JavaScript code back to the browser, so it can update the page and handle input events.

Building a Better Game Loop Timer

For a long time building a game loop timer was done with the timer functions that have always existed in the browser: setTimeout and setInterval. Although this worked acceptably to a certain degree, it suffered from a few drawbacks.

The first drawback was that, especially on slower computers and browsers, the game might try to update the game more often than the browser could handle, resulting in a visual slow-down. The second drawback was that even when the browser had a different tab active, the game would continue running at full speed, slowing down the computer and giving JavaScript games a bad name.

Starting in 2011, browsers began adding support for the requestAnimationFrame API, which allowed the browser to control the rate at which the game loop was called based on how fast the browser can actually update the screen. Since it first appeared, the requestAnimationFrame specification has settled out and is now consistent across the browsers that support it. For browsers that don't support it, Paul Irish (with the help of a number of other folks on the Internet) developed a polyfill that backports requestAnimationFrame support to all browsers using setTimeout where necessary. You can see Paul's post on the subject on his blog from 2011 at http://paulirish.com/2011/requestanimationframe-for-smart-animating/.

Adding the code from Listing 9-4 to the top of your quintus.js file (outside of the definition for Quintus at the top of the file) can expose a consistent requestAnimationFrame method on the window object to all browsers.

LISTING 9-4: requestAnimationFrame polyfill

```
(function() {
    var lastTime = 0;
    var vendors = ['ms', 'moz', 'webkit', 'o'];
    for(var x = 0; x < vendors.length && !window.requestAnimationFrame; ++x) {
        window.requestAnimationFrame = window[vendors[x]+'RequestAnimationFrame'];
        window.cancelAnimationFrame =
            window[vendors[x]+'CancelAnimationFrame'] ||
window[vendors[x]+'CancelRequestAnimationFrame'];
    }

    if (!window.requestAnimationFrame)
        window.requestAnimationFrame = function(callback, element) {
            var currTime = new Date().getTime();
            var timeToCall = Math.max(0, 16 - (currTime - lastTime));
            var id = window.setTimeout(function() { callback(currTime +
timeToCall); },
                timeToCall);
            lastTime = currTime + timeToCall;
            return id;
        };

    if (!window.cancelAnimationFrame)
        window.cancelAnimationFrame = function(id) {
            clearTimeout(id);
        };
}());
```

As you can see, if the nonvendor-prefixed version of requestAnimationFrame isn't available, the code loops through each of the potential vendor-specific prefixes and uses that prefix as the nonprefixed version. If that fails, the code approximates requestAnimationFrame and cancelAnimationFrame using setTimeout and cancelTimeout. These polyfilled methods, because they don't have native browser support, do suffer from the drawbacks previously mentioned, but they are the best you can use.

Adding the Optimized Game Loop to Quintus

Having created a consistent polyfill to an optimized timer method, up next is creating the game loop itself. The traditional game loop has two main pieces that execute each frame: update and render. The update piece is responsible for stepping the game logic through a small chunk of time, handling any user input, motion, and collisions between objects and updating each game object to a consistent state.

Next, the game needs to render itself onto the screen. How the rendering step is done depends on how your game is built. For Canvas-based games, you usually want to clear the entire Canvas and then redraw all the necessary sprites on to the page, for CSS and SVG games. Provided you updated the properties of the objects on the page correctly, your job is actually done—the browser takes care of moving and updating the objects.

Armed with this knowledge, you can add a game loop method to Quintus and `pause` and `unpause` methods. Open up `quintus.js` and add the code from Listing 9-5 before the final `return` statement.

LISTING 9-5: Adding a game loop

```
Q.gameLoop = function(callback) {
  Q.lastGameLoopFrame = new Date().getTime();

  Q.gameLoopCallbackWrapper = function(now) {
    Q.loop = requestAnimationFrame(Q.gameLoopCallbackWrapper);
    var dt = now - Q.lastGameLoopFrame;
    if(dt > 100) { dt = 100; }
    callback.apply(Q,[dt / 1000]);
    Q.lastGameLoopFrame = now;
  };

  requestAnimationFrame(Q.gameLoopCallbackWrapper);
};

Q.pauseGame = function() {
  if(Q.loop) {
    cancelAnimationFrame(Q.loop);
  }
  Q.loop = null;
};

Q.unpauseGame = function() {
  if(!Q.loop) {
    Q.lastGameLoopFrame = new Date().getTime();
    Q.loop = requestAnimationFrame(Q.gameLoopCallbackWrapper);
  }
}
```

The `Q.gameLoop` method takes in a callback that expects a `dt` parameter representing the difference in seconds from the last frame (this is a small fraction close to 1/60th of a second) and wraps that callback in a method that calculates this difference from the current time that is passed into the `requestAnimationFrame` callback. This wrapped callback is saved in `Q.gameLoopCallbackWrapper` and used in `Q.pauseGame` and `Q.unpauseGame` to start and stop the game timer.

Testing the Game Loop

Quintus now has enough functionality to at least drop it on the page and try out the game loop and the `pause` and `unpause` code.

Open a new HTML file called **gameloop_test.html** and put in the HTML in Listing 9-6 into the file. Make sure the dependencies of jquery and underscore.js are in the directory as well as your `quintus.js` code to this point.

LISTING 9-6: Game loop test gameloop_test.html

```html
<!DOCTYPE HTML>
<html lang="en">
  <head>
    <meta charset="UTF-8">
    <title></title>
    <script src='jquery.min.js'></script>
    <script src='underscore.js'></script>
    <script src='quintus.js'></script>
  </head>
  <body>
    <div id='timer'>0</div>
    <div id='fps'>0</div>
    <button id='pause'>Pause</button>
    <button id='unpause'>Unpause</button>
    <script>
      var TimerTest = Quintus();

      var totalFrames = 0,
          totalTime = 0;

      TimerTest.gameLoop(function(dt) {
          totalTime += dt;
          totalFrames += 1;
          $("#timer").text(Math.round(totalTime * 1000) + " MS");
          $("#fps").text(Math.round(totalFrames / totalTime) + " FPS");
      });

      $("#pause").on('click',TimerTest.pauseGame);
      $("#unpause").on('click',TimerTest.unpauseGame);
    </script>
  </body>
</html>
```

Loading this page should execute the game loop function and enable you to pause and unpause the game using the two buttons.

All the game loop in this exercise does is keep track of the total time and the total number of frames that have run in two global variables and then update two <divs> using jQuery to display the time the loop has already run in milliseconds and the frames per second that the animation runs.

It uses the jQuery.fn.on method to bind the Q.pauseGame and Q.unpauseGame methods to button clicks. One nice side effect of the way the Quintus code is built is that nowhere in quintus.js have you referred to the this object. The Quintus object is always referred to by the local variable Q, which is bound in a closure. This means that one of the trickiest parts of JavaScript, knowing what object this refers to at any given time won't affect the main Quintus code. As such, you can pass Quintus methods such as Q.pauseGame and Q.unpauseGame into callbacks without worrying about binding them to their object.

This type of binding won't be possible to do when sprites are introduced because in that case you'll want to use the prototype property to save memory and creation time as discussed in Chapter 2, but since very few instances of the Quintus engine will ever be created (generally only one per page) this method of object creation makes life easier.

ADDING INHERITANCE

In the past, most game engines used the idea of object inheritance ubiquitously. For example, animated sprites are built up from moving sprites that are built up from Base Objects. Part of this inheritance hierarchy developed because of the static nature of languages such as C++, which lend themselves to using inherited classes and virtual functions to treat different types of objects uniformly.

Using Inheritance in Game Engines

As game engines grew in size, people realized that a static hierarchy of classes quickly became unwieldy. Even though you might want some shallow hierarchy in your classes for where objects share the same base functionality, artificially creating a single deep hierarchy doesn't usually make sense.

Take the example of a shooter game with a number of different weapons the player can pick up. Say you have the following three weapons:

➤ A crowbar, which can be used only to hit people and doesn't have ammunition

➤ A pistol, which can be used as a projectile weapon or can be used to hit people as a mêlée weapon and has a limited amount of ammunition for shooting

➤ A grenade, which can be used only as a projectile weapon but also has a ranged damage effect

Even in this simple case, coming up with a single hierarchy that allows for code reuse, while at the same time preventing weapons from being burdened with functionality they don't need, is difficult. You might be tempted to create the following set of base classes:

```
Weapon
   MeleeWeapon
      RangedWeapon
         AreaDamageWeapon
```

Although this isn't perfect—a grenade, for example, would subclass `AreaDamageWeapon` but would need to override any mêlée weapon functionality and disable it—at first glance it at least seems like a workable base. Adding new types of weapons, however, quickly becomes clunky and redundant. Imagine how to handle a rifle with an attached grenade launcher, which would be a weapon with ranged, mêlée, and area damage. Something such as a landmine that is set somewhere and causes area damage when stepped on (much like a mêlée weapon) would also be a challenge. When you start jumping through hoops to make a class hierarchy work correctly, it becomes clear it's time to move on to something else.

That something else is known as the *component/entity model*. The idea is that you don't define a linear class hierarchy to build up to your wanted level of functionality; rather, you define a number of loosely coupled components that know nothing about each other and just go about their own business. For example, in the case of the weapons defined previously, you could define separate components for Melee Attacks, Ranged Attacks, and Area Damage Attacks and bind the triggering of those components to the different firing inputs. (For example, when the weapon is equipped and fire1 is pressed, do a mêlée attack; when fire2 is pressed do a ranged attack.)

The only downside to components is that there tends to be a lot of them, and adding a long string of components on object creation and dealing with not knowing what base level of functionality all objects support can be challenging. Components also tend to be self-contained, which means that when you do want them to interact, you have additional problems.

To this end Quintus uses a compromise between inheritance and components by supporting both, enabling you to use inheritance where it makes sense and components when you need more flexibility. To support the former, the engine needs to add a classical inheritance model to JavaScript. To support the latter, it needs to add a component system and have low-level support for events to allow for as much decoupling between components as possible.

Adding Classical Inheritance to JavaScript

JavaScript doesn't suffer from the limitation of statically typed interfaces and instead usually takes advantage of the concept of duck typing. duck typing, which has been mentioned previously, revolves around the idea that the type of an object doesn't matter; all that matters are the properties and methods that an object responds to.

JavaScript does support a prototypical inheritance model that enables a more traditional type of inheritance. The three main issues with using prototypical inheritance out-of-the-box are that it doesn't support calling inherited functionality via a super-type method; creating descendant objects feels slightly kludgey; and there's no way to inherit constructors.

You can solve this in a number of ways and add a more traditional class hierarchy to JavaScript. One of the most popular is jQuery creator John Resig's Simple JavaScript inheritance, which takes its cues from base2 and another JavaScript library called Prototype.js. It's a piece of open-source code released under the MIT license originally described on John's website: `http://ejohn.org/blog/simple-javascript-inheritance/`.

Add the code from Listing 9-7 somewhere to the top of `quintus.js`, outside of the Quintus constructor method. (Near the top of the file, after the `requestAnimationFrame` code outside of any curly braces, is fine.)

LISTING 9-7: Simple JavaScript inheritance

```
/* Simple JavaScript Inheritance
 * By John Resig http://ejohn.org/
 * MIT Licensed.
 */
// Inspired by base2 and Prototype
(function(){
  var initializing = false,
      fnTest = /xyz/.test(function(){xyz;}) ? /\b_super\b/ : /.*/;
  // The base Class implementation (does nothing)
  this.Class = function(){};
```

```
    // Create a new Class that inherits from this class
    Class.extend = function(prop) {
      var _super = this.prototype;

      // Instantiate a base class (but only create the instance,
      // don't run the init constructor)
      initializing = true;
      var prototype = new this();
      initializing = false;

      // Copy the properties over onto the new prototype
      for (var name in prop) {
        // Check if we're overwriting an existing function
        prototype[name] = typeof prop[name] == "function" &&
          typeof _super[name] == "function" &&
                fnTest.test(prop[name]) ?
          (function(name, fn){
            return function() {
              var tmp = this._super;

              // Add a new ._super() method that is the same method
              // but on the super-class
              this._super = _super[name];

              // The method only need to be bound temporarily, so we
              // remove it when we're done executing
              var ret = fn.apply(this, arguments);
              this._super - tmp;

              return ret;
            };
          })(name, prop[name]) :
          prop[name];
      }

      // The dummy class constructor
      function Class() {
        // All construction is actually done in the init method
        if ( !initializing && this.init )
          this.init.apply(this, arguments);
      }

      // Populate our constructed prototype object
      Class.prototype = prototype;

      // Enforce the constructor to be what we expect
      Class.prototype.constructor = Class;
      // And make this class extendable
      Class.extend = arguments.callee;

      return Class;
    };
  })();
```

The main gist of this code is to allow new classes to be extended from existing ones using the `extend` method. Inherited objects can share the same instance methods as the parent objects and call parent methods using `this._super()` from the child method. This special case is handled by the loop in the middle, which, instead of just copying the entire method over blindly, checks for an existing method on the parent and then creates a wrapper function that temporarily sets the `this._super` method to the parent's definition during the call:

```
// Copy the properties over onto the new prototype
for (var name in prop) {

  // Check if we're overwriting an existing function
  prototype[name] = typeof prop[name] == "function" &&
    typeof _super[name] == "function" && fnTest.test(prop[name]) ?
    (function(name, fn){
      return function() {
        var tmp = this._super;

        // Add a new ._super() method that is the same method
        // but on the super-class
        this._super = _super[name];

        // The method only need to be bound temporarily, so we
        // remove it when we're done executing
        var ret = fn.apply(this, arguments);
        this._super = tmp;

        return ret;
      };
    })(name, prop[name]) :
    prop[name];
}
```

The preceding code checks if the property already exists on the superclass; if it does, it creates a function that does the temporary `this._super` reassignment before calling the new method again. If the method doesn't exist, the code simply assigns the property, preventing adding in any additional overhead.

The `Class` code also adds in a constructor function that automatically calls the `init()` method of the object, allowing for the chaining of initializers as well:

```
// The dummy class constructor
function Class() {
  // All construction is actually done in the init method
  if ( !initializing && this.init )
    this.init.apply(this, arguments);
}
```

Finally, it adds the `extend` method to the class so that it can further be subclassed:

```
// And make this class extendable
Class.extend = arguments.callee;
```

Calling `arguments.callee` returns the method that was called (in this case `extend`) and that method is then assigned to the property `extend` of the returned `Class` object, allowing further subclassing down the line.

Exercising the Class Functionality

To get a sense of how to use this code, try exercising this functionality in the console of the browser as follows:

```
var Person = Class.extend({
  init: function() { console.log('Created Person'); },
  speak: function() { console.log('Person Speaking:'); }
});

var p = new Person();
// Logs: Created Person

p.speak();
// Logs: Person Speaking:

var Guy = Person.extend({
  init: function() { this._super(); console.log('Created Guy'); },
  speak: function() { this._super(); console.log("I'm a Guy!"); }
});

var bob = new Guy();
// Logs: Created Person
//       Created Guy

bob.speak();
// Logs: Person Speaking
//       I'm a Guy!

// Girl doesn't call the super method
var Girl = Person.extend({
  init: function() { console.log('Created Girl'); },
  speak: function() { console.log("I'm a Girl!"); }
});

var jill = new Girl();
// Logs: Created Girl

jill.speak();
// Logs: I'm a Girl!
```

As you can see, the class functionality makes it possible to cleanly create and extend classes that ensure that methods of the super class are called when appropriate.

```
bob instanceof Person;   // true
bob instanceof Guy;      // true
bob instanceof Girl;     // false
jill instanceof Person;  // true
jill instanceof Guy;     // false
jill instanceof Girl;    // true
```

This functionality also makes it easy to use the type of an object where necessary. Notice that bob and jill respond as expected to the instanceof operator.

SUPPORTING EVENTS

Adding support for events in a game engine makes it easier to keep different parts of the engine from becoming too tightly coupled. It means one part of the game can communicate events and actions to other parts of the game without needing to know anything about the objects it's communicating with.

When you add components into the mix, it even allows a sprite to communicate with itself without needing to know all the components that make it up. A Physics component on a sprite might trigger a collision event, and two components listening for the event could separately handle triggering the appropriate sound effect and animation effect.

Designing the Event API

Quintus uses a base class called Evented that is the jumping-off point for any object that needs to subscribe to and trigger events. As usual, you must think about the API first and then build the code around that API afterward.

Given a player sprite and a scene object, now walk through an example event functionality:

```
// Play the intro animation on the player
// when the scene starts
scene.bind('start',player,function() {
  this.showIntro();
});

// Bind a method on player using the method name
scene.bind('finish',player,'showFinal');

// Trigger the start event on the scene
scene.trigger('start');

// Unbind the player from the start event
scene.unbind('start',player);

// Release the player from listening
// to all events (such as if it's blown up)
player.debind();
```

This API provides a way to bind, trigger, and unbind events as well as release an object from any events (such as when it is removed from the game) so that sprites that have been destroyed don't continue to respond to events.

Writing the Evented Class

As you've seen, the base Evented class needs to support four methods: bind, unbind, trigger, and debind. Open up quintus.js and add in a definition for Q.Evented from Listing 9-8 below the gameLoop code (but before the final return). You fill in each of the method calls in turn in the subsequent sections.

LISTING 9-8: Evented outline code

```
Q.Evented = Class.extend({
  bind: function(event,target,callback) {
    // TODO: Fill in bind code
  },

  trigger: function(event,data) {
    // TODO: Fill in trigger code
  },

  unbind: function(event,target,callback) {
    // TODO: Fill in unbind code
  },

  debind: function() {
    // TODO Fill in the debind code
  }
});
```

To keep subclassing the Evented class simple, the class doesn't use the init constructor method but will initialize any objects on-the-fly as necessary.

Filling in the Evented Methods

First, consider the bind method. Its job is to bind a listener to a specific event and trigger the callback on the target. The target is an optional argument that provides a context for the callback and allows the callback to be removed with a call to debind on the target to prevent stale events from hanging around. Fill in the code in Listing 9-9 into the bind method:

LISTING 9-9: The event bind method

```
bind: function(event,target,callback) {
  // Handle the case where there is no target provided
  if(!callback) {
    callback = target;
    target = null;
  }
  // Handle case for callback that is a string
  if(_.isString(callback)) {
    callback = target[callback];
  }

  this.listeners = this.listeners || {};
  this.listeners[event] = this.listeners[event] || [];
  this.listeners[event].push([ target || this, callback]);
  if(target) {
    if(!target.binds) { target.binds = []; }
    target.binds.push([this,event,callback]);
  }
},
```

At its base, the `bind` method is relatively straightforward: The only pieces of essential code are the three lines in the center that add a listener to an object, called `this.listeners`, keyed by the name of the event. Each listener consists of a two-element array made up of a context object and the callback itself. The code first needs to check that the `this.listeners` array exists because `Evented` doesn't have an `init` constructor method.

The rest of the code is in line with Quintus's goal of being friendly to developers by enabling a few different input formats. The `bind` method can be called three different ways:

```
scene.bind('start',function() { ... });
scene.bind('start',player,function() { ... });
scene.bind('start',player,'methodName');
```

The first signature is useful when you don't need to worry about context or objects unbinding themselves when they are removed from the game. The latter two both provide the same result, but one takes a string for the name of the method property on the target object, and the other takes the method itself.

Next consider the `trigger` method, the simplest method of the four. Fill the method in with the code from Listing 9-10. (Don't forget to separate each of the four method definitions with a comma.)

LISTING 9-10: Evented trigger method

```
trigger: function(event,data) {
  if(this.listeners && this.listeners[event]) {
    for(var i=0,len = this.listeners[event].length;i<len;i++) {
      var listener = this.listeners[event][i];
      listener[1].call(listener[0],data);
    }
  }
},
```

`trigger` just checks to see if there are any listeners listening to that specific event. If so, each of the listeners is looped over, and the callback is called with the provided context. Because each listener is made up of an array with the context and callback, the code for actually making the call looks like this:

```
listener[1].call(listener[0],data);
```

Given the flexibile notion of context and the `this` object in JavaScript, you should always be explicit with what the context of a method call is.

With events bound and triggerable, you can unbind them when an object is destroyed or no longer needs to be triggered on specific events. Fill in the code for `unbind` from Listing 9-11.

LISTING 9-11: Evented unbind method

```
unbind: function(event,target,callback) {
  if(!target) {
    if(this.listeners[event]) {
      delete this.listeners[event];
    }
  } else {
```

```
      var l = this.listeners && this.listeners[event];
      if(l) {
        for(var i = l.length-1;i>=0;i--) {
          if(l[i][0] == target) {
            if(!callback || callback == l[i][1]) {
              this.listeners[event].splice(i,1);
            }
          }
        }
      }
    }
  },
```

The unbind method can take one, two, or three parameters, each providing more specificity for the exact event to be removed. In the first case, where no target is provided, the object removes the entire list of listeners for that event by simply removing the key from the object.

In the second and third cases, where you are unbinding only one or a few of all the possible listeners to that event, the method needs to actually loop through each of the listeners and remove the ones that are being unbound using the built-in Array.splice method. Looping over an array and removing elements from it at the same time is a somewhat tricky proposition because if you loop over the array normally and then change its length, you can end up with a problem. One way around this is to loop from the end of the array on down to the beginning. If an element needs to be removed, it won't affect the index of elements previous to it in the array.

The last method on Evented is the debind method, which removes an object from any listeners it's registered with. unbind is used to remove listeners from an object, while debind is used when an object is being destroyed to remove all of its listeners to prevent memory leaks and unexpected behavior. Fill in the code for debind from Listing 9-12.

LISTING 9-12: Evented debind method

```
debind: function() {
   if(this.binds) {
     for(var i=0,len=this.binds.length;i<len;i++) {
       var boundEvent = this.binds[i],
           source = boundEvent[0],
           event = boundEvent[1];
       source.unbind(event,this);
     }
   }
}
```

This code loops over each of the elements in the this.binds array and calls unbind to remove them.

SUPPORTING COMPONENTS

The last core piece of functionality necessary to bootstrap Quintus is adding in component support. As described earlier in the section "Using Inheritance in Game Engines," components make it simpler to create small pieces of reusable functionality that can be mixed and matched among the various sprites and objects that need it.

`Crafty.js` a popular, mature HTML5 Game engine based entirely around a component-entity architecture, as discussed in Chapter 26, "Using an HTML5 Game Engine," and was the inspiration for the Quintus component methods.

Designing the Component API

As usual, think about the API first and how you want to use components in the game. Components need to be added and removed from sprites quickly and concisely. They should be accessible from the objects but also not overly pollute the object's namespace. Listing 9-13 shows and example of how you could define and use components.

LISTING 9-13: Imagining a component system

```
var exGame = Quintus();
var player = new exGame.GameObject();
exGame.register('sword',{
 added: function() {
  // When whatever we are registered with triggers
  // a fire event, call the attack method
  this.entity.bind('fire',this,'attack');
 },
 attack: function() {
  // Code to attack
 },
 // Methods copied directly over to the entity
 extend: {
   attack: function() {
    this.sword.attack();
   }
 }

});
// Add the sword component
player.add('sword');

// Calls attack via event
player.trigger('fire');

// Call attack directly from extended event
player.attack();

// Remove the sword component
player.del('sword');

// Should cause an error
player.attack();
```

The component system in Quintus needs to register components, add components, remove components, and let the base sprite be extended with additional methods.

Implementing the Component System

The actual implementation for the component system has three separate parts. The first is the register method to register components. The register functionality is handled by the Q.register method, and under the hood it creates a new class for the component and stores it in Q.components, indexed by name.

Add the code in Listing 9-14 in the usual spot to the bottom of quintus.js, before the final return statement.

LISTING 9-14: The base Quintus components functionality

```
Q.components = {};

Q.register = function(name,methods) {
  methods.name = name;
  Q.components[name] = Q.Component.extend(methods);
};
```

All this code does is register the component into a Q.components object and extend the Q.Component class with the passed-in method. Next is the creation of the Q.Component class that handles the heavy lifting of adding itself and removing itself from an object.

Add the code in Listing 9-15 below the code you just added in to create the Q.Component class.

LISTING 9-15: The Q.Component class

```
Q.Component = Q.Evented.extend({
  init: function(entity) {
    this.entity = entity;
    if(this.extend) _.extend(entity,this.extend);
    entity[this.name] = this;
    entity.activeComponents.push(this.name);
    if(this.added) this.added();
  },

  destroy: function() {
    if(this.extend) {
      var extensions = _.keys(this.extend);
      for(var i=0,len=extensions.length;i<len;i++) {
        delete this.entity[extensions[i]];
      }
    }
    delete this.entity[this.name];
    var idx = this.entity.activeComponents.indexOf(this.name);
    if(idx != -1) {
      this.entity.activeComponents.splice(idx,1);
    }
    this.debind();
    if(this.destroyed) this.destroyed();
  }
});
```

The base component class has only two main responsibilities: to handle being added to an entity and to handle being removed from that entity. When the component is added to an entity (which is done in the `init` constructor) the component does five things:

1. It sets a property so that it can refer back to the entity.

2. It extends the entity with new properties from its `extend` attribute.

3. It adds itself to the entity as a property under its name. (So, for example, the sword component would be accessible via `entity.sword`.)

4. It also adds itself to the entity's list of active components.

5. It calls the `added` method on the component to set up any post-initialization requirements like listeners.

The `Q.Component` class extends from the `Q.Evented` object, so it can bind and be bound to.

When a component is destroyed, it needs to do the reverse, which amounts to removing any extensions by removing properties that match the keys of the extend object from the entity. Next, it needs to destroy the property named after the component from the entity and remove the entry from the active components list. Finally, it calls `debind` to remove any event handlers it has bound and calls the custom `destroyed()` handler if one is defined.

The last piece for the component system is the `Q.GameObject` class, which inherits from `Q.Evented` and is responsible for adding and removing components. The `Q.GameObject` class is the base class from which all active game objects, such as sprites, inherit from.

Add the definition of `Q.GameObject` in Listing 9-16 to the spot at the bottom of `quintus.js` before the final return.

LISTING 9-16: Q.GameObject definition

```
Q.GameObject = Q.Evented.extend({
  has: function(component) {
    return this[component] ? true : false;
  },
  add: function(components) {
    components = Q._normalizeArg(components);
    if(!this.activeComponents) { this.activeComponents = []; }
    for(var i=0,len=components.length;i<len;i++) {
      var name = components[i],
          comp = Q.components[name];
      if(!this.has(name) && comp) {
        var c = new comp(this);
        this.trigger('addComponent',c);
      }
    }
    return this;
  },
  del: function(components) {
    components = Q._normalizeArg(components);
```

```
      for(var i=0,len=components.length;i<len;i++) {
        var name = components[i];
        if(name && this.has(name)) {
          this.trigger('delComponent',this[name]);
          this[name].destroy();
        }
      }
      return this;
    },

    destroy: function() {
      if(this.destroyed) { return; }
      this.debind();
      if(this.parent && this.parent.remove) {
        this.parent.remove(this);
      }
      this.trigger('removed');
      this.destroyed = true;
    }
  });
```

The base `Q.GameObject` class again inherits from `Q.Evented`, allowing it to listen for and trigger events. The code has four main methods: `add`, `has`, `del`, and `destroy`. The first three are used to add, check for, and remove components from an object respectively. The last method, `destroy`, is used to destroy the object itself.

First is the `has` method, which checks if a `Q.GameObject` already has a certain component by checking if the object has a property by the same name. This is a little risky because it relies on the developer to be careful about component names and extended properties, but if there's a name conflict, other issues can result regardless.

Next the `add` and `del` methods add and remove components from a `Q.GameObject`, and they are almost mirror images of each other. The `add` method loops over all the components to be added, looks them up in `Q.components`, and then creates the new component object. The `del` method does the reverse, looping over the components to remove and calling the component's `remove` method for each.

Both methods have some additional logic in them to prevent the developer from adding or removing a component more than once. Each also triggers an event with the component instance itself passed as the data argument.

The `destroy` method calls `debind` on the object, tries to remove it from its parent if it has one, and triggers a `removed` event to allow any components to clean up if necessary. It also adds a `destroyed` property to prevent the `destroy` method from being called more than once.

SUMMARY

You now have the building blocks to create a reusable HTML5 game engine. You created the initial game container object, the game loop, and some base classes for working with events and components. Having a solid base on which to build the rest of the engine in a modular way is going to help a lot down the line. The next chapter covers loading some game elements onto the page and building a reusable user input handling system.

10

Bootstrapping the Quintus Engine: Part II

WHAT'S IN THIS CHAPTER?

➤ Capturing input

➤ Drawing onscreen controls

➤ Loading assets

WROX.COM CODE DOWNLOADS FOR THIS CHAPTER

The wrox.com code downloads for this chapter are found at www.wrox.com/remtitle
.cgi?isbn=9781118301326 on the Download Code tab. The code is in the chapter 10
download and individually named according to the names throughout the chapter.

INTRODUCTION

In the last chapter the seeds of a reusable engine were planted. This chapter fills out that base
with classes to get something onto the screen, accept user input, and load assets.

ACCESSING A GAME CONTAINER ELEMENT

For the game to render anything on the screen, it must have an object to draw on. For Canvas
games this is a Canvas element. For other types of games, it will be either a regular <div> or
an SVG element. To this end you'll create a flexible setup method on Quintus that grabs a container from a passed-in ID or creates an element from scratch if necessary. The setup method
also grabs the context from the element if it's supported.

Add the code in Listing 10-1 to the bottom of `quintus.js` from Chapter 9 above the final `return Q` statement.

LISTING 10-1: The Quintus setup and clear methods

```
Q.setup = function(id, options) {
  var touchDevice = 'ontouchstart' in document;
  options = options || {};
  id = id || "quintus";
  Q.el = $(_.isString(id) ? "#" + id : id);

  if(Q.el.length === 0) {
    Q.el = $("<canvas width='320' height='420'></canvas>")
           .attr('id',id).appendTo("body");
  }

  var maxWidth = options.maxWidth || 5000,
      maxHeight = options.maxHeight || 5000,
      resampleWidth = options.resampleWidth,
      resampleHeight = options.resampleHeight;

  if(options.maximize) {
    $("html, body").css({ padding:0, margin: 0 });
    var w = Math.min(window.innerWidth,maxWidth);
    var h = Math.min(window.innerHeight - 5,maxHeight)

    if(touchDevice) {
      Q.el.css({height: h * 2});
      window.scrollTo(0,1);

      w = Math.min(window.innerWidth,maxWidth);
      h = Math.min(window.innerHeight - 5,maxHeight);
    }

    if(((resampleWidth && w > resampleWidth) ||
        (resampleHeight && h > resampleHeight)) &&
       touchDevice) {
      Q.el.css({  width:w, height:h })
          .attr({ width:w/2, height:h/2 });
    } else {
      Q.el.css({  width:w, height:h })
          .attr({ width:w, height:h });
    }

  }

  Q.wrapper = Q.el
              .wrap("<div id='" + id + "_container'/>")
              .parent()
              .css({ width: Q.el.width(),
```

```
                    margin: '0 auto' });

   Q.el.css('position','relative');

   Q.ctx = Q.el[0].getContext &&
           Q.el[0].getContext("2d");


   Q.width =  paraseInt(Q.el.attr('width'),10);
   Q.height = parseInt(Q.el.attr('height'),10);

   $(window).bind('orientationchange',function() {
     setTimeout(function() { window.scrollTo(0,1); }, 0);
   });

   return Q;
 };


 Q.clear = function() {
   Q.ctx.clearRect(0,0,Q.el[0].width,Q.el[0].height);
 };
```

This setup code performs a simple task but has some complications because it tries to accommodate different usage patterns: `setup` can be called with no parameters, with an `id` of an element, or with the element itself. If no `id` is passed in, the engine defaults to using an id of `quintus`. If it can't find an element, it creates a new `<canvas>` element. It then creates a wrapper element used to center the element on the page by default with a size of 320 x 420, enough to fill up an iPhone screen. Finally, it checks for a `getContext` method on the object, and if it finds one, it grabs the `2d` context and stores it in `Q.ctx` for later use.

The method also accepts an options hash with an optional `maximize` option that resizes the main element to match the screen. The screen maximization techniques to remove the address bar from Chapter 6 are added for touch devices. When maximizing, the method also accepts optional `maxWidth`, `maxHeight`, `resampleWidth`, and `resampleHeight` parameters. The first two set a maximum width and height for the game and the second two set an optional width and height at which to resample down by half on mobile devices.

The method also returns the `Q` object, allowing to be chained with further calls on Quintus if necessary.

The `clear` method is much simpler and just clears the entirety of the Canvas.

To try this simple functionality out, open an HTML file called **canvas_test.html** and put in the HTML in Listing 10-2:

LISTING 10-2: Canvas test example

```
<!DOCTYPE HTML>
<html lang="en">
  <head>
    <title>Canvas Test</title>
    <meta charset="UTF-8">
    <script src='jquery.min.js'></script>
```

continues

LISTING 10-2 *(continued)*

```
    <script src='underscore.js'></script>
    <script src='quintus.js'></script>
  </head>
  <body>
    <script>
      var Q = Quintus().setup();
      Q.el.css('backgroundColor','red');
    </script>
  </body>
</html>
```

This example just creates a new Quintus instance and then turns the background color of the created Canvas element red to give an indication of where the element is on the page. If you load it in a browser, you should see a slender red Canvas element running down the center of your browser. If you modify the setup line to read

```
      var q = Quintus().setup("quintus", { maximize: true });
```

you should be able to maximize the red area on both desktop and mobile devices.

CAPTURING USER INPUT

You can't actually make a game without giving the player some way to interact with your game. Following the same pattern as *Alien Invasion* built in Chapters 1 through 3, Quintus handles user input from both the keyboard and via a touch interface. Supporting the keyboard is useful in development as well as when players play your game via the desktop.

Creating an Input Subsystem

The simplest way to do input is to directly bind some action (for example, pressing the right arrow key) to an action in the game, like moving the player to the right. The problem with this mechanism becomes obvious after you add additional input options to your game.

In the case of a game that needs to work on both mobile and desktop, you have at least two input mechanisms: keyboard or mouse and touch. Abstracting your game logic away from what's actually generating the input and providing a consistent interface to the engine can make developing games much easier.

Quintus uses a module called `Quintus.Input` to handle input. Keeping the input code separate from the rest of the Quintus engine helps keep the dependencies in check and makes it easier to swap out a different input engine if necessary.

The input module will eventually support five different input mechanisms:

➤ Keyboard (desktop input)

➤ Mouse (desktop input)

➤ Direct manipulation (touch input)

➤ Keypad (touch input)

➤ Joypad (touch input)

Keyboard and mouse hopefully need no extra description. Direct manipulation refers to the capability to move stuff on the screen directly. (Think firing the Angry Birds slingshot.) Keypad input is the use of onscreen buttons as used in *Alien Invasion*. Joypad input refers to the small, analog-style touch pad that works like a four-way control pad. It can be used as an analog control (providing a strength and an angle) or as a digital control (providing movement in four discrete directions).

In this chapter the keyboard, keypad, and joystick inputs will be built; Chapter 14, "Building Games with SVG and Physics," covers direct manipulation and mouse input.

Bootstrapping the Input Module

The main goal of the input module is to bind some sort of input action, whether a keypress, an onscreen keypad press, or a joypad movement to a specific action, such as `left` or `right`. It shouldn't matter how the action gets triggered; the game should see the same stream of input coming in.

The game receives input in two ways. The first is by looking at the `Q.inputs` object:

```
Q.inputs['fire'] // true if fire is being held down
```

Each bound action has an object key set to `true` if that key is currently held down. This is useful for movement in which you want to check each frame to see if the user is moving and, if so, update their position appropriately.

For actions triggered on a specific press rather than just holding down the button, the input module inherits from `Evented` to allow the binding of listeners. For example:

```
Q.input.bind('fire',function() {
    console.log("Fire pressed");
});

Q.input.bind('fireUp',function() {
    console.log("Fire released");
});
```

Supporting both methods can help keep your game step code from needing to poll every input each frame to check for changes.

Each of the input methods will be configurable with what events are triggered, but some defaults can handle the most common cases to prevent the need for too much configuration.

To start with the module, open a new file called **quintus_input.js** in the same directory as `quintus.js` and add the code in Listing 10-3.

LISTING 10-3: The base Quintus.Input module

```
Quintus.Input = function(Q) {
  var KEY_NAMES = { LEFT: 37, RIGHT: 39, SPACE: 32,
                    UP: 38, DOWN: 40,
```

continues

LISTING 10-3 *(continued)*

```
                      Z: 90, X: 88
              };

      var DEFAULT_KEYS = { LEFT: 'left', RIGHT: 'right',
                           UP: 'up',    DOWN: 'down',
                           SPACE: 'fire',
                           Z: 'fire',
                           X: 'action' };

      var DEFAULT_TOUCH_CONTROLS  = [ ['left','<' ],
                                      ['right','>' ],
                                      [],
                                      ['action','b'],
                                      ['fire', 'a' ]];

      // Clockwise from midnight (a la CSS)
      var DEFAULT_JOYPAD_INPUTS =  [ 'up','right','down','left'];

      Q.inputs = {};
      Q.joypad = {};

      var hasTouch =  !!('ontouchstart' in window);

      Q.InputSystem = Q.Evented.extend({
       // TODO: Fill in Input System code
      });

      Q.input = new Q.InputSystem();

  };
```

As you can see, this code sets up four constant-style variables used in the input module. The first, KEY_NAMES, is a convenience array that matches input keycodes with more developer friendly names. Listing 10-3 defines codes for only the arrow keys, the spacebar, and the Z and X keys because that is what this book uses, but you can add additional keycodes if needed.

The remaining three arrays define the default input action bindings for the keyboard, keypad touch controls, and the joypad.

Next up are the Q.inputs and Q.joypad objects, which hold the current state of the action inputs. These are initialized to empty objects, and a boolean variable, hasTouch, is defined to check if support for the touch events is available in the browser.

Finally, a stub for the InputSystem class is added, which inherits from Evented so that, as shown in the listing, objects can bind to input events.

Handling Keyboard Events

Keyboard events are the easiest to handle, and the code bears a striking similarity to the code from Chapter 1, "Flying Before You Walk." You can fill in the TODO in Q.InputSystem from Listing 10-3 with the code in Listing 10-4.

LISTING 10-4: Keyboard events

```
Q.InputSystem = Q.Evented.extend({
  keys: {},
  keypad: {},
  keyboardEnabled: false,
  touchEnabled: false,
  joypadEnabled: false,

  bindKey: function(key,name) {
    Q.input.keys[KEY_NAMES[key] || key] = name;
  },

  keyboardControls: function(keys) {
    keys = keys || DEFAULT_KEYS;
    _(keys).each(function(name,key) {
     this.bindKey(key,name);
    },Q.input);
    this.enableKeyboard();
  },

  enableKeyboard: function() {
    if(this.keyboardEnabled) return false;

    // Make selectable and remove an :focus outline
    Q.el.attr('tabindex',0).css('outline',0);

    Q.el.keydown(function(e) {
      if(Q.input.keys[e.keyCode]) {
        var actionName = Q.input.keys[e.keyCode];
        Q.inputs[actionName] = true;
        Q.input.trigger(actionName);
        Q.input.trigger('keydown',e.keyCode);
      }
      e.preventDefault();
    });

    Q.el.keyup(function(e) {
      if(Q.input.keys[e.keyCode]) {
        var actionName = Q.input.keys[e.keyCode];
        Q.inputs[actionName] = false;
        Q.input.trigger(actionName + "Up");
        Q.input.trigger('keyup',e.keyCode);
      }
      e.preventDefault();
    });
    this.keyboardEnabled = true;
  },
```

The keyboard controls consist of three methods:

➤ bindKey is responsible for binding a key code (the numeric identifier of the key pressed, not the ASCII representation) to a specific action by setting a value on the Q.input.keys object. It accepts either a key name from the KEY_NAMES array (such as "LEFT") or a straight keycode.

➤ keyboardControls is used to actually enable keyboard controls on the game. It binds any passed-in keys (or uses the DEFAULT_KEYS defined in Listing 10-4) by calling bindKey on each and then calls enableKeyboard, which does the browser event binding.

➤ enableKeyboard defines both a keydown and a keyup event on the element. To make the <canvas> element selectable but disable any outline focus, you first need to add the tabindex property and then set the outline style to 0.

Next, the keydown event looks up the action associated with that keycode, if any, and then sets that input to true. It also triggers an event with the same name as the input and then prevents any default browser actions from taking place by calling e.preventDefault().

The keyup event does the exact opposite, setting the action to false and triggering an action matching the event name with "Up" appended.

Adding Keypad Controls

Next are the keypad controls, a version of which was also built in Chapter 3, "Finishing Up and Going Mobile." The goal of these controls is to add a number of different buttons to bottom of the screen. What makes these slightly more difficult than the keyboard events is that you can't match touchstart and touchend events directly to keypad presses. If you did, users couldn't slide their fingers around the screen as they are apt to do.

Instead, Quintus takes advantage that every touch event includes with it all the touches currently on the screen along with any touches that have changed. It loops over these touch events each time there is any event and updates the actions pressed regardless of what event occurs.

Using this mechanism requires a little more housekeeping to trigger events when a key is pressed or released, but you'll end up with a behavior that mimics keypresses while still allowing users to slide their hands around.

The engine assumes that the controls are to be drawn across the bottom of the screen and should stretch the entirety of the device. As such, the size of the controls is calculated by the number of entries in the controls array. Five entries in the array mean that each control can take up one-fifth of the screen, minus the size of the gutter between the controls. The controls array also allows blank entries that represent empty spots that shouldn't trigger.

Add the code in Listing 10-5 below the key functions inside the definition of Q.InputSystem below the code you added in Listing 10-4.

LISTING 10-5: Touch controls

```
touchLocation: function(touch) {
  var el = Q.el,
      pageX = touch.pageX,
      pageY = touch.pageY,
      pos = el.offset(),
      touchX = (el.attr('width') || Q.width) *
               (pageX - pos.left) / el.width(),
```

```
        touchY = (el.attr('height')||Q.height) *
                 (pageY - pos.top) / el.height();
  return { x: touchX, y: touchY };
},

touchControls: function(opts) {
  if(this.touchEnabled) return false;
  if(!hasTouch) return false;

  Q.input.keypad = opts = _({
    left: 0,
    gutter:10,
    controls: DEFAULT_TOUCH_CONTROLS,
    width: Q.el.attr('width') || Q.width,
    bottom: Q.el.attr('height') || Q.height
  }).extend(opts||{});

  opts.unit = (opts.width / opts.controls.length);
  opts.size = opts.unit - 2 * opts.gutter;

  function getKey(touch) {
    var pos = Q.input.touchLocation(touch);
    for(var i=0,len=opts.controls.length;i<len;i++) {
      if(pos.x < opts.unit * (i+1)) {
        return opts.controls[i][0];
      }
    }
  }

  function touchDispatch(event) {
    var elemPos = Q.el.position(),
        wasOn = {},
        i, len, tch, key, actionName;

    // Reset all the actions bound to controls
    // but keep track of all the actions that were on
    for(i=0,len = opts.controls.length;i<len;i++) {
      actionName = opts.controls[i][0];
      if(Q.inputs[actionName]) { wasOn[actionName] = true; }
      Q.inputs[actionName] = false;
    }

    for(i=0,len=event.touches.length;i<len;i++) {
      tch = event.touches[i];
      key = getKey(tch);

      if(key) {
        // Mark this input as on
        Q.inputs[key] = true;

        // Either trigger a new action
        // or remove from wasOn list
        if(!wasOn[key]) {
          Q.input.trigger(key);
```

continues

LISTING 10-5 *(continued)*

```
        } else {
          delete wasOn[key];
        }
      }
    }
  }

  // Any remaining were on the last frame
  // and need to trigger an up action
  for(actionName in wasOn) {
    Q.input.trigger(actionName + "Up");
  }

  return null;
}

Q.el.on('touchstart touchend touchmove touchcancel',function(e) {
  touchDispatch(e.originalEvent);
  e.preventDefault();
});

this.touchEnabled = true;
},

disableTouchControls: function() {
  Q.el.off('touchstart touchend touchmove touchcancel');
  this.touchEnabled = false;
},
```

The code in Listing 10-5 defines three top-level methods: `touchLocation`, `touchControls`, and `disableTouchControls`. Touch location is used to find the correct pixel location on the `<canvas>` element (or non-`<canvas>` element) even if the Canvas has been rescaled to different dimensions from its pixel dimensions (which can be done via CSS styling). To allow the touch code to work with DOM-based games, the code uses the `Q.width` variable if the main Q.el doesn't have a width attribute (as it won't in the event of a DOM-based game). From a performance perspective, this code could be improved by caching the `jQuery` calls instead of calculating them each call, but to keep the code straightforward and resilient to change events, this is left as an exercise for you.

The primary setup method, `touchControls`, further defines two additional methods inside of it that do most of the actual work for handling keypad events.

1. `getKey` calls `touchLocation` to get the pixel location on the Canvas and then returns the keypad button (if any) that corresponds to that element.

2. `touchDispatch` is called each time a touch event occurs. `touchDispatch` consists primarily of three loops:

   ➤ The first loop sets the `Q.inputs` array to `false` for all entries to turn all the keypad bound inputs off and takes note of any inputs that are on in the `wasOn` object.

   ➤ The second loop loops over all the current touches on the device and maps them to keypad presses, setting the appropriate input. If the input isn't already on, the loop triggers an event on Q.input; otherwise, the action is removed from the wasOn array.

➤ The last loop loops over whatever inputs were on before touchDispatch was called and triggers the appropriate up event.

The last part of touchControls binds any of the touch events—touchstart, touchend, touchmove, and touchcancel—to call touchDispatch.

The last method, disableTouchControls, simply removes the event handlers from the element, disabling the onscreen keypad. It also marks the joypad as disabled if that happened to be set up.

Adding Joypad Controls

The last supported input mechanism, the joypad, is also the most complicated, primarily because it needs to work as both an analog and a digital keypad that maps keypad locations to actions to make it compatible with the keyboard and keypad input.

The idea behind the joypad is that the user can initiate a touch anywhere in the joypad area to center the control, and then the joypad should detect movement relative to that location. Again, the joypad is configurable in size, colors, and alpha, as well as the actions it triggers. To make the most common use case simple to initialize, however, defaults are set for most of the options. The joypad also triggers the same default actions as the keyboard and keypad: up, right, left, and down.

Unlike the keypad, the joypad needs to treat each of the touch events differently. The touchstart event is used to start and center the joypad, capturing the identifier of the touch so that only that touch adjusts the joypad from then on. touchmove events are used to actually move the center of the joypad around. Finally, the touchend event removes the joypad.

Add the code in Listing 10-6 below the keypad functions inside the definition of Q.InputSystem after the code from Listing 10-5.

LISTING 10-6: Joypad controls

```
joypadControls: function(opts) {
  if(this.joypadEnabled) return false;
  if(!hasTouch) return false;
  var joypad = Q.joypad = _.defaults(opts || {},{
    size: 50,
    trigger: 20,
    center: 25,
    color: "#CCC",
    background: "#000",
    alpha: 0.5,
    zone: (Q.el.attr('width')||Q.width) / 2,
    joypadTouch: null,
    inputs: DEFAULT_JOYPAD_INPUTS,
    triggers: []
  });

  Q.el.on('touchstart',function(e) {
```

continues

LISTING 10-6 *(continued)*

```
      if(joypad.joypadTouch === null) {
        var evt = e.originalEvent,
        touch = evt.changedTouches[0],
        loc = Q.input.touchLocation(touch);

        if(loc.x < joypad.zone) {
          joypad.joypadTouch = touch.identifier;
          joypad.centerX = loc.x;
          joypad.centerY = loc.y;
          joypad.x = null;
          joypad.y = null;
        }
      }
    });

    Q.el.on('touchmove',function(e) {
      if(joypad.joypadTouch !== null) {
        var evt = e.originalEvent;

        for(var i=0,len=evt.changedTouches.length;i<len;i++) {
          var touch = evt.changedTouches[i];

          if(touch.identifier === joypad.joypadTouch) {
            var loc = Q.input.touchLocation(touch),
                dx = loc.x - joypad.centerX,
                dy = loc.y - joypad.centerY,
                dist = Math.sqrt(dx * dx + dy * dy),
                overage = Math.max(1,dist / joypad.size),
                ang =  Math.atan2(dx,dy);

            if(overage > 1) {
              dx /= overage;
              dy /= overage;
              dist /= overage;
            }

            var triggers = [
              dy < -joypad.trigger,
              dx > joypad.trigger,
              dy > joypad.trigger,
              dx < -joypad.trigger
            ];

            for(var k=0;k<triggers.length;k++) {
              var actionName = joypad.inputs[k];
              if(triggers[k]) {
                Q.inputs[actionName] = true;

                if(!joypad.triggers[k]) {
                  Q.input.trigger(actionName);
                }
```

```
          } else {
            Q.inputs[actionName] = false;
            if(joypad.triggers[k]) {
              Q.input.trigger(actionName + "Up");
            }
          }
        }

        _.extend(joypad, {
          dx: dx, dy: dy,
          x: joypad.centerX + dx,
          y: joypad.centerY + dy,
          dist: dist,
          ang: ang,
          triggers: triggers
        });

        break;
      }
    }
  }
  e.preventDefault();

});

Q.el.on('touchend touchcancel',function(e) {
    var evt = e.originalEvent;

    if(joypad.joypadTouch !== null) {
      for(var i=0,len=evt.changedTouches.length;i<len;i++) {
      var touch = evt.changedTouches[i];
        if(touch.identifier === joypad.joypadTouch) {
          for(var k=0;k<joypad.triggers.length;k++) {
            var actionName = joypad.inputs[k];
            Q.inputs[actionName] = false;
          }
          joypad.joypadTouch = null;
          break;
        }
      }
    }
    e.preventDefault();
});

this.joypadEnabled = true;
},
```

Much like the keypad, the primary method `joypadControls` sets up the configuration and then a number of event handlers for the joypad. Because the game may need access to the joypad analog information such as the strength and angle of the movement, the joypad information is stored in `Q.joypad` instead of `Q.input.joypad` for easier access.

The first handler, `touchstart`, is responsible for identifying a touch to activate the joypad. This is done by first checking that the joypad isn't already activated by ensuring `joypad.joypadTouch` is set to `null`. (Notice the three equal signs: `===`. This is necessary because the touch identifier might be 0, which would be `true` when compared with `null` if type-coercion is allowed.) Next the method checks if the touch is within the joypad zone, which defaults to the left side of the play area, and if so it captures the identifier and center of the touch and sets the inner circle position to `null` to prevent any initial movement.

The bulk of the work for the joypad calculations is done in the `touchmove` handler. This handler first checks that the joypad is activated by making sure `joypad.joypadTouch` isn't `null`; then it checks any changed touches for one that matches the identifier stored in `joypad.joypadTouch`. When this is found, the location of the center is calculated. To prevent the center from reaching outside the bounds of the joypad, the location of the center is limited to the size of the joypad. The total distance and angle of the joypad are also calculated to allow the game to pull the analog information about the joypad direction and strength.

Next, the `touchmove` handler checks against each of the four action triggers to see if the joypad has moved far enough to count as a triggered movement. If there is a new trigger that is activated or an old trigger that is no longer activated, the handler fires the appropriate event. Then the current state of the joypad updates.

Finally, the `touchend` handler checks if one of the changed touches matches the identifier of the joypad, and if so disables the joypad.

Drawing the Onscreen Input

To this point, the `Quintus.Input` module has everything it needs to capture user input. What it doesn't have is any way to draw those controls on the screen. The keypad buttons are drawn as a series of boxes with text in them (refer to Chapter 3), and the joypad is drawn as a pair of concentric circles. Add the four methods in Listing 10-7 below the `joypadControls` method.

LISTING 10-7: Drawing the onscreen input

```
drawButtons: function() {
  var keypad = Q.input.keypad,
      ctx = Q.ctx;

  ctx.save();
  ctx.textAlign = "center";
  ctx.textBaseline = "middle";

  for(var i=0;i<keypad.controls.length;i++) {
    var control = keypad.controls[i];

    if(control[0]) {
      ctx.font = "bold " + (keypad.size/2) + "px arial";
      var x = i * keypad.unit + keypad.gutter,
          y = keypad.bottom - keypad.unit,
          key = Q.inputs[control[0]];

      ctx.fillStyle = keypad.color || "#FFFFFF";
      ctx.globalAlpha = key ? 1.0 : 0.5;
```

```
            ctx.fillRect(x,y,keypad.size,keypad.size);

            ctx.fillStyle = keypad.text || "#000000";
            ctx.fillText(control[1],
                          x+keypad.size/2,
                          y+keypad.size/2);
        }
    }

    ctx.restore();
},

drawCircle: function(x,y,color,size) {
  var ctx = Q.ctx,
      joypad = Q.joypad;

  ctx.save();
  ctx.beginPath();
  ctx.globalAlpha=joypad.alpha;
  ctx.fillStyle = color;
  ctx.arc(x, y, size, 0, Math.PI*2, true);
  ctx.closePath();
  ctx.fill();
  ctx.restore();
},

drawJoypad: function() {
  var joypad = Q.joypad;
  if(joypad.joypadTouch !== null) {
    Q.input.drawCircle(joypad.centerX,
                       joypad.centerY,
                       joypad.background,
                       joypad.size);

    if(joypad.x !== null) {
      Q.input.drawCircle(joypad.x,
                         joypad.y,
                         joypad.color,
                         joypad.center);
    }
  }

},

drawCanvas: function() {
  if(this.touchEnabled) {
    this.drawButtons();
  }

  if(this.joypadEnabled) {
    this.drawJoypad();
  }
}
```

The `drawCanvas` method is the primary method that needs to be called each frame to draw the controls. This method works only for Canvas-based games. This method calls two helper methods: `drawButtons` and `drawJoypad`. `drawJoypad` further calls a helper method called `drawCircle` to draw the outer and inner joypad circles.

`drawButtons` loops over each of the controls and draws a square with a text character on top of it to identify the button. It also checks the state of each keypad button so that buttons currently depressed are drawn highlighted. The method uses the `textAlign` and `textBaseline` attributes of the Canvas to center the text in the buttons. These are discussed in detail in Chapter 15, "Learning Canvas, the Hero of HTML5." The `fillText` method can be slow, so in production you'll most likely want to replace the text buttons with images.

`drawCircle` uses the `arc` command with a fill to draw a circle. `drawJoypad` calls this twice: once for the outer larger circle and once for the center circle. See Chapter 15 for a description of the Canvas API in depth.

Finishing and Testing the Input

The `Quintus.Input` module is now feature complete. The only thing that could still be added is a little bit of helper glue code—to help users get up and running quickly—and an HTML file to test the whole thing.

Based on the assumption that the most common usage for the input system is either a two-way keypad with a and b buttons or a four-way joypad with a and b buttons, you can add a simple helper method to the top-level Quintus module to set up just that, along with the desktop fallback keyboard controls. Add the code in Listing 10-8 below the definition for `Q.input`.

LISTING 10-8: The controls helper method

```
Q.input = new Q.InputSystem();

Q.controls = function(joypad) {
  Q.input.keyboardControls();

  if(joypad) {
    Q.input.touchControls({
      controls: [ [],[],[],['action','b'],['fire','a']]
    });
    Q.input.joypadControls();
  } else {
    Q.input.touchControls();
  }

  return Q;
  };
};
```

This code takes only one parameter, a boolean option about whether to turn on the joypad or just use the keypad.

Next, this code needs to be tested. Create a file called **input_test.html** and fill in the code from Listing 10-9.

LISTING 10-9: input_test.html input test

```html
<!DOCTYPE HTML>
<html lang="en">
  <head>
    <meta charset="UTF-8">
    <title>Input Test</title>
    <meta name='viewport' content='width=device-width, user-scalable=no'>
    <script src='jquery.min.js'></script>
    <script src='underscore.js'></script>
    <script src='quintus.js'></script>
    <script src='quintus_input.js'></script>
  </head>
  <body>
    <script>
      var Q = Quintus()
              .include("Input")
              .setup("quintus",{ "maximize": true })
              .controls(true);
      Q.input.bind('fire',function() {
        console.log('fire!');
      });
      Q.input.bind('fireUp',function() {
        console.log('fire up');
      });
      Q.gameLoop(function() {
        Q.clear();
        Q.input.drawCanvas();
      });
      Q.el.css('backgroundColor','#666');
    </script>
  </body>
</html>
```

You'll see this code walks through the steps of setting up Quintus, including the `Quintus.Input` module you just wrote, and then turning on the controls with the joypad. It also binds a couple of event handlers to test that events are triggered. You can try binding some additional inputs, including the movement inputs left, right, up, and down. On a mobile device you should see the console logs if you turn the console on.

On desktop and WP7, you won't see any controls as touch events aren't supported, but the fire key triggers will work on the desktop.

You should use the left side of the screen as a joypad and the right side to press the buttons, as shown in Figure 10-1.

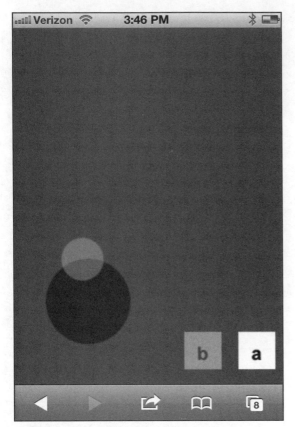

FIGURE 10-1: The joypad and button inputs.

LOADING ASSETS

Unless you're building a game entirely out of squares, at some point you need to load some assets into the game. Assets include images, audio, sprite and level data, and anything else that your game needs to run stored in a separate file.

In one sense HTML5 handles asset loading for you automatically. If you create an `Image` object, set the source, and then draw it, the browser can happily comply without throwing an error message. It won't, however, actually draw the image on the screen until it's been fully downloaded. This means that you'll have game elements that just "pop" into the page. A better strategy is to preload any assets during a loading screen and wait to start the game until everything is ready to go. The following code is an example of how the asset loading functionality should work:

```
var Q = Quintus().setup();
Q.load(['sprites.png','correct.ogg'],function() {
  alert('Everything loaded!');
});
```

To make the loading method more flexible, Q.load will be designed to be flexible in what it accepts for arguments, accepting either a single asset name string, an array of assets, or an object that maps asset names to filenames to load.

This book has dealt with image loading a of couple times, first in Chapter 1 and then in Chapter 8, "Running JavaScript on the Command Line." This will be the last time. You'll build a general-purpose asset loader into Quintus, which will be reused in the rest of the book.

Defining Asset Types

To know how to load a specific file, the engine needs to have a list of file extensions it can convert into specific asset types. This is actually a small list because the engine cares only about images and audio files at this point. Quintus should also return the asset type given a filename, which means the engine needs a method to pull off the extension and look up the type in the asset type list.

Open up quintus.js again, and add the code in Listing 10-10 just before the final return to do just that.

LISTING 10-10: Asset type functionality

```
// Augmentable list of asset types
Q.assetTypes = {
  // Image Assets
  png: 'Image', jpg: 'Image', gif: 'Image', jpeg: 'Image',
  // Audio Assets
  ogg: 'Audio', wav: 'Audio', m4a: 'Audio', mp3: 'Audio'
};

// Determine the type of an asset with a lookup table
Q.assetType = function(asset) {
  // Determine the lowercase extension of the file
  var fileExt = _(asset.split(".")).last().toLowerCase();

  // Lookup the asset in the assetTypes hash, or return other
  return Q.assetTypes[fileExt] || 'Other';
};
```

The first piece of code defines an object that maps a lowercase file extension to an uppercase asset type. Because this object is defined as a public object on Q, it can be easily extended to handle additional asset types.

The method Q.assetType does the job of transforming a filename into a lowercase extension and then looks up the asset type in the Q.assetTypes object. The one-liner to take a filename and get the extension splits the filename by periods into an array and then grabs the last element of that array as the extensions and converts it to lowercase. Finally, the method returns the looked-up value or a special type of 'Other' for other types of files.

Loading Specific Assets

The next task is to write methods to the different asset types. Image and Audio assets are loaded by creating an object of the appropriate type. Other assets are just loaded via an AJAX get request using jQuery. The assumption is that if developers want to load a random file type, they can figure out what to do with it if you give them the data.

Add the three loading methods in Listing 10-11 to the bottom of `quintus.js` in the usual spot before the final `return`.

LISTING 10-11: Asset loading methods

```javascript
// Loader for Images
Q.loadAssetImage = function(key,src,callback,errorCallback) {
  var img = new Image();
  $(img).on('load',function() { callback(key,img); });
  $(img).on('error',errorCallback);
  img.src = Q.options.imagePath + src;
};


Q.audioMimeTypes = { mp3: 'audio/mpeg',
                     ogg: 'audio/ogg; codecs="vorbis"',
                     m4a: 'audio/m4a',
                     wav: 'audio/wav' };

// Loader for  Audio
Q.loadAssetAudio = function(key,src,callback,errorCallback) {
  if(!document.createElement("audio").play || !Q.options.sound) {
    callback(key,null);
    return;
  }

  var snd = new Audio(),
      baseName = Q._removeExtension(src),
      extension = null,
      filename = null;

  // Find a supported type
  extension =
    _(Q.options.audioSupported)
    .detect(function(extension) {
      return snd.canPlayType(Q.audioMimeTypes[extension]) ?
                            extension : null;
  });

  // No supported audio = trigger ok callback anyway
  if(!extension) {
    callback(key,null);
    return;
  }

  // If sound is turned off,
  // call the callback immediately
  $(snd).on('error',errorCallback);
  $(snd).on('canplaythrough',function() {
    callback(key,snd);
  });
```

```
    snd.src = Q.options.audioPath + baseName + "." + extension;
    snd.load();
    return snd;
  };

  // Loader for other file types, just store the data
  // returned from an ajax call
  Q.loadAssetOther = function(key,src,callback,errorCallback) {
    $.get(Q.options.dataPath + src,function(data) {
      callback(key,data);
    }).fail(errorCallback);
  };
```

Each of the three loader methods performs the same task with a different asset type, which amounts to providing a consistent call to a callback containing the passed in key and the loaded object in question. A helper method to remove the extension from a filename is also defined.

`Q.loadAssetImage` creates an `Image` object and links the callback to the load event method. `Q.loadAssetOther` just uses the jQuery `get` method to load data into a buffer and trigger the callback when it's loaded.

Finally, the `Q.loadAssetAudio` creates an `Audio` element and then determines if the `Audio` tag is available or whether sound is turned on normally. In cases in which the sound tag isn't supported, or the sound is turned off, the method calls the callback immediately and returns.

The `Audio` loader also needs to do some extra work to ensure the audio file loaded is supported by the browser. To do this it keeps a hash called `Q.audioMimeTypes` that maps file extensions to audio mime types. Armed with the mime type of an extension, it can check if a file of the supported type is playable by calling `Audio.canPlayType` with the mime type.

The reason for all these file-type gymnastics is that there isn't a single audio format supported across all browsers. As such, it falls onto the developers to make sure they provide audio files in as many formats as are necessary for the supported browsers. In general this means making audio assets available in `.mp3` and `.ogg` format. To make the developer's life easier, the code in the preceding listing strips off the extension of any audio file and tries to find a file in one of formats the developers have indicated support for in `Q.options.audioSupported` that is also supported by the browser.

If no supported audio is available, the engine just acts like everything is still okay and lets the user play the game without audio. This means that if developers want to support only one audio format such as `.mp3`, they can do so and still have the game play, albeit without sound.

Each of the preceding methods also takes an `errorCallback` that is triggered if something were to go wrong with the loading of the asset.

Finishing the Loader

To round out the basic loader functionality, the engine needs a spot to keep track of assets along with a method to do the dirty work of synchronizing the loading of assets.

Before getting to this, though, you need to add some defaults to the engine to make loading assets more succinct and provide a list of supported audio formats for your game. Near the top of the Quintus definition, you defined an options hash that can hold any defaults for the engine. Update the hash to match the code in Listing 10-12.

LISTING 10-12: Default options for Quintus

```
var Quintus = function(opts) {
  var Q = {};
  Q.options = {
    imagePath: "images/",
    audioPath: "audio/",
    dataPath:  "data/",
    audioSupported: [ 'mp3','ogg' ],
    sound: true
  };
  if(opts) { _(Q.options).extend(opts); }
```

Assets are held in the system in a simple object and indexed by name. To look up a hash, you just need to call `Q.asset(name)`. The actual dirty work for loading a list of assets is handled by the `Q.load` method. Its duty is to take whatever the programmer passed in for assets to load (it could be a string, an array, or an object), turn it into a consistent data structure, and then loop over each of the objects, calling the appropriate loader method (as defined in Listing 10-12).

Add the code in Listing 10-13 to the usual spot in `quintus.js` before the final `return`.

LISTING 10-13: Asset loading

```
// Return a name without an extension
Q._removeExtension = function(filename) {
  return filename.replace(/\.(\w{3,4})$/,"");
};

// Asset hash storing any loaded assets
Q.assets = {};


// Getter method to return an asset
Q.asset = function(name) {
  return Q.assets[name];
};

// Load assets, and call our callback when done
Q.load = function(assets,callback,options) {
  var assetObj = {};

  // Make sure we have an options hash to work with
  if(!options) { options = {}; }

  // Get our progressCallback if we have one
  var progressCallback = options.progressCallback;

  var errors = false,
      errorCallback = function(itm) {
        errors = true;
        (options.errorCallback ||
         function(itm) { alert("Error Loading: " + itm ); })(itm);
```

```
      };

    // If the user passed in an array, convert it
    // to a hash with lookups by filename
    if(_.isArray(assets)) {
      _.each(assets,function(itm) {
        if(_.isObject(itm)) {
          _.extend(assetObj,itm);
        } else {
          assetObj[itm] = itm;
        }
      });
    } else if(_.isString(assets)) {
      // Turn assets into an object if it's a string
      assetObj[assets] = assets;
    } else {
      // Otherwise just use the assets as is
      assetObj = assets;
    }

    // Find the # of assets we're loading
    var assetsTotal = _(assetObj).keys().length,
        assetsRemaining = assetsTotal;

    // Closure'd per-asset callback gets called
    // each time an asset is successfully loadded
    var loadedCallback = function(key,obj) {
      if(errors) return;

      // Add the object to our asset list
      Q.assets[key] = obj;

      // We've got one less asset to load
      assetsRemaining--;

      // Update our progress if we have it
      if(progressCallback) {
          progressCallback(assetsTotal - assetsRemaining,assetsTotal);
      }

      // If we're out of assets, call our full callback
      // if there is one
      if(assetsRemaining === 0 && callback) {
        // if we haven't set up our canvas element yet,
        // assume we're using a canvas with id 'quintus'
        callback.apply(Q);
      }
    };

    // Now actually load each asset
    _.each(assetObj,function(itm,key) {

      // Determine the type of the asset
      var assetType = Q.assetType(itm);

      // If we already have the asset loaded,
```

continues

LISTING 10-13 *(continued)*

```
        // don't load it again
        if(Q.assets[key]) {
          loadedCallback(key,Q.assets[key]);
        } else {
          // Call the appropriate loader function
          // passing in our per-asset callback
          // Dropping our asset by name into Q.assets
          Q["loadAsset" + assetType](key,itm,
                                 loadedCallback,
                                 function() { errorCallback(itm); });
        }
      });

    };
```

The first definition is the assets hash, defined as an empty object on Q and the simple `Q.asset` getter method that just looks up a key in the `assets` hash. Defining a getter method instead of just exposing the `Q.assets` hash directly allows someone to override the method to create, for example, dynamically generated assets.

The `load` method is the main method for loading the assets. Its functionality can be broken down into three sections:

➤ The first section converts whatever assets the developer wants to load into a consistent format that looks like the following:

```
  { "assetname.ext": "assetname.ext",
    "assetname2.ext": "assetname2.ext" }
```

➤ Next, a `loadedCallback` is defined. This method is passed as the callback method to each of the asset-type-specific loading methods. It keeps track of the number of remaining assets and finally triggers the final callback when everything has loaded correctly. If any errors have been noted, the callback returns early to prevent the game from trying to start with invalid assets. If a progress callback has been provided (such as to show a loading screen with a progress bar), the callback calls it each time a new asset loads.

➤ The last section loops over each element in the assets hash, determines the correct type of the asset, and then dispatches to the appropriate loader function.

This method of asset loading allows developers to create new asset types based on file extensions and add new loader methods if necessary.

Adding Preload Support

Although the `Q.load` method does most of the heavy lifting, the engine could make the developer's life easier by providing preloading support to allow the developer to mark assets for preloading prior to making the actual call to load. This is useful when putting together scenes or when different modules are responsible for determining what assets need to be loaded.

Add the code in Listing 10-14 to the regular spot in the bottom of `quintus.js` before the final `return`.

LISTING 10-14: Preload support

```
// Array to store any assets that need to be
// preloaded
Q.preloads = [];

// Let us gather assets to load
// and then preload them all at the same time
Q.preload = function(arg,options) {
  if(_(arg).isFunction()) {
    Q.load(_(Q.preloads).uniq(),arg,options);
    Q.preloads = [];
  } else {
    Q.preloads = Q.preloads.concat(arg);
  }
};
```

The preloading code provides a simple interface consisting of a single method called `Q.preload` that either takes a callback method or one or more assets to load. It looks at the argument and decides whether to add more items to the preload list or to actually perform the loading by calling `Q.load`. Items are added to the preload list by simply calling `Array.concat`, which either add an element to the end of the array, or if the passed in argument is also an array, concatenate the two arrays into a single array.

Here's how the preload code might be used:

```
var Q = Quintus({ audioSupported: [ 'wav','ogg']}).setup();

Q.preload('sprites.png');
Q.preload(['fire.mp3','explosion.mp3']);
Q.preload(function() {
  alert("All loaded!");
});
```

Separating calls to generate a list of resources to load from the loading call allows more flexibility in which components are responsible for tracking the resources they require. You can take a look at the file `asset_test.html` in the chapter code for a working example of loading a couple of files.

SUMMARY

You now have some of the additional pieces of glue necessary for an HTML5 game engine: setup, input, and assets. Setting up the visual container for the game is important to get anything on the screen at all. Input on mobile devices is a little trickier than on a desktop because any type of input requires a visual element to display to the user, such as buttons or a joypad. Asset loading, although not a sexy topic, is an important one to get right. Nothing destroys the professionalism of a game more than a bunch of elements popping onto the screen while you play.

11

Bootstrapping the Quintus Engine: Part III

INTRODUCTION

The first two chapters on building the Quintus engine laid the groundwork for building a
game. This chapter rounds out the engine by adding support for sprites and stages. Sprites
are the primary visual GameObject used in the engine to display graphics and elements on
the screen. Sprites use either basic assets or SpriteSheets to draw themselves onto the
game. Scenes provide a way to package up a discrete piece of your game, such as a level,
into a nice reusable package. Lastly, Stages are the primary containers for the state of your
game and are responsible for tracking lists of GameObjects and ensuring they are updated
and drawn on each frame.

DEFINING SPRITESHEETS

Before tackling sprites, the engine is going to add support for sprite sheets. Sprite Sheets, as you've seen in previous chapters, allow any number of images to be stored in a single image, making your game quicker to load and animations easier to work with. The sprite sheet functionality ties into the code from Chapter 8, "Running JavaScript on the Command Line," that generated spritesheets from the command line so you don't need to spend your time multiplying sprite *x* and *y* positions in your head.

Creating a SpriteSheet Class

In this case, a single `Sprite Sheet` object refers only to a single set of like-sized frames of the same sprite. A single-loaded image asset might be compiled into a number of `SpriteSheet` objects.

The sprite functionality in Quintus is going to go into its own module. Open up a new file called **quintus_sprites.js** and place the code from Listing 11-1 into it to define the `SpriteSheet` class functionality.

LISTING 11-1: The Q.SpriteSheet class

```
Quintus.Sprites = function(Q) {

  // Create a new sprite sheet
  // Options:
  //   tilew - tile width
  //   tileh - tile height
  //   w     - width of the sprite block
  //   h     - height of the sprite block
  //   sx    - start x
  //   sy    - start y
  //   cols  - number of columns per row
  Q.SpriteSheet = Class.extend({
    init: function(name, asset,options) {
      _.extend(this,{
        name: name,
        asset: asset,
        w: Q.asset(asset).width,
        h: Q.asset(asset).height,
        tilew: 64,
        tileh: 64,
        sx: 0,
        sy: 0
        },options);
      this.cols = this.cols ||
                  Math.floor(this.w / this.tilew);
    },

    fx: function(frame) {
      return (frame % this.cols) * this.tilew + this.sx;
    },

    fy: function(frame) {
```

```
      return Math.floor(frame / this.cols) * this.tileh + this.sy;
    },

    draw: function(ctx, x, y, frame) {
      if(!ctx) { ctx = Q.ctx; }
      ctx.drawImage(Q.asset(this.asset),
                    this.fx(frame),this.fy(frame),
                    this.tilew, this.tileh,
                    Math.floor(x),Math.floor(y),
                    this.tilew, this.tileh);

    }

  });

  return Q;
};
```

The SpiteSheet class is relatively short, clocking in at fewer than 40 lines of code. The init constructor does nothing but set up the initial values in the object given an asset object and a set of options. It has only three methods other than its constructor: the fx and fy methods which calculate the frame *x* and *y* position in the sheet; and the draw method, which draws a specific frame of the SpriteSheet at an *x* and *y* location on the passed-in context.

fy (short for frame y) is calculated by using Math.floor to get the row that a specific frame is in. The row number is then multiplied by the height of each tile. fx is calculated by using the modulus operator to find how many tiles to index horizontally into each row. The resulting number is then multiplied by the width of each tile to get the final result. Because of poor support for subpixel rendering (especially on mobile devices), the draw method also turns whatever *x* and *y* values that are passed in into integers using Math.floor.

The end result is that given a SpriteSheet object, you can quickly draw a specific frame at an *x* and *y* location on the canvas.

Tracking and Loading Sheets

Creating sprite sheets that can draw individual frames gets you a good portion of the way to engine support for sprite sheets, but Quintus needs a central mechanism for compiling and tracking sheets to make them easy to reference and look up. Add the code from Listing 11-2 to the bottom of quintus_sprites.js before the final closing curly brace.

LISTING 11-2: Loading and tracking sheets

```
Q.sheets = {};
Q.sheet = function(name,asset,options) {
  if(asset) {
    Q.sheets[name] = new Q.SpriteSheet(name,asset,options);
  } else {
    return Q.sheets[name];
  }
```

continues

LISTING 11-2 *(continued)*

```
    };

    Q.compileSheets = function(imageAsset,spriteDataAsset) {
      var data = Q.asset(spriteDataAsset);
      _(data).each(function(spriteData,name) {
        Q.sheet(name,imageAsset,spriteData);
      });
    };
```

The Q.sheets object provides a central location to store sheets.

The Q.sheet method works double duty as both a setter and a getter method to either return a sheet by name or create a new SpriteSheet. Using one method for multiple purposes (called *method overloading* when done in languages that have native support) helps keep the number of method names a developer needs to remember at a more manageable number. You can see that Q.sheet checks if the user has passed in an asset, and if so the method creates a new SpriteSheet object, looking up the asset in the Quintus engine by calling Q.asset(asset) and passing along any additional options. If no asset is passed in, then the method just looks for a sheet by that name and returns it.

The last method shown in Listing 11-2, Q.compileSheets, combines an asset name with a JSON sprite data asset to generate one or more sprite sheets automatically from the data generated by the spriter generator from Chapter 8.

Testing the SpriteSheet class

To test the sprite sheet functionality, load up a page with some sprites and play back an animation or two. Fire up a new HTML document called spritesheet_test.html and fill in the code from Listing 11-3.

LISTING 11-3: Testing the SpriteSheet class

```
<!DOCTYPE HTML>
<html lang="en">
  <head>
    <meta charset="UTF-8">
    <title>Sprite Test</title>
    <script src='jquery.min.js'></script>
    <script src='underscore.js'></script>
    <script src='quintus.js'></script>
    <script src='quintus_sprites.js'></script>
  </head>
  <body>
    <script>
      var Q = Quintus().include('Sprites').setup();
      Q.load(['sprites.png','sprites.json'],function() {
        Q.compileSheets('sprites.png','sprites.json');

        var slowDown = 4,
```

```
            frame1 = 0,
            frame2 = 0;

      Q.gameLoop(function() {
        Q.clear();

        var sheet1 = Q.sheet('man');
        sheet1.draw(Q.ctx,50,50,Math.floor(frame1/slowDown));
        frame1 = (frame1+1) % (sheet1.frames  * slowDown);

        var sheet2 = Q.sheet('blob');
        sheet2.draw(Q.ctx,150,50,Math.floor(frame2/slowDown));
        frame2 = (frame2+1) % (sheet2.frames * slowDown);
      });
    });
  </script>
 </body>
</html>
```

To run the example, ensure that you have an `images/` directory with `sprites.png` and a `data/` directory containing `sprites.json`. You may also need to run the code from a server (or off localhost) to prevent the browser's security protections against loading local files via AJAX (the `sprites.json` in this case).

Dissecting the preceding code, you can see it starts off by loading and compiling the sprite sheet. After that it runs a simple game loop that draws a frame of two different named sprites, looping two counters—frame1 and `frame2`—over each of the frames, slowing the code down by a `slowDown` factor to keep the animations from playing too fast.

The end result is two animations playing back on the page on the Canvas element.

ADDING SPRITES

With sprite sheets defined, the next task is to create the sprite object. Because sprites are important to Quintus and games in general, the actual sprite class is most likely going to come as a bit of a surprise: It clocks in at fewer than 40 lines and doesn't have a lot of built-in functionality. The reason it doesn't have all that much going on is that most of the important functionality has already been built and resides elsewhere: Events are handled by `Evented`, components are handled by `GameObject`, and graphics are handled by assets and `SpriteSheet`.

This means that all that's left for the sprite class to do is tie all these pieces together into a single package. The sprite class built in this chapter will be called `Sprite`. Chapter 13, "Crafting a CSS3 RPG," discusses a `DomSprite` class which inherits from `Sprite` that you'll use when you build a game with HTML and CSS3.

Writing the Sprite Class

Add the sprite code from Listing 11-4 into the `quintus_sprites.js` file before the final closing curly brace.

LISTING 11-4: The Sprite class

```javascript
// Properties:
//    x
//    y
//    z - sort order
//    sheet or asset
//    frame
Q.Sprite = Q.GameObject.extend({
   init: function(props) {
     this.p = _({
       x: 0,
       y: 0,
       z: 0,
       frame: 0,
       type: 0
       }).extend(props||{});
     if((!this.p.w || !this.p.h)) {
       if(this.asset()) {
         this.p.w = this.p.w || this.asset().width;
         this.p.h = this.p.h || this.asset().height;
       } else if(this.sheet()) {
         this.p.w = this.p.w || this.sheet().tilew;
         this.p.h = this.p.h || this.sheet().tileh;
       }
     }
     this.p.id = this.p.id || _.uniqueId();
   },

   asset: function() {
     return Q.asset(this.p.asset);
   },

   sheet: function() {
     return Q.sheet(this.p.sheet);
   },

   draw: function(ctx) {
     if(!ctx) { ctx = Q.ctx; }
     var p = this.p;
     if(p.sheet) {
       this.sheet().draw(ctx, p.x, p.y, p.frame);
     } else if(p.asset) {
       ctx.drawImage(Q.asset(p.asset),
                     Math.floor(p.x),
                     Math.floor(p.y));
     }
     this.trigger('draw',ctx);
   },

   step: function(dt) {
     this.trigger('step',dt);
   }
});
```

As you can see, there's not a whole lot to the base sprite code. This is intentional. The basic sprite is designed to be as lightweight and minimal as possible, relying on descendant classes and components for any specific functionality.

The longest method is the constructor `init` method, which ensures that the object has a valid properties object—p—and grabs the `width` and `height` of the object from the asset or `SpriteSheet` assigned to the object. It also grabs a globally unique ID from `underscore.js` to give each sprite its own unique identifier.

The `Sprite` class next defines two getter methods—`asset` and `sheet`—to pull out an assigned asset or `SpriteSheet` if applicable. Again, using a getter method means that descendant classes (or even components) could override the method.

The `draw` method is responsible for actually drawing the sprite's asset onto the Canvas. It has some conditional code to check for either a single asset or a `SpriteSheet` and can handle both. The `draw` method is a candidate for being overridden by descendant classes that have more complicated or nested drawing functionality. The method also triggers a `draw` event in case components need to do any additional drawing. As with the `SpriteSheet`, because of different support for subpixel rendering, the `draw` method also turns whatever x and y values that are passed in into integers using `Math.floor`.

The `step` method is just a stub that triggers a `step` event for any listening components.

Referencing Sprites, Properties, and Assets

As you saw in Chapter 10, "Bootstrapping the Quintus Engine: Part II," the engine keeps a hash of all loaded assets to make them easily and quickly referenced by name. `SpriteSheets` are similarly referenced, as you just saw, in the `Q.sheets` object.

This is done intentionally because the goal is to have sprites refer to the assets and sheets by name instead of passing around instances of the sheet itself. The reason for this is that it's a major goal of Quintus to make sprites serializable, meaning that their current state can be written out to disk and local storage, or sent over the network to be reconstituted intact on the other end of the network pipe.

For this to work, the engine must make sure that only simple types, such as strings and numbers, are used as properties and that serializable properties are kept separate from other properties and methods. You can see that the sprite class keeps a separate properties hash under the property p. This makes accessing object properties a little more verbose, but it has the added advantage that any pieces of state are segregated from all the object's other properties.

Because giving each sprite its own name would get tedious, every sprite is identified by a unique identifier stored in `p.id`. This allows other objects to store and pass around objects by their identifiers instead of by actual references to the objects, making garbage collection and network syncing simpler.

Exercising the Sprite Object

With a Canvas `Sprite` object in place, it's time to start a quick sample game to show how the `Sprite` class could be used. This chapter builds a simple breakout-style game. You start by adding a paddle at the bottom of the game that the user can control. Figure 11-1 shows how the game will look at the end of the chapter.

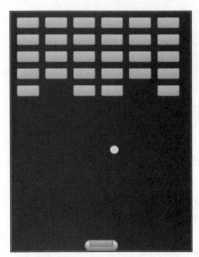

FIGURE 11-1: The final game.

Open the file called `blockbreak.html` and put in the boilerplate HTML code in Listing 11-5 to get a page started. You'll also need to include the `quintus.js` and `quintus_input.js` files from the last chapter and the `jquery.min.js` and `underscore.js` dependencies.

LISTING 11-5: blockbreak.html boilerplate

```html
<!DOCTYPE HTML>
<html lang="en">
  <head>
    <meta charset="UTF-8">
    <meta name="viewport" content="width=device-width, user-scalable=0,
minimum-scale=1.0, maximum-scale=1.0"/>
    <title>Block Break</title>
    <script src='jquery.min.js'></script>
    <script src='underscore.js'></script>
    <script src='quintus.js'></script>
    <script src='quintus_input.js'></script>
    <script src='quintus_sprites.js'></script>
    <script src='blockbreak.js'></script>
    <style>
      body { padding:0px; margin:0px; }
      canvas { background-color:black; }
    </style>
  </head>
  <body>
  </body>
</html>
```

Next, create the `blockbreak.js` file referenced in Listing 11-5 and enter the code in Listing 11-6 to get a simple paddle up and running. To run the game, you need to run it from a server on localhost because of the loaded sprite file. You also need to copy in the `blockbreak.png` file from the game assets into images/ and the blockbreak.json file into data/ subdirectories under the game to make the assets available.

LISTING 11-6: blockbreak.js

```
$(function() {
  var Q = window.Q = Quintus()
                     .include('Input,Sprites')
                     .setup();

  Q.input.keyboardControls();
  Q.input.touchControls({
          controls:  [ ['left','<' ],[],[],[],['right','>' ] ]
        });

  Q.Paddle = Q.Sprite.extend({
    init: function() {
      this._super({
        sheet: 'paddle',
        speed: 200,
        x: 0
      });
      this.p.x = Q.width/2 - this.p.w/2;
      this.p.y = Q.height - this.p.h;
      if(Q.input.keypad.size) {
        this.p.y -= Q.input.keypad.size + this.p.h;
      }
    },

    step: function(dt) {
      if(Q.inputs['left']) {
        this.p.x -= dt * this.p.speed;
      } else if(Q.inputs['right']) {
        this.p.x += dt * this.p.speed;
      }
      if(this.p.x < 0) {
        this.p.x = 0;
      } else if(this.p.x > Q.width - this.p.w) {
        this.p.x = Q.width - this.p.w;
      }
      this._super(dt);
    }
  });

  Q.Ball = Q.Sprite.extend({
    init: function() {
      this._super({
        sheet: 'ball',
        speed: 200,
        dx: 1,
        dy: -1,
      });
      this.p.y = Q.height / 2 - this.p.h;
```

continues

LISTING 11-6 *(continued)*

```javascript
      this.p.x = Q.width / 2 + this.p.w / 2;
    },

   step: function(dt) {
     var p = this.p;

     p.x += p.dx * p.speed * dt;
     p.y += p.dy * p.speed * dt;

     if(p.x < 0) {
       p.x = 0;
       p.dx = 1;
     } else if(p.x > Q.width - p.w) {
       p.dx = -1;
       p.x = Q.width - p.w;
     }

     if(p.y < 0) {
       p.y = 0;
       p.dy = 1;
     } else if(p.y > Q.height - p.h) {
       p.dy = -1;
       p.y = Q.height- p.h;
     }
     this._super(dt);


   }


 });

 Q.load(['blockbreak.png','blockbreak.json'], function() {
   Q.compileSheets('blockbreak.png','blockbreak.json');

   var paddle = new Q.Paddle();
   var ball = new Q.Ball();

   Q.gameLoop(function(dt) {
     Q.clear();

     paddle.step(dt);
     paddle.draw();

     ball.step(dt);
     ball.draw();

     Q.input.drawCanvas();
   });

 });

});
```

The setup portion and the loading portion of the code should be familiar. Because the game is now loaded via a separate JavaScript file and not inline with the document, the entire file is a wrapper in a jQuery document-ready callback: `$(function() { .. });`. Next the game object Q is created and set up. Because the code is wrapped in a closure, the variable Q is also added to the window object so that it can be accessible via the console via `window.Q` in case you want to play around with the game's API directly. The game also sets up the default keyboard controls and some custom `touchControls` to remove the a and b buttons that aren't needed in this game.

Next up is the `Q.Paddle` sprite, which inherits from `Sprite`. The `init` method for the sprite calls the `Sprite` constructor `init` with the initial properties of the object, including the name of the `SpriteSheet` that will be used to draw the object. The `init` method does a little bit of calculation on the x position to center the paddle and the y position of the object because on a desktop computer the paddle can be on the bottom of the page, whereas on a touch device, it should be moved up to leave room for the keypad controls.

The paddle `step` method then overrides the default `step` method inherited from `Sprite` and uses the `Q.inputs` object to determine if the paddle should be moving left or right.

The `Q.Ball` sprite is also added in. This sprite simply bounces around the game, reversing direction when it runs into a wall. Currently it doesn't interact with the paddle. The `step` method uses the speed and direction of the ball to update its position each frame.

Finally the game runs the `gameLoop`, which clears the Canvas, steps, draws the paddle, and then draws the input elements.

Fire up the example, and you should be able to move the paddle left and right.

SETTING THE STAGE WITH SCENES

Looking at the `gameLoop` in the example from the last section, it's easy to see how unwieldy the code for an actual game could become if each object needed to be individually updated and drawn on each step. Add in collision detection and suddenly things could get complicated quickly. The solution, as you saw in the `GameBoard` object in Chapter 2, "Making It a Game," is the idea of an object that manages the updating and drawing of many sprites. Quintus will call this object a `Stage`. Quintus will add the additional concept of a `Scene` object that will be used to set up a stage object into a particular stage. One use of a `Scene` would be to make it easy to set up levels and then switch between levels.

Creating the Quintus.Scenes Module

To start with the scene functionality, Quintus adds a new module called `Quintus.Scenes` to encompass the `Q.Stage` and `Q.Scene` classes. The `Q.Scene` object is actually going to be incredibly simple. Its only purpose is to wrap a function that sets up a passed-in stage object.

`Q.Stage` will be a bit more complicated, but it will look similar to the `GameBoard` from Chapter 2 with some extra functionality for events.

Create a new JavaScript file called `quintus_scenes.js` and put the code from Listing 11-7 in it.

LISTING 11-7: Scenes functionality

```
Quintus.Scenes = function(Q) {

  Q.scenes = {};
  Q.stages = [];

  Q.Scene = Class.extend({
    init: function(sceneFunc,opts) {
      this.opts = opts || {};
      this.sceneFunc = sceneFunc;
    }
  });

  // Set up or return a new scene
  Q.scene = function(name,sceneObj) {
    if(!sceneObj) {
      return Q.scenes[name];
    } else {
      Q.scenes[name] = sceneObj;
      return sceneObj;
    }
  };
};
```

The scene functionality is concise. It consists of a class called `Q.Scene` that has a simple purpose: Capture a callback method and an optional options hash. Next it has a `Q.scene` method that acts as both a getter (when passed one argument) and setter method (when passed two arguments).

The idea behind the scene functionality is that you want a self-contained way to set up a level or section of your game, and putting in a self-contained method makes it easy to swap between different scenes.

Writing the Stage Class

The `Q.Stage` class is responsible for keeping track of a list of sprites and letting them update and render themselves. It's a good bit beefier than the `Q.Scene` class but does a lot more as well. Much of the code should look familiar to the class from Chapter 2.

Add the definition of the `Stage` class from Listing 11-8 to the bottom of the `Quintus.Scenes` module before the final closing curly braces.

LISTING 11-8: The Overlap method and Stage class

```
Q.overlap = function(o1,o2) {
  return !((o1.p.y+o1.p.h-1<o2.p.y) || (o1.p.y>o2.p.y+o2.p.h-1) ||
           (o1.p.x+o1.p.w-1<o2.p.x) || (o1.p.x>o2.p.x+o2.p.w-1));
};

Q.Stage = Q.GameObject.extend({
  // Should know whether or not the stage is paused
  defaults: {
```

```
      sort: false
    },

  init: function(scene) {
    this.scene = scene;
    this.items = [];
    this.index = {};
    this.removeList = [];
    if(scene)  {
      this.options = _(this.defaults).clone();
      _(this.options).extend(scene.opts);
      scene.sceneFunc(this);
    }
    if(this.options.sort && !_.isFunction(this.options.sort)) {
        this.options.sort = function(a,b) { return a.p.z - b.p.z; };
    }
  },

  each: function(callback) {
    for(var i=0,len=this.items.length;i<len;i++) {
     callback.call(this.items[i],arguments[1],arguments[2]);
    }
  },

eachInvoke: function(funcName) {
  for(var i=0,len=this.items.length;i<len;i++) {
    this.items[i][funcName].call(
      this.items[i],arguments[1],arguments[2]
    );
  }
},

detect: function(func) {
  for(var i = 0,val=null, len=this.items.length; i < len; i++) {
    if(func.call(this.items[i],arguments[1],arguments[2])) {
      return this.items[i];
    }
  }
  return false;
},

insert: function(itm) {
  this.items.push(itm);
  itm.parent = this;
  if(itm.p) {
    this.index[itm.p.id] = itm;
  }
  this.trigger('inserted',itm);
  itm.trigger('inserted',this);
  return itm;
},

remove: function(itm) {
  this.removeList.push(itm);
```

continues

LISTING 11-8 *(continued)*

```javascript
    },

    forceRemove: function(itm) {
      var idx = _(this.items).indexOf(itm);
      if(idx != -1) {
        this.items.splice(idx,1);
        if(itm.destroy) itm.destroy();
        if(itm.p.id) {
          delete this.index[itm.p.id];
        }
        this.trigger('removed',itm);
      }
    },

    pause: function() {
      this.paused = true;
    },

    unpause: function() {
      this.paused = false;
    },

    _hitTest: function(obj,type) {
      if(obj != this) {
        var col = (!type || this.p.type & type) && Q.overlap(obj,this);
        return col ? this : false;
      }
    },

    collide: function(obj,type) {
      return this.detect(this._hitTest,obj,type);
    },

    step:function(dt) {
      if(this.paused) { return false; }

      this.trigger("prestep",dt);
      this.eachInvoke("step",dt);
      this.trigger("step",dt);

      if(this.removeList.length > 0) {
        for(var i=0,len=this.removeList.length;i<len;i++) {
          this.forceRemove(this.removeList[i]);
        }
        this.removeList.length = 0;
      }
    },

    draw: function(ctx) {
      if(this.options.sort) {
        this.items.sort(this.options.sort);
      }
      this.trigger("predraw",ctx);
```

```
            this.eachInvoke("draw",ctx);
            this.trigger("draw",ctx);
        }
    });
```

The Q.Stage object inherits from the Q.GameObject, as you might expect, allowing it to bind and trigger events as well as add additional behaviors via components. The init method sets up the initial properties on the object and executes the scene method if a scene object were passed in. The Quintus stage object also supports the idea of z order, allowing objects to be sorted prior to rendering.

The three following methods—each, eachInvoke, and detect—are the same as the ones described in Chapter 2. They exist as helper methods to make it easier to perform operations on the items list. The difference between each and eachInvoke is that the former takes an actual callback method, whereas the latter calls a method stored as a property on the object. You'll notice each of these methods calls the Function.call method with exactly two parameters instead of Function.apply, which could support any number of parameters passed as an array. The reason for this is that to call Function.apply a new array object needs to be created, which is something that any good HTML5 Engine should try to avoid wherever possible for methods that are called frequently to limit the stutters caused by the garbage collector.

> **NOTE** *As an HTML5 game programmer, you have only one real enemy: the garbage collector. JavaScript is a garbage-collected language, which means that the developer doesn't need to worry about allocating and freeing memory. The downside to this, however, is that at certain intervals JavaScript needs to clean up no-longer-used pieces of memory itself by running a garbage collector. The collector can take some time to run, sometimes more than 100ms, leading to a noticeable stutter in gameplay. The goal of any JavaScript engine should be to create as few objects as possible over the course of a normal frame and save the creation of objects for situations where real game objects like sprites need to be created.*

The functionality for adding and removing objects also works the same as in Chapter 2, with the add, remove, and forceRemove methods performing the same tasks as before with only the addition of a call to the object's destroy method and some triggered events. There is also an additional index on the id of the object. If you remember the Q.GameObject code from Chapter 10, the destroy method also calls remove, which could lead to an infinite recursive loop. This is the reason you added the GameObject.destroyed property, which allows you to remove an object by calling GameObject.destroy() or Stage.remove(object) and have the engine behave correctly either way.

To make it easier to look up objects on the stage by their id, the stage object keeps both the sorted items' array as well as an object that is used as a hash to key objects to their ids.

The collision methods are also similar to what you saw in Chapter 2. The overlap method has been pulled out and is placed as a method directly on Q primarily to make it easier to reach for scoping reasons. The primary method for doing bounding box collisions—Stage.collide—calls a helper method called _hitTest that uses the Q.collide method. The definition for _hitTest could have been embedded as an anonymous function directly inside of Q.collide, but this would have led to the function definition being parsed on every call, slowing down the engine slightly and adding to the garbage that needs to be collected.

Finally, the `step` and `draw` methods loop over each of the objects in the list and call the appropriate method on each as well as trigger events before and after. The `draw` method also calls the optional sort function to make sure objects are drawn in the correct z order.

Rounding Out the Scene Functionality

The last bit of code needed for scenes are some helper methods for staging, clearing, pausing, unpausing, and looping the game. These utility methods are added directly onto the Q object instance.

Add the code in Listing 11-9 to the bottom of the `Quintus.Scenes` module before the final closing curly brace.

LISTING 11-9: Scene and stage utility methods

```
Q.activeStage = 0;

Q.stage = function(num) {
  // Use activeStage is num is undefined
  num = (num === void 0) ? Q.activeStage : num;
  return Q.stages[num];
};

Q.stageScene = function(scene,num,stageClass) {
  stageClass = stageClass || Q.Stage;
  if(_(scene).isString()) {
    scene = Q.scene(scene);
  }

  num = num || 0;

  if(Q.stages[num]) {
    Q.stages[num].destroy();
  }

  Q.stages[num] = new stageClass(scene);

  if(!Q.loop) {
    Q.gameLoop(Q.stageGameLoop);
  }
};

Q.stageGameLoop = function(dt) {
  if(Q.ctx) { Q.clear(); }

  for(var i =0,len=Q.stages.length;i<len;i++) {
    Q.activeStage = i;
    var stage = Q.stage();
    if(stage) {
      stage.step(dt);
      stage.draw(Q.ctx);
    }
```

```
      }

    Q.activeStage = 0;

    if(Q.input && Q.ctx) { Q.input.drawCanvas(Q.ctx); }
  };

  Q.clearStage = function(num) {
    if(Q.stages[num]) {
      Q.stages[num].destroy();
      Q.stages[num] = null;
    }
  };

  Q.clearStages = function() {
    for(var i=0,len=Q.stages.length;i<len;i++) {
      if(Q.stages[i]) { Q.stages[i].destroy(); }
    }
    Q.stages.length = 0;
  };
```

Much like Q.scene, the Q.stage helper method returns a specific stage. It has a little bit of added complication in that the engine keeps track of an activeStage, which represents the stage currently stepped and drawn so that it can be referenced more easily by sprites and other parts of the engine.

Unlike Q.scene, which worked as both a getter and a setter, to add a new stage to the game, the engine provides a different method, called Q.stageScene, to take a scene and present it on a stage. This method can be called with anywhere from 0 to 3 parameters. In the first case, when no parameters are passed, the method creates a new, empty stage on at the first slot. When passed all three parameters, the developer has control over the scene to be staged: the stage slot used and the stage class. Because Q.Stage is a normal, extensible class, it stands to reason the module that would want to extend the default stage functionality (such as adding in more advanced collision detection algorithms) can do so and call Q.stageScene with that stage class.

The actual code of Q.stageScene is straightforward. It looks up a scene object if a string is passed in, destroys the existing stage at that slot if there is one, and then creates a new stage object at the proper slot. Finally, it checks to see if the game loop has already been started; if not, it runs the loop with a special Q.stageGameLoop method (defined next) that ensures all the active steps are updated and rendered for each scene. This means the first time you call Q.stageScene the engine takes care of starting the appropriate game loop automatically.

The Q.stageGameLoop method, which is passed to Q.gameLoop as just described, clears the context, if there is one, and then loops over each of the stages in the Q.stages array (which may not have values at each index, so care is needed to ensure there is a valid stage object at any index). It then calls the step and draw methods of each stage, setting the Q.activeStage property so that any sprites on that stage can call Q.stage() to get the currently active stage object because they will need to for collision detection, for example.

> **NOTE** *You might be wondering why the engine spends extra effort on supporting multiple stages active at a time when one stage can happily support as many objects as necessary. Although there are other reasons, the primary reason is to make it easy to add layered game interface screens on top of the current game. If you were developing an RPG, for example, you would want to easily pop up an inventory screen on top of the game screen and pause the game. By adding a little bit of engine support for both of these features, the engine makes life much easier down the road for this sort of functionality without adding too much complexity to the engine.*

FINISHING BLOCKBREAK

With the rest of the scene functionality hammered out, you can finish up the *Blockbreak* game. First, you need to open the `blockbreak.html` file and add in the `quintus_scenes.js` file you just created to the initial `script` tags:

```
<script src='jquery.min.js'></script>
<script src='underscore.js'></script>
<script src='quintus.js'></script>
<script src='quintus_input.js'></script>
<script src='quintus_sprites.js'></script>
<script src='quintus_scenes.js'></script>
<script src='blockbreak.js'></script>
```

Next the initial setup code must pull in the `Scenes` module. Update the `include` call at the top of `blockbreak.js` to read:

```
$(function() {
  var Q = window.Q = Quintus()
                   .include('Input,Sprites,Scenes')
                   .setup();
  Q.input.keyboardControls()
  Q.input.touchControls({
          controls: [ ['left','<' ],[],[],[],['right','>' ]]
        });
```

Next modify the code inside of the `Q.load` callback at the bottom of the file that starts the game to use the scene and stage functionality:

```
Q.load(['blockbreak.png','blockbreak.json'], function() {
  Q.compileSheets('blockbreak.png','blockbreak.json');
  Q.scene('game',new Q.Scene(function(stage) {
    stage.insert(new Q.Paddle());
    stage.insert(new Q.Ball());
  }));
  Q.stageScene('game');
});
```

You can see the actual code is shortened to a scene definition and the staging of that scene. Resetting the game is now as simple as calling `Q.stageScene('game')`. Reload the game page and make sure everything still works exactly as before.

With the boilerplate changes out of the way, the first thing to do is add in support for collisions between the ball and anything else it might come into contact with. In the definition of the `Q.Ball` in `blockbreak.js`, add some collision detection code to the top and some code to reset the game if the ball goes below the bottom of the screen. To keep the code simple, *Blockbreak* will have only one level and you get only one life.

```
step: function(dt) {
  var p = this.p;
  var hit = Q.stage().collide(this);
  if(hit) {
    if(hit instanceof Q.Paddle) {
      p.dy = -1;
    } else {
      hit.trigger('collision',this);
    }
  }

  p.x += p.dx * p.speed * dt;
  p.y += p.dy * p.speed * dt;

  if(p.x < 0) {
    p.x = 0;
    p.dx = 1;
  } else if(p.x > Q.width - p.w) {
    p.dx = -1;
    p.x - Q.width - p.w;
  }
  if(p.y < 0) {
    p.y = 0;
    p.dy = 1;
  } else if(p.y > Q.height) {
    Q.stageScene('game');
  }
}
```

This makes it so that the paddle interacts with the ball. The game starts over if you miss the ball and let it go off the bottom of the screen. Although chasing a ball around an empty screen is probably more fun than you can handle, now add to the excitement some actual blocks.

The block class isn't going to be anything special. The only explicit functionality it's going to have is some extra code when the ball triggers a collision. Add the code in Listing 11-10 to `blockbreak.js` above the `Q.load` statement:

LISTING 11-10: The Blockbreak Q.Block class

```
Q.Block = Q.Sprite.extend({
  init: function(props) {
    this._super(_(props).extend({ sheet: 'block'}));
    this.bind('collision',function(ball) {
      this.destroy();
      ball.p.dy *= -1;
```

continues

LISTING 11-10 *(continued)*

```
            Q.stage().trigger('removeBlock');
        });
    }
});
```

If you look at the changes made to the Q.Ball class a couple of snippets ago, you can notice the ball is already triggering a collision callback when it hits anything that's not the paddle. The block object listens for that collision callback, removes itself, and flips the direction the ball was heading vertically. It also triggers an event called removeBlock on the stage.

Next you need to modify the actual loading code at the bottom of blockbreak.js to add some blocks onto the screen and do something when all the blocks have been destroyed. That something is going to be the simple act of resetting the game back to start. Modify the following highlighted code to finish up *Blockbreak*:

```
Q.load(['blockbreak.png','blockbreak.json'], function() {
    Q.compileSheets('blockbreak.png','blockbreak.json');
    Q.scene('game',new Q.Scene(function(stage) {
      stage.add(new Q.Paddle());
      stage.add(new Q.Ball());

      var blockCount=0;
      for(var x=0;x<6;x++) {
        for(var y=0;y<5;y++) {
          stage.insert(new Q.Block({ x: x*50+10, y: y*30+10 }));
          blockCount++;
        }
      }
      stage.bind('removeBlock',function() {
        blockCount--;
        if(blockCount == 0) {
          Q.stageScene('game');
        }
      });
    }));

    Q.stageScene('game');
});
```

Notice the use of the variable blockCount to keep track of the number of blocks still left to destroy. To set up the blocks, the scene method loops over the *x* and *y* dimensions with some hardcoded values and adds those elements onto the page. When it receives a removeBlock event, it counts down until there are no more blocks left and then unceremoniously restarts the game.

That's about as far as this book is going to take the *Blockbreak* game because its primary purpose was to be an example of how to build a game with the scene and sprite functionality—and clocking in at just under 100 lines of code, the game does its job. To be a complete game, it still would have a while to go: The collision detection doesn't take into consideration side impacts; the paddle position doesn't control the bounce; and the game has no lives, no points, and no welcome or game-over screens. Some power-ups wouldn't hurt either, but all that is left as an exercise for you.

SUMMARY

You have now completed the initial Quintus functionality, adding in sprites, sprite maps, scenes, and the stage. The engine is now complete enough to be used to build a Canvas game, as was shown in the simple *Blockbreak* game built at the end of the chapter. As you'll see in the next few chapters, with a few more extensions, the engine will be capable of building CSS3 and SVG games.

PART IV
Building Games with CSS3 and SVG

12

Building Games with CSS3

- ➤ Deciding on using a scene graph
- ➤ Adding DOM functionality to Quintus
- ➤ Running a DOM-based version of the sample game

WROX.COM CODE DOWNLOADS FOR THIS CHAPTER

The wrox.com code downloads for this chapter are found at www.wrox.com/remtitle
.cgi?isbn=9781118301326 on the Download Code tab. The code is in the chapter 12
download and individually named according to the names throughout the chapter.

INTRODUCTION

This chapter takes a detour from the use of Canvas to build games to show how to create
games with CSS3 using DOM elements and still get good performance on mobile. This chapter
adds DOM support to the Quintus engine. The next chapter builds on the functionality from
this chapter to build the beginnings of a simple nethack-style dungeon crawler.

DECIDING ON A SCENE GRAPH

Before delving into how to build games with CSS3, this question should be answered first:
When does it make sense to build a game with each of the three available HTML5-family
technologies—Canvas, CSS3, and SVG? The answer is that the technology to use depends
heavily on three factors: your target audience and devices, your interaction method, and your
performance requirements.

Your Target Audience

For the first factor, target audience, you should be aware that Canvas and SVG are natively supported only on IE9 and above on the desktop, meaning that if you want to target older IE browsers, those technologies are both out. Conversely, the Canvas element is hardware-accelerated on mobile only in iOS 5 and up, Chrome for Android, and WP7.5. Older smartphones cannot push a lot of pixels (full-screen redraws are probably out at any reasonable Canvas resolutions) so if you target those devices, you need to consider your choice of technology carefully.

Your Interaction Method

The type of game and the interaction method required should drive your decision on technology. The <canvas> tag, in all its glory, does not natively provide a scene graph. A *scene graph* is a hierarchical representation of the state of each element in the current scene. For CSS3 (DOM) and SVG, you have nested sets of elements that have discrete representations that you can modify (by changing the left or top position of a DOM element, for example). For Canvas, all you have is a bunch of pixels on the page.

Say you draw a car and you want to move the car. With CSS3 or SVG, you could pick up the car object as represented in the scene graph and move it by changing its transform, or left and top, CSS property. Wherever you move it to, it will stay until you move it again. If the car had child objects that were wheels, those would automatically move along with the car.

For the Canvas you have only a representation of the car as drawn on the Canvas as a bunch of pixels. If you tried to move it, you'd just end up moving some pixels from one spot to another on the Canvas. To move the car, you need to either clear the Canvas and redraw everything in its proper new position, or erase the car by drawing the background and then drawing the car in a different spot. If your car has wheels that move, you need to draw the car and then its wheels each time the wheels rotate. Although the Canvas gives you control over every last pixel you draw in your game, it requires more work by the developer or game engine.

Scene graphs have another advantage. Because the scene graph knows about the positions of elements, the browser can handle touch and mouse events and route the event to the correct object. With Canvas games you need to write the logic to do picking and target specific objects.

All this discussion of scene graphs means is that if you have a game that's going to work via direct interaction—in other words by having the user interact directly with elements on the screen—using a technology that has a scene graph can make your life easier. For example, a poker game where the user clicks and possibly drags cards would benefit from a scene graph. An action game where the controls are just a left and right arrow and a jump button would not.

Your Performance Requirements

The last consideration is performance. As mentioned previously, the type of game you build and its performance needs influence your technology decision. CSS3 and SVG tend to perform better on more devices providing you aren't moving too many individual elements at a time. If you are moving only a few elements at any given time, CSS3 in particular has hardware-accelerated support for transitions.

With hardware acceleration, objects will move smoothly at a high frame rate without your needing to worry about animating them yourself.

On the flip side, for a fast-scrolling platformer, hardware-accelerated Canvas generally performs better on the browsers that support it than using CSS3.

IMPLEMENTING DOM SUPPORT

Quintus can add DOM support to the engine via a module called `Quintus.DOM`. This module creates DOM-based equivalents of the `Sprite` and `Stage` classes called, perhaps not surprisingly, `DOMSprite` and `DOMStage`. The `setup` method can also have a DOM-based equivalent called `setupDOM`.

Considering DOM Specifics

At an API level, the Quintus DOM classes behave much like their Canvas counterparts. On the inside, however, because the DOM provides a persistent scene graph, the classes behave quite differently. The step method of `DOMStage` still steps though each sprite, but the `DOMSprite` step method has the additional duty to update the element that represents the sprite on the document. Because the browser takes care of actually drawing the element, the `draw` method consists of nothing but a trigger call.

Sprites will be added to the page as `<div>` elements of set width and height with a background image adjusted using an offset position calculated by the element's sprite map. Changing the frame consists of moving the background position around.

Next the sprites need to be positioned. Although this might at first glance seem to be as easy as using the traditional `left` and `top` CSS properties along with absolute positioning, to get the best performance you must use the new CSS3 `transform` property, which benefits from hardware-accelerated rendering.

Because the `transform` property comes with the usual host of vendor-specific prefixes, the engine looks at what's supported in the browser and generates a single method for positioning that falls back to `left` and `top` support if necessary.

Finally there's the issue of animation. Manually animating a bunch of DOM elements every frame can certainly be done, but at a large scale it gets quite taxing on the browser, especially on mobile. Luckily CSS3 has support for animation baked in via transitions and key frame animations. In this case using transitions makes a lot of sense because the game can update an object's state once and count on the browser to transition the property from one spot to another.

CSS3 transitions are unfortunately in the same vendor-prefix quagmire as `transforms`, so you need a method to detect the best way to add support to all browsers as well.

Bootstrapping the Quintus DOM Module

Start the `Quintus.DOM` module by opening a new file called **quintus_dom.js** and entering the code from Listing 12.1 into it.

LISTING 12.1: Bootstrapped Quintus DOM module

```
Quintus.DOM = function(Q) {
  Q.setupDOM = function(id,options) {
    options = options || {};
    id = id || "quintus";
    Q.el = $(_.isString(id) ? "#" + id : id);
    if(Q.el.length === 0) {
      Q.el = $("<div>")
                .attr('id',id)
                .css({width: 320, height:420 })
                .appendTo("body");
    }
    if(options.maximize) {
      var w = $(window).width();
      var h = $(window).height();
      Q.el.css({width:w,height:h});
    }
    Q.wrapper = Q.el
                  .wrap("<div id='" + id + "_container'/>")
                  .parent()
                  .css({ width: Q.el.width(),
                         height: Q.el.height(),
                         margin: '0 auto' });
    Q.el.css({ position:'relative', overflow: 'hidden' });
    Q.width = Q.el.width();
    Q.height = Q.el.height();
    setTimeout(function() { window.scrollTo(0,1); }, 0);
    $(window).bind('orientationchange',function() {
      setTimeout(function() { window.scrollTo(0,1); }, 0);
    });
    return Q;
  };
};
```

This code creates the initial module wrapper method and also creates the setupDOM method. This is the counterpart to Q.setup() for Canvas-based games. It either uses an existing DOM element or creates a new one to be a wrapper for the game. If the maximize option is passed in, the method resizes the container to fit the screen. Next, it creates a wrapper container around that element to center it on the page. It also sets the element to be positioned to allow elements inside it to be positioned absolutely as necessary, and it sets the overflow property to hidden to prevent any elements in the game from appearing outside of the game container.

Creating a Consistent Translation Method

Before adding in the DOMSprite and DOMStage classes to actually get something onto the screen, the issue to get a consistent positioning method needs to be solved.

The idea is to find the best-performing method the browser in question supports and then bind that to a consistent method name so that the rest of the DOM support doesn't need to know how exactly elements are positioned. CSS3 defines support for the transform property, which depending on the browser supports translate(..) and translate3d(..) values that can move elements around more efficiently than using the traditional `left` and `top` properties. `translate3d` in particular results in hardware-accelerated transforms being applied to DOM elements.

> **NOTE** *The downside to using transforms is that none of the transform properties are guaranteed to be vendor-prefix free, so each of the vendor prefixes needs to be considered when trying to find support for the best positioning method available. If `translate3d` isn't supported, `translate` will be used; otherwise plain old `top` and `left` positioning will be done.*

The code is first going to check if CSS3 transform support is available, and if it is, check if `translate3d` (which triggers hardware-accelerated support in WebKit) is available. If so, a method called `translate3DBuilder` is called that returns another method that is customized to the proper prefix. JavaScript makes it easy to create methods that return methods through the power of closures. The `translate3d` isn't supported; `translateBuilder` is called to return a method that does non-3d transforms.

Add the code in Listing 12-2 to the bottom of `quintus_dom.js` before the final closing curly brace.

LISTING 12-2: Checking for translation support

```
(function() {
  function translateBuilder(attribute) {
    return function(dom,x,y) {
      dom.style[attribute] =
      "translate(" + Math.floor(x) + "px," +
      Math.floor(y) + "px)";
    };
  }
  function translate3DBuilder(attribute) {
    return function(dom,x,y) {
      dom.style[attribute] =
      "translate3d(" + Math.floor(x) + "px," +
      Math.floor(y) + "px,0px)";
    };
  }
  function scaleBuilder(attribute) {
    return function(dom,scale) {
      dom.style[attribute + 'Origin'] = "0% 0%";
      dom.style[attribute] = "scale(" + scale + ")";
    };
  }
  function fallbackTranslate(dom,x,y) {
    dom.style.left = x + "px";
    dom.style.top = y + "px";
  }
  var has3d = ('WebKitCSSMatrix' in window &&
               'm11' in new WebKitCSSMatrix());
  var dummyStyle = $("<div>")[0].style;
  var transformMethods = ['transform',
```

continues

LISTING 12-2 *(continued)*

```
                              'webkitTransform',
                              'MozTransform',
                              'msTransform' ];
      for(var i=0;i<transformMethods.length;i++) {
        var transformName = transformMethods[i];
        if(!_.isUndefined(dummyStyle[transformName])) {
          if(has3d) {
            Q.positionDOM = translate3DBuilder(transformName);
          } else {
            Q.positionDOM = translateBuilder(transformName);
          }
          Q.scaleDOM = scaleBuilder(transformName);
          break;
        }
      }
      Q.positionDOM = Q.positionDOM || fallbackTranslate;
      Q.scaleDOM = Q.scaleDOM || function(scale) {};
    })();
```

To keep the functions from polluting the main `Quintus.DOM` namespace, notice the entire expression is wrapped in an immediately invoked functional expression (IIFE). This enables the entire bit of code to result in only two definitions being added to `Q`: `Q.positionDOM` and `Q.scaleDOM`.

The first part of the listing consists of three methods that return methods. This is a relatively tricky concept to understand if you haven't seen it a lot before, so take a deeper look at one of those methods:

```
      function translateBuilder(attribute) {
        return function(dom,x,y) {
          dom.style[attribute] =
          "translate(" + Math.floor(x) + "px," +
          Math.floor(y) + "px)";
        };
      }
```

Notice that the entirety of `translateBuilder` consists of a `return` statement that returns a function. The function returned uses the `attribute` parameter passed into the original method. This is allowed in JavaScript because the language supports closures, which bind the definition of function to the scope in which they were originally defined. The returned method can be used anywhere in the code base at a later point and can keep track of the previously bound value of the attribute when it is called.

After the definition of the various binding methods, the code creates a `<div>` element and checks the style attributes of that element for prefixed transform support of each of the different vendor prefixes.

It also does a WebKit-specific check for 3-D support. If you want a more general check for `translate3d`, take a look at Modernizr. Because most mobile browsers are WebKit-based, the WebKit-specific check gets you a significant amount of mileage.

The code also creates a `Q.scaleDOM` method, which is used to perform a scale transform. Because there isn't a 3-D equivalent necessary for this, the creation of the scale method is simpler.

Creating a Consistent Transition Method

Having created a consistent way to translate DOM elements as efficiently as possible for performance, you need to do the whole thing over again to create an easy way to add transition support for browsers that support it.

Add the code in Listing 12-3 at the bottom of quintus_dom.js above the final closing curly brace.

LISTING 12-3: Checking for transition support

```
(function() {
  function transitionBuilder(attribute,prefix){
    return function(dom,property,sec,easing) {
      easing = easing || "";
      if(property == 'transform') {
        property = prefix + property;
      }
      sec = sec || "1s";
      dom.style[attribute] = property + " " + sec + " " + easing;
    };
  }
  // Dummy method
  function fallbackTransition() { }
  var dummyStyle = $("<div>")[0].style;
  var transitionMethods = ['transition',
                           'webkitTransition',
                           'MozTransition',
                           'msTransition' ];
  var prefixNames = [ '', '-webkit-', '-moz-', '-ms-' ];
  for(var i=0;i<transitionMethods.length;i++) {
    var transitionName = transitionMethods[i];
    var prefixName = prefixNames[i];
    if(!_.isUndefined(dummyStyle[transitionName])) {
      Q.transitionDOM = transitionBuilder(transitionName,prefixName);
      break;
    }
  }
  Q.transitionDOM = Q.transitionDOM || fallbackTransition;
})();
```

This block follows the same pattern as the code in the previous section except its goal is to create a method that lets the developer add a transition on a property in a consistent manner. In this case, if there isn't built-in support, the fallback is to just do nothing. The game still runs as expected, but all transitions are instant instead of animated.

Implementing a DOM Sprite

Next up is the DOM equivalent of the Canvas Sprite class. This class actually extends the base Q.Sprite class. (So the Quintus.DOM module must be loaded after the Quintus.Sprites module.)

As mentioned previously, the primary difference between a DOM and Canvas sprite is that a DOM sprite doesn't need to worry about drawing itself, but it does need to make sure it keeps the properties of the DOM element in sync with itself.

Add the code in Listing 12-4 to the bottom of `quintus_dom.js` before the final closing curly-brace.

LISTING 12-4: The DOMSprite class

```
Q.DOMSprite = Q.Sprite.extend({
  init: function(props) {
    this._super(props);
    this.el = $("<div>").css({
      width: this.p.w,
      height: this.p.h,
      zIndex: this.p.z || 0,
      position: 'absolute'
    });
    this.dom = this.el[0];
    this.rp = {};
    this.setImage();
    this.setTransform();
  },

  setImage: function() {
    var asset;
    if(this.sheet()) {
      asset = Q.asset(this.sheet().asset);
    } else {
      asset = this.asset();
    }
    if(asset) {
      this.dom.style.backgroundImage = "url(" + asset.src + ")";
    }
  },

  setTransform: function() {
    var p = this.p;
    var rp = this.rp;
    if(rp.frame !== p.frame) {
      if(p.sheet) {
        this.dom.style.backgroundPosition =
            (-this.sheet().fx(p.frame)) + "px " +
            (-this.sheet().fy(p.frame)) + "px";
      } else {
        this.dom.style.backgroundPosition = "0px 0px";
      }
      rp.frame = p.frame;
    }
    if(rp.x !== p.x || rp.y !== p.y) {
      Q.positionDOM(this.dom,p.x,p.y);
      rp.x = p.x;
      rp.y = p.y;
    }
```

```
      },

      hide: function() {
        this.dom.style.display = 'none';
      },

      show: function() {
        this.dom.style.display = 'block';
      },

      draw: function(ctx) {
        this.trigger('draw');
      },

      step: function(dt) {
        this.trigger('step',dt);
        this.setTransform();
      },

      destroy: function() {
        if(this.destroyed) return false;
        this._super();
        this.el.remove();
      }
    });
```

The init method has the responsibility to create the actual DOM <div> that contains the background image. It uses jQuery to create the <div> and sets the dimensions and zIndex on the object. Using jQuery adds a little bit of overhead to any DOM operation, so for operations that will potentially be done each frame, the method also grabs the actual DOM object and stores it in this.dom.

Next, it creates an object called rp, which stores the real properties of the DOM as they have been set. Making changes to DOM objects is relatively expensive performance-wise, so in lieu of updating those properties in each frame, the sprite's step method compares its properties hash p against the values in rp and only updates the DOM object when there is a discrepancy. Finally, the init method calls this.setImage(), which sets the backgroundImage on the div, and setTransform(), which sets the element's position in the container as well as the background image position (which corresponds to the frame of the sprite map).

The setImage method is straightforward because all it does is set the backgroundImage property by grabbing it from the spritesheet or from the asset.

setTransform is more complicated. You can see it checks for a difference in the frame, and x and y properties between the p and rp objects as described. If the frame needs to be updated, it calculates the position using either the spritesheet helper methods fx and fy or just sets the position to 0 if there isn't a spritesheet attached to the Sprite.

For the position, the Q.positionDOM method created earlier is used to set the position in whatever best way is supported by the browser.

Because the rp object is initialized to the empty object, the first time setTransform is run. The frame and position are guaranteed to be set.

The show and hide methods adjust the display property of the element to either none or block, which results in the element either being hidden or visible on the page, respectively.

The draw method is just a stub that triggers a draw event because the browser takes care of actually drawing the object. The step similarly triggers the step event, but it also calls setTransform afterward in case any of the positioned attributes are modified.

Lastly, the destroy method needs to clean up the DOM object and its internal record keeping, so it calls the jQuery remove() method to remove the element from the page after letting the inherited method do its work.

The Q.DOMSprite class now has a compatible interface to Q.Sprite. However, if you try to use the standard Q.Stage object to keep track of DOMSprites, you'll be seriously disappointed because nothing actually appears on the screen.

Creating a DOM Stage Class

For DOMSprite objects to work correctly, they need to be added to a stage object that has its own container DOM element and knows how to add DOM elements on to the page. Because the CSS scaling tricks that were possible using the <canvas> tag aren't possible with DOM elements, the engine must use a different mechanism for scaling up content when necessary. Luckily, the same transform CSS3 style used to translate content also supports the scale value. To make it easier to keep scaling and translating separated on the stage object (the stage follows the player in the example in the next chapter), the DOMStage class creates a separate wrapper element used for scaling the view.

Because the Sprite and Stage functionality are stored in different modules, the DOMStage class puts in a check in case someone tries to build a game with DOMSprites but does not use the scene and stage module.

Add the code from Listing 12-5 to the bottom of the quintus_dom.js file in the usual spot before the final closing curly-brace. This rounds out the basic DOM sprite functionality.

LISTING 12-5: DOMStage class

```
if(Q.Stage) {
  Q.DOMStage = Q.Stage.extend({
    init: function(scene) {
      this.el = $("<div>").css({
        top:0,
        position:'relative'
      }).appendTo(Q.el);
      this.dom = this.el[0];
      this.wrapper = this.el.wrap('<div>').parent().css({
        position:'absolute',
        left:0,
        top:0
      });
      this.scale = 1;
      this.wrapper_dom = this.wrapper[0];
      this._super(scene);
```

```
      },

      insert: function(itm) {
        if(itm.dom) { this.dom.appendChild(itm.dom); };
        return this._super(itm);
      },

      destroy: function() {
        this.wrapper.remove();
        this._super();
      },

      rescale: function(scale) {
        this.scale = scale;
        Q.scaleDOM(this.wrapper_dom,scale);
      },

      centerOn: function(x,y) {
        this.x = Q.width/2/this.scale -  x;
        this.y = Q.height/2/this.scale - y;
        Q.positionDOM(this.dom,this.x,this.y);
      }
    });
  }
```

The Q.DOMStage class extends the basic Canvas stage class, so all the methods in the normal Q.Stage class, including pausing and unpausing are available. The init method has the task to create the DOM element that acts as a container and the wrapper element that will be used for scaling the container up and down. After that it just calls the init method of the inherited class to take care of the rest.

The insert and destroy methods similarly call the corresponding method of the super class. In addition, insert appends the DOM element of the Sprite being added to the container element of the stage. The destroy method also makes sure the wrapper element is removed from the page, which removes all the child elements with it.

The rescale method is new. It uses the Q.scaleDOM method created earlier in the chapter to rescale the wrapper. This will be used the same way the Canvas was scaled with CSS in earlier chapters to fill the screen on larger devices such as tablets. The centerOn method repositions the stage, taking into consideration the current scale and will be used as a camera to follow the player around.

Replacing the Canvas Equivalents

With Q.setupDOM and the Q.DOMSprite and Q.DOMStage classes written, the basic functionality is done. However, using the DOM equivalents is a little cumbersome. For example, to stage a scene using the Q.DOMStage class, you need to override the stageClass and write

```
Q.stageScene(sceneObj,0,Q.DOMStage)
```

instead of simply

```
Q.stageScene(sceneObj);
```

If you write a DOM-based game, this adds some unnecessary noise to the code, so to keep the code simpler, add a method that replaces Canvas-based methods and classes with their DOM-based equivalents. You can call this method before setup to make it easier to work with DOM games.

Add the code in Listing 12-6 to the usual spot at the bottom of quintus_dom.js.

LISTING 12-6: The Q.domOnly method

```
Q.domOnly = function() {
  Q.Stage = Q.DOMStage;
  Q.setup = Q.setupDOM;
  Q.Sprite = Q.DOMSprite;
  return Q;
};
```

Chaining in this call to the beginning of a game's setup makes it easier to convert a game from Canvas to DOM.

Testing the DOM Functionality

Before delving into building a CSS3 nethack-style game, try out the DOM functionality by converting the simple *Blockbreak* game from the previous chapter into a DOM-based one.

Open up your blockbreak.html from the previous chapter (or copy the code over to a new directory) and add a <script> tag to load the quintus_dom.js file you just wrote. You'll also need to change the style tag to reference #quintus instead of just the canvas element:

```
<!DOCTYPE HTML>
<html lang="en">
  <head>
    <meta charset="UTF-8">
    <meta name="viewport" content="width=device-width, user-scalable=0,
minimum-scale=1.0, maximum-scale=1.0"/>
    <title>Block Break</title>
    <script src='jquery.min.js'></script>
    <script src='underscore.js'></script>
    <script src='quintus.js'></script>
    <script src='quintus_input.js'></script>
    <script src='quintus_sprites.js'></script>
    <script src='quintus_scenes.js'></script>
    <script src='quintus_dom.js'></script>
    <script src='blockbreak.js'></script>
    <style>
      body { padding:0px; margin:0px; }
      #quintus { background-color:black; }
    </style>
  </head>
  <body>
  </body>
</html>
```

Next, open up the `blockbreak.js` file and modify the initial setup calls to include the DOM module and chain in a call to `domOnly()`.

```
$(function() {
  var Q = window.Q = Quintus()
                     .include('Input,Sprites,Scenes,DOM')
                     .domOnly()
                     .setup();
  Q.input.keyboardControls()
```

Because the `domOnly()` method replaces all the Canvas classes with their DOM-based equivalents, no other changes to the code need to be made.

Fire up the game in a browser. You'll need to run it off of localhost as usual, as it loads JSON data.

You should see the same game as in the previous chapter, with the exception of the movement controls on the bottom of the screen on mobile. The hotspots for controlling the paddle still work but because no code has been written to display the buttons, nothing appears on the screen on mobile.

If you inspect the page in Chrome, you can notice that all the blocks along with the paddle and ball are actual DOM elements. You now have an HTML5 game that runs in IE6!

SUMMARY

In this chapter you learned how to build games using DOM elements by using performance-optimized transforms and transitions. You also added DOM element support to the Quintus engine and converted the *Blockbreak* example to a DOM based game with just a few lines of code.

13

Crafting a CSS3 RPG

WHAT'S IN THIS CHAPTER?

➤ Creating a scrolling tilemap

➤ Building an RPG

➤ Adding enemies and power-ups

WROX.COM CODE DOWNLOADS FOR THIS CHAPTER

The wrox.com code downloads for this chapter are found at www.wrox.com/remtitle
.cgi?isbn=9781118301326 on the Download Code tab. The code is in the chapter 13
download and individually named according to the names throughout the chapter.

INTRODUCTION

This chapter exercises the DOM-based code from Chapter 12 to build a simple a nethack-style
RPG. This game requires tiled background support, so the engine also adds a class in the next
section called DOMTileMap, which is designed just for that purpose.

CREATING A SCROLLING TILE MAP

To build a nethack-style game, the engine needs to add a 2-D tile map to the game in an efficient manner. One naive way to do this would be to just add an absolutely positioned sprite at
each position. This does work; however, as the map gets larger, it slows the browser down to a
crawl. Instead, you want to create a single large sprite that can be moved around as a unit and
treated like a single element.

Understanding the Performance Problem

If you take a medium-sized map that might be 50 tiles tall by 50 tiles wide, this would result in 2,500 sprites, each of which needs to be stepped every frame. In addition, every time you make a modification to an element, the browser needs to repaint the container, resulting in a significant slowdown in frame rate from constantly updating. If you don't create a more efficient mechanism of collision detection than looping over every potential object, then every moving sprite would need to be tested in each iteration. All this would lead to exceedingly small map sizes or horrible performance.

A better plan of attack would be to create a single tile map sprite that contains all the tiles and that can be stepped and moved around as a single entity. Because the individual tiles aren't moving, collision detection is as simple as dividing a position by the size of each tile to get a tile position and checking that one location.

Implementing the DOM Tile Map Class

For all these reasons the engine adds in a class called `Q.DOMTileMap`, which encapsulates all this functionality. The individual levels of the RPG extend this class to add additional game-specific functionality.

Each tile in the tile map is added as a floated DOM element to increase browser performance. Provided the width and height of the containing `<div>` is set correctly, all the floated elements will end up in the right spot visually.

To prevent the user from seeing the entire dungeon at once, the tile map also supports showing and hiding individual tiles. (The player reveals the tiles of the level as they move.) Because setting the display method to `none` would result in all the floated tiles shifting, the class instead just toggles the visibility property of the element. As every time the browser reaches in and affects the DOM there is a performance penalty, the tile map class keeps track of which tiles are shown and hidden in a data structure and changes only the DOM element when absolutely necessary.

Listing 13-1 shows the code for the `Q.DOMTileMap` class. Add it to the bottom of `quintus_dom.js` in the usual spot before the final closing curly-brace.

LISTING 13-1: The DOMTileMap class

```
Q.DOMTileMap = Q.DOMSprite.extend({
  // Expects a sprite sheet, along with cols and rows properties
  init:function(props) {
    var sheet = Q.sheet(props.sheet);
    this._super(_(props).extend({
      w: props.cols * sheet.tilew,
      h: props.rows * sheet.tileh,
      tilew: sheet.tilew,
      tileh: sheet.tileh
    }));
    this.shown = [];
    this.domTiles = [];
```

```
    },

    setImage: function() { },

    setup: function(tiles,hide) {
      this.tiles = tiles;
      for(var y=0,height=tiles.length;y<height;y++) {
        this.domTiles.push([]);
        this.shown.push([]);
        for(var x=0,width=tiles[0].length;x<width;x++) {
          var domTile = this._addTile(tiles[y][x]);
          if(hide) { domTile.style.visibility = 'hidden'; }
          this.shown.push(hide ? false : true);
          this.domTiles[y].push(domTile);
        }
      }
    },

    _addTile: function(frame) {
      var p = this.p;
      var div = document.createElement('div');
      div.style.width = p.tilew + "px";
      div.style.height = p.tileh + "px";
      div.style.styleFloat = div.style.cssFloat = 'left';
      this._setTile(div,frame);
      this.dom.appendChild(div);
      return div;
    },

    _setTile: function(dom,frame) {
      var asset = Q.asset(this.sheet().asset);
      dom.style.backgroundImage = "url(" + asset.src + ")";
      dom.style.backgroundPosition = (-this.sheet().fx(frame)) +"px "
 + (-this.sheet().fy(frame)) + "px";
    },

    validTile: function(x,y) {
      return (y >= 0 && y < this.p.rows) &&
             (x >= 0 && x < this.p.cols);
    },

    get: function(x,y) { return this.validTile(x,y) ?
                                 this.tiles[y][x] : null; },

    getDom: function(x,y) { return this.validTile(x,y) ?
                                  this.domTiles[y][x] : null; },
    set: function(x,y,frame) {
      if(!this.validTile(x,y)) return;
      this.tiles[y][x] = frame;
      var domTile = this.getDom(x,y);
      this._setFile(domTile,frame);
    },

    show: function(x,y) {
      if(!this.validTile(x,y)) return;
```

continues

LISTING 13-1 *(continued)*

```
      if(this.shown[y][x]) return;
      this.getDom(x,y).style.visibility = 'visible';
      this.shown[y][x] = true;
    },

  hide: function(x,y) {
    if(!this.validTile(x,y)) return;
    if(!this.shown[y][x]) return;
    this.getDom(x,y).style.visibility = 'hidden';
    this.shown[y][x] = false;
  }
});
```

This class is a little complicated so break it down into three chunks. The first part, the `init` method, sets up the tile map's properties:

```
Q.DOMTileMap = Q.DOMSprite.extend({
  init:function(props) {
    var sheet = Q.sheet(props.sheet);
    this._super(_(props).extend({
      w: props.cols * sheet.tilew,
      h: props.rows * sheet.tileh,
      tilew: sheet.tilew,
      tileh: sheet.tileh
    }));
    this.shown = [];
    this.domTiles = [];
  },
  setImage: function() { },
```

`init` pulls out the spritesheet and the number of rows, columns, and tiles from the passed-in properties and uses that to calculate the width and height of the sprite. It calls the `this._super()` method to let the DOMSprite class finish the initialization and creation of the actual DOM element. The `init` method of DOMSprite also calls `setImage` to set a background image on the sprite, but because the DOMTileMap element doesn't need a background image, this method is overridden to be an empty stub method.

Next are the three methods used to take a 2-D array of tile frames and create the tile map:

```
  setup: function(tiles,hide) {
    this.tiles = tiles;
    for(var y=0,height=tiles.length;y<height;y++) {
      this.domTiles.push([]);
      this.shown.push([]);
      for(var x=0,width=tiles[0].length;x<width;x++) {
        var domTile = this._addTile(tiles[y][x]);
        if(hide) { domTile.style.visibility = 'hidden'; }
        this.shown.push(hide ? false : true);
        this.domTiles[y].push(domTile);
      }
    }
```

```
  },

  _addTile: function(frame) {
    var p = this.p;
    var div = document.createElement('div');
    div.style.width = p.tilew + "px";
    div.style.height = p.tileh + "px";
    div.style.styleFloat = div.style.cssFloat = 'left';
    this._setTile(div,frame);
    this.dom.appendChild(div);
    return div;
  },

  _setTile: function(dom,frame) {
    var asset = Q.asset(this.sheet().asset);
    dom.style.backgroundImage = "url(" + asset.src + ")";
    dom.style.backgroundPosition = (-this.sheet().fx(frame)) +"px " +
                                   (-this.sheet().fy(frame)) + "px";
  },
```

The setup method takes in the 2-D array, creates the DOM element by calling the internal helper method _addTile, and updates the domTiles and shown arrays with the appropriate values. The domTiles array contains a 2-D array that matches the tiles array, except it points to the actual DOM elements so that they can be manipulated. The shown array is a 2-D array of booleans that keeps track of which tiles are visible and which are hidden.

The _addTile method takes in a frame and returns the DOM element set to that frame. Because lots of DOM elements are going to be created, the engine uses the native document.createElement method as opposed to the usual jQuery method to get a little speed advantage where possible. Setting the float property is also a little tricky because different browsers refer to it differently when it's accessed via JavaScript. Rather than try to determine which way is correct, the method takes the shortcut of just setting both options. It also calls _setTile as a shortcut to set the background image and background image position correctly based on the frame.

The last section of the class retrieves and updates the tiles in the tile map:

```
      validTile: function(x,y) {
        return (y >= 0 && y < this.p.rows) &&
               (x >= 0 && x < this.p.cols);
      },
      get: function(x,y) { return this.validTile(x,y) ?
                                  this.tiles[y][x] : null; },
      getDom: function(x,y) { return this.validTile(x,y) ?
                                     this.domTiles[y][x] : null; },
      set: function(x,y,frame) {
        var domTile = this.getDom(x,y);
        if(!domTile) return;
        this.tiles[y][x] = frame;
        this._setFile(domTile,frame);
      },

      show: function(x,y) {
        var domTile = this.getDom(x,y);
        if(!domTile) return;
        if(this.shown[y][x]) return;
```

```
      domTile.style.visibility = 'visible';
      this.shown[y][x] = true;
    },

    hide: function(x,y) {
      var domTile = this.getDom(x,y);
      if(!domTile) return;
      if(!this.shown[y][x]) return;
      domTile.style.visibility = 'hidden';
      this.shown[y][x] = false;
    }
```

To keep the individual game code simpler, when a game calls any of the preceding tile manipulation routines, the engine should fail silently if an invalid tile location is passed in. This allows the game to try to hide or show tiles outside of the map without needing to do bounds checking. To facilitate this, the validTile checks a passed in *x* and *y* location against the range of rows and columns passed in and returns false if the elements are out of bounds.

This method is used by the get and getDOM methods to prevent indexing incorrectly into the tiles or domTiles array and causing an exception. The set method lets the game update the frame at a specific tile. This can be used to do animation or change the state of the tile map (for example, when a door opens). The show and hide methods toggle the visibility of an individual square.

BUILDING THE RPG

With all the pieces in place, it's time to turn your attention to actually building the RPG that graces the title of the chapter. The basic game plan is to load a text file that contains an ASCII map of a level, with monsters and loot strewn about in various places, and turn that into a tile map and a set of sprites for the player to interact with.

Creating the HTML File

The first step, as usual, is to create the necessary HTML wrapper file to hold the game. Create a new file called **rpg.html** and enter the code from Listing 13-2 into it.

LISTING 13-2: The RPG wrapper file

```html
<!DOCTYPE HTML>
<html lang="en">
  <head>
    <meta charset="UTF-8">
    <meta name="viewport" content="width=device-width, user-scalable=0,
minimum-scale=1.0, maximum-scale=1.0"/>
    <title>RPG</title>
    <script src='jquery.min.js'></script>
    <script src='underscore.js'></script>
    <script src='quintus.js'></script>
    <script src='quintus_input.js'></script>
    <script src='quintus_sprites.js'></script>
```

```
<script src='quintus_scenes.js'></script>
<script src='quintus_dom.js'></script>
<script src='rpg.js'></script>
<style>
  * { padding:0px; margin:0px; }
  #quintus { background-color:black; }
</style>
</head>
<body>
</body>
</html>
```

As before, this file is almost completely empty except for a few reset styles and the script tags to load the game.

Setting Up the Game

To start the game, set up a basic structure for the game that sets up the window and loads some art assets.

Rather than reinvent the wheel for a nethack (also known as rogue-like) tileset, some friendly folks on the Internet have released public domain tilesets that you can use to build the game: `http://rltiles.sourceforge.net/`.

The RPG in this chapter uses three of the files from RLTiles to get up and running. These tiles need a little bit of background removal work to fit nicely into the game, but otherwise they should work well. The `images/` directory of this chapter's files have the images set up as needed. Each of the images has a large set of 32-pixel by 32-pixel images. This game isn't going to put much of the tile set to good use, but rather is just going to pull random enemy and item images for visual effect.

With these three files in hand, it's time to bootstrap the game. Create the **rpg.js** file that was mentioned in the preceding HTML wrapper file and put in the boilerplate code in Listing 13-3. You also need a level data text file called **level1.txt** in a `data/` subfolder of your game to run. Right now it doesn't matter what is in the file: You can copy the one from the chapter assets or just create your own and save an empty file.

LISTING 13-3: Bootstrapping the RPG

```
$(function() {
  var Q = window.Q = Quintus()
                   .include('Input,Sprites,Scenes,DOM')
                   .domOnly()
                   .setup('quintus',{ maximize: true });
  var tileSize = 32;
  var TILE = {
    WALL: 10,
    FLOOR: 30,
    STAIRS: 45
  };
  var impassableTiles = {
    10: true
```

continues

LISTING 13-3 *(continued)*

```
  };
  Q.input.keyboardControls();
  Q.input.joypadControls({zone: Q.width});
  Q.load(['characters.png',
          'dungeon.png',
          'items.png',
          'level1.txt'], function() {

    Q.sheet('characters', 'characters.png',
            { tilew: tileSize, tileh: tileSize });

    Q.sheet('tiles', 'dungeon.png',
            { tilew: tileSize, tileh: tileSize });

    Q.sheet('items', 'items.png',
            { tilew: tileSize, tileh: tileSize });

    Q.scene('level1',new Q.Scene(function(stage) {
      if(Q.width > 600 || Q.height > 600) {
        stage.rescale(2);
      }
      alert("Loaded!");

    }));
    Q.stageScene('level1');
  });
});
```

The code sets up the Q object, sets a couple of global variables you'll use later, and then sets up the default keyboard controls and a full-width joypad.

Next, the code loads four assets—three images and a level data text file—and sets up three spritesheets after those are loaded.

Next, it creates a new scene called level1. Right now that scene doesn't do much except rescale the game if the width or height of the browser is greater than 600. This allows the iPad and desktop browser to get a zoomed-in view of the game. (For browsers that support transforms, older browsers see everything smaller.)

Finally, the game calls Q.stageScene("level1") to load that first scene into the game. If everything goes according to plan, you should get an alert on the page that says "Loaded."

Adding a Tile Map

It's time to get tiles onto the board. To do this the game subclasses the DOMTileMap class to create a class that can take in the level data text file asset and turn it into something the DOMTileMap class can use.

To make it easy to create levels, the level format will be an ASCII file where Xs represent walls and periods (.) represent corridors and rooms. Additional sprites such as monsters and treasures will be demarked by other letters. The game can figure out the width and height of the map from the data. See Figure 13-1 for an example of what a level might look like.

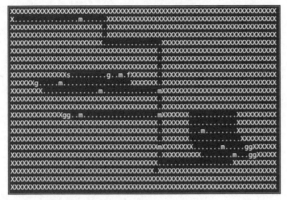

FIGURE 13-1: Level text file.

Open up `rpg.js` again, and add the `Q.Level` class defined in Listing 13-14 to the file above the `Q.load` method.

LISTING 13-4: The Q.Level class

```
Q.Level = Q.DOMTileMap.extend({
  legend: {
    "X": "wall",
    ".": "floor"
  },

  init:function(asset,stage) {
    this.stage = stage;
    this.level = [];
    this.sprites = [];
    var data = Q.asset(asset);
    this.extra = [];
    _.each(data.split("\n"),function(row) {
      var columns = row.split("");
      if(columns.length > 1) {
        this.level.push(columns);
        this.sprites.push([]);
      }
    },this);

    this._super({
      cols:this.level[0].length,
      rows:this.level.length,
      sheet: 'tiles'
```

continues

LISTING 13-4 (continued)

```
        });

      var tiles =[];
      for(var y=0;y<this.level.length;y++) {
        tiles[y] = [];
        for(var x =0;x<this.level[0].length;x++) {
          var square = this.level[y][x],
              frame = null,
              method = this.legend[square] || "wall";

          frame = this[method](x*tileSize,y*tileSize);
          tiles[y].push(frame);
        }
      }
      this.setup(tiles,false);
    },

    insert: function(sprite) {
      this.stage.insert(sprite);
      this.sprites[sprite.p.tileY][sprite.p.tileX] = sprite;
      return sprite;
    },

    wall: function(x,y) { return TILE.WALL; },
    floor: function(x,y) { return TILE.FLOOR; }
  });
```

Now the class primarily modifies the `init` method to take in an asset and a stage and set up the tile map by looking up what it should do with each tile in the `legend` property. Currently, only two tile types are supported, `floor` and `wall`; each just controls the look of the tile. You'll add functionality to keep track of the sprites at each tile location, so in anticipation of that functionality the `this.sprites` array is created with the same number of rows as the main tile data. It also has a helper method for inserting sprites into the stage that adds them to the `this.sprites` array.

To test this out, remove the alert and modify the code inside of the `Q.scene` definition for the `level1` scene to read:

```
Q.scene('level1',new Q.Scene(function(stage) {
    if(Q.width > 600 || Q.height > 600) {
      stage.rescale(2);
    }
    stage.level = stage.insert(
                  new Q.Level("level1.txt",stage)
                );
  }));
  Q.stageScene('level1');
```

If you load up the game, you should see your level rendered onto the screen. Because the `level1.txt` file loads via AJAX, you must ensure you load the page via localhost, not using a file:// URL.

Creating Some Useful Components

Sprites in a tiled environment need to behave differently than sprites in a 2-D platformer might. They should move in `tileSize` increments around the board, avoid running over walls and each other, and keep the level sprites array up-to-date as they wander around the dungeon.

It would be nice to encapsulate this functionality in a reusable way. One way would be to create a `TileSprite` base class from which all sprites would inherit, but this might prove cumbersome if you want to reuse sprites from other places. Another way to handle this is to create a component that adds tile-aware positioning and movement to any sprite. You'll take the latter option.

This component hooks into the `step` event and looks at a sprite's `dx` and `dy` properties (short for direction *x* and direction *y*) to see if the sprite tries to move in any direction. If it does, it checks to make sure that there aren't any other tiles or sprites in the way; if not it moves the sprite. If there is another sprite in the way, it can let the sprite know it ran into something by triggering an event and passing the sprite with which it collided.

Open up `rpg.js` again and add the `tiled` component as defined in Listing 13-5 above the definition for `Q.Level`.

LISTING 13-5: The tiled component

```
Q.register('tiled', {
  added:function() {
    var p = this.entity.p;
    _(p).extend({
      wait: 0,
      delay: 0.15,
      tileX: Math.floor(p.x / tileSize),
      tileY: Math.floor(p.y / tileSize),
      dx: 0,
      dy: 0
    });
    this.direction = {};
    this.entity.bind('step',this,'move');
    this.entity.bind('removed',this,'removed');
  },

  move: function(dt) {
    var p -this.entity.p,
        stage = this.entity.parent;

    if(p.wait <= 0) {
      var destX = p.tileX, destY = p.tileY;

      if(p.attacking) {
          this.entity.trigger('attack',this.direction);
      } else if(p.dx || p.dy) {
        if(p.dx > 0) { destX += 1; }
        else if(p.dx < 0) { destX -= 1 };
```

continues

LISTING 13-5 *(continued)*

```
            if(p.dy > 0) { destY += 1; }
            else if(p.dy < 0) { destY -= 1; }

            if(!impassableTiles[stage.level.get(destX,destY)]) {
              var sprite = stage.level.sprites[destY][destX];
              this.direction.dx = destX - p.tileX;
              this.direction.dy = destY - p.tileY;
              this.direction.sprite = sprite;
              if(!sprite) {
                this.moved(destX,destY);
                this.setPosition();
                p.wait = p.delay;
              } else {
                p.wait = p.delay * 2;
              }
              this.entity.trigger(sprite ? 'hit' : 'moved',
                                  this.direction);
            }
          }
        } else {
          p.wait -= dt;
        }
      },
      setPosition: function() {
        var p =this.entity.p;
        p.x = p.tileX * tileSize;
        p.y = p.tileY * tileSize;
      },
      moved: function(destX,destY) {
        var stage = this.entity.parent;
        var p =this.entity.p;
        stage.level.sprites[p.tileY][p.tileX] = null;
        p.tileX = destX;
        p.tileY = destY;
        stage.level.sprites[p.tileY][p.tileX] = this.entity;
      },
      removed: function() {
        var stage = this.entity.parent;
        var p =this.entity.p;
        stage.level.sprites[p.tileY][p.tileX] = null;
      }
    });
```

This is one of the first significant components for Quintus that has been used in the book, so it's worth taking an in-depth look at what this component does.

The initial `added()` method, if you remember, is called when the component is initially added to a game object. As is often the case, this method does two main things: extend the properties hash of the game object and bind to some object events. Here the component adds in some properties to get the current tile location, movement delay, and movement direction. Next, it binds to the `step` and `removed` events.

The step event handler, which corresponds to the move method is the most complicated one. It has the responsibility to move the object if it's not waiting between steps. (This is tracked in the wait property.) It also checks for an attacking property that is used for timing when attacking another object.

Finally, the main check determines a destination *x* and *y* location, checks if there are any impassable tiles in the way, and then checks if there is a sprite in the way. If there is no sprite, the object is moved using two helper methods—moved and setPosition—and the delay is reset to prevent the object from moving too quickly. If not, the delay is reset and the sprite is added to the direction object. Finally, either a hit or a moved event is triggered, passing in the data in the direction object.

The direction object is the event object passed with every triggered event. It is reused from call to call to save on memory.

The helper method setPosition is used to update the *x* and *y* location of the object based in the tile location. The method moved keeps the level's sprites array in sync to make it easy to check for collisions at the tile level.

While you're in the component creation mood, you need to add another quick component called transition to the codebase. Add the code in Listing 13-6 below the definition of the tiled component.

LISTING 13-6: The transition component

```
Q.register('transition', {
  added: function() {
    Q.transitionDOM(this.entity.dom,'transform','0.25s');
  }
});
```

This simple component just adds transition support on the transform to allow smooth movement when objects are moved an entire tile.

The next component, which you should add directly below the transition component, is a camera component to track the user around the level. This is done simply by binding to the player's moved event and telling the stage to center on the player when it moves, as shown in Listing 13-7.

LISTING 13-7: The camera component

```
Q.register('camera', {
  added: function() {
    this.entity.bind('moved',this,'track');
  },
  track: function() {
    var p = this.entity.p,
        stage = this.entity.parent;
    stage.centerOn(p.x, p.y);
  }
});
```

The component can grab the stage from the entity, which has it as a parent, and then simply call the centerOn method to adjust the view.

Finally, the last component needs to grab user input. You can add this below the camera component definition. This component, called player_input, simply looks at the inputs and sets the p.dx and p.dy variables (used previously in the tiled component) to indicate the direction the player is trying to move. This component is listed in Listing 13-8.

LISTING 13-8: The player input component

```
Q.register('player_input', {
  added: function() {
    this.entity.bind('step',this,'input');
  },
  input: function() {
    var p = this.entity.p;
    if(Q.inputs['left']) { p.dx = -1 }
    else if(Q.inputs['right']) { p.dx = 1;}
    else { p.dx = 0;}
    if(Q.inputs['up']) { p.dy = -1 }
    else if(Q.inputs['down']) { p.dy = 1;}
    else { p.dy = 0;}
  }
});
```

Because the input system is abstracted away, the player_input component doesn't need to worry about where the input is coming from, whether it is the joypad or keyboard.

Adding in the Player

With all these components in place, up next is adding in a player class. This player class will represent the player as they move around the game and encapsulate all their functionality. All you need to do is subclass the Q.Sprite class, set some basic properties in the constructor, and add the components that were built in the last section.

Add the Q.Player class, as shown in Listing 13-9, below the components defined previously.

LISTING 13-9: The Player class

```
Q.Player = Q.Sprite.extend({
  init: function(props) {
    this._super(_({
      sheet: 'characters',
      frame: 65,
      wait: 0,
      z: 10,
      attack: 5,
      health: 40,
      maxHealth: 40,
      gold: 0,
```

```
      xp: 0
    }).extend(props));
    this.add('player_input, tiled, camera, transition');
  }
});
```

The player defines a number of initial properties that won't be used immediately, such as `health`, `maxHealth`, `gold`, and `xp`, but these will be used later in the chapter. As you can see, however, using components makes it easy to add reusable chunks of functionality to sprites without creating a deep class hierarchy.

To get a player on the screen, add the player to the stage in the level1 scene at the bottom of the file, and while you're there, add the transition component to the stage as well, so the stage can track the player smoothly.

```
Q.scene('level1',new Q.Scene(function(stage) {
  if(Q.width > 600 || Q.height > 600) {
    stage.rescale(2);
  }
  stage.level = stage.insert(
                  new Q.Level("level1.txt",stage)
                );
  stage.add('transition');
  var player = stage.insert(new Q.Player({ x: 1 * tileSize,
                                          y: 1 * tileSize }));
  player.camera.track();
  player.bind('removed',stage,function() {
    Q.stageScene('level1');
  });
}));
Q.stageScene('level1');
```

With these pieces in place, you should load the `rpg.html` file and have the player move around the stage in response to the keyboard arrow keys or the joypad. (The joypad won't actually be visible, but the player character will respond if you drag your finger around.)

Adding Fog, Enemies, and Loot

Wandering around an empty dungeon isn't a lot of fun for anyone but the most risk adverse adventurer. To make things more interesting, it's time to add in some enemies to battle with and some loot to pick up.

The first step is to add a sprite class for each of the different types of objects that are needed. In this case three different types of objects are created:

➤ Enemies for the player to attack

➤ Loot for the player to pick up

➤ A health fountain for the player to replenish their health

Each of these is a short sprite class that has an `interact` method that can dictate how the object interacts with the player.

Add the three sprite types to `rpg.js` below the `Q.Player` class, as shown in Listing 13-10.

LISTING 13-10: The Enemy, Fountain and Loot classes

```
Q.Enemy = Q.Sprite.extend({
  init: function(props) {
    this._super(_({
      sheet: 'characters',
      z: 10,
      health: 10,
      maxHealth: 10,
      damage: 5,
      xp: 100
    }).extend(props));
    this.add('tiled, transition');
    this.bind('interact',this,'interact');
    this.hide();
  },

  interact: function(data) {
    this.p.health -= data.damage;
    if(this.p.health <= 0) {
      this.destroy();
      data.source.trigger('xp',this.p.xp);
    } else {
      var damage = Math.round(Math.random() * this.p.damage);
      data.source.trigger('interact',
                          { source: this, damage: damage });
    }
    this.trigger('health',this);
  }
});

Q.Fountain= Q.Sprite.extend({
  init: function(props) {
    this._super(_({
      sheet: 'tiles',
      frame: 71,
      z: 10,
      power: 10
    }).extend(props));
    this.add('tiled');
    this.bind('interact',this,'interact');
    this.hide();
  },

  interact: function(data) {
    data.source.trigger('heal',{ amount: this.p.power });
  }
});

Q.Loot = Q.Sprite.extend({
  init: function(props) {
```

```
        this._super(_({
          sheet: 'items',
          frame: Math.floor(Math.random() * 30 * 9) + 150,
          z: 10,
          gold: Math.floor(Math.random() * 100)
        }).extend(props));
        this.add('tiled');
        this.bind('interact',this,'interact');
        this.hide();
      },
      interact: function(data) {
        data.source.trigger('gold',this.p.gold);
        this.destroy();
      }
    });
```

In each case the sprite consists of an `init` constructor function that sets up the object's properties and binds to the aforementioned `interact` method. Because each of the sprites are also selectively unhidden when the player is near, each is also hidden at the start.

The `interact` method for each of the elements is where the interesting behavior occurs. In the case of the `Q.Enemy` class, the user is viewed to be attacking the enemy when they interact. (This seems reasonable. Do you normally ask enemies for directions?) The method reduces the enemy's health by the passed-in amount and either dies a quick death or attacks the player. If the enemy dies, it triggers an `xp` (experience point) event on the player, which could be used to level-up the player. The attack also triggers a health event on the enemy, which is used in the next section to update a health bar.

The `interact` method for the `Q.Fountain` class calls a `heal` method on the player to restore some amount of health to the player. Finally, the `Q.Loot` class triggers a `gold` event on the player.

By binding to an event in each case rather than calling a specific method on the destination, the source and recipient are uncoupled, meaning that one doesn't need to know anything about the other and that interdependencies are reduced. It also means that components can easily hook into the system to add additional functionality to the core sprite behaviors.

For the player to interact with other elements, the class needs to be extended to handle collision and attack events. It also needs an `interact` method to handle when it is attacked by an enemy.

Modify the `Q.Player` class to match the code in Listing 13-11.

LISTING 13-11: The modified player sprite

```
    Q.Player = Q.Sprite.extend({
      init: function(props) {
        this._super(_({
          sheet: 'characters',
          frame: 65,
          wait: 0,
          z: 10,
          attack: 5,
          health: 40,
          maxHealth: 40,
```

continues

LISTING 13-11 *(continued)*

```
    gold: 0,
    xp: 0
  }).extend(props));
  this.add('player_input, tiled, camera, transition');
  this.bind('hit',this,'collision');
  this.bind('attack',this,'attack');
  this.bind('interact',this,'interact');
  this.bind('heal',this,'heal');
},

collision: function(data) {
  this.p.x += data.dx * tileSize/2;
  this.p.y += data.dy * tileSize/2;
  this.p.attacking = true;
},

attack: function(data) {
  var damage = Math.round(Math.random() * this.p.attack);
  data.sprite.trigger('interact',
                      { source: this, damage: damage });
  this.p.attacking = false;
  this.tiled.setPosition();
},

interact: function(data) {
  this.p.health -= data.damage;
  if(this.p.health <= 0) {
    this.destroy();
  }
  this.trigger('health');
},

heal: function(data) {
  this.p.health += data.amount;
  if(this.p.health > this.p.maxHealth) {
    this.p.health = this.p.maxHealth;
  }
  this.trigger('health');
}
});
```

The Player is sent an initial collision event when it runs into a sprite. (This is handled by the `tiled` component earlier.) It reacts to that event by moving half the distance into the square in question and setting the `attacking` property to `true`. The tiled component then sends an `attack` event a short time later. Receiving this, the Player calculates a random amount of damage based on their `attack` property and sends the `interact` event to whatever it ran into. If it's an enemy, that enemy absorbs the damage and either dies or returns the attack, triggering an interact event on the player.

The `heal` method does the reverse and increases the players' health by a set amount. In the case of both `heal` and `interact`, a `health` event fires off for later to use to indicate that the player's health has been changed.

Extending the Tile Map with Sprites

With the player class updated and the additional sprite classes created, all that's left is to update the Q.Level class to add sprites onto the board where necessary. In addition, the viewport for large browsers is currently too large and allows the player to see too much of the dungeon. A better option would be to narrow down the viewport so that map tiles are exposed only when the player is near them. If you remember, the Q.DOMTileMap class had an option to turn on and off the visibility of individual tiles, and that can now be used to slowly expose the dungeon as the player goes through it.

To get the additional sprites into the tile map, the legend Q.Level class needs to be extended to point to the new creator methods for the different types of tiles. These new methods, in addition to returning the appropriate tile, each insert an object into the stage. Add the code highlighted in Listing 13-12 to the Q.Level class.

LISTING 13-12: The final Level class

```
Q.Level = Q.DOMTileMap.extend({
  legend: {
    "X": "wall",
    ".": "floor",
    "m": "monster",
    "f": "fountain",
    "d": "door",
    "g": "gold",
    "s": "stairs"
  },
  init:function(asset,stage) {
    this.stage = stage;
    this.level = [];
    this.sprites = [];
    var data = Q.asset(asset);
    this.extra = [];
    _.each(data.split("\n"),function(row) {
      var columns = row.split("");
      if(columns.length > 1) {
        this.level.push(columns);
        this.sprites.push([]);
      }
    },this);

    this._super({
      cols:this.level[0].length,
      rows:this.level.length,
      sheet: 'tiles'
    })

    var tiles =[];
    for(var y=0;y<this.level.length;y++) {
      tiles[y] = [];
      for(var x =0;x<this.level[0].length;x++) {
        var square = this.level[y][x],
```

continues

LISTING 13-12 *(continued)*

```
                 frame = null,
                 method = this.legend[square] || "wall";

           frame = this[method](x*tileSize,y*tileSize);
           tiles[y].push(frame);
         }
       }
    this.setup(tiles,true);
  },

  insert: function(sprite) {
    this.stage.insert(sprite);
    this.sprites[sprite.p.tileY][sprite.p.tileX] = sprite;
    return sprite;
  },

  unfog: function(x,y) {
    for(var sx=x-2,ex=x+2;sx<=ex;sx++) {
      for(var sy=y-2,ey=y+2;sy<=ey;sy++) {
        this.show(sx,sy);
        if(this.validTile(sx,sy) && this.sprites[sy][sx]) {
          this.sprites[sy][sx].show();
        }
      }
    }
  },
  wall: function(x,y) { return TILE.WALL; },

  floor: function(x,y) { return TILE.FLOOR; },

  stairs: function(x,y) {
    this.startX = x;
    this.startY = y;
    return TILE.STAIRS;
  },

  gold: function(x,y) {
    this.insert(new Q.Loot({ x:x, y:y }));
    return TILE.FLOOR;
  },

  fountain: function(x,y) {
    this.insert(new Q.Fountain({ x:x, y:y }));
    return TILE.FLOOR;
  },

  monster: function(x,y) {
    var frame = Math.floor(Math.random()*64);
    this.insert(new Q.Enemy({ x:x, y:y, frame:frame }));
    return TILE.FLOOR;
  }

});
```

Although the code is long, each of the sprite methods is the same. It just creates a sprite of the wanted type, adds it to the stage, and then returns the floor tile that should be underneath the sprite. The stairs sprite is special because it marks the place where the player should start the level, and that starting position is stored in the startX and startY properties.

The unfog method also deserves a mention. Its job is to take a square of tiles and sprites around the player and make them visible by unhiding them as the play approaches. This allows the level to be slowly exposed as the player moves around. This method needs to be triggered in the camera component for it to work, so add the highlighted line to that component:

```
Q.register('camera', {
    added: function() {
      this.entity.bind('moved',this,'track');
    },
    track: function() {
      var p = this.entity.p,
          stage = this.entity.parent;
      stage.centerOn(p.x, p.y);
      stage.level.unfog(p.tileX,p.tileY);
    }
});
```

Next, the spot where the player is created needs to be updated to use the level's startX and startY position. Modify the level1 scene creation method to read

```
Q.scene('level1',new Q.Scene(function(stage) {
    if(Q.width > 600 || Q.height > 600) {
      stage.rescale(2);
    }
    stage.level = stage.insert(new Q.Level("level1.txt",stage));
    stage.add('transition');
    var player = stage.insert(new Q.Player({ x: stage.level.startX ,
                                             y: stage.level.startY }));
    player.camera.track();
    player.bind('removed',stage,function() {
      Q.stageScene('level1');
    });
}));
```

With those two changes, you can now wander around the dungeon attacking random monsters and picking up loot. Although this works, there's a major problem because you cannot tell how much health each of the enemies has left or how much gold and experience points (xp) you picked up. The next section remedies this issue as the game wraps up.

Adding a Health Bar and HUD

To wrap up the simple RPG, add in some visual feedback for how much health enemies have left and how the player is doing in terms of health, gold, and xp.

One of the nice things about building a DOM game is that it's easy to add new persistent elements onto the game. For the case of the health bar that you are about to add, a simple set of CSS rectangles should do the trick.

To make the health bar reusable, it's going to be created as a component that can be added to sprites and updated by listening to the `health` events that the sprites have strewn about.

Add the `healthbar` component in Listing 13-13 to the spot in `rpg.js` where the rest of the components are located, below the definition for the `player_input` component.

LISTING 13-13: The healthbar component

```
Q.register('healthbar', {
  added: function() {
    this.entity.bind('health',this,'update');

    this.bg = $("<div>").appendTo(this.entity.dom).css({
      width: "100%",
      height: 5,
      position: 'absolute',
      bottom: -6,
      left: 0,
      backgroundColor: "#000",
      border: "1px solid #999"
    }).hide();

    this.bar = $("<div>").appendTo(this.entity.dom).css({
      width: "100%",
      height: 5,
      position: 'absolute',
      bottom: -5,
      left: 1,
      backgroundColor: "#F00"
    }).hide();

    Q.transitionDOM(this.bar[0],'width');

  },

  large: function() {
    this.bg.css({ height: 20, bottom: -1 }).show();
    this.bar.css({ height: 20, bottom: 0 }).show();
    return this;
  },

  update: function(sprite) {
    this.bar.show();
    this.bg.show();
    var p = sprite.p;
    var width = Math.round(p.health / p.maxHealth * 100);
    this.bar.css('width',width + "%");
  }
});
```

You can see this component creates two `<div>`s and then an `update` method that sets the width of the inner `<div>` based on the health that the sprite in question has left. Both `<div>`s are hidden in the beginning because it's usual not to show a health bar unless the sprite has less than full health to keep the screen uncluttered. To add an animated effect to the bar decreasing, the Q.transitionDOM method is called on the bar to add a transition to its width.

To see the bar in action, add the health bar component to the Q.Enemy sprite as highlighted here:

```
Q.Enemy = Q.Sprite.extend({
  init: function(props) {
    this._super(_({
      sheet: 'characters',
      z: 10,
      health: 10,
      maxHealth: 10,
      damage: 5,
      xp: 100
    }).extend(props));
    this.add('tiled, transition, healthbar');
    this.bind('interact',this,'interact');
    this.hide();
  },
```

If you now go around the dungeon attacking enemies, you should see the health of enemies decrease as you attack them before they die.

The last bit of functionality needed is a HUD to display the player's health with the gold and xp that they picked up along the way. To achieve this the game reuses the health bar you just created (in a larger form, if you picked up on the previous large method) and adds in a new sprite to display stats on the screen called Q.Stat.

The game also launches an additional stage to be used as a container for the HUD elements so that the first stage is moved around to follow the player as needed.

Again, because this game uses DOM elements, it's easy to add text sprites into the game by just setting the content of the sprite's <div>. For the player health bar, the engine cheats by creating a dummy sprite of a set size and calls the large method on the healthbar component to size it up.

Add the definition for the two sprites, as shown in Listing 13-14, to rpg.js above the Q.load call.

LISTING 13-14: The Stat sprite

```
Q.Stat = Q.Sprite.extend({
  init: function(props) {
    this._super(_(props).extend({
      w: 100, h: 20, z: 100
    }));

    this.el.css({color: 'white', fontFamily: 'arial' })
         .text(this.p.text + ": 0");
  },

  update: function(data) {
    this.el.text(this.p.text + ": " + data.amount);
  }
```

continues

LISTING 13-14 *(continued)*

```
  });

  Q.PlayerHealth = Q.Sprite.extend({
    init: function(props) {
      this._super(_(props).extend({
        w: Q.width / 4, h: 20, z: 100
      }));
      this.add('healthbar');
      this.healthbar.large();
    },
    update: function(sprite) {
      this.trigger('health',sprite);
    }
  });
```

As you can see these two sprites are simple. The first sets some CSS on its element and then uses the jQuery `text` method to set the content of the `div`. The second `Q.PlayerHealth` sprite cheats a little bit by reusing the `healthbar` component from the last section but calls the helper method `large` to resize the bar larger. It then passes any update events it receives through to the health bar by triggering a health event.

Now for the grand finale: A new scene called `hud` must be set up that creates the HUD elements and binds the update methods so that they are updated. Next, the `level1` scene needs to launch the HUD scene when it is created and bind the appropriate events on the player to events fired on the HUD stage.

This all sounds more complicated than it actually is. Modify the code at the bottom of `rpg.js` to match the highlighted code, as shown in Listing 13-15, and you should get the wanted effect.

LISTING 13-15: The HUD scene

```
      Q.scene('hud',new Q.Scene(function(stage) {
        var health, gold, xp;
        health = stage.insert(new Q.PlayerHealth({ x: 0, y: 10 }));
        stage.bind('health',health,'update');
        gold = stage.insert(new Q.Stat({
                                text: "gold", x: Q.width-100, y: 10
                             }));

        stage.bind('gold',gold,'update');
        xp = stage.insert(new Q.Stat({ text: "xp", x: Q.width-200, y: 10 }));
        stage.bind('xp',xp,'update');
      }));

      Q.scene('level1',new Q.Scene(function(stage) {
        Q.stageScene('hud',1);
        if(Q.width > 600 || Q.height > 600) {
          stage.rescale(2);
        }
        stage.level = stage.insert(new Q.Level("level1.txt",stage));
        stage.add('transition');
        var player = stage.insert(new Q.Player({ x: stage.level.startX ,
                                        y: stage.level.startY }));
```

```
player.camera.track();
player.bind('removed',stage,function() {
  Q.stageScene('level1');
});

player.bind('health',stage,function() {
  Q.stage(1).trigger('health',player);
});

Q.stage(1).trigger('health',player);
player.bind('gold',stage,function(amount) {
  player.p.gold += amount;
  Q.stage(1).trigger('gold',{ amount: player.p.gold });
});

player.bind('xp',stage,function(amount) {
  player.p.xp += amount;
  Q.stage(1).trigger('xp',{ amount: player.p.xp });
});

}));
```

The level1 scene triggers events on the hud scene by calling the Q.stage(1) method to trigger the call. In the hud each of the three interface elements are created and then their update methods are bound to events on the stage.

Keeping the hud stage and the main level stage separate from each other makes it easy to reuse the hud for multiple levels and keeps each of the individual pieces smaller.

If you reload the game, you should now accumulate gold and attack random (although all equally difficult) enemy sprites. See Figure 13-2.

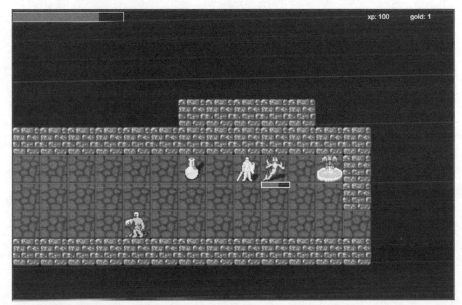

FIGURE 13-2: The final game (shown on an iPad).

With a few hundred lines of code, you've now built the backbone of a nethack-style CSS3-based RPG, as shown in Figure 13-2. There are a lot of features that can still be added to fill out the functionality, including enemy movement, different strengths and rewards from enemies, random levels and pathfinding, inventory, and all the other trappings of a good nethack-style RPG. If you want to keep hacking on it, the code is open source under the MIT license and on GitHub.

SUMMARY

In this chapter you built a game using CSS and DOM elements. There are more CSS3 features such as animations and 3-D transforms that haven't been covered that could fill another book. If you are looking for more things that you can do in CSS3, check out some of the resources in the bibliography. Although the new CSS3 features are neat, with hardware-accelerated canvas appearing on more and more devices and browsers, one of the primary advantages of CSS is its backward compatibility, so building a game from the ground up that relies on cutting-edge CSS features might not be the best idea. This chapter showed you how to build a game that works all the way back to IE6 on the desktop, whereas still providing a nice smooth-animated experience for newer desktop and mobile browsers.

14

Building Games with SVG and Physics

WHAT'S IN THIS CHAPTER?

➤ Understanding scalable vector graphics (SVG)

➤ Manipulating SVG from JavaScript

➤ Creating SVG sprites

➤ Implementing a physics engine

➤ Adding enemies and power-ups

WROX.COM CODE DOWNLOADS FOR THIS CHAPTER

The wrox.com code downloads for this chapter are found at www.wrox.com/remtitle .cgi?isbn=9781118301326 on the Download Code tab. The code is in the chapter 14 download and individually named according to the names throughout the chapter.

INTRODUCTION

SVG (scalable vector graphics) is the closest thing that HTML5 has to a direct competitor to Flash. SVG provides the capability to draw vector graphics that can be scaled, rotated, and transformed to your heart's content while still providing a scene graph to interact with, meaning SVG elements can receive mouse and touch events. This chapter uses SVG with a 2-D physics engine, called Box2d, which has been ported from C++ to JavaScript (by way of ActionScript) to create a physics playground and cannon game.

UNDERSTANDING SVG BASICS

SVG is an odd bird. It's been around since time eternal (1999), but it never caught on. One reason for this is that previously, Internet Explorer didn't support the standard, opting for its own proprietary Vector Markup Language (VML) for the same task. Until IE9 was released, using SVG meant cutting out IE users completely or using a library such as Raphael.js that supported both SVG and VML.

With the release of IE9, the future started looking up for SVG with the capability to build vector graphics in an HTML5-approved way. Mobile Safari along with Android 3.0 and up as well as the newest version of all the desktop browsers have excellent SVG support, so building a game that relies on SVG is a viable option provided you are okay with leaving out users of older versions of Internet Explorer and Android. Performance still leaves a little bit to be desired, however; so run some tests on your target platforms before committing to SVG as a game technology.

Getting SVG on Your Page

SVG is an XML-based markup language that provides support for a number of vector primitives, including text, rectangles, circles, ellipses, and arbitrary paths. These primitives can use different strokes and fills, including pattern and gradient fills. SVG also supports advanced features such as clipping, masking, compositing, and animation.

Browsers provide an overabundance of ways to place SVG on the page, including as the source in an `<img>` tag, linked from an `<embed>` tag, linked from an `<object>` tag, and embedded using an `<iframe>`, or dropped directly onto the page in an `<svg>` tag. Having all those options is a little confusing, but you don't actually need to know all of them. There are three separate use cases, each with a preferred embedding mechanism:

➤ First, if you just want a simple way to get an external SVG document on the page, use an `<img>` tag. You can't script the tag, and users of Firefox pre 4.0 will be out of luck (this is currently approximately 4% of Firefox users and getting smaller all the time), but it's the easiest way to put an SVG document onto the page that you just need to work as an image.

```
<img src='mydocument.svg' />
```

➤ Second, if you have an external SVG document that you want to script and interact with, use the `<embed>` tag, which enables you to reach into the document and add event handlers and the like:

```
<embed src="mydocument.svg" type="image/svg+xml" />
```

➤ Finally, the last and most common usage from a game development perspective is to embed your SVG document directly into the page:

```
<svg id="mysvg" xmlns="http://www.w3.org/2000/svg" version="1.1">
  <rect x="20" y="20" width="50" height="50" fill="black" />
</svg>
```

Often you want to start with an empty `<svg>` tag (much like the `<canvas>` tag) and add all your objects dynamically. This is how the Quintus engine will be extended in this chapter to support SVG. One thing you'll notice is the inclusion of the version attribute and the `xmlns` (short for XML namespace) attribute.

The namespace is important because you're embedding a different type of document into your HTML and need to tell the browser how to handle it. In this case the browser is clever enough to render the document without the namespace, but trying to create elements via JavaScript without the namespace won't work.

Getting to Know the Basic SVG Elements

As you saw briefly, SVG documents are simple XML documents that can be embedded directly into the page. You can also load an SVG document directly into the browser by loading it from a URL or your local machine.

Listing 14-1 shows a simple, hand-written SVG file embedded in an HTML5 document. You'll need the penguin.png file in your images/ directory to make it work yourself. The output of the file is shown in Figure 14-1.

LISTING 14-1: A simple SVG file

```
<!DOCTYPE HTML>
<html lang="en">
<head>
      <meta charset="UTF-8">
      <title>A Birdhouse</title>
</head>
<body>
<svg id="mysvg" xmlns="http://www.w3.org/2000/svg" version="1.1"
     width="400" height="400"
     viewBox="0 0 150 150" >
  <g transform="rotate(-5,75,75)">
    <rect id="rect" x="50" y="50" rx="5" ry="5"
          width="50" height="50" fill="black" />
    <circle id="circle" cx="75" cy="75" r="10" fill="#CCC"/>
    <path d="M 50 50 L 75 50 L 75 0 z"
          fill="black" stroke="#CCC" stroke-width="2"/>
    <polygon points="75,50 100,50 75,0"
          fill="#CCC" stroke="black" stroke-width="2"/>
  </g>

  <image xlink:href='images/penguin.png'
     width='32' height='32'
     transform="translate(75,75)"
     onclick="alert('Penguin Click');"Click
     ontouchstart="alert('Penguin Touch');" />
  <text x="75" y="125" text-anchor="middle"
        font-family="Verdana" font-size="10" fill="black" >
    A tilted birdhouse
  </text>
</svg>

</body>
</html>
```

As mentioned, SVG provides a number of different primitives for drawing. Unlike Canvas, after you create an element, it sticks around in the scene graph the same way that DOM elements do. You can move the element around by modifying its *x* and *y* properties or by adding a `transform` property. SVG elements can also have event handlers attached. If you click the image of the penguin on the desktop, you can trigger the `onclick` handler. If you touch it on a WebKit device, you'll trigger a "Penguin Touch" alert.

Each primitive element also has a set of properties specific to the element in question. Although a full overview of all the details of the SVG spec is out of scope for a single chapter, the following sections discuss some of the details of a few of the primitive elements used previously. If you want to learn more about SVG, check out the specification at `www.w3.org/TR/SVG/`.

A tilted birdhouse

FIGURE 14-1: An example SVG page.

<svg>

The base `<svg>` container element has already been briefly described, but a couple of additional attributes will be important later in the chapter. (Attributes in SVG are case-sensitive, so make sure you match the case shown in the text.) The `width` and `height` attributes are self-explanatory because they define the width and height of the element inside of the HTML document. The `viewBox` attribute (the "B" in box is capitalized) is interesting. It defines the portion of the SVG document that is visible inside of the SVG container. `viewBox` takes four integer parameters (separated by spaces, not commas):

```
<svg width='WIDTH' height='HEIGHT' viewBox="X Y WIDTH HEIGHT"> ... </svg>
```

As you may have figured out, from a game perspective you can use the `viewBox` as a camera into your game. If you set a `WIDTH` and `HEIGHT` in the `viewBox` that is smaller than the `WIDTH` and `HEIGHT` on the `<svg>` element, objects in the SVG container appear zoomed in. If you set the `WIDTH` and `HEIGHT` to be larger than the container, elements zoom out. Setting the `X` and `Y` parameters essentially pans the camera around the page.

If the aspect ratio of the `<svg>` element and the `viewBox` don't line up, how the content displays inside of the container depends on the value of the `preserveAspectRatio` attribute. The default options ensure that the content is scaled down, so the entire `viewBox` is visible inside of the container, with content centered in the *x* and *y* direction. `preserveAspectRatio` has a lot of configurable values, so if you need control over how elements display, you can see the full description of the available options on the w3.org website: `www.w3.org/TR/SVG/coords.html#PreserveAspectRatioAttribute`.

In most cases your game sets a viewport that matches the aspect ratio of the element, so you won't need to reconfigure `preserveAspectRatio` often.

Your SVG document must have a top-level `<svg>` tag, but it can also have child `<svg>` tags that can be transformed and moved independently.

<rect>

The `<rect>` tag defines a rectangle or a square. It takes a `width` and `height` parameter to define the size of the rectangle along with optional `rx` and `ry` parameters to add a border radius to the rectangle. The *x* and *y* locations indicate the top-left corner of the rectangle.

<circle> and <ellipse>

The `<circle>` tag defines a circle. It takes a `cx` and `cy` parameter, which defines the center of the circle, and then an `r` parameter that defines the radius. If you don't want a symmetric circle, you can also use the `<ellipse>` and define different *x* and *y* radii using `rx` and `ry` in addition to the center parameters.

<path>

The `<path>` tag is an extremely useful tag, which is the Swiss-army-knife of SVG that can be used to draw arbitrary paths and shapes. The `d` attribute sets the path data used to draw the object. The path data is a string in the form of commands followed by arguments. The example shown earlier to draw a triangle was as follows:

```
<path d="M 50 50 L 75 50 L 75 0 Z" fill="black"
      stroke="#CCC" stroke-width="2"/>
```

The `<path>` tag uses three commands:

➤ `M`: For absolute move to

➤ `L`: For absolute line to

➤ `Z`: To close the path

Using a lowercase `m` or `l` means the points provided after would be relative to the previous command instead of absolute positions (except in the case of an initial `m`, which would be interpreted as an absolute position regardless). These commands draw straight lines, but you can also draw cubic Bézier curves and quadratic Bézier curves using `C` and `S` or `Q` and `T` commands, respectively. Drawing Bézier curves by hand, however, is no fun, so you'll most likely want to generate your path using a program such as Adobe Illustrator or the open-source Inkscape, both of which export to SVG.

Again, for more details the w3.org specification documentation provides a comprehensive resource: `www.w3.org/TR/SVG/paths.html#DAttribute`.

<polygon> and <polyline>

The `<polygon>` and `<polyline>` elements are much like a version of the `<path>` element limited to straight lines. Each takes a `points` attribute that defines the set of points that makes up the shape. `<polygon>` elements are closed shapes where the last point is automatically connected back to the first while `<polyline>` elements have only strokes and aren't filled.

```
<polygon points="75,50 100,50 75,0"
         fill="#CCC" stroke="black" stroke-width="2"/>
```

As you can see, each point is defined as a comma-separated *x* and *y* value, and the points are separated by spaces.

<image>

You can also embed images in your SVG, but be aware that your bitmap-based images won't magically become vector-based and will show their roots if scaled too large. As shown in the previous example, `<image>` tags are written as follows:

```
<image xlink:href='images/penguin.png'  width='32' height='32' />
```

`<image>` tags require an `xlink:href` attribute to define the equivalent of the DOM `<img>` tag `src` and then an explicit `width` and `height`. If you don't provide a width and height, the element defaults to 0 by 0.

<text>

As you might expect, you can also draw text inside of SVG. You can set the font and size using the same names as CSS—`font-family` and `font-size`—as well as position the text with *x* and *y* or transforms. The actual text goes inside the text tag, as shown in the following example:

```
<text x="75" y="125" text-anchor="middle"
      font-family="Verdana" font-size="10" fill="black" >
   A tilted birdhouse
</text>
```

You can control the position of the text relative to the *x* and *y* location provided by using the `text-anchor` attribute with possible values of `start`, `middle`, or `end`. This corresponds to left-aligned, centered-aligned or right-aligned text.

Inside of the `<text>` element, you can use the `<tspan>` tag to mark up various pieces of text with different styles and positions, for example:

```
<text x="75" y="125" font-family="Verdana" font-size="10" fill="black" >
   A tilted <tspan fill="red">birdhouse</tspan>
</text>
```

This would result in the word *birdhouse* being colored red.

If you want dynamic multiline text, SVG is not the place to do it. You need to explicitly break up your text using `<tspan>` elements with modified *x* and *y* locations or use multiple `<text>` elements. Consider placing DOM elements over the SVG and using zIndex to control the layering order.

<g>

The final tag this section covers, `<g>`, is used to group elements together so that they can be styled and transformed as a unit. From the preceding example:

```
<g transform="rotate(-5,75,75)">
  <rect id="rect" x="50" y="50" rx="5" ry="5"
        width="50" height="50" fill="black" />
  <circle id="circle" cx="75" cy="75" r="10" fill="#CCC"/>
  <path d="M 50 50 L 75 50 L 75 0 z"
        fill="black" stroke="#CCC" stroke-width="2"/>
```

```
<polygon points="75,50 100,50 75,0"
       fill="#CCC" stroke="black" stroke-width="2"/>
</g>
```

All the elements inside of the `<g>` tag are rotated by -5 degrees around a center of 75, 75. Using groups allows you to define complicated subshapes that can be easily animated.

Transforming SVG Elements

All the elements discussed share an attribute called `transform` that enables SVG elements to be arbitrarily positioned, rotated, and scaled, much like the `transform` property available in CSS3.

The `transform` property takes a list of transforms to apply in sequence, one after the other. The available transforms are shown in Table 14-1:

TABLE 14-1: Transform Properties

TRANSFORM	DESCRIPTION
`translate(tx,ty)`	Move the element `tx` and `ty` units to the right and down. If `ty` is left out, it is assumed to be 0.
`scale(sx, sy)`	Scale the element `sx` times in the horizontal direction and `sy` times in the vertical direction. If `sy` is left out, it is assumed to be the same as `sx`. The number can be greater than 1 to make the element larger and less than 1 to make it smaller.
`rotate(angle)` `rotate(angle, cx, cy)`	Rotate the element by angle degrees. If `cx` and `cy` are provided, the element is rotated around that point; if not it is rotated around 0,0. Supplying a `cx` and `cy` is a shortcut to calling `translate(cx,cy) rotate(angle) translate(-cx,-y)`.
`skewX(angle)` `skewY(angle)`	Less useful for games, this does either a horizontal or vertical skew.
`matrix(a,b,c,d,e,f)`	This enables you to perform an arbitrary 2-D transformation using a 3 × 3 matrix. In 2-D, the row of the matrix is always 0,0,1 so only 6 values a–f need to be specified. Each of the preceding transforms can be expressed in matrix form, so setting the matrix explicitly provides a shortcut for applying arbitrary transforms.

Applying Strokes and Fills

All the vector elements shown previously can be given a stroke, which defines how the outline of the element is drawn, and a fill, which defines what the interior of the object looks like. (`<polyline>`s don't have interiors, so the fill doesn't apply.)

There are many stroke and fill properties available, but the most common ones are shown in Table 14-2.

TABLE 14-2: Stroke and Fill Properties

PROPERTY	DESCRIPTION
`stroke`	A color or reference to a gradient or pattern used to draw the outline.
`stroke-width`	The size of the outline.
`stroke-linejoin`	Set to one of `miter`, `round`, `bevel` or `inherit`, which defines how different line segments are connected. `miter` is the default, which defines a sharp angle.
`stroke-opacity`	A number between 0 and 1 defining the opacity of the outline.
`fill`	A color or reference to a gradient or pattern used to draw the fill.
`fill-opacity`	A number between 0 and 1 defining the opacity of the fill.

> **NOTE** *There are additional properties for creating dashed lines, fine-tuning the line joins, and controlling the fill algorithm that you probably won't use often, but you can check out the spec for all the available options at* www.w3.org/TR/SVG/painting.html.

The `stroke` and `fill` properties can be defined using simple CSS colors, but they can also use gradients. SVG supports two types of gradients: linear and radial. Linear gradients define `x1,y1` and `x2,y2` properties that represent the start and end of the gradient. Radial gradients define `cx,cy` and `fx,fy` properties along with an `r` radius that represents the center of the outer circle and the focal point of the gradient. Both types of gradients then use color `<stop>` tags to represent the color at specific percentages from the start to finish.

Gradients are created inside of a `<defs>` section and identified with `id` attributes. They are then referenced using the `id` preceded by a pound sign inside of the URL value.

All this makes more sense with an example. Listing 14-2 defines two gradients, a linear and a radial one, and uses them on two equal size squares. The result is shown in Figure 14-2.

LISTING 14-2: SVG gradients

```
<!DOCTYPE HTML>
<html lang="en">
<head>
  <meta charset="UTF-8">
  <title>SVG Gradients</title>
</head>
<body>
<svg id="mysvg" xmlns="http://www.w3.org/2000/svg"
```

```
            version="1.1" width="800" height="800" >
    <defs>
      <linearGradient id="linear-test"
                        x1="1" y1="0" x2="0" y2="0">
        <stop offset="5%" stop-color="black" />
        <stop offset="55%" stop-color="white" />
        <stop offset="95%" stop-color="black" />
      </linearGradient>
      <radialGradient id="radial-test"
                        cx="0" cy="0" r="1" fx="0" fy="0">
        <stop offset="5%" stop-color="black" />
        <stop offset="55%" stop-color="white" />
        <stop offset="95%" stop-color="black" />
      </radialGradient>
    </defs>
    <rect x="0" y="50" width="375" height="375" fill="url(#linear-test)" />
    <rect x="400" y="50" width="375" height="375" fill="url(#radial-test)" />
    </svg>
  </body>
  </html>
```

FIGURE 14-2: SVG gradients.

Both types of gradients also support a gradientUnits attribute, which determines what the units the x1,y1,x2,y2 and cx,cy,r,fx,fy attributes use. By default the objectBoundingBox value is used, which means that all values are expected to be in the range of 0 to 1. If the alternative option userSpaceOnUse is applied, the values would be set in the same range as the element on the Canvas.

SVG also supports pattern fills, which enable you to define a set of SVG elements to be used as a repeated fill pattern. The pattern is defined by a <pattern> element with an id that can take a width and height along with a viewBox that works the same way as described in the <svg> element. Inside the <pattern> element, you can draw the SVG element that makes up the pattern. The fill then needs to reference the id in the fill attribute the same way as with gradients. Again, an example makes this easier to understand. Listing 14-3 shows a pattern created with a circle and a diagonal polyline, which when applied to an ellipse results in what is shown in Figure 14-3.

LISTING 14-3: An example SVG pattern

```
<!DOCTYPE HTML>
<html lang="en">
<head>
  <meta charset="UTF-8">
  <title>SVG Patterns</title>
</head>
<body>
<svg id="mysvg" xmlns="http://www.w3.org/2000/svg" version="1.1"
width="800" height="800" >
 <defs>
    <pattern id="pattern-test" patternUnits="userSpaceOnUse"
             x="0" y="0" width="50" height="50"
             viewBox="0 0 10 10" >
      <circle cx="5" cy="5" r="5" fill="black" />
      <polyline points="0,0 10,10" stroke="white" stroke-width="2"/>
    </pattern>
  </defs>
  <ellipse fill="url(#pattern-test)" stroke="black" stroke-width="5"
           cx="400" cy="200" rx="350" ry="150" />
</svg>
</body>
</html>
```

FIGURE 14-3: SVG patterns.

Again the full specification has some less-used options you can take a look at that this book doesn't have space to cover.

Beyond the Basics

SVG is a large specification that includes a large number of additional pieces including Animation, Filters, Clipping, Masking, and Compositing that aren't going to be used in this chapter. However, there are a number of cases in which these features might be useful in game development, so take a moment to look through the full SVG specification if you are interested in learning more: www .w3.org/TR/SVG.

If you haven't taken a look at the specification yet, you should become familiar with it because going straight to the source is usually the best way to get answers quickly (often quicker than searching Google).

WORKING WITH SVG FROM JAVASCRIPT

As you might expect, SVG elements have an interface exposed via JavaScript that enables you to manipulate any SVG properties. Unfortunately, the method to do this is different than normal DOM elements, so jQuery can't do its normal thing. There are jQuery plug-ins for extending jQuery with SVG support, such as Keith Wood's jQuery SVG: `http://keith-wood.name/svg.html`.

However, rather than introduce another dependency, this section examines how to add and manipulate SVG documents directly. Doing so ensures that when SVG support is added to the Quintus engine in the next section that the engine doesn't get bogged down performance-wise with too many layers of abstraction. (The CSS3 RPG from the last chapter similarly used DOM methods directly when there was a performance advantage to do so.)

Creating SVG Elements

The general mechanism to create a new DOM node without using jQuery is to use the `document` `.createElement` method. Using this method to create an `<svg>` element on the page unfortunately won't quite do the trick. It will add an element called `<svg>` to the page, but that element will act just like a normal DOM element and won't have any SVG-like properties.

To create an SVG element dynamically, you need to use the less well-known `document` `.createElementNS`, which creates an element within the specified name space.

In the case of SVG, the namespace is defined as:

```
http://www.w3.org/2000/svg
```

To create an SVG element, you need to call `createElementNS` and pass in the SVG namespace:

```
var SVGNS = "http://www.w3.org/2000/svg";
var svg = document.createElementNS(SVGNS,"svg");
```

This element is now a normal SVG element that will render elements inside of it as proper SVG elements.

This pattern continues if you need to create other SVG elements. For example, to create a `<rect>` element, you would need to use `createElementNS` as well:

```
var SVGNS = "http://www.w3.org/2000/svg";
var rect = document.createElementNS(SVGNS,"rect");
```

Adding that `<rect>` to the `<svg>` element can be done using the standard `appendChild()` command:

```
svg.appendChild(rect);
```

This adds the child (`<rect>` in this case) to the end of the SVG container. Because SVG doesn't have the idea of a zIndex, the order of SVG elements in the container is actually quite important as later elements are drawn over previous elements.

Setting and Getting SVG Attributes

Armed with an `<svg>` container and the ability to create elements inside of that container, you might think that setting properties on those elements is as easy as setting the attribute the way you would on a DOM element:

```
// This won't work
rect.width = 500;
```

Unfortunately, that's not the case. Trying to set attributes on SVG elements directly isn't going to work. To set attributes you need to use the `setAttribute` or `setAttributeNS` methods, which set a named property either without a namespace or in a specific provided namespace.

Most `svg` element properties aren't in a namespace, so using the `setAttribute` method works for properties like `width`, `height`, and the like. For example, to set the width on a `rect` object, you could write:

```
// This will work
rect.setAttribute('width',500);
```

Some elements, however, do have properties in a namespace. One example is the `xlink:href` property from the `<image>` tag discussed earlier:

```
<image xlink:href='images/penguin.png'  width='32' height='32' />
```

To set this property, you need to use `setAttributeNS` and provide the correct namespace:

```
image.setAttributeNS("http://www.w3.org/1999/xlink","href","image.png");
```

There is an equivalent set of methods—`getAttribute` and `getAttributeNS`—that act as getters of specific attributes. To retrieve the `width` of a `rect` object, for example, you could write:

```
var width = rect.getAttribute('width');
```

Armed with the ability to create and manipulate SVG elements, it's now time to use an extension to the Quintus engine that adds support for SVG elements.

ADDING SVG SUPPORT TO QUINTUS

SVG elements are going to be added to the engine in much the same way that DOM elements were: by adding in a custom `Q.setupSVG` method to set up an `<svg>` element and then creating a custom `Q.SVGSprite` class that knows to create a corresponding SVG element.

The major complication to creating a game with SVG elements is that the collision detection becomes tricky if you allow elements made up of arbitrary polygons that can be rotated at random angles. Luckily, this isn't a problem that the engine must solve because the 2-D physics engine, Box2dweb that is going to be added in the next section is responsible for the details of handling collisions.

Creating an SVG Module

Armed with the knowledge of how to interact with SVG via JavaScript, it's time to create the Quintus SVG module. Open up a new file called **quintus_svg.js**, and enter the code from Listing 14-4.

LISTING 14-4: The base Quintus.SVG module

```javascript
Quintus.SVG = function(Q) {
  var SVG_NS ="http://www.w3.org/2000/svg";
  Q.setupSVG = function(id,options) {
    options = options || {};
    id = id || "quintus";
    Q.svg = $(_.isString(id) ? "#" + id : id)[0];
    if(!Q.svg) {
      Q.svg = document.createElementNS(SVG_NS,'svg');
      Q.svg.setAttribute('width',320);
      Q.svg.setAttribute('height',420);
      document.body.appendChild(Q.svg);
    }

    if(options.maximize) {
      var w = $(window).width()-1;
      var h = $(window).height()-10;
      Q.svg.setAttribute('width',w);
      Q.svg.setAttribute('height',h);
    }

    Q.width = Q.svg.getAttribute('width');
    Q.height = Q.svg.getAttribute('height');
    Q.wrapper = $(Q.svg)
                   .wrap("<div id='" + id + "_container'/>")
                   .parent()
                   .css({ width: Q.width,
                          height: Q.height,
                          margin: '0 auto' });

    setTimeout(function() { window.scrollTo(0,1); }, 0);
    $(window).bind('orientationchange',function() {
      setTimeout(function() { window.scrollTo(0,1); }, 0);
    });
    return Q;
  };
};
```

The `Q.setupSVG` method follows a lot of the same patterns as the `Q.setup` and `Q.setupDOM` methods before it. The major difference is that this method needs to use the `document.createElementNS` method and `setAttribute` to create and modify elements instead of trusty old jQuery or setting object properties directly.

The SVG namespace is set at the top of the page for later reuse. After you create an SVG element, it still behaves like a normal DOM element, so the `Q.wrapper` element can be created the same way it is normally created.

Adding SVG Sprites

Up next is the SVG sprite class, which shares a lot of the same ideas as the DOMSprite: It must actually create a browser element and set properties on that element to move it around. The difference here is that the type of element created is dependent on the shape that the SVGSprite is set to.

Open up `quintus_svg.js` again, and add the code from Listing 14-5 to the bottom of the file before the final closing curly brace.

LISTING 14-5: The Q.SVGSprite class

```
Q.SVGSprite = Q.Sprite.extend({
    init: function(props) {
      this._super(_(props).defaults({
        shape: 'block',
        color: 'black',
        angle: 0,
        active: true,
        cx: 0,
        cy: 0
      }));
      this.createShape();
      this.svg.sprite = this;
      this.rp = {};
      this.setTransform();
    },

    set: function(attr) {
      _.each(attr,function(value,key) {
        this.svg.setAttribute(key,value);
      },this);
    },

    createShape: function() {
      var p = this.p;
      switch(p.shape) {
        case 'block':
          this.svg = document.createElementNS(SVG_NS,'rect');
          _.extend(p,{ cx: p.w/2, cy: p.h/2 });
          this.set({ width: p.w, height: p.h });
          break;
        case 'circle':
          this.svg = document.createElementNS(SVG_NS,'circle');
          this.set({ r: p.r, cx: 0, cy: 0 });
          break;
        case 'polygon':
          this.svg = document.createElementNS(SVG_NS,'polygon');
          var pts = _.map(p.points,
                          function(pt) {
                            return pt[0] + "," + pt[1];
                          }).join(" ");
          this.set({ points: pts });
```

```
        break;

      }
      this.set({ fill: p.color });
      if(p.outline) {
        this.set({
          stroke: p.outline,
          "stroke-width": p.outlineWidth || 1
        });
      }
    },

    setTransform: function() {
      var p = this.p;
      var rp = this.rp;
      if(rp.x !== p.x ||
         rp.y !== p.y ||
         rp.angle !== p.angle ) {
        var transform = "translate(" + (p.x - p.cx) + "," +
                                      + (p.y - p.cy) + ") " +
                        "rotate(" + p.angle +
                                   "," + p.cx +
                                   "," + p.cy +
                                   ")";
        this.svg.setAttribute('transform',transform);
        rp.angle = p.angle;
        rp.x = p.x;
        rp.y = p.y;
      }
    },

    draw: function(ctx) {
      this.trigger('draw');
    },

    step: function(dt) {
      this.trigger('step',dt);
      this.setTransform();
    },

    destroy: function() {
      if(this.destroyed) return false;
      this._super();
      this.parent.svg.removeChild(this.svg);
    }
  });
```

The init method of Q.SVGSprite doesn't do anything particularly special except set some defaults on the shape and color of the default object. It then calls createShape to create the element. Finally, it calls setTransform to set the transform property on the SVG element.

The set method is a helper method that accepts hash properties and uses setAttribute to set each of them. Although there is some overhead with this and it probably shouldn't be used during each step, it does provide a convenient way to set multiple properties at once in a jQuery-like fashion.

The `createShape` method is perhaps the most interesting. The meat of the method is a `switch` statement that looks at the `p.shape` property and creates the appropriate type of SVG element.

For a `block` shape, it creates a `<rect>` element and sets the `width` and `height` properties on it. For a `circle` shape, it creates a `<circle>` element and sets the radius. It sets the center *x* and *y* location to `0` as the element will be moved with the `transform` property. Finally, for the `polygon` shape, it needs to create a string of points to pass in to the `points` attribute.

After `createShape` has created the element, the `createShape` method looks at the `fill` and `outline` properties to set the fill and the stroke.

The `setTransform` method again looks a good deal like the method of the same name from `Q.DOMSprite`. Its main job is to see if any of the property attributes have changed since the last frame and update the transform of the SVG element appropriately. To do this it first crafts a `translate` transform followed by a `rotate` transform set to rotate around the center of the object. The order here is important because changing the order of the two would result in a rotation around the point 0,0, which would lead to all sorts of problems down the road.

Creating an SVG Stage

The last bit of SVG functionality needed for the engine is to create an SVG-aware stage class that can act as a container for `Q.SVGSprite`.

To keep different stages separate, the `SVGStage` class creates its own child `<svg>` element that sits inside of the primary SVG element. The class also exposes methods to move the viewport around. The code for `Q.SVGStage` is shown in Listing 14-6 and should be added before the final closing curly brace at the end of `quintus_svg.js`.

LISTING 14-6: Q.SVGStage

```
Q.SVGStage = Q.Stage.extend({
  init: function(scene) {
    this.svg = document.createElementNS(SVG_NS,'svg');
    this.svg.setAttribute('width',Q.width);
    this.svg.setAttribute('height',Q.height);
    Q.svg.appendChild(this.svg);

    this.viewBox = { x: 0, y: 0, w: Q.width, h: Q.height };
    this._super(scene);
  },

  insert: function(itm) {
    if(itm.svg) { this.svg.appendChild(itm.svg); }
    return this._super(itm);
  },

  destroy: function() {
    Q.svg.removeChild(this.svg);
    this._super();
  },

  viewport: function(w,h) {
```

```
      this.viewBox.w = w;
      this.viewBox.h = h;
      if(this.viewBox.cx || this.viewBox.cy) {
        this.centerOn(this.viewBox.cx,
                      this.viewBox.cy);
      } else {
        this.setViewBox();
      }
    },

    centerOn: function(x,y) {
      this.viewBox.cx = x;
      this.viewBox.cy = y;
      this.viewBox.x = x - this.viewBox.w/2;
      this.viewBox.y = y - this.viewBox.h/2;
      this.setViewBox();
    },

    setViewBox: function() {
      this.svg.setAttribute('viewBox',
                            this.viewBox.x + " " + this.viewBox.y + " " +
                            this.viewBox.w + " " + this.viewBox.h);
    },

    browserToWorld: function(x,y) {
      var m = this.svg.getScreenCTM();
      var p = this.svg.createSVGPoint();
      p.x = x; p.y - y;
      return p.matrixTransform(m.inverse());
    }
  });

  Q.svgOnly = function() {
    Q.Stage = Q.SVGStage;
    Q.setup = Q.setupSVG;
    Q.Sprite = Q.SVGSprite;
    return Q;
  };
```

Listing 14-6 also includes the Q.svgOnly method that, much like the Q.domOnly method from the last chapter, replaces the non-SVG classes with their SVG counterparts for easier access.

The init, insert, and destroy methods should look similar to those from Q.DOMStage. The init method is responsible for creating the <svg> child element and adding it to the primary Q.svg object. The insert method augments the inherited method by calling appendChild to add the element to the stage's <svg> tag. Finally, destroy ensures the stage's <svg> tag is cleaned up when the stage is removed.

More interesting are the viewport, centerOn, and setViewBox methods. These allow you to use the stage's <svg> element's viewBox like a camera, panning by calling centerOn and zooming in and out by setting the width and height of the viewBox by calling viewport. The viewport method is also smart enough to check if the user has called centerOn previously; if so it uses the stored cx and cy coordinates to re-center the screen after it has reset the viewBox.

Finally, the `browserToWorld` method deserves some explanation. To determine where in the SVG world the user has touched or clicked, you need to transform that event's pixel position to the corresponding position inside of the world. This is made more difficult because the `viewBox` has been set and so the SVG element may only be partially zoomed in depending on the aspect ratio of the `view-Box` compared to the aspect ratio of the screen (imagine a portrait shaped `viewBox` on a landscape turned device—figuring out the pixel size of `viewBox` will take some doing).

All these complications mean that figuring out a priori of the SVG location of an event given the event's pixel location on the screen is a huge hassle. Luckily, the SVG spec provides a method that gets you halfway there. `getScreenCTM` returns the transformation matrix that goes the other way: from SVG units to screen units. However, with a little bit of matrix math, you can use the inverse of that matrix by calling `m.inverse()` to go the other way: from screen to SVG units.

Testing the SVG Class

With all this SVG engine code written, it's time to render something on the screen using SVG. The first step, as usual, is to create a template HTML file that loads the necessary JavaScript files. Create a file called **cannon.html**, and add the code in Listing 14-7.

LISTING 14-7: cannon.html

```
<!DOCTYPE HTML>
<html lang="en">
  <head>
    <meta charset="UTF-8">
    <meta name="viewport"
          content="width=device-width, user-scalable=0,
                   minimum-scale=1.0, maximum-scale=1.0"/>
    <title>SVG Test</title>
    <script src='jquery.min.js'></script>
    <script src='underscore.js'></script>
    <script src='quintus.js'></script>
    <script src='quintus_input.js'></script>
    <script src='quintus_sprites.js'></script>
    <script src='quintus_scenes.js'></script>
    <script src='quintus_svg.js'></script>
    <script src='cannon.js'></script>
    <style>
      * { padding:0px; margin:0px; }
    </style>
  </head>
  <body>
  </body>
</html>
```

Next create a file called **cannon.js** referenced in the preceding file. It eventually holds the Box2D-powered cannon game built later in this chapter, but for now, it just holds some basic SVG testing code.

Add the code in Listing 14-8 to cannon.js to the new file. Its goal is to test out the three different supported shapes—blocks, circles, and polygons—and test out the browserToWorld method to ensure you can add objects at points where the user touches the screen.

LISTING 14-8: Initial cannon.js file

```javascript
$(function() {
  var Q = window.Q = Quintus()
                    .include('Input,Sprites,Scenes,SVG')
                    .svgOnly()
                    .setup('quintus',{ maximize: true });

  Q.scene('level',new Q.Scene(function(stage) {

    stage.insert(new Q.Sprite({
      x: 100, y: 250, w: 500, h: 50
    }));

    stage.insert(new Q.Sprite({
      w: 30, h:20, x: 0, y: 100
    }));

    stage.insert(new Q.Sprite({
      r: 30, x: 50, y: 100, shape:'circle'
    }));

    stage.insert(new Q.Sprite({
      x: 120, y: 100, shape: 'polygon', color: "red",
      points: [[ 0, 0 ], [ 100, 0 ],[ 120, 25],[ 50, 50]]
    }));

    stage.viewport(400,400);
    stage.centerOn(100,200);

    $(Q.wrapper).on('touchstart',function(e) {
      var touch = e.originalEvent.changedTouches[0];
      if(touch.target.sprite) {
        touch.target.sprite.destroy();
      } else {
        var point = stage.browserToWorld(touch.pageX,touch.pageY);
        var box = stage.insert(new Q.Sprite({
                    x: point.x, y: point.y, w: 20, h: 20
        }));
      }
      e.preventDefault();
    });
  }));
  Q.stageScene("level");
});
```

Much of this code should start to look familiar. The initial call to `Quintus()` chains in some includes and then calls `svgOnly` to replace the Canvas sprites. Finally, `setup` is called with `options` passed in to maximize the SVG element to the size of the page.

The `scene` method sets up a scene called `level` that adds a number of sprites onto the page. These sprites, however, don't have assets or spritesheets as usual, rather they have a `shape` property defined (or use the default `block` shape) along with either a width and height or a radius (for circles). For the `polygon` sprite a set of points that define the points that make up the shape are needed.

The stage is set to a smaller viewport and is centered on the first larger block. If you want to see the effect this has, you can comment out those lines and reload the page.

Finally, the last bit of code checks for a new touch anywhere on the page. If it gets one, it first checks if the target element has a `sprite` property. If it does it destroys the sprite; if the target element doesn't have a `sprite` property, it uses the `stage.browserToWorld` method to convert the first changed touch to a point inside of the SVG element and then adds a new box sprite at that location.

The end result is that if you touch an existing object on the page, it removes it; whereas if you touch an empty spot on the page, it adds in a new block.

Now, open the page on a supported mobile browser (iOS or Android 3+) and give it a try. You should see one each of the three different types of sprites: blocks, circles, and polygon. You should also remove existing sprites by clicking them and add a new sprite by clicking a white spot.

The hit boxes for the SVG elements are precise: Unless you touch directly in the element, it won't disappear. (No square hit boxes here.)

ADDING PHYSICS WITH BOX2D

A bunch of static elements hanging out in space isn't a whole lot of fun. To make things more interactive and save the hassle of trying to figure out collisions on arbitrary convex polygons, Quintus adds support for a JavaScript port of a well-known 2-D physics engine called Box2D, which is available at: `http://box2d.org/`.

Box2D, created by Erin Catto, is written in C++, but a few adventurous souls manually created an ActionScript 3.0 port called Box2DFlash (available at `http://box2dflash.sourceforge.net/`) to allow Flash developers to use Box2D. A few other adventurous folks, taking advantage of the similarities between ActionScript and JavaScript, created an ActionScript to JavaScript converter that could convert the ActionScript code to JavaScript. Got all that?

The easiest to use and most up-to-date JavaScript port is currently box2dweb, available on Google Code: `http://code.google.com/p/box2dweb/`.

Although it's not a perfect fit for the JavaScript environment because Box2web creates a lot of objects each frame and so can challenge the JavaScript garbage collector, it works surprisingly well, and integrating it with the SVG code already written is straightforward.

There is no full documentation for Box2Dweb, but that's because it shares the same definitions as box2dflash, which has good API documentation: `www.box2dflash.org/docs/2.1a/reference/`.

The SVG code in this chapter was implemented specifically with the idea to add in a physics engine, but it stands to reason that a Canvas game might also want to do the same. For that reason, the physics functionality of Quintus is created as a set of components rather than as classes extending SVGSprite and SVGStage. The basic Canvas Sprite class and default Stage wouldn't use the physics components without adding in support for rotated sprites, but that's something that could be added to the base class easily.

Understanding Physics Engines

Before getting into the details of integrating a physics engine, you need to understand what a physics engine actually does.

The reason for integrating a physics engine into the system is that the way objects interact in the real world is quite involved. If you want to accurately simulate the behavior of a ball flying into a stack of blocks in 2-D space, which results in the tower tumbling over and blocks spinning and careening off each other, you'd be in for some work.

The first challenge would be to calculate pixel-perfect collisions between the various boxes and the ball. With boxes rotated at various angles, the simple box collision detection from earlier chapters would fall far short.

The next challenge would be to accurately simulate the behavior after a collision happens: Do the two boxes bounce off each other? Does a box slide on the ground or stick because of friction? How should an arbitrary polygon rotate when it's hit?

Physics engines handle both of these challenges for you. Your job is to define the shape and physical properties of the bodies that make up the simulation. From that point you can hand those details off to the physics, and tell it to advance the simulation by 1/60th of a second and give you the new angles and positions of objects. The physics engine can take care of updating objects according to their velocities and any forces (including gravity) acting on them and take care of properly resolving any collisions and interactions.

Implementing the World Component

Box2D, like many other physics engines, relies on a central `world` object to act as a container for any physical bodies that will be added to the game. Because this is fairly analogous to the `stage` object in Quintus, it makes sense for the `world` to be a component added onto the stage.

The method calls to set up and simulate a Box2D world are actually simple. All you need to do is create a new `Box2D.Dynamics.b2World` object, passing in the world's gravity. Then, for every frame, you need to call the world's `step` method with the time elapsed since the last time step and the number of velocity and position iterations. Running more iterations means that each simulation step is smaller, and the results of the simulation will be better and more stable (that is, objects won't go flying off or fall through other objects) at the cost of more rendering time.

Box2D provides an extensive API, which this book doesn't cover in depth, so instead the engine is just going to cherry-pick a limited subset of features to get some objects joyously flying around the screen.

The world component needs to make only few calls to get a Box2D world set up and running. To let objects and collisions reach back out into the engine, it's also going to need to add in a listener that has its callbacks triggered whenever there is a collision.

To start implementing the `Quintus.Physics` module, create a new file called **quintus_physics.js**, and add the code in Listing 14-9.

LISTING 14-9: The Quintus.Physics bootstrap

```
Quintus.Physics = function(Q) {
  var B2d = Q.B2d = {
      World: Box2D.Dynamics.b2World,
      Vec: Box2D.Common.Math.b2Vec2,
      BodyDef: Box2D.Dynamics.b2BodyDef,
      Body: Box2D.Dynamics.b2Body,
      FixtureDef: Box2D.Dynamics.b2FixtureDef,
      Fixture: Box2D.Dynamics.b2Fixture,
      PolygonShape: Box2D.Collision.Shapes.b2PolygonShape,
      CircleShape: Box2D.Collision.Shapes.b2CircleShape,
      Listener:  Box2D.Dynamics.b2ContactListener
    };

  var defOpts = Q.PhysicsDefaults = {
    gravityX: 0,
    gravityY: 9.8,
    scale: 30,
    velocityIterations: 8,
    positionIterations: 3
  };

  Q.register('world',{
    added: function() {
      this.opts = _(defOpts).clone();
      this._gravity = new B2d.Vec(this.opts.gravityX,
                                  this.opts.gravityY);
      this._world = new B2d.World(this._gravity, true);
      _.bindAll(this,"beginContact","endContact","postSolve");

      this._listener = new B2d.Listener();
      this._listener.BeginContact = this.beginContact;
      this._listener.EndContact = this.endContact;
      this._listener.PostSolve = this.postSolve;
      this._world.SetContactListener(this._listener);

      this.col = {};
      this.scale = this.opts.scale;
      this.entity.bind('step',this,'boxStep');
    },

    setCollisionData: function(contact,impulse) {
      var spriteA = contact.GetFixtureA().GetBody().GetUserData(),
```

```
            spriteB = contact.GetFixtureB().GetBody().GetUserData();

      this.col["a"] = spriteA;
      this.col["b"] = spriteB;
      this.col["impulse"] = impulse;
      this.col["sprite"] = null;
    },

    beginContact: function(contact) {
      this.setCollisionData(contact,null);
      this.col.a.trigger("contact",this.col.b);
      this.col.b.trigger("contact",this.col.a);
      this.entity.trigger("contact",this.col);
    },

    endContact: function(contact) {
      this.setCollisionData(contact,null);
      this.col.a.trigger("endContact",this.col.b);
      this.col.b.trigger("endContact",this.col.a);
      this.entity.trigger("endContact",this.col);
    },

    postSolve: function(contact, impulse) {
      this.setCollisionData(contact,impulse);
      this.col["sprite"] = this.col.b;
      this.col.a.trigger("impulse",this.col);
      this.col["sprite"] = this.col.a;
      this.col.b.trigger("impulse",this.col);
      this.entity.trigger("impulse",this.col);
    },

    createBody: function(def) {
      return this._world.CreateBody(def);
    },

    destroyBody: function(body) {
      return this._world.DestroyBody(body);
    },

    boxStep: function(dt) {
      if(dt > 1/20) { dt = 1/20; }
      this._world.Step(dt,
                       this.opts.velocityIterations,
                       this.opts.positionIterations);
    }
  });
};
```

`Box2D.Dynamics.b2World` is an example of one of the nicely namespaced objects that Box2D defines. The only problem with this namespacing is that it is a little burdensome to type. For this reason it's common to create a scoped set of shortened class names; Quintus follows this pattern as well by adding elements to a `B2d` object.

Next, the module defines a number of defaults that you can use to create and run the world. These include the *x* and *y* components of gravity, a scale multiplier, and counters for the number of velocity and position iterations to run.

The scale option is an interesting one. Although you might think that it shouldn't matter what size objects are, Box2D works better when objects are measured on a smaller scale, such as in the range of 1–10, as opposed to, say 100–1000. This means that the normal scale of pixels doesn't match well with Box2D's preferred object scale. That's the reason for the `scale` option in the defaults. It's a divisor used to scale down objects from a pixel-size scale to a smaller range. If you think of a single unit as a meter, and work with objects in the range of one to a few meters, you can hit the sweet spot for Box2D's calculations.

Next, the `added` method does the primary work to create the world. This is actually easier than it sounds. All that's needed is to create a gravity vector from the options hash and then create a new `B2d.World` object. With that, you could start adding entities to Box2D and simulate the world.

The only problem would be that you'd have no information about when an object collided with another object. Objects would still not overlap, as Box2D handles that part, but you'd lack any meaningful information about interactions that is necessary to build a game. (Do you want that bullet just bouncing off the enemy?) To get around this, Box2D provides the ability to set a contact listener. The `world` component ties into this and then passes forward any collisions it receives to the sprites that received the collision by triggering `contact`, `endContact`, and `impulse` events that correspond to Box2D's `BeginContact`, `EndContact`, and `PostSolve` callbacks. The first two—`BeginContact` and `EndContact`—are called when two entities start touching and stop touching, respectively.

The last, `PostSolve`, is called every time there is an impulse caused by another body. This can be quite often (imagine a ball rolling down a hill), so you must to be careful to keep the `impulse` event handlers quick. To keep the memory usage down, all the collision handlers also reuse the same `col` object among all the events and use the helper method `setCollisionData` to populate the data for the callbacks.

Each callback triggers three events, one on each object and then one on the stage. This allows you to centralize collision detection in the stage in lieu of on each object if necessary.

With the contact listener set, the `added` method binds itself to the stage's step method to trigger the `boxStep` callback. `boxStep` is responsible for stepping the world at the correct rate using the `dt` passed into the callback along with the number of velocity and position iterations.

The only other methods—`createBody` and `destroyBody`—act as proxies for the Box2D world's methods of the same name.

Implementing the Physics Component

With the world component built, up next is a component to add physics support to the sprites. This component will be called, not surprisingly, `physics`. Its job is to create a Box2d body that matches the sprite's size and shape when added, update the sprite's position based on Box2D's simulation, and remove the body when the sprite is removed.

Box2D supports two types of objects: static and dynamic. Static objects don't do anything but wait for dynamic objects to collide into them. They are also much lighter on the processor because they don't need to be actively updated each step. The component enables the creation of either type based on a `type` property, with the default being dynamic objects.

The main complexity of the component resides in the `insert` method, which is called after the sprite has been added to the stage. This method is responsible to create the `body` object that will be added into the Box2D world. Bodies have a number of properties, including a position and whether the body is static or dynamic. These properties need to be set to initial values before the body is created.

None of those properties, however, tell Box2D anything about the shape. That job is the responsibility of one or more fixtures added to the body. Each fixture must be a convex shape (meaning it has no dents), and although multiple fixtures are supported in Box2D, the physics component will just support one. The fixtures also have details like the object's density, friction, and restitution (bounciness).

To get the `physics` component into the engine, add the code in Listing 14-10 to the bottom of `quintus_physics.js`, before the final closing curly brace.

LISTING 14-10: The physics component

```
var entityDefaults = Q.PhysicsEntityDefaults = {
  density: 1,
  friction: 1,
  restitution: .1
};

Q.register('physics',{
  added: function() {
    if(this.entity.parent) {
      this.inserted();
    } else {
      this.entity.bind('inserted',this,'inserted');
    }
    this.entity.bind('step',this,'step');
    this.entity.bind('removed',this,'removed');
  },

  position: function(x,y) {
    var stage = this.entity.parent;
    this._body.SetAwake(true);
    this._body.SetPosition(new B2d.Vec(x / stage.world.scale,
                                       y / stage.world.scale));
  },

  angle: function(angle) {
    this._body.SetAngle(angle / 180 * Math.PI);
  },

  velocity: function(x,y) {
    var stage = this.entity.parent;
    this._body.SetAwake(true);
    this._body.SetLinearVelocity(new B2d.Vec(x / stage.world.scale,
                                             y / stage.world.scale));
```

continues

LISTING 14-10 *(continued)*

```
  },

  inserted: function() {
    var entity = this.entity,
        stage = entity.parent,
        scale = stage.world.scale,
        p = entity.p,
        ops = entityDefaults,
        def = this._def = new B2d.BodyDef,
        fixtureDef = this._fixture = new B2d.FixtureDef;

    def.position.x = p.x / scale;
    def.position.y = p.y / scale;
    def.type = p.type == 'static' ?
               B2d.Body.b2_staticBody :
               B2d.Body.b2_dynamicBody;
    def.active = true;

    this._body = stage.world.createBody(def);
    this._body.SetUserData(entity);
    fixtureDef.density = p.density || ops.density;
    fixtureDef.friction = p.friction || ops.friction;
    fixtureDef.restitution = p.restitution || ops.restitution;

    switch(p.shape) {
      case "block":
        fixtureDef.shape = new B2d.PolygonShape;
        fixtureDef.shape.SetAsBox(p.w/2/scale, p.h/2/scale);
        break;
      case "circle":
        fixtureDef.shape = new B2d.CircleShape(p.r/scale);
        break;
      case "polygon":
        fixtureDef.shape = new B2d.PolygonShape;
        var pointsObj = _.map(p.points,function(pt) {
          return { x: pt[0] / scale, y: pt[1] / scale };
        });
        fixtureDef.shape.SetAsArray(pointsObj, p.points.length);
        break;
    }

    this._body.CreateFixture(fixtureDef);
    this._body._bbid = p.id;
  },
  removed: function() {
    var entity = this.entity,
        stage = entity.parent;
    stage.world.destroyBody(this._body);
  },
  step: function() {
    var p = this.entity.p,
        stage = this.entity.parent,
        pos = this._body.GetPosition(),
```

```
        angle = this._body.GetAngle();
      p.x = pos.x * stage.world.scale;
      p.y - pos.y * stage.world.scale;
      p.angle = angle / Math.PI * 180;
    }
  });
```

When this component is added to a sprite, it first checks if the sprite has already been added to a stage. If so it calls `inserted` immediately; otherwise, it waits until the `inserted` event is triggered.

The bulk of the code for the `physics` component, as you can see, is in the `inserted` method. This method creates the Box2D body, sets up the fixture definition based on the shape of the object, and creates the fixture on the body.

Two helper methods—`position` and `velocity`—let you set those properties onto the sprite's body. Both of those methods also call `SetAwake(true)` on the body. Box2D puts objects that aren't moving and causing collisions "asleep" after a period of time to save on CPU cycles. To ensure that the object "wakes up" and starts responding to forces again when it is artificially moved, `SetAwake` needs to be called manually. (Normally, box 2D handles this for you anytime an object is involved in a collision.)

The `removed` method simply ensures that the body is destroyed from the Box2D world, in addition to the sprite being removed from the screen.

Finally the `step` method, which is called after every step, has the responsibility to translate the position and angle of the body in the Box2D back into the position of the sprite, taking into consideration the scale property discussed earlier.

Adding Physics to the Example

With the physics component wrapped up, it's time to see the Box2D in action. This can be done fairly simply by adding the `world` component to the stage and the `physics` component to each of the sprites. First, open `cannon.html` and add Box2dWeb and the `quintus_physics.js` file to the HTML file as shown here (you'll need to grab a copy of Box2dWeb-2.1.a.3.js from the chapter code or download your own version):

```
<script src='quintus_sprites.js'></script>
<script src='quintus_scenes.js'></script>
<script src='quintus_svg.js'></script>
<script src='Box2dWeb-2.1.a.3.js'></script>
<script src='quintus_physics.js'></script>
<script src='cannon.js'></script>
```

Update the highlighted code in `cannon.js`, as shown in Listing 14-11, to add physics support to the SVG example.

LISTING 14-11: Adding physics to the SVG example

```
$(function() {
  var Q = window.Q = Quintus()
                   .include('Input,Sprites,Scenes,SVG,Physics')
                   .svgOnly()
```

continues

LISTING 14-11 *(continued)*

```
                        .setup('quintus',{ maximize: true });

    Q.scene('level',new Q.Scene(function(stage) {

      stage.insert(new Q.Sprite({
        x: 100, y: 250, w: 500, h: 50, type:"static"
      }));
      stage.insert(new Q.Sprite({
        w: 30, h:20, x: 0, y: 100
      }));
      stage.insert(new Q.Sprite({
        r: 30, x: 50, y: 100, shape:'circle'
      }));

      stage.insert(new Q.Sprite({
        x: 120, y: 100, shape: 'polygon', color: "red",
        points: [[ 0, 0 ], [ 100, 0 ],[ 120, 25],[ 50, 50]]
      }));

      stage.add("world");
      stage.each(function() { this.add("physics"); });

      stage.viewport(400,400);
      stage.centerOn(100,200);
      $(Q.wrapper).on('touchstart',function(e) {
        var touch = e.originalEvent.changedTouches[0];
        if(touch.target.sprite) {
          touch.target.sprite.destroy();
        } else {
          var point = stage.browserToWorld(touch.pageX,touch.pageY);
          var box = stage.insert(new Q.Sprite({
            x: point.x, y: point.y, w: 20, h: 20
          }));
          box.add("physics");
          box.bind("contact",function(sprite) {
            sprite.set({fill:"blue"});
          });
        }
        e.preventDefault();
      });
    });
```

The first block also needs to be updated to type static so that it can act as a platform for the other objects. Finally, the box elements added when you touch on an empty part of the screen add in a listener to the contact event to turn any object they touch blue. The result is shown in Figure 14-4.

CREATING A CANNON SHOOTER

With physics and SVG in Quintus, you now have all the pieces you need to build a simple physics-based, knock-things-down game. (Box2D, after all, is the 2-D physics engine that powered *Angry Birds*.)

FIGURE 14-4: Box2D Physics applied to SVG.

The fun part of physics-based gameplay is that as a developer you don't need to do much to get the basic functionality working: The physics engine handles a lot of it for you. The flip side of this, however, is that the physics-based games require a lot of parameter tweaking to be fun and work well.

Planning the Game

Using the physics components built in this chapter, the idea behind the cannon game is quite simple: Throw some round objects around the page trying to hit some small round targets.

The game uses the location of a touch to control the angle of the cannon and release a cannon ball whenever the touch is released. (On a desktop `mousemove` and `mouseup` events are used.)

The cannon is a polygon sprite that won't have the physics component enabled, so it can move and adjust as necessary. It fires `Q.CannonBall` sprites that have physics enabled, so they can collide with everything else.

Finally, the `Q.Target` object is just a small, pink ball that has physics turned on. It listens to its `contact` event and checks if the object it is in contact with is a `Q.CannonBall`. If it is, it can destroy itself and update the counter of the number of targets left on the page. When that number reaches 0, it restarts the level. In a real game it would be time to move to the next level. Check out Figure 14-5 for an in-game screen shot.

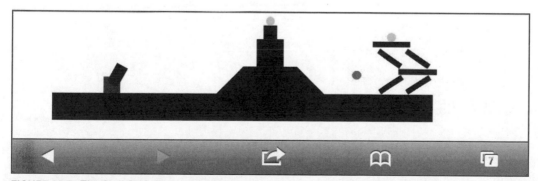

FIGURE 14-5: The final SVG Cannon shooter.

Building the Necessary Sprites

It's time to create the final game code. Open `cannon.js` and rip out all the existing code. The first pieces of code needed are the three sprite classes described in the last section: the `Q.CannonBall`, the `Q.Cannon`, and the `Q.Target`. Add the code in Listing 14-12 to the top of the `cannon.js` file, below the initial Quintus setup code.

LISTING 14-12: Cannon sprites

```
$(function() {
  var Q = window.Q = Quintus()
                    .include('Input,Sprites,Scenes,SVG,Physics')
                    .svgOnly()
                    .setup('quintus',{ maximize: true });


  Q.CannonBall = Q.Sprite.extend({
    init: function(props) {
      this._super({
        shape: 'circle',
        color: 'red',
        r: 8,
        restitution: 0.5,
        density: 4,
        x: props.dx * 50 + 10,
        y: props.dy * 50 + 210,
        seconds: 5
      });
      this.add('physics');
      this.bind('step',this,'countdown');
    },

    countdown: function(dt) {
      this.p.seconds -= dt;
      if(this.p.seconds < 0) {
        this.destroy();
      } else if(this.p.seconds < 1) {
        this.set({ "fill-opacity": this.p.seconds });
      }
    }
  });

  Q.Cannon = Q.Sprite.extend({
    init: function(props) {
      this._super({
        shape:'polygon',
        color: 'black',
        points: [[ 0,0 ], [0,-5], [5,-10], [8, -11], [40, -11],
                 [ 40, 11], [8, 11], [5, 10], [0, 5] ],
        x: 10,
        y: 210
      });
```

```
      },

      fire: function() {
        var dx = Math.cos(this.p.angle / 180 * Math.PI),
            dy = Math.sin(this.p.angle / 180 * Math.PI),
            ball = new Q.CannonBall({ dx: dx, dy: dy, angle: this.p.angle });
        Q.stage().insert(ball);
        ball.physics.velocity(dx*400,dy*400);
      }
    });

    var targetCount = 0;
    Q.Target = Q.Sprite.extend({
      init: function(props) {
        this._super(_.extend(props,{
          shape: 'circle',
          color: 'pink',
          r: 8
        }));
        targetCount++;
        this.add('physics');
        this.bind('contact',this,'checkHit');
      },

      checkHit: function(sprite) {
        if(sprite instanceof Q.CannonBall) {
          targetCount--;
          this.parent.remove(this);
          if(targetCount == 0) { Q.stageScene('level'); }
        }
      }
    });
  });
```

As expected, the code for each of the three sprites is quite short, consisting of mostly property setup code.

The Q.CannonBall class, which represents the ball fired from the cannon, has only one additional method, countdown, which ensures that the ball is removed from the page after five seconds. It also makes the ball fade out when there is less than 1 second left in its lifetime. The initial position x and y are set by taking the base position of the cannon and using the passed-in dx and dy values calculated from the angle of the cannon when it is fired.

The Q.Cannon class is defined as a cannon-like polygon. As mentioned, it doesn't need the physics component added because it won't be partaking in any collisions but will be controlled by having its angle set. As such the points passed in are set in such a way that rotating the polygon rotates it around the base of the cannon because the base is set to the point 0,0. The only additional method on the cannon is the fire method, which calculates the position of the tip of the cannon using the angle and the sin and cos methods.

If you remember your high-school geometry, cos returns a number from 0 to 1 that represents the horizontal components of a right triangle with a hypotenuse of length 1. sin can do the same thing for the vertical component. This means the tip of the cannon, so the starting point for the cannonball can be calculated by multiplying `dx` and `dy` by the length of the cannon plus some space for the radius of the cannonball, which is exactly what the `Q.CannonBall` class does.

The `fire` method then inserts the newly-created cannon ball into the stage and then assigns it a velocity using the calculated `dx` and `dy` values so that the ball flies in the correct direction based on the angle of the cannon.

Finally, the `Q.Target` object just creates a small, pink ball that listens for a `contact` event and checks if the thing hitting it is a cannon ball. If so, it removes itself from its parent and checks if there are any targets left. If not the level is restarted. Because the contact event happens during the world step loop, the sprite needs to be careful not to destroy itself immediately (which is what would happen if it called `this.destroy()`). Instead it calls remove on the parent, which cues the sprite up to be removed at the end of the step.

Gathering User Input and Finishing the Game

The last bit of the game is simply to grab the user's input to control the angle of the cannon and set up some blocks and targets in an interesting formation on the page.

The code uses a single listener to move the cannon angle that runs on `touchstart` and `touchmove` on a mobile and `mousemove` on a desktop. Then the user lifts up their finger or releases the mouse, and the game fires the cannon at the previously-calculated angle.

Next, the scene is set up with a number of different blocks for the user to knock down and a couple of targets to aim at. Add the code in Listing 14-13 to the bottom of `cannon.js` before the final curly brace.

LISTING 14-13: The rest of the cannon code

```
$(Q.wrapper).on('touchstart touchmove mousemove',function(e) {
  var stage = Q.stage(0),
      cannon = stage.cannon,
      touch = e.originalEvent.changedTouches ?
              e.originalEvent.changedTouches[0] : e,
      point = stage.browserToWorld(touch.pageX,touch.pageY);

  var angle = Math.atan2(point.y - cannon.p.y,
                         point.x - cannon.p.x);
  cannon.p.angle = angle * 180 / Math.PI;
  e.preventDefault();
});

$(Q.wrapper).on('touchend mouseup',function(e) {
  Q.stage(0).cannon.fire();
  e.preventDefault();
});

Q.scene('level',new Q.Scene(function(stage) {
```

```
targetCount = 0;
stage.add("world");
stage.insert(new Q.Sprite({
  x: 250, y: 250, w: 700, h: 50, type:"static"
}))

stage.insert(new Q.Sprite({ w: 10, h:50, x: 500, y: 200 }));
stage.insert(new Q.Sprite({ w: 10, h:50, x: 550, y: 200 }));
stage.insert(new Q.Sprite({ w: 70, h:10, x: 525, y: 170 }));
stage.insert(new Q.Sprite({ w: 10, h:50, x: 500, y: 130 }));
stage.insert(new Q.Sprite({ w: 10, h:50, x: 550, y: 130 }));
stage.insert(new Q.Sprite({ w: 70, h:10, x: 525, y: 110 }));

stage.insert(new Q.Sprite({
  points: [[ 0,0 ], [ 50, -50 ],[150, -50],[200,0]],
  x: 200,
  y: 225,
  type:'static',
  shape: 'polygon'
}));

stage.insert(new Q.Sprite({ w: 50, h:50, x: 300, y: 150 }));
stage.insert(new Q.Sprite({ w: 25, h:25, x: 300, y: 115 }));

stage.each(function() { this.add("physics"); });

stage.insert(new Q.Target({ x: 525, y: 90 }));
stage.insert(new Q.Target({ x: 300, y: 90 }));
stage.insert(new Q.Sprite({ w: 30, h:30, x: 10, y: 210,
                            color: 'blue' }));

stage.cannon = stage.insert(new Q.Cannon());
stage.viewport(600,400);
stage.centerOn(300,100);

}));
Q.stageScene("level");
```

As you can see there's not much new here from the previous examples. The touchstart handler has a little bit of math to calculate the angle of the cannon using atan2 (this was discussed when calculating the angle of the joypad), but other than that, the event handlers don't have any tricks up their sleeves. They are positioned outside of the level definition, as the level may be reset (or you might want to define multiple levels), and in lieu of unbinding the handlers and rebinding, the same handler can be used over and over again provided it doesn't need any local variables from the scene definition method. To get around this the cannon object is stored as a property of the stage.

If you have the desire, there's plenty left that could be added to the game, including multiple levels, points, and a limit on the number of cannonballs the user can fire. You can also use the impulse handler to track the force of the contact with the targets and remove them only when they are impacted with enough force to prevent a slowly rolling cannonball from doing damage.

SUMMARY

You covered a lot of ground, learning how to use SVG to create a game with arbitrary shapes and how to wire those shapes to a 2-D physics engine. There's still lots of details in Box2D, including joints and impulses, that this chapter didn't cover, but the basics should be enough to build a simple game (or maybe the next Angry Birds!). SVG is still a spec that's flying a little bit under the radar from a game development perspective. As soon as performance reaches an acceptable level across devices, you'll likely see a lot more games make use of SVG given the flexibility it provides to draw arbitrary vector elements with a browser-provided scene graph. Advanced features like filters and animations are also becoming better supported, so expect to see lots more cool SVG demos coming in the near future.

PART V
HTML5 Canvas

15

Learning Canvas, the Hero of HTML5

WHAT'S IN THIS CHAPTER?

➤ Adding and sizing the canvas element

➤ Creating images from Canvas

➤ Drawing images, text, and paths

➤ Creating gradients and patterns

➤ Using transforms

➤ Learning additional Canvas effects

WROX.COM CODE DOWNLOADS FOR THIS CHAPTER

The wrox.com code downloads for this chapter are found at www.wrox.com/remtitle.cgi?isbn=9781118301326 on the Download Code tab. The code is in the chapter 15 download and individually named according to the names throughout the chapter.

INTRODUCTION

This chapter examines the Canvas API in depth. Although you've seen in the past two chapters that you can build HTML5 games using technologies besides Canvas, from a game perspective Canvas still remains the most flexible technology to build a game with. Previous chapters have shown how you can use Canvas to make games using bitmapped spritesheets. Canvas, however, offers more than just a way to draw some images. It has a full repertoire of vector drawing methods for drawing shapes and curves along with support for text, transforms, and a variety of composition modes.

GETTING STARTED WITH THE CANVAS TAG

You've already seen that getting a `<canvas>` element onto your page is as easy as adding the element into your HTML document with the `width` and `height` attributes:

```
<canvas id="mycanvas" width='640' height='480'></canvas>
```

This creates an element 640 pixels wide by 480 pixels tall on the page, and by default the CSS width and height of the `<canvas>` element are set up to match the pixel width and height.

Understanding CSS and Pixel Dimensions

The CSS dimensions and pixel dimensions of the page don't have to be the same, however. You can set the CSS width and height (which determines the size of the element on the page) completely independent of the pixel width and height. To make this clear, Listing 15-1 shows some code that puts a random colored, 1-pixel rectangle at every pixel position of each of four different pixel-sized Canvas elements. All canvas elements are set—via a CSS `<style>` tag—to 200 pixels wide by 200 pixels tall.

LISTING 15-1: Examining CSS size versus pixel size

```
<script src='jquery.min.js'></script>
<style>
 canvas { width: 200px; height: 200px; }
</style>

<canvas width="2" height="2"></canvas>
<canvas width="10" height="10"></canvas>
<canvas width="50" height="50"></canvas>
<canvas width="10" height="100"></canvas>

<script>
  $("canvas").each(function() {
    var ctx = this.getContext("2d");
    for(var y=0,h=this.height;y<h;y++) {
      for(var x=0,w=this.width;x<w;x++) {
        var r = Math.floor(Math.random()*255),
            g = Math.floor(Math.random()*255),
            b = Math.floor(Math.random()*255);
        ctx.fillStyle = "rgb(" + r + "," + g + "," + b + ")";
        ctx.fillRect(x,y,1,1);
      }
    }
  });
</script>
```

Figure 15-1 shows the result of running this code. Notice that although all canvas elements are set to the same size on the page, they each have different pixel densities.

You can also notice on the first two elements that when the canvas element is scaled up, the browser attempts to smooth the generated image between pixels. By default all modern browsers apply either bicubic (IE) or bilinear (everyone else) upsampling algorithms to images to make them look smoother when shown at a size larger than their pixel dimensions. This upsampling rule also applies to canvas tags, so if you set the width and height of the element to be larger than the pixel dimensions, some upsampling occurs.

> **NOTE** *Bicubic and bilinear upsampling are two algorithms for taking an image of a certain size and making it look better when scaled up. Without any upsampling the larger image would have a "jagged" look made up of larger pixels. Both algorithms use a method of interpolating colors so that the larger image appears smooth and not jagged, at a cost of some processing time and a loss of detail in the final image. Bicubic tends to do a better job at preserving detail than bilinear but can cause strange "halo" effects on occasion.*

This is usually okay, but if you create an 8-bit retro game, you may prefer to have a crisper pixelated look. To support this, some browsers have support for a CSS property called `image-rendering` that gives a small modicum of control over the resampling algorithm. As of this writing this is possible only in Firefox and Internet Explorer, but WebKit has merged a patch into its nightly builds, so support in Safari, iOS, Chrome, and Chrome for Android should be available by the time you read this. The goal is to force the browser to use the faster nearest-neighbor algorithm, which doesn't do any interpolation between pixels. Only Microsoft enables you to explicitly set the algorithm to use, whereas the other browsers give this style different names.

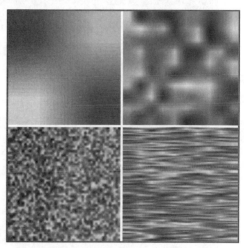

FIGURE 15-1: Canvas CSS versus pixel size.

To make this work, you must be in vendor prefix land for a while, and Microsoft is still going its own way with a `-ms-interpolation-mode` property, but the following CSS style should future-proof you for when WebKit adds support:

```
canvas {
    image-rendering: -moz-crisp-edges;          /* Firefox 6.0+ */
    image-rendering: -webkit-optimize-contrast; /* Webkit */
    image-rendering: optimize-contrast;         /* Standards compliant */
    -ms-interpolation-mode: nearest-neighbor;   /* MS Specific extension*/
}
```

Figure 15-2 shows how this looks in Firefox 11; the edges are crisper.

As discussed in Chapter 6, "Being a Good Mobile Citizen," CSS pixels don't correspond to display pixels on high-resolution devices such as the iPhone 4, iPad 3, and Galaxy Nexus. This means that if you leave the canvas element at its default resolution without setting a CSS width, you wouldn't be using the display to its best capability. This means that text drawn on the canvas element, for example, won't be crisp.

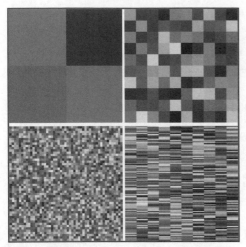

FIGURE 15-2: Resized Canvas with crisp edges.

To get around this, you can check for a property on the window variable called `window` `.devicePixelRatio`, which can give you the multiplier of the ratio of a device to CSS pixels. Using that multiplier you can scale up the canvas element's pixel size while keeping the CSS size fixed. By adding in a `scale` onto the context, your game won't need to know that the `<canvas>` element has been rescaled, and you can continue to use CSS pixels to position elements in the game. Listing 15-2 shows how to do this.

LISTING 15-2: Rescaling for high-resolution devices

```
var $canvas = $("#mycanvas"),
    Canvas = $canvas[0],
    ctx = canvas.getContext("2d");

if (window.devicePixelRatio) {
  var pixelWidth = canvas.width,
      pixelHeight = canvas.height;

  canvas.width = pixelWidth * window.devicePixelRatio;
  canvas.height = pixelHeight * window.devicePixelRatio;

  $canvas.css({ width: pixelWidth, height: pixelHeight });
  ctx.scale(window.devicePixelRatio, window.devicePixelRatio);
}
```

The code grabs the original width and height properties on the `<canvas>` element and then rescales the pixel width and height up by the `devicePixelRatio`. It then sets the CSS width and height to their original size, so the canvas element isn't resized. Finally, it uses the `scale` method (more on transforms later in this chapter) to scale up all calls on the context.

Grabbing the Rendering Context

The majority of the interesting stuff you might do with the `<canvas>` tag is done using the element's context, which as you've seen in a lot of places throughout this book is retrieved by calling:

```
var ctx = canvas.getContext("2d");
```

2-D is the only context currently supported across all modern browsers. All drawing calls are always performed on the context and not the canvas element.

If Canvas isn't supported by the browser, the `getContext` method won't be present on the canvas element. As you've also seen earlier in this book, you can determine whether a browser supports the tag by checking for the presence of the `getContext` method on a newly created `<canvas>` element:

```
var hasCanvas = document.createElement("canvas").getContext ? true : false;
```

You can also check for the presence of the method on an existing `<canvas>` element on the page.

The variable `ctx` refers to an arbitrary 2-D rendering context throughout this chapter, but you can of course stick the context in any variable, and you might have multiple contexts for multiple canvas elements on the page.

> **NOTE** There is also a `webgl` context (sometimes available as `experimental-webgl` depending on the browser) that exposes the WebGL rendering API, but because most mobile devices don't have WebGL enabled, this isn't covered in this book.

Creating an Image from Canvas

The only other method with good cross-browser support is the `canvas.toDataURL` method, which returns a data URL that represents a snapshot image of the current state of the Canvas. This image can generate an `<img>` tag or save the image to a server. The method accepts an optional parameter indicating the file type to save, either `"image/png"` or `"image/jpeg"` (Chrome also supports a new image type called `"image/webp"`). If this parameter isn't passed, the method defaults to generating a png. For JPEGs and webp you can also pass a second optional quality parameter.

To generate images from a canvas tag you could write:

```
// Generate a PNG image
png = canvas.toDataURL();
png = canvas.toDataURL("image/png");
// Generate a JPG with quality 0.8
jpg = canvas.toDataURL("image/jpeg", 0,8);
```

You can test the `toDataURL` method by running the code in Listing 15-3, which grabs a snapshot every time you click or touch the Canvas.

LISTING 15-3: to-data-url.html

```
<script src='jquery.min.js'></script>
<canvas id="mycanvas", width="400" height="400"></canvas>
<div id='snapshots'></div>

<script>
  var canvas = $("#mycanvas")[0],
      ctx = canvas.getContext("2d");
  function randInt(max) {
    return Math.floor(Math.random() * max);
  }
  function drawRandomRectangle() {
    var r = randInt(255), g = randInt(255), b = randInt(255),
        s = randInt(100), x = randInt(400), y = randInt(400);
    ctx.fillStyle = "rgb(" + r + "," + g + "," + b + ")";
    ctx.fillRect(x,y,s,s);
  }
  setInterval(drawRandomRectangle,50);
  $(canvas).on("click touchstart",function(e) {
    var url = canvas.toDataURL("image/png");
    $("<img>").({ src: url, width: 100, height:100 }).prependTo("#snapshots");
    e.preventDefault();
  });
</script>
```

This code creates a canvas element and adds a randomly colored and sized square onto the page every 50 milliseconds. Clicking or touching the canvas element calls the toDataURL method, creates a new <img> tag, sets the src attribute to that URL, and then prepends that <img> tag to a snapshots <div>. Each click generates a new image, and because the width of the <img> is set to 100, you can see a time lapse of how the Canvas changes with each click you make.

The W3C specification also defines a toBlob method that outputs a File object, which saves on memory because the file may be written to disk and is easier to work with. Unfortunately, as of this writing that method is not implemented in any browser, so it should be avoided. (Firefox defines a mozGetAsFile method, but this is nonstandard and uses a different syntax.)

DRAWING ON CANVAS

The Canvas context provides a number of different ways to draw onto the <canvas> element. The four primary methods are drawing rectangles, paths, text, and images. (The context also has methods to modify pixel data directly that are discussed in Chapter 17, "Playing with Pixels.") With the exception of the images, the other drawing methods can be drawn as a stroke, meaning only the outline is drawn, or as a fill, meaning the interior is drawn. Much like SVG, Canvas also has support for a number of different line join styles and end caps. Also like SVG, Canvas can do strokes and fills using gradients and patterns.

Setting the Fill and Stroke Styles

The Canvas context keeps the state of the current stroke and fill styles in the `strokeStyle` and `fillStyle` properties, respectively. These properties can be both read and written to. The simplest values you can set for stroke and fill are CSS color values. These color values can be in the form of a normal pound-sign-prefixed hexadecimal color string such as `"#F00"` or `"#FF0000"`, as an RGB triplet string in the form `"rgb(255,0,255)"`, or as a named color such as `"red"`.

For example:

```
ctx.fillStyle = "teal";

ctx.strokeStyle = "rgb(128,64,64)";

ctx.fillStyle = "#FF0000";

console.log(ctx.fillStyle);
// Logs the last value "#FF0000"

console.log(ctx.strokeStyle);
// Logs the strokeStyle converted hexadecimal as "#804040"
```

Both `fillStyle` and `strokeStyle` can also be set to gradients or patterns. Canvas supports two types of gradients: linear and radial. These types are created by calling the chosen method on the context:

```
var linearGradient = ctx.createLinearGradient(x0, y0, x1, y1);
var radialGradient = ctx.createRadialGradient(x0, y0, r0, x1, y1, r1);
```

Linear gradients start at x0, y0 and go until x1, y1. They are drawn as an infinitely-wide band that is perpendicular to the line created by the passed-in points.

Radial gradients are generated as a cone created between the two circles defined by the passed-in parameters. Areas outside of both circles are transparent. If you just want to create a single circular gradient, you can set the first radius to 0 and both points x0, y0 and x1, y1 to be the same point.

After you create a gradient, you need to add color stops to it. These define the color at a specific percentage of the way from the start to the end of the gradient. To add a stop, you need to call `addColorStop` on the gradient and pass a number from 0 to 1 that represents the position of the stop and the color:

```
gradient.addColorStop(position, color);
```

For example, to create a gradient that goes from black to white at the midpoint and then back to black, you could write

```
linearGradient.addColorStop(0,"#000");
linearGradient.addColorStop(0.5,"#FFF");
linearGradient.addColorStop(1,"#000");
```

You can use any valid CSS color definition to pass in as the second parameter to `addColorStop`.

The last stroke or fill style you can create is a pattern. A *pattern* is an image repeated over the area of the fill and is created by calling

```
var pattern = ctx.createPattern(sourceImage, repeatString);
```

sourceImage can be an <img> element; this includes objects created with new Image(), a <video> element, or a <canvas> element. repeatString is one of the following values: "repeat", "repeat-x", "repeat-y", or "no-repeat". You should recognize these strings as the repeat values you can set on a backgroundImage in CSS. They map to the pattern repeated in both directions, repeated horizontally only, repeated vertically only, and not repeated at all.

Listing 15-4 shows an example of both types of gradients created along with a simple pattern generated from an offscreen <canvas> element. The result is shown in Figure 15-3.

LISTING 15-4: Creating canvas gradients

```
<script src='jquery.min.js'></script>
<style> canvas { background-color:black; } </style>

<canvas id="mycanvas", width="600" height="400"></canvas>
<script>
  var canvas = $("#mycanvas")[0],
      ctx = canvas.getContext("2d"),
      width = canvas.width,
      height = canvas.height;
  var linearGradient = ctx.createLinearGradient(0,0,100,300),
      radialGradient = ctx.createRadialGradient(300,200,0,
                                                300,300,200);
  linearGradient.addColorStop(0,"#000");
  linearGradient.addColorStop(0.5,"#FFF");
  linearGradient.addColorStop(1,"#000");

  radialGradient.addColorStop(0,"#000");
  radialGradient.addColorStop(0.5,"#FFF");
  radialGradient.addColorStop(1,"#000");

  ctx.fillStyle = linearGradient;
  ctx.fillRect(0,0,200,400);
  ctx.fillStyle = radialGradient;
  ctx.fillRect(200,0,200,400);

  var patternCanvas = $("<canvas width='20' height='20'>")[0],
      patternCtx = patternCanvas.getContext("2d")

  patternCtx.fillStyle = "#777";
  patternCtx.fillRect(0,0,10,10);

  patternCtx.fillStyle = "#FFF";
  patternCtx.fillRect(10,10,10,10);

  ctx.fillStyle = ctx.createPattern(patternCanvas,"repeat");
  ctx.fillRect(400,0,200,400);
</script>
```

FIGURE 15-3: Canvas gradients.

The code creates a Canvas that is 600 pixels wide and 400 pixels tall and draws three rectangles each with a different fill. The first contains a linear gradient, the second a radial gradient, and the third a simple pattern fill created from an offscreen 20 x 20 canvas element.

The gradients are created with positions relative to the entire canvas and not the individual rectangle. This means that moving the `fillRect` results in a shifting of the gradient on the rectangle. If you need to use a gradient on a sprite, you need to use the translate, rotate, and scale methods described in "Using the Canvas Transformation Matrix" to move elements around that contain gradients rather than drawing them at particular canvas positions.

Setting the Stroke Details

Although gradients and patterns work on both strokes and fills, a number of stroke-specific settings enable you to control how the line that defines the stroke is drawn. These properties are:

```
// Sets the line width in current units (default 1)
ctx.lineWidth = width;

// Sets the cap style on the end of lines
// possible values are "butt", "round", "square" (default "butt")
ctx.lineCap = "butt";

// Sets the style at corners between two lines
// possible values are "round", "bevel", "miter" (default "miter")
ctx.lineJoin = "miter";

// Sets the max size of a miter join in current units
// Prevents mitered corners from getting too large at small angles.
ctx.miterLimit = 10;
```

There's not much more to say about stroke details other than the `lineWidth` and `miterLimit` properties are affected by the current transform state, so if you do a scale on the context, your line width increases as well.

Adjusting the Opacity

The rendering context also provides a `globalAlpha` property that enables you to control the opacity of whatever is rendered. This can be set to a number between 0 (fully transparent) and 1 (fully opaque).

```
// Fully opaque
ctx.globalAlpha = 1;

// 50% transparent
ctx.globalAlpha = 0.5;
```

This property persists between paths and rendering calls, so if you change it somewhere you must make sure to change it back afterward or adjust your code to set it to 1 before each rendering call.

Drawing Rectangles

The simplest drawing method that Canvas supports is the drawing of arbitrarily-sized rectangles. It has three methods supported: clearing the rectangle, creating a filled-in rectangle, and creating a rectangle outline:

```
// Clear the specified rectangle,
// setting each pixel to black and transparent
ctx.clearRect(x, y, w, h)

// Create a filled-in rectangle using the current fillStyle
ctx.fillRect(x, y, w, h)

// Create a rectangle outline using the current strokeStyle
ctx.strokeRect(x, y, w, h)
```

These methods tend to execute quickly (except when using a gradient or pattern fill) and `clearRect` is often used to clear the canvas between frames.

Drawing Images

You've already seen the three `drawImage` methods in Chapter 1, "Flying Before You Walk." They are repeated here for reference:

```
// Draw an image at x,y at its full size
ctx.drawImage(image, x, y)

// Draw an image at x,y rescaled to width w and height h
ctx.drawImage(image, x, y, w, h)

// Draw the portion of the image defined by the rectangle sx,sy and sw,sh
// at x,y with width w and height h
ctx.drawImage(image, sx, sy, sw, sh, x, y, w, h)
```

The first version draws a full image at its full size at a location on the canvas.

The second version draws a full image that has been resized to w by h. If the Canvas has been rescaled using CSS or a transform has been applied, this may not mean w pixels by h pixels. For example, if you scale the Canvas down by half as shown earlier for retina iOS devices, you might want to load images that have twice the resolution and draw them at half width and half height to get the best visual results.

The third version is the one used throughout the Quintus code to pull a portion of an image from a spritesheet and draw it onto the canvas.

The image argument in each case can be an Image object (which is equivalent to an <img> DOM element), another <canvas> element, or a <video> element.

Drawing Paths

Paths are the most complicated drawing tool available for use in Canvas, but they are also the most powerful. They enable you to draw arbitrary shapes and curves onto the Canvas. When a path is completed, you can either call stroke to draw the path as an outline or fill to draw the path as a filled-in shape. If the path hasn't been closed, the path will be implicitly closed when you call fill.

Instead of calling stroke or fill, you can also define a clipping region using the existing path by calling clip. This can limit future drawing commands to the previously drawn path until you call restore. The HTML5 specification defines a method called resetClip, but as of this writing it's not well implemented in any browsers.

Paths are defined by points and the connecting segments between them. Those segments can be straight lines, arcs, or curves. Each path consists of one or more subpaths, which can be closed (meaning the last point connects to the first) or open.

To create a path call ctx.beginPath(); followed by any number of path commands, and then call ctx.fill() or ctx.stroke(). If you want to create multiple subpaths, you can also call ctx .closePath() to close the subpath and implicitly create a new one starting at the last point of the previous path. You can also call ctx.moveTo(x,y) to move the starting point for the next command and implicitly create the new subpath if the previous path had more than 1 point. Calling moveTo does not, however, implicitly close the previous subpath. When you call stroke or fill, all the subpaths in the current path are affected.

Canvas provides seven different commands for drawing the various segments of a path that can be mixed and matched. The details for each command are shown here:

➤ ctx.lineTo(x, y): Adds a new point at x,y and connects the previous point with a straight line.

➤ ctx.quadraticCurveTo(cpx, cpy, x, y): Adds a new point at x,y and connects the previous point with a quadratic Bézier curve with the control point cpx, cpy.

➤ ctx.bezierCurveTo(cp1x, cp1y, cp2x, cp2y, x, y): Adds a new point x,y to the subpath and connects the previous point with a cubic Bézier curve defined by the control points cp1x, cp1y and cp2x, cp2y.

➤ ctx.arcTo(x1, y1, x2, y2, radiusX, [,radiusY, rotation]): Adds an arc between x1,y1 and x2,y2 with the radius defined. It also connects the previous point on the subpath with a straight line to x1,y1. If `radiusY` and `rotation` are provided, `arcTo` draws a portion of an ellipse that has been rotated `rotation` radians counterclockwise from the positive x axis.

➤ `ctx.arc(x, y, radius, startAngle, endAngle [, anticlockwise ] )`: This draws an arc starting at x,y of the passed in radius between `startAngle` and `endAngle` (defined in radians). If anticlockwise is set to `true`, the arc will be drawn counterclockwise.

➤ `ctx.ellipse(x, y, radiusX, radiusY, rotation, startAngle, endAngle, anticlockwise)`: This draws the portion of an ellipse between `startAngle` and `endAngle` starting at x and y with the given radii whose semi-major axis is rotated `rotation` radians counterclockwise from the positive x-axis. It connects any previous point on the subpath to the start of the drawn ellipse arc.

➤ `ctx.rect(x, y, w, h)`: This draws a new subpath rectangle consisting of four points defined as the corners of the rectangle and closes that subpath. Similar to `fillRect` or `strokeRect` but it generates a subpath instead.

As you can see, there are lots of ways to draw vector paths. After a path is drawn on the canvas, however, it is converted into pixel data, and the details of the path are lost. The spec has been updated to create a new Path object that can be reused by calling `ctx.stroke(path)` or `ctx.fill(path)`, but as of this writing that element hasn't made it into any browsers.

NOTE *Bézier curves are parametric curves commonly used in computer graphics. They are defined by a start and end point and either one (in quadratic curves) or two control points (in cubic curves). These control points define the size and shape of the curve between the start and end points.*

The equation for a point on a Quadric Bézier curve at a given time t is between 0 and 1 and can be written as a quadratic vector equation:

$$P(t) = (1-t)2P_0 + 2t(1-t)P_c + t^2P_1$$

or in JavaScript as

```
var x = (1-t)*(1-t)*p0.x + 2*t*(1-t)*pc.x + t*t*p1.x

var y = (1-t)*(1-t)*p0.y + 2*t*(1-t)*pc.y + t*t*p1.y
```

Given start and end points are p0 and p1 and the control point is pc. The Cubic Bézier equation is even more involved; luckily the browser handles drawing the curves for you. To get a sense of how the control point affects the arc, check out the file `bezier.html` *in the included code.*

Rendering Text on Canvas

As you saw in the title screen in Chapter 1, "Flying Before You Walk," Canvas also has the capability to render text onto the canvas element. Much like a rectangle drawing, Canvas provides two methods to render text:

```
ctx.fillText(str, x, y);
  ctx.strokeText(str, x, y);
```

The first method, `fillText`, draws a string of text with the characters fill-in (as text normally is) at the location `x, y` whereas the second, `strokeText`, draws only the outline. By default the text is aligned to the left (in left-to-right languages at least), but you can change this by using the `ctx` `.textAlign` property for any of the following values:

```
ctx.textAlign = "left";   // Left aligned from x,y
ctx.textAlign = "right";  // Right aligned from x,y
ctx.textAlign = "center"; // Centered on x,y
ctx.textAlign = "start";  // Same as "left" in left-to-right languages
ctx.textAlign = "end";    // Same as "right" in left-to-right languages
```

The default is `"start"`, but to center text horizontally on a specific point, you can use `"center"`.

Vertical alignment is controlled via the `ctx.textBaseline` property. By setting this property to different values, you can control where text is positioned relative to the passed in *y* value:

```
ctx.textBaseline = "top";        // text baseline is top of the em square
ctx.textBaseline = "middle";     // text baseline is middle of the em square
ctx.textBaseline = "alphabetic"; // text is on normal alphabetic baseline
ctx.textBaseline = "bottom";     // text baseline is bottom of the em square
```

A couple of additional options are currently unsupported (`"ideographic"` and `"hanging"`) as of this writing. The default `textBaseline` value is `"alphabetic"`. This value can sometimes be difficult to work with when positioning text; setting the `textBaseline` to `"top"` or `"bottom"` may be easier to get text exactly where you want it.

The final property, `ctx.font`, enables you to set the font using a CSS-style font string. This string can contain anything from just a size and font-family declaration up to a full style, variant, weight, size, and family declaration. If you pass an invalid font declaration, the assignment fails silently.

```
ctx.font = "20px Arial";    // Set the font to 20px

// Font set to italic, bold 40px Lobster, line height isn't actually used
ctx.font = "italic normal bold 40px/20px Lobster";

// Setting just the size or family isn't valid and is ignored
ctx.font = "40px";  // INVALID
ctx.font = "Arial"; // INVALID

// Still returns "italic normal bold 40px/20px Lobster"
console.log(ctx.font);
```

Any font available on the page is available in canvas. This means any fonts you load via `@font-face` are fair game.

You can also measure the width of a string of text using the `ctx.measureText` method. It returns a `TextMetrics` object which, from the HTML5 specification, looks like it should have lots of interesting properties such as horizontal and vertical bounding boxes and em height information. In practice, browsers have only implemented the width property of the text that you render.

```
var m = ctx.measureText("This is some text");
// Width of "This is some text" with the current font
console.log(m.width);
```

More properties may appear at some point, but the primary use case now is to precalculate the width of a piece of text for positioning or hit-testing.

USING THE CANVAS TRANSFORMATION MATRIX

Although it's been referenced previously, this book hasn't yet described in detail the transformation matrix that Canvas provides. This matrix enables you to translate, rotate, and scale any element you draw in Canvas, including images and paths.

This matrix works much the same way as the transforms in SVG from Chapter 14 ("Building Games with SVG and Physics") do, but in addition canvas provides a way to easily save and restore the matrix state to enable easy nesting of drawing commands. (SVG didn't have this problem because elements were nested under each other in the DOM.)

Understanding the Basic Transformations

Similar to SVG and CSS3, Canvas provides the standard basic 2-D transformations: translate, scale, and rotate. After you apply a transform, it applies to everything you draw until you change it.

```
ctx.translate(x,y);

ctx.scale(sx,sy);

// Rotate takes an angle in radians
ctx.rotate(angle * Math.PI / 180);
```

If you need to apply a custom transform (such as a skew) that is not handled by the built-in translate, scale, or rotate, you can also call `ctx.transform` directly with the matrix values:

```
ctx.transform(a, b, c, d, e, f);
```

When you call any of the preceding methods, internally the browser creates a transform matrix that performs the wanted transform and multiplies the current transformation matrix by it. This means that the order of operations is important—and is something that people often have trouble with.

The best practice is to apply transforms from global to local. This means that if you want to move an object to some spot on the canvas and have it appear rotated to a certain angle, you would first apply the more global transform (the translation) and then apply the more local transform (the rotation). If you apply it the other way around, you imply that the rotation is the global transform, so the element should be rotated around its translation.

If the element needs to be rotated around its center and was not centered at 0,0, you also need to wrap translations to center and then uncenter them around the rotation.

For example, to rotate a square around its own center and then translate it somewhere on the canvas, apply those transforms in the reverse order. (It's easier if you read the following code from bottom to top.)

```
// Move the object to the correct spot
ctx.translate(250,200);

// Uncenter the element back to its original spot
ctx.translate(50,50);

// Rotate it
```

```
ctx.rotate(45 * Math.PI / 180);

// Center it
ctx.translate(-50,-50);

// Draw it
ctx.fillRect(0,0,100,100);
```

If you change the order of any of these (with the exception of the first two translations, which are commutative), you end up with a rectangle that changes position as you try to change the angle of rotation.

Saving, Restoring, and Resetting the Transformation Matrix

Because you often want to nest transforms, the Canvas context provides a couple of handy methods to save and restore the state of the transformation matrix:

```
ctx.save(); // Save the state
  ctx.translate(...);
  ctx.scale(...);
  ctx.rotate(...);
    ...
ctx.restore(); // Restore the matrix
```

Using save and restore enables you to apply any number of child transforms and then restore the state back without affecting any other code that might rely on the state of the transformation matrix.

You can also reset the transformation matrix back to a known state with setTransform:

```
ctx.setTransform(a, b, c, d, e, f)
```

If you need to reset the matrix to the identity matrix (which doesn't do any transforms), you can run

```
ctx.setTransform(1,0,0,1,0,0);
```

You must be careful with resetting the transform completely because this may cause unexpected results if you adjust the canvas size for retina graphics, for example, as shown earlier.

Drawing Snowflakes

To drive home the power of transforms, build a recursive random "snowflake generator" that generates interesting recursive fractal-like patterns.

The idea is that each snowflake can be defined as a number of branches that spread out in a different direction. Each branch then has a set number of smaller child branches spread out over some range of angles and so on to a set limit. Because each step of the recursion is the same, a single method can be used that calls itself. The only difference with the nested calls is that the state of the transformation matrix is set up so that the child branches are drawn underneath the parent branches.

Figure 15-4 shows one of the more interesting outputs of the nearly infinite number of possible snowflakes. The code for the snowflake generator is shown in Listing 15-5.

FIGURE 15-4: Snowflake output.

LISTING 15-5: Generating random snowflakes

```
<script src='jquery.min.js'></script>
<style> canvas { background-color:white; } </style>

<canvas id="mycanvas", width="600" height="400"></canvas>

<script>
  var canvas = $("#mycanvas")[0],
      ctx = canvas.getContext("2d");

  function randInt(max) {
    return Math.floor(Math.random() * max);
  }
  function randomSnowflake() {
    var rootBranches = randInt(8)+1,
        childBranches = randInt(8)+2,
        childSpread = Math.random()*0.5 + 0.5,
        size = 50 + randInt(50),
        level = randInt(4)+1,
        distance = Math.random()*0.5 + 0.5;

    function drawSnowflake(branches,spread,level) {
      var angle;
      for(var i=0;i<branches;i++) {
        if(spread == 1) {
          // Don't overlap branches of we are rotating fully
          angle = Math.PI * 2 * spread * (-0.5 + i/branches);
        } else {
          angle = Math.PI * 2 * spread * (-0.5 + i/(branches-1));
        }

        ctx.save();

        // Rotate to point straight up for this branch
```

```
        ctx.rotate(angle);

        // Draw this branch
        ctx.beginPath();
        ctx.moveTo(0,0);
        ctx.lineTo(0,size*distance);
        ctx.stroke();

        // Draw child branches if necessary
        if(level > 0) {
            // Move to the end of the branch and scale down
            ctx.translate(0,size*distance);
            ctx.scale(distance,distance);
            drawSnowflake(childBranches,childSpread,level-1);
        }
        ctx.restore();
    }
}

ctx.clearRect(0,0,600,400);
ctx.save();

// Generate a random color
var r = randInt(255), g = randInt(255), b = randInt(255);
ctx.strokeStyle = "rgb(" + r + "," + g + "," + b + ")";
ctx.lineWidth = 2;

// Center the initial branches
ctx.translate(300,200);

drawSnowflake(rootBranches,1,level);
ctx.restore();
}
randomSnowflake();
$(canvas).on('click',randomSnowflake);
</script>
```

The exterior method `randomSnowflake` generates a number of random property values setting the number of branches, spread angle, size, level of recursion, and a random color for the snowflake. It then calls the recursive method `drawSnowflake`, which draws a single line for each branch rotated to the correct angle and then sets up the transformation matrix for the child branches. It then checks if there are more levels to draw, and if so, calls itself again with some updated parameters.

Because all drawing calls are wrapped in `ctx.save()` and `ctx.restore()` calls, each branch can pass along its transformation matrix to its child branches without affecting any of the other ones.

Each time you click the Canvas, a new snowflake generates. The variety of possibilities by just drawing some lines and varying a few parameters shows the power of nested transforms.

APPLYING CANVAS EFFECTS

As this chapter wraps up, there are a couple additional effects worth covering that Canvas provides: shadows and composition effects.

Adding Shadows

The Canvas context provides a way to add drop shadows to any drawn element, including text, rectangles, paths, and images. This is controlled via a set of four properties on the context:

```
          // CSS color shadow, accepts RGBA, RGB, hexadecimal
ctx.shadowColor = "rgba(255,255,255,0.5)";

ctx.shadowOffsetX = 4;     // horizontal shadow offset
ctx.shadowOffsetY = 4;     // vertical shadow offset
ctx.shadowBlur = 10;       // distance for shadow to fade out
```

You can use shadows to generate normal drop-shadow effects by using darker `shadowColor` values or give a subtle glow effect by setting the shadow offset values to zero and using a lighter color.

> **WARNING** *Elements with shadows are significantly more processor-intensive to draw than elements without, so use shadows sparingly and consider prerendering effects to an offscreen canvas buffer.*

Using Composition Effects

The Canvas context also provides a property called `globalCompositeOperation`, which controls how Canvas combines existing content with new elements drawn on canvas. The specification defines 11 different possible values for this property, with the default value `source-over` placing newly drawn elements over the existing content as you would expect.

Unfortunately as of this writing, consistent cross-browser support for the interesting composite operations is poor, so this property is something to keep track of as it evolves rather than using it now.

The intended results of each operation, as pulled directly from the specification, are listed in Table 15-1.

TABLE 15-1: Composite Operations

OPERATION	DESCRIPTION
source-atop	A atop B. Display the source image wherever both images are opaque. Display the destination image wherever the destination image is opaque but the source image is transparent. Display transparency elsewhere.
source-in	A in B. Display the source image wherever both the source image and destination image are opaque. Display transparency elsewhere.
source-out	A out B. Display the source image wherever the source image is opaque and the destination image is transparent. Display transparency elsewhere.
source-over (default)	A over B. Display the source image wherever the source image is opaque. Display the destination image elsewhere.
destination-atop	B atop A. Same as `source-atop` but using the destination image instead of the source image and vice versa.
destination-in	B in A. Same as `source-in` but using the destination image instead of the source image and vice versa.

OPERATION	DESCRIPTION
destination-out	B out A. Same as `source-out` but using the destination image instead of the source image and vice versa.
destination-over	B over A. Same as `source-over` but using the destination image instead of the source image and vice versa.
lighter	A plus B. Display the sum of the source image and destination image, with color values approaching 255 (100%) as a limit.
copy	A (B is ignored). Display the source image instead of the destination image.
xor	A xor B. Exclusive OR of the source image and destination image.

Safari is unfortunately one of the browsers that doesn't handle a few of these operations correctly, including incorrect rendering of `"source-in"`, `"source-out"`, `"destination-in"`, `"destination-atop"`, and `"copy"`.

Firefox doesn't handle `"copy"` correctly. The latest version of Chrome for the desktop and Chrome for Android do apply all the operations correctly. You can see how each operation looks in Figure 15-5 or try it out by running the `composition.html` file from this chapter's code.

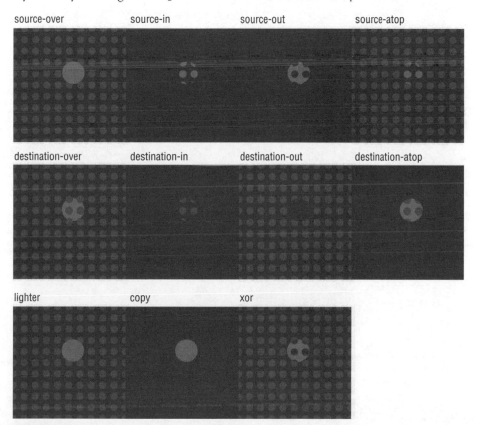

FIGURE 15-5: Results of composite operations.

The only operations, as of this writing, supported well by all browsers are the `"source-over"` (the default), `"source-atop"`, `"destination-over"`, `"destination-out"`, and `"lighter"`.

SUMMARY

You now know more about using the API for the canvas element, including how to use 2-D canvas to the full extent of its capabilities, including the peculiarities of the pixel dimensions along with the different rendering capabilities of the 2-D context. You also saw the variety of vector drawing capabilities of canvas along with how to set up gradient and patterns fills. Finally, you learned how to use canvas effects such as shadow and composition effects.

16

Getting Animated

WHAT'S IN THIS CHAPTER?

➤ Defining an animation API

➤ Building an animation system

➤ Creating a Canvas-based viewport

➤ Creating parallax backgrounds

WROX.COM CODE DOWNLOADS FOR THIS CHAPTER

The wrox.com code downloads for this chapter are found at www.wrox.com/remtitle .cgi?isbn=9781118301326 on the Download Code tab. The code is in the chapter 16 download and individually named according to the names throughout the chapter.

INTRODUCTION

The spritesheet support from Chapter 11, "Bootstrapping the Quintus Engine: Part III," allowed Sprites with spritesheets to play back animations by modifying the frame property of a sprite. Although this approach works for simple games with single animations, more complicated games such as the platformer built in Chapter 18, "Creating a 2-D Platformer," require a more robust system to handle animation. This chapter builds an animation system that enables more complex behaviors. This chapter also examines what you need to build and animate Canvas-based parallax scrolling backgrounds.

BUILDING ANIMATION MAPS

A robust animation system for Quintus should have two main goals. The first goal is to make it easy to trigger animations by name and not have to worry about the speed or the frame that the animation is playing at. The second goal is to have the animation system hook into the entity's events so that animations can trigger events to make it easier to time actions and behaviors.

Deciding on an Animation API

To begin, think about what a good API for an animation system might look like. There are two main pieces to consider. The first is the method to define animation. The second is the way animations are played. The first is straightforward: You need a way to set the frames that make up the animation as well as any additional details about the animation. Listing 16-1 shows how this can work.

LISTING 16-1: The animation api

```
Q.animations('player', {
  run_right: { frames: _.range(0,10) },
  run_left:  { frames: _.range(10,20) },
  stand:     { frames: _.range(30,25), rate: 1/5 },
  fire:      { frames: _.range(25,30), loop: false, rate: 1/30 },
  die:       { frames: _.range(30,45), rate: 1/5, next: 'dead' },
  dead:      { frames: [ 45 ] }
});
```

In the preceding code, `Q.animations` creates a sprite animation map called `player` and passes in a hash defining the frames and any additional details about the animation, including whether it shouldn't loop, whether it has a rate override, and whether another animation should play after it is done.

As a shortcut to pass in a long array of frames, such as [0, 1, 2, 3, 4, 5, 6], you can use the underscore shortcut method `_.range` to do the same by calling `_.range(0,7)`. (Notice that `_.range` goes up, too, but does not include the second number.)

In the preceding case, the player has left and right running animation that loops as well as a looping standing animation that plays at a slower rate. A fire animation runs at a faster rate and doesn't loop. Next is a die animation that automatically plays a 1-frame dead animation when it's done.

With the animations defined, it's now time to figure out how they should be played. Because `play` is the term often associated with animation, a simple play method takes the name of the animation to play along with an optional priority value. Adding in a priority to play allows animations that are higher priority (such as an attack) to override lower priority animations (such as a run or walk).

Listing 16-2 shows what a player sprite might look like powered by animations.

LISTING 16-2: An animated player sprite

```
Q.sheet('player_animations', 'dummy.png',{ tilew: 96, tileh: 96});

Q.Player = Q.Sprite.extend({
  init:function(props) {
    this._super(_(props).extend({
      sprite: 'player',
      sheet: 'player_animations',
      rate: 1/15
    }));

    this.add('animation');
    this.bind('animEnd.fire',this,function() { console.log("Fired!"); });
    this.bind('animLoop.run_right',this,function() {
      console.log("run right");
    });

    this.bind('animLoop.run_left',this,function() {
      console.log("run left"); }
    );
    Q.input.bind('fire',this,"fire");
  },

  fire: function() {
    this.play('fire',1);
  },

  step: function(dt) {
    if(Q.inputs['right']) {
      this.play('run_right');
    } else if(Q.inputs['left']) {
      this.play('run_left');
    } else {
      this.play('stand');
    }
    this._super(dt);
  }
});
```

The player `init` method defines a `rate` property that sets the default speed with which animations on the sprite play as well as a `sprite` property that defines the controlling animation sprite and the standard `sheet` property that ties the player to a spritesheet. Next it adds the `animation` component that adds the `play` method into the object. Then it defines a number of callbacks to play when specific animations are either finished or have gone through a single loop of frames. The former can be useful to trigger other actions, whereas the latter can be used to trigger periodic behavior, like a player running out of breath while running or running out of oxygen slowly while underwater.

Separating out sprite animation maps from spritesheets makes it easy to swap one or the other. You could, for example, have a number of spritesheets that match animation frames but have different characters.

The step method is set to play a specific animation at the lowest default priority level depending on the user's movement actions. The fire method, on the other hand, plays the fire animation at a higher priority level (1) so that it takes precedence over the movement animations. Because fire was set to be a nonlooping animation, when it finishes the movement animation takes over.

Writing the Animation Module

With the API for animations defined, you can implement the module. The module will be called Quintus.Anim and will consist of little more than some helper methods to define and retrieve animations and an animation component that can be added to Sprite objects (or actually anything with a frame property and a step method).

The animation component extends the Sprite with a play method that calls animation.play and sets up the animation. It also ties in to the step event to update the current frame and trigger events as necessary.

The code for the module is shown in Listing 16-3. It should be added to a new file called **quintus_anim.js**.

LISTING 16-3: The Quintus.Anim module

```
Quintus.Anim = function(Q) {
  Q._animations = {};
  Q.animations = function(sprite,animations) {
    if(!Q._animations[sprite]) Q._animations[sprite] = {};
    _.extend(Q._animations[sprite],animations);
  };

  Q.animation = function(sprite,name) {
    return Q._animations[sprite] && Q._animations[sprite][name];
  };

  Q.register('animation',{
    added: function() {
      var p = this.entity.p;
      p.animation = null;
      p.animationPriority = -1;
      p.animationFrame = 0;
      p.animationTime = 0;
      this.entity.bind("step",this,"step");
    },
    extend: {
      play: function(name,priority) {
        this.animation.play(name,priority);
      }
    },
    step: function(dt) {
      var entity = this.entity,
          p = entity.p;
      if(p.animation) {
        var anim = Q.animation(p.sprite,p.animation),
            rate = anim.rate || p.rate,
```

```
              stepped = 0;
          p.animationTime += dt;
          if(p.animationChanged) {
            p.animationChanged - false;
          } else {
            p.animationTime += dt;
            if(p.animationTime > rate) {
              stepped = Math.floor(p.animationTime / rate);
              p.animationTime -= stepped * rate;
              p.animationFrame += stepped;
            }
          }
          if(stepped > 0) {
            if(p.animationFrame >= anim.frames.length) {
              if(anim.loop === false || anim.next) {
                p.animationFrame = anim.frames.length - 1;
                entity.trigger('animEnd');
                entity.trigger('animEnd.' + p.animation);
                p.animation = null;
                p.animationPriority = -1;
                if(anim.trigger) {
                  entity.trigger(anim.trigger,anim.triggerData)
                }
                if(anim.next) { this.play(anim.next,anim.nextPriority); }
                return;
              } else {
                entity.trigger('animLoop');
                entity.trigger('animLoop.' + p.animation);
                p.animationFrame - p.animationFrame % anim.frames.length;
              }
            }
            entity.trigger("animFrame");
          }
          p.sheet = anim.sheet || p.sheet;
          p.frame = anim.frames[p.animationFrame];
        }
      },

      play: function(name,priority) {
        var entity = this.entity,
            p = entity.p;
        priority = priority || 0;
        if(name != p.animation && priority >= p.animationPriority) {
          p.animation = name;
          p.animationChanged = true;
          p.animationTime = 0;
          p.animationFrame = 0;
          p.animationPriority = priority;
          entity.trigger('anim');
          entity.trigger('anim.' + p.animation);
        }
      }

    });
  };
```

As you can see, the meat of the component is the `step` method, which is responsible for updating the `frame` if enough time has passed and then triggering events. But before getting to that, it's time to walk through the code a piece at a time.

The first three declarations are the connective tissue that enables you to set and retrieve animations. Animations are stored in a nested hash in the property `Q._animations`. Calling `Q.animations` with a name and a set of `animations` adds those to the animations available for that sheet. Calling `Q.animation` with a name and an animation name returns the details for that animation.

Each animation is required to have an array of frames, but for additional flexibility you need to support a number of other properties to make it easier to customize individual animations and chain animations together:

```
{
    frames: [0,1,2,3],   /* An array of frames in the sheet */
                         /* can be created with _.range(0,3) */
    /* Optional Parameters */
    sheet: 'sheetName',  /* An override for the sheet, if used,
                            must be on all animations */
    loop: false,         /* Loop animation (default: true) */
    rate: 1/30,          /* Frame rate override for this animation */
    next: 'animName',    /* Animation to auto-play after this one */
    trigger: 'event',    /* Custom event to trigger when done */
    trigerData: { .. }   /* Optional custom trigger data */
}
```

The animation component adds only a single exposed method to the entity's interface: `play`, which as already described, takes an animation name and an optional priority.

The `play` method extended onto the entity is just a proxy for the method directly on the component (listed at the bottom). That method first checks that you're actually trying to change the animation, as a call to play with the same animation that is already playing just continues to play that animation. Next if the animation has changed and the priority passed in is higher than the currently running animation, the animation properties are updated, and two `anim` events are triggered: one general one and one that's specific to the animation being played.

The `step` method does the most work. It first checks if there is an animation being played, and if so it takes over control of the sprite's `frame` property.

It then checks if this is the first frame of a new animation. If not it updates the animation time based on the rate (either from the sprite or the per-animation rate override) and advances the animation by the required number of frames depending on the time step.

Next it checks if the animation has updated itself this frame. If so, it needs to do some more work. First, the code checks if the current frame has reached the end of the animation. If so it checks if this is a single-loop animation or if there is an animation to play next. If either of those conditions are true, the method sets the frame to the last frame of the animation to be safe and then triggers two `animEnd` events. It then resets the animation and `animationPriority` to default values. Finally it triggers a custom event or plays the next animation if either of those properties is set.

If it's a looping animation, the method triggers `animLoop` events to signal an individual loop has played through and then uses the modulus operator to ensure the `animationFrame` is within the range of frames.

Finally, when everything else is done, the method sets the sprite's `frame` property and optionally the animation sheet if the animation has that property set.

Testing the Animation

To test the animation functionality, create a simple animated sprite that can meander around the stage. To start, create a new HTML file called **animation.html**, and enter the code in Listing 16-4:

LISTING 16-4: The animation bootstrap html

```html
<!DOCTYPE HTML>
<html lang="en">
  <head>
    <meta charset="UTF-8">
    <meta name="viewport" content="width=device-width,
user-scalable=0, minimum-scale=1.0, maximum-scale=1.0"/>
    <title>Animation</title>
    <script src='js/jquery.min.js'></script>
    <script src='js/underscore.js'></script>
    <script src='js/quintus.js'></script>
    <script src='js/quintus_input.js'></script>
    <script src='js/quintus_sprites.js'></script>
    <script src='js/quintus_scenes.js'></script>
    <script src='js/quintus_anim.js'></script>
    <script src='animation.js'></script>
    <style>
      * { padding:0px; margin:0px; }
    </style>
  </head>
  <body>
  </body>
</html>
```

This is just the basic Quintus bootstrap code with the new `quintus_anim.js` module added in. To start keeping the jQuery and underscore dependencies along with the slowly building `Quintus` code separated from per-example code, the engine code has been relegated to a separate `js/` directory.

Next, create the **animation.js** file mentioned earlier and put the code from Listing 16-5 into it. This code defines a slimmed-down version of the user-controlled player character from the beginning of the chapter that walks around and can trigger a fire animation. To run the code, you need the images from the chapter code and the `sprites.json` files in the `images/` and `data/` subfolders respectively. You also need to launch the example from localhost because of the AJAX-loaded `sprites.json` file.

LISTING 16-5: A basic walking demo

```
$(function() {
  var Q = window.Q = Quintus()
                    .include('Input,Sprites,Scenes,Anim')
                    .setup('quintus', { maximize: true })
                    .controls()
  Q.Player = Q.Sprite.extend({
    init:function(props) {
      this._super(_(props).extend({
        sheet: 'man',
        sprite: 'player',
        rate: 1/15,
        speed: 700
      }));
      this.add('animation');
      this.bind('animEnd.fire',this,function() {
                                  console.log("Fired!");
                                });
      this.bind('animLoop.run_right',this,function() {
                                         console.log("right");
                                       });
      this.bind('animLoop.run_left',this,function() {
                                        console.log("left");
                                      });
      Q.input.bind('fire',this,"fire");
    },
    fire: function() {
      this.play('fire',1);
    },
    step: function(dt) {
      var p = this.p;
      if(p.animation != 'fire') {
        if(Q.inputs['right']) {
          this.play('run_right');
          p.x += p.speed * dt;
        } else if(Q.inputs['left']) {
          this.play('run_left');
          p.x -= p.speed * dt;
        } else {
          this.play('stand');
        }
      }
      this._super(dt);
    }
  });

  Q.Block = Q.Sprite.extend({
    init:function(props) {
      this._super(_(props).extend({ sheet: 'woodbox' }));
    }
  });

  Q.scene('level',new Q.Scene(function(stage) {
```

```
    stage.insert(new Q.Player({ x:100, y:50, z:2 }));
    stage.insert(new Q.Block({ x:800, y:160, z:1 }));
    stage.insert(new Q.Block({ x:550, y:160, z:1 }));
  }, { sort: true }));

  Q.load(['sprites.png','sprites.json',,'background-floor.png',
          'background-wall.png'],function() {
    Q.compileSheets('sprites.png','sprites.json');
    Q.animations('player', {
      run_right: { frames: _.range(7,-1,-1), rate: 1/10},
      run_left: { frames: _.range(0,8), rate:1/10 },
      fire: { frames: [8,9,10,8], next: 'stand', rate: 1/30 },
      stand: { frames: [8], rate: 1/5 }
    });
    Q.stageScene("level");
  });
});
```

The player class matches the one from the beginning of the chapter in most ways. It defines a `Q.Player` sprite controlled by the player and animated based on the actions the player takes. It also logs a few events when animations finish. In a real game these events could be used to actually trigger a bullet firing or deplete a user's stamina.

The block class grabs an item from the spritesheet to display a crate. Next, the scene "level" is defined to set up a `Player` object and a couple of blocks for reference. Because the player should be in front of everything else, you also need to add a `sort` option onto the stage.

Finally, the `Q.load` method loads the assets, compiles the spritesheets and then creates the animations. The animations could easily be loaded via a .json file if you want to separate them from the game logic or generate them automatically. (The background images will be used later in this chapter.)

If you fire up this example in a browser or mobile device, you can walk the man around a static, white-background area relative to a couple of blocks, as shown in Figure 16-1.

FIGURE 16-1: The walking man.

ADDING A CANVAS VIEWPORT

SVG made the engine's life easy to add in a camera; the built-in `viewport` attribute enables you to control the viewport of the SVG element and act as a camera on the action.

With the Canvas tag's transforms, however, this functionality can easily be added to a stage using a component you can call `viewport`. The `viewport` component can have a few methods to allow a game to adjust the center of the viewport as well as add a sprite to follow, which means to center on the screen at all times.

This component ties into the `step` event to update the viewport position and then the `predraw` and `draw` events to wrap all the rendering calls in the appropriate saves, transforms, and restores based on the state of the viewport.

Add the code for the viewport from Listing 16-6 to the bottom of the `quintus_anim.js` file before the final closing curly brace.

LISTING 16-6: The viewport component

```
Q.register('viewport',{
  added: function() {
    this.entity.bind('predraw',this,'predraw');
    this.entity.bind('draw',this,'postdraw');
    this.x = 0,
    this.y = 0;
    this.centerX = Q.width/2;
    this.centerY = Q.height/2;
    this.scale = 1;
  },

  extend: {
    follow: function(sprite) {
      this.unbind('step',this.viewport);
      this.viewport.following = sprite;
      this.bind('step',this.viewport,'follow');
      this.viewport.follow();
    },

    unfollow: function() {
      this.unbind('step',this.viewport);
    },

    centerOn: function(x,y) {
      this.viewport.centerOn(x,y);
    }
  },

  follow: function() {
    this.centerOn(this.following.p.x + this.following.p.w/2,
                  this.following.p.y + this.following.p.h/2);
  },

  centerOn: function(x,y) {
    this.centerX = x;
    this.centerY = y;
```

```
      this.x = this.centerX - Q.width / 2 / this.scale;
      this.y = this.centerY - Q.height / 2 / this.scale;
    },

    predraw: function() {
      Q.ctx.save();
      Q.ctx.translate(Q.width/2,Q.height/2);
      Q.ctx.scale(this.scale,this.scale);
      Q.ctx.translate(-this.centerX, -this.centerY);
    },

    postdraw: function() {
      Q.ctx.restore();
    }
  });
```

The initial `added` method doesn't do much except set up the viewport parameters as necessary. This sets up the initial `centerX` and `centerY` positions; a scale mulitiplier to control how large the game should rescale the sprites and events; and the *x* and *y* to determine the position of the top left of the window.

Next, the stage is extended with three methods: `follow`, `unfollow`, and `centerOn`. These enable the developer to tell the view to follow the position of a specific sprite, unfollow that sprite, and manually center the viewport on a specific pixel location. `follow` and `unfollow` simply bind and unbind an event handler that calls the component's `centerOn` each step. The entity's `centerOn` method also is just a proxy for the component's method.

Next, the component's `centerOn` method sets the `centerX` and `centerY` and then calculates the *x* and *y* locations from the center, width of the Canvas, and the scale.

The `predraw` method does all the work to set up the viewport transform. It saves the current transform, centers the context in the window, does any necessary rescaling, and then moves the top left of the window by the wanted center values.

The `postdraw` method undoes all the transforms by simply calling `restore` on the context.

To test this method, modify the `Q.scene` code in `animation.js` as highlighted in the following code:

```
Q.scene('level',new Q.Scene(function(stage) {
  var player = stage.insert(new Q.Player({ x:100, y:50, z:2 }));
  stage.insert(new Q.Block({ x:800, y:160, z:1 }));
  stage.insert(new Q.Block({ x:550, y:160, z:1 }));

  stage.add('viewport');
  stage.follow(player);
  Q.input.bind('action',stage,function() {
    stage.viewport.scale = stage.viewport.scale == 1 ? 0.5 : 1;
  });
}, { sort: true }));
```

This adds a viewport onto the stage, sets it to follow the player, and then adds a handler to allow the user to play with the scale amount by pressing the action key (the b button on mobile devices).

GOING PARALLAX

Parallax scrolling is a technique used to give the appearance of depth in a 2-D scrolling game by having different background layers scrolling at different speeds. For example, if you have a sky layer scrolling at a slower speed than a mountain layer, it can give the appearance, at a simplistic level, that the sky is farther away than the mountains.

To put this into the engine, a new sprite called the Repeater must be added. This sprite works hand-in-hand with the just-defined viewport component to allow some extra background elements. It works by repeating itself in either the *x* and *y* direction or in one individual direction, and stays in a consistent spot on the screen. Repeating in one direction is useful for side-scrolling or top-scrolling games that have a background that repeats only in a single direction.

Add the Repeater sprite in Listing 16-7 to the bottom of quintus_anim.js.

LISTING 16-7: The repeater sprite

```
Q.Repeater = Q.Sprite.extend({
  init: function(props) {
    this._super(_(props).defaults({
      speedX: 1,
      speedY: 1,
      repeatY: true,
      repeatX: true
    }));
    this.p.repeatW = this.p.repeatW || this.p.w;
    this.p.repeatH = this.p.repeatH || this.p.h;
  },

  draw: function(ctx) {
    var p = this.p,
        asset = this.asset(),
        sheet = this.sheet(),
        scale = this.parent.viewport.scale,
        viewX = this.parent.viewport.x,
        viewY = this.parent.viewport.y,
        offsetX = p.x + viewX * this.p.speedX,
        offsetY = p.y + viewY * this.p.speedY,
        curX, curY, startX;
    if(p.repeatX) {
      curX = Math.floor(-offsetX % p.repeatW);
      if(curX > 0) { curX -= p.repeatW; }
    } else {
      curX = p.x - viewX;
    }
    if(p.repeatY) {
      curY = Math.floor(-offsetY % p.repeatH);
      if(curY > 0) { curY -= p.repeatH; }
    } else {
      curY = p.y - viewY;
    }
    startX = curX;
```

```
      while(curY < Q.height / scale) {
        curX = startX;
        while(curX < Q.width / scale) {
          if(sheet) {
            sheet.draw(ctx,curX + viewX, curY + viewY,p.frame);
          } else {
            ctx.drawImage(asset,curX + viewX, curY + viewY);
          }
          curX += p.repeatW;
          if(!p.repeatX) { break; }
        }
        curY += p.repeatH;
        if(!p.repeatY) { break; }
      }
    }
  });
```

The init method, per usual, just sets up some initial defaults. It also defaults to the repeat width and height to match the size of the image or asset so that tiles repeat perfectly by default.

The draw method is more complex; it needs to calculate the offset of each repeated tile. The preceding code takes the easy way out. Instead of calculating the exact partial image to draw each of the corners, the class overdraws tiles as necessary. Optimized code that handles the edge cases of rendering partial tiles at the edges and corners is left as an exercise for you.

Some complication is added because the background might repeat only in the vertical or the horizontal direction. If the element isn't set to repeat in a direction, instead of calculating an offset using the modulus, the position of the tile is set to the x or y position of the sprite minus the view.

On the other hand, if a tile repeats in a direction, first, the offset is calculated by using the sprite's position, and the view's position is multiplied by the scrolling speed.

Finally, the drawing loop goes over each direction and starts from before the left side of the Canvas until after the right side of the Canvas and from before the top side of the Canvas until after the bottom of the Canvas. If the repeater is turned off in either direction, the loop just breaks out after the first cycle.

To try out the repeater, add a couple of scrolling backgrounds to the level:

```
Q.scene('level',new Q.Scene(function(stage) {
  stage.insert(new Q.Repeater({ asset: 'background-wall.png',
                                speedX: 0.50, repeatY: false, y:-225 }));
  stage.insert(new Q.Repeater({ asset: 'background-floor.png',
                                speedX: 1.0, repeatY: false,  y:260}));
  var player = stage.insert(new Q.Player({ x:100, y:50, z:2 }));
  stage.insert(new Q.Block({ x:800, y:160, z:1 }));
  stage.insert(new Q.Block({ x:550, y:160, z:1 }));
  stage.add('viewport');
  stage.follow(player);
  Q.input.bind('action',stage,function() {
    stage.viewport.scale = stage.viewport.scale == 1 ? 0.25 : 1;
  });
}, { sort: true }));
```

The final result should look like Figure 16-2 depending on the device or size of the browser.

FIGURE 16-2: The final result.

SUMMARY

You built a simple animation system that allows the use of named, timed animation to control character animation. Abstracting away the details of which frame is playing on a character at any given time makes it easier to add more complicated behaviors to your characters. In preparation for Chapter 18's platform game, this chapter also covered adding in an animated camera that follows the player along with support for scrolling parallax backgrounds.

17

Playing with Pixels

INTRODUCTION

One of the much-heralded features of the new HTML5 Canvas tag is the capability to access pixel data directly. So far you haven't played around with pixels, but in this chapter you see what it takes to inspect and manipulate pixels directly. As a practical application to use pixel data, you build a *Lander*-style game that involves flying a ship around a map using small bursts of thruster (see Figure 17-1). But first, this chapter takes a brief diversion into 2-D physics to get the basis to build Lander.

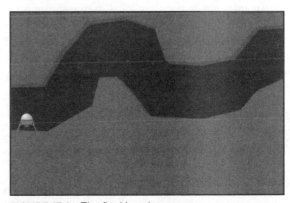

FIGURE 17-1: The final Lander game.

REVIEWING 2-D PHYSICS

You played with physics in Chapter 14, "Building Games with SVG and Physics," when you used the JavaScript port of Box2D for physics and collision detection, but the Physics library handled the details of what you were doing without really diving into exactly what was going on. This is okay when you want a full-blown physics simulation without worrying about the nitty-gritty details, but often you just need some basic 2-D motion, so a full physics library would be overkill. For *Lander*, you want pixel-perfect collision detection, which would put a lot of strain on a traditional physics engine where theoretically each pixel must be modeled as a simulation object.

> **HIGH-LEVEL MATH**
>
> Warning: This section discusses some high school level algebra and basic calculus. If it's been a while, this should be a good refresher. If this seems a little difficult, fight through it. Game programming tends to involve a fair amount of math, with more advanced techniques requiring progressively more complicated stuff. It will be worth it in the long run to get comfortable reading the occasional equation.

Understanding Force, Mass, and Acceleration

For those of you who took high school physics, the following equations should look familiar:

$$\text{Equation 1: } f = m \times a \text{ or } a = f / m$$

$$\text{Equation 2: } v = v_0 + a \times dt$$

$$\text{Equation 3: } p = p_0 + v \times dt$$

These are the basic 2-D dynamics equations that define the acceleration on a body as a function of its mass and the forces acting on it, and the position of a rigid body in relation to a combination of its starting position, its velocity, and its acceleration.

Equation 1 spells out that the acceleration on an object is equal to the force being applied to it divided by the object's mass. Equation 2 calculates the current velocity v if you know the initial velocity v_0 and the acceleration from Equation 1. The symbol dt represents an instantaneous delta of time. Finally, Equation 3 calculates the position of the object given the initial position and the current velocity from Equation 2.

Assuming that force and thus acceleration is a constant, with a little bit of calculus, you can unify the last two equations down to a single equation:

$$\text{Equation 4: } p = p_0 + v_0 \times t + \tfrac{1}{2} \times a \times t^2$$

This equation tells you that the position of an object with constant acceleration can be determined as a function of its initial position p_0, initial velocity v_0, and constant acceleration a. For any number of t seconds that you plug into the equation, you can calculate the position. What's a good example of constant acceleration? Well, gravity, for one, can be modeled as a constant force of 9.8 m/s^2.

Modeling a Projectile

Given the preceding equation, you can easily model a projectile launched into the air because its vertical acceleration will just be governed by gravity (a constant), and its horizontal acceleration will be 0 (which also happens to be a constant). Because you haven't created any sort of vector classes, the easiest way to handle a 2-D position is to evaluate the equation twice each frame, once for the x direction and once for the y direction.

For the x direction, you can simplify the equation further by completely dropping the x acceleration component, but leave it in for completeness.

Listing 17-1 takes the preceding equation and uses Quintus to run a simple simulation of a projectile launched into the air. You can modify any of the initial values to see how they affect behavior.

LISTING 17-1: Modeling a projectile with a closed form solution

```
var Q = Quintus().include("Sprites").setup()

Q.load(['cannonball.png','cannonball2.png'],function() {

  var ball1 = new Q.Sprite({
    asset: 'cannonball.png',
    x0:     0,  // Initial X position
    vx0:   20,  // X velocity
    ax:     0,  // X acceleration
    y0:   380,  // Initial Y position
    vy0:-100,   // Y velocity
    ay:    20,  // Constant Y acceleration
    t:      0   // Starting time
  });

  ball1.step = function(dt) {
    var p = this.p;
    p.t += dt;

    p.x = p.x0 + p.vx0 * p.t + 0.5 * p.ax * (p.t * p.t);
    p.y = p.y0 + p.vy0 * p.t + 0.5 * p.ay * (p.t * p.t);
  }


  Q.gameLoop(function(dt) {
    Q.clear();

    ball1.step(dt);
    ball1.draw(Q.ctx);
  });

});
```

Much of the code consists of setting up the initial values for the ball's position and velocity, and the actual position is calculated using just the two lines at the bottom of the update function. These two lines mirror Equation 4 exactly, once for the x direction and once for the y direction. Finally, the `gameLoop` function is written explicitly; it clears the Canvas before updating the ball's position and calling the draw method. If you want to follow the path of the ball explicitly, you can remove the call to `this.clear()` and the ball leaves a trail.

Switching to an Iterative Solution

Equation 4 is a closed form solution in that you can express the exact position of the cannonball at any point in time just by plugging t into the one equation. You can do this because you are modeling such a simple object. The minute you get something more complex, such as an object involving interactions with other objects or input from the user, you won't come up with a closed form solution without hiring some mathematicians from MIT.

Instead, you need to go back to your first set of differential equations (Equations 1 through 3) and turn them into something more computer-friendly. The easiest way to do this is to use a *discrete integration technique*. Discrete integration means instead of using calculus to determine an exact solution, you can use an actual, albeit small value for *dt* to find an approximate solution. The most commonly used method for discrete integration also happens to be the simplest and is known as *Forward Euler*, named after the famous Swiss mathematician Leonhard Euler. This method translates well to computer simulation. This means you can assume that over any small chunk of time, any of your potentially changing values, such as acceleration or velocity, are constant. The velocity and position equations now become the following:

$$\text{Equation 5: } v = v_{t-1} + a_t \times dt$$

$$\text{Equation 6: } p = p_{t-1} + v_t \times dt$$

In the preceding equations, *dt* is no longer an instantaneous delta but rather is a small but measurable amount of time. In the game, it will be approximately 1/30th of a second, or one frame of animation.

These equations aren't written in terms of v_0 and p_0 (velocity and position at time zero) but rather in terms of v_{t-1} and p_{t-1} (velocity and position at the last simulation step). This means that you can't say exactly where the ball is at any given point just by plugging in a value of *t*; rather you can incrementally calculate only the position based on the previous position.

This limitation is fine for most cases, because you usually just care about what the current state of the game is, but you're going to keep track of what happened previously for the purposes of replay or time travel (like in a game such as *Braid*); you must put in some extra work and keep track of your history somewhere.

Now it's time to compare your closed form solution with your iterative solution by running both at the same time. Create a second `CanvasSprite` called `ball2` and update its position using the Forward Euler method described previously. Add in the code for `ball2`, as shown in Listing 17-2, below the `ball1` step method:

LISTING 17-2: Modeling a projectile with an iterative solution

```
var ball2 = new Q.Sprite({
  asset: 'cannonball2.png',
  x:      0,
```

```
        vx:    20,
        ax:     0,
        y:    380,
        vy:  -100,
        ay:    20
    });

    ball2.step = function(dt) {
      var p = this.p;

      p.vy += p.ay * dt;

      p.x += p.vx * dt;
      p.y += p.vy * dt;
    }
```

To get the second ball to appear, you need to update the gameLoop to update both balls as shown here:

```
Q.gameLoop(function(dt) {
        this.clear();

        ball1.step(dt);
        ball1.draw(this.ctx);

        ball2.step(dt);
        ball2.draw(this.ctx);
    });
```

Because the second simulation uses an approximation of the solution to the movement equation, you would expect to see some error slowly creeping in that is in the form of a divergence of the two ships; the actual result isn't visibly different from the closed form solution. This is a good sign because it means that the approximation that is used doesn't change the behavior much from the actual solution.

Extracting a Reusable Class

Now it's time to take your existing Quintus Sprite object from Chapter 11, "Bootstrapping the Quintus Engine: Part III," and extend it with a modified step method to abstract away your movement methods. The only changes you need to make are to update the init method to initialize the velocity and acceleration to zero, and then copy over your updated code to the new object to the update for the new object (see Listing 17-3). Add the MovingSprite class to the bottom of quintus_sprites.js before the final closing brace.

LISTING 17-3: The Quintus MovingSprite class

```
Q.MovingSprite = Q.Sprite.extend({
  init: function(props) {
    this._super(_({
      vx: 0,
      vy: 0,
```

continues

LISTING 17-3 *(continued)*

```
        ax: 0,
        ay: 0
      }).extend(props));
    },

    step: function(dt) {
      var p = this.p;

      p.vx += p.ax * dt;
      p.vy += p.ay * dt;

      p.x += p.vx * dt;
      p.y += p.vy * dt;

      this._super(dt);
    }
  });
```

The `MovingSprite` class adds in the initial velocity and acceleration to the base properties and then modifies the `step` method to run an iterative solution.

IMPLEMENTING LANDER

Now put your newfound Forward-Euler sprite class to good use and build a simple physics-based game where you spelunk around in a moon lander. Why is this a good use of your physics details? Well, unlike other games, where you generally get to control the velocity of your protagonist directly, in *Lander*-style games, you control only acceleration, meaning that movements need to be planned out in advance. You have three controls: thrust left, thrust right, and thrust up. You need to carefully plan your ascent because if you use too much upward thrust, you'll watch helplessly as your lander crashes into the ceiling.

Bootstrapping the Game

Create a new file called **lander.html** and add the code in Listing 17-4 to create the basic outline and setup for your game.

LISTING 17-4: lander.html

```
<!DOCTYPE HTML>
<html lang="en">
  <head>
    <meta charset="UTF-8">
    <title>Simple Cannon example</title>
    <script src='js/jquery.min.js'></script>
    <script src='js/underscore.js'></script>
    <script src='js/quintus.js'></script>
    <script src='js/quintus_input.js'></script>
    <script src='js/quintus_sprites.js'></script>
```

```
      <script src='js/quintus_scenes.js'></script>

      <meta name="viewport" content="width=device-width,user-scalable=no">
      <style>
        body { padding:0px; margin:0px; }
        #quintus { background-color:#CCC; }
      </style>
    </head>
    <body>
      <canvas id='quintus' width='480' height='320'></canvas>

      <script>
        var Q = Quintus().include("Input,Sprites,Scenes")
                         .setup()
                         .controls();


      </script>
    </body>
  </html>
```

Because the lander game isn't going to have all that much code, the entire game will be built within the single lander.html file.

Building the Ship

Now create a basic ship sprite controlled by the keyboard using only force. You extend MovingSprite and add in a new update method that takes in user input to calculate the new position.

To give the game a small bit of dynamism, set up the ship to show a thruster image when the vertical thrust is on (see Listing 17-5). Also add in some constraints to prevent the lander from flying off the screen by just stopping the ship if it flies outside of the Canvas bounds.

This code goes in lander.html before the closing </script> tag.

LISTING 17-5: A basic ship class

```
      Q.Ship = Q.MovingSprite.extend({
        step: function(dt) {
          var p = this.p;

          // Set our horizontal force
          p.fx = 0;
          if(Q.inputs['left']) { p.fx -= p.thrustX; }
          if(Q.inputs['right']) { p.fx += p.thrustX; }

          // Set our vertical force
          if(Q.inputs['fire']) {
            p.fy = -p.thrustY;
            p.asset = "lander_thrust.png";
          } else {
```

continues

LISTING 17-5 *(continued)*

```
        p.fy = 0;
        p.asset = "lander.png";
    }

    // Calculate our y and x acceleration
    p.ay = p.gravity + p.fy / p.m;
    p.ax = p.fx / p.m;

    // Let our super-class update our x and y
    this._super(dt);

    // Force our lander to stay in our box
    // and zero out our velocity when we hit a wall
    if(p.y < 0) { p.y = 0;  p.vy = 0; }
    if(p.y > Q.height- p.h) { p.y = Q.height - p.h; p.vy = 0; }
    if(p.x < 0) { p.x = 0; p.vx = 0; }
    if(p.x > Q.width - p.w) { p.x = Q.width - p.w; p.vx = 0; }
  }
});
```

The `Ship` class extends the `MovingSprite` class from the last section and overrides the step method to enable player input and some extra behavior. The update method includes a few different sections. The first section calculates the forces acting on the ship by looking at the player input. Pressing the right or left keys adds a horizontal force, whereas pressing the spacebar adds a vertical force. The class also swaps the asset for the sprite to show the `lander_thrust.png` graphic when the ship accelerates upward. Next, the current acceleration is calculated from those forces, a gravity constant and the ship's mass property. With the acceleration updated, the parent's method to update the velocity and position is called. Finally, a bounds check to make sure the ship stays on the screen is needed.

Next the `Ship` needs to actually be put into the game. After the standard perfunctory loading and stage setup details, you create a background sprite and a new `ship` object with an initial *x* and *y* location, along with an initial mass and gravity. Add the code from Listing 17-6 to the bottom of `lander.html` before the closing `</script>` tag.

LISTING 17-6: The basic Lander game code

```
Q.load(['lander.png','background.png',
        'lander_thrust.png','map.png'], function() {

  Q.scene("level",new Q.Scene(function(stage) {
    stage.insert(new Q.Sprite({ asset: "background.png" }));
    stage.insert(new Q.Sprite({ asset: "map.png" }));

    var ship = stage.insert(new Q.Ship({
      asset: 'lander.png',
      x:        10, // X Position
      y:        170, // Y Position
      gravity: 20,  // Gravity
```

```
        m:       1,   // Ship's Mass
      thrustX: 40,   // Horizontal Thrust
      thrustY: 80,   // Vertical Thrust
    }));

  }));

  Q.stageScene("level");
});
```

Fire up your code or run the `lander_basic.html` example from the chapter code and use the left arrow, right arrow, and spacebar keys to move the ship. You can play with the mass and gravity options in the simple blank loader to get a sense of how adjusting those variables affect the movement of the ship.

Even though the background is loaded in, the ship doesn't interact with it yet but just flies over it. This will be remedied in the next section.

Getting Pixel Perfect

Armed with your simple ship floating around the screen, now you can start working on the biggest missing element: the cave walls.

Although you could build your game as you did in the previous SVG exercise in Chapter 14 and do only object-to-object collision detection, it makes much more sense to take advantage of the Canvas tag's capability to access pixel data of bitmaps to do pixel-to-pixel collision detection between the lander bitmap and level map.

You could look directly at the `canvas` tag used to draw the whole game, but as you will be drawing a couple of layers and the ship, you'd have to be clever to figure out which parts are your wall and which are your ship (such as by looking for a specific color.) To make the game more flexible you can redraw the background to an off-screen Canvas and pull the pixel data from there. To facilitate this flexibility, you can add a new method into the core of Quintus to return pixel data from a loaded image.

Use the `getImageData` method (see the W3C specification at `www.w3.org/TR/2dcontext/ #pixel-manipulation`), which returns the image data from a Canvas object.

> **TROUBLE RUNNING THE EXAMPLES**
>
> Different browsers have different restrictions for accessing pixel data from the local filesystem (in other words, from URLs that begin with *file://*). If you have trouble running the examples (check your JavaScript console to look for errors), run them off a local server as you have previously for examples that loaded JSON data.

If you have an image instead of a Canvas object, as with the background image, you can use jQuery to create a new Canvas element and then draw the background image onto that Canvas element. As shown in Listing 17-7, you can then return the pixel's image data from the Canvas context by calling `getImageData` and passing in the coordinates of the image you want (such as the whole Canvas).

LISTING 17-7: Returning pixel data from an image

```
Q.imageData = function(img) {
  var canvas = $("<canvas>").attr({
                        width: img.width,
                        height: img.height })[0];

  var ctx = canvas.getContext("2d");
  ctx.drawImage(img,0,0);

  return ctx.getImageData(0,0,img.width,img.height);
}
```

Retrieving the image data is a somewhat expensive operation, so unless you are updating the image it's best to do this once and cache the result.

Add the code in Listing 17-7 to the bottom of `quintus.js` before the final `return Q` statement.

Playing with ImageData

Now that you have an `ImageData` object, how can you determine whether there is a "collidable" pixel at a specific *x* and *y* location? Well, this task is equivalent to finding the color value at a specific pixel, and to do this you need to do a little bit of simple math. `ImageData` objects have width and height attributes, but the main meat of the information is in `ImageData.data`. This is a one-dimensional array of the actual pixel data, in 4-byte RGBA (red, green, blue, and alpha) chunks. This means all four elements of the array constitute 1 pixel from the Canvas. Within those four elements, each of which represents a number from 0–255, you can examine the red, green, blue, and alpha values that make up the pixel.

As Figure 17-2 shows, the alpha value determines how opaque the pixel is, with a value of 0 meaning the pixel is completely transparent, whereas a value of 255 means it is completely opaque. You can use the alpha value to determine if there is anything at that particular pixel in the image.

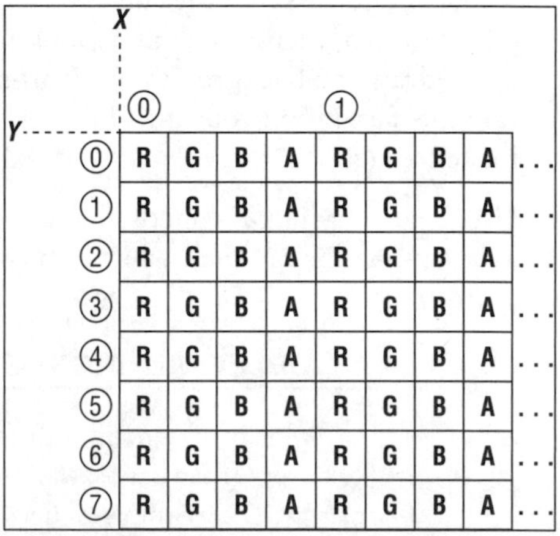

To get to the data for a specific pixel in an image, you need to determine the number of elements that pixel is in from the start of the array. Because each pixel consists of four elements, the length of each row of data is therefore four times the pixel width of the image. To get the row offset, you need to multiply that number by the *y* position. To index into the row the correct number of elements, take the *x* value and multiply by 4. Next, because you want the alpha value of that pixel, add 3 to the result, which results in the following code:

FIGURE 17-2: Alpha values and transparency.

```
alpha = imageData.data[y*4*imageData.width + x*4 + 3];
```

Got that? Good because you actually need to do it twice over each iteration of a two-dimensional loop. You're going to loop over all the pixels of your little lander, and for every pixel on the ship that is not transparent, compare it with the matching pixel of the background.

To keep the inner loop a little simpler, you can precalculate the starting location of the Ship in relation to the background pixel data. You do this, as shown in Listing 17-8, and stick it in the variable bgOffset. Add the following checkCollision method to the Ship class.

LISTING 17-8: Checking collision between ship and background

```
checkCollision: function() {
  var bgData = Q.backgroundPixels;

  // Get a integer based position from our
  // x and y values
  var bgx = Math.floor(this.p.x);
  var bgy = Math.floor(this.p.y);

  // Calculate the initial offset into our background
  var bgOffset = bgx * 4 + bgy * bgData.width * 4 + 3;

  // Pull out our data easy access
  var pixels = this.imageData.data;
  var bgPixels = bgData.data;

  for(var sy=0;sy < this.imageData.height;sy++) {
    for(var sx=0;sx < this.imageData.width;sx++) {
      // Check for an existing pixel on our ship
      if(pixels[sx*4 + sy * this.imageData.width * 4 + 3]) {

        // Then check for a matching existing pixel
        // on the background starting from our bgOffest
        // and then indexing in from there
        if(bgPixels[bgOffset + sx*4 + sy * bgData.width * 4]) {

          // Next check if we are at the bottom of the lander
          // if so return 1, to indicate that we might be landing
          // instead of crashing
          if(sy > this.imageData.height - 2) {
            return 1;
            } else {
            // Otherwise return 2 and...Boom!
            return 2;
          }
        }
      }
    }
  }
  return 0;
}
```

The collision code attempts to differentiate between a "landing" and a "crash" by checking if the collision is on the bottom of the ship object. If so, the method returns 1; otherwise, if the collision takes place anywhere else on the object, it returns 2 to indicate that it's time to blow the ship up.

Now you need to update the Ship class to check for collisions during the step function. Add the following to the top of the step method to stop the Ship in its tracks when it's dead:

```
step: function(dt) {
  if(this.dead) return;
```

Next, at the bottom of that same function, add in a call to the checkCollision method and handle the response appropriately:

```
this._super(dt);

var col;
if(col = this.checkCollision()) {
  if(col == 1 && Math.abs(p.vy) < 30) {
    if(p.vy > 0) {
      p.vy = 0;
    }
  } else {
    this.dead=true;
  }
}
}
```

You need to verify the return value of checkCollision. If it returns a 1, you collided with the bottom of the lander, and if you go slowly, you can land. Otherwise, you mark the Ship as dead.

Next you'll need to modify the game code itself to grab the backgroundPixels for the ship to compare against. Add the highlighted lines to scene definition in lander.html to read:

```
Q.load(['lander.png','background.png',
        'lander_thrust.png','map.png'], function() {

  Q.scene("level",new Q.Scene(function(stage) {
    stage.insert(new Q.Sprite({ asset: "background.png" }));
    stage.insert(new Q.Sprite({ asset: "map.png" }));

    var ship = stage.insert(new Q.Ship({
      asset: 'lander.png',
      x:       10, // X Position
      y:       230, // Y Position
      gravity: 20,  // Gravity
      m:       1,   // Ship's Mass
      thrustX: 40,  // Horizontal Thrust
      thrustY: 80,  // Vertical Thrust
    }));

    Q.backgroundPixels = Q.imageData(Q.asset('map.png'));
    ship.imageData = Q.imageData(Q.asset('lander.png'));

  }));

  Q.stageScene("level");
});
```

Congratulations! You now have pixel-perfect collisions between your background and your ship, so creating a new level is as easy as creating a new level image. If you want to see the results, you can run `lander_collision.html` from the chapter code. When you crash, you need to press the Reload button on your browser to restart the game.

Although the code in Listing 17-7 works, it's ripe for some optimization. If this were a production game, you'd take a deep look at the best way to optimize the inner loop of the `checkCollision` code. One quick optimization would be to modify the loop variables to increment by a number other than 1 to prevent the need for multiplications in the pixel data lookups. (Multiplications take more time for CPUs to perform than additions.) This optimization is left as an exercise to try on your own.

RESTRICTIONS WITH getImageData

Using Canvas with `getImageData` has a few restrictions associated with it that you should be aware of. If you pull an image into your Canvas from a different domain, that Canvas becomes "tainted," so you can't use `getImageData` on that Canvas. This was a restriction that was put in place to prevent access to images that might contain personal information from other websites because images are loaded with full cookies sent to that domain.

Making It Go Boom

Right now in the current version of Lander, you don't get a dramatic ship death—the ship just stops. You can fix that with the help of some exploding pixels. You create a new class that takes the pixels of the lander and explodes them when you die. This amounts to a simplified pixel-based particle engine.

Adding an Explosion Class

To start, you need to create a new class called `Explosion`. Although it's going to act like the sprites you are familiar with, in that it'll have an `update` and a `draw` method, you can inherit it straight from the base class because you don't need any existing functionality.

The `init` method is going to take in some information about the about-to-be-particlized lander—specifically its location, velocity, and image data—and create a series of particles, each with their own location and velocity representing one pixel from the input lander image. For performance reasons you won't turn every pixel of the lander into a particle; rather you just sample every fourth pixel and create particles of 3 pixels by 3 pixels in size. This is an arbitrary decision—play with the `init` code to generate different-sized particles to get a sense of performance. Listing 17-9 shows the commented `init` code.

LISTING 17-9: Explosion init method

```
Q.Explosion = Q.GameObject.extend({
  init: function(x,y,vx,vy,imgData) {

    // Set up a container for our pixels
    this.particles = []

    // Grab the lander's image data
    var landerData = imgData.data;


    // Create a 3x3 pixel-data
    // image data container to use for blitting down the road
    this.pixelData = Q.ctx.createImageData(3,3);
    this.drawPixel = this.pixelData.data;

    // Pixels are going to be exploding out from
    // the center of the lander
    var centerX = imgData.width / 2;
    var centerY = imgData.height / 2;

    // Loop over each fourth pixel of the lander image
    for(var sy=0;sy < imgData.height;sy+=4) {
      for(var sx=0;sx < imgData.width;sx+=4) {

        // Offset into the 1 dimension pixel data array
        var loc = sx*4 + sy * imgData.width * 4;

        // If there's a lander pixel here
        if(landerData[loc + 3]) {

          // Get the direction of the pixel from center
          var distX = sx - centerX;
          var distY = sy - centerY;

          // Add a new particle
          this.particles.push({
            x: x + sx,   // starting position x
            y: y + sy,   // starting position y
            lifetime: 5,   // remaining lifetime
            r: landerData[loc] + 20,   // make it a little redder
            g: landerData[loc+1],
            b: landerData[loc+2],
            a: landerData[loc+3],
            // For particle velocity, use the ship's
            // velocity, plus a random direction emanating
            // from the center of the ship
            vx: vx/6 +  distX * 5 *(Math.random()+0.5),
            vy: vy/6 + distY * 5 * (Math.random()+0.5)
          });
        }
      }
    }
  },
```

After the `init` method has run, the `Explosion` will have a set of pixels that match the original color of the pixels from the ship that can spread out and move independently.

Drawing Pixels

With the particles created, you need to take care of the two remaining sprite functions to finish off the `Q.Explosion` class: `update` and `draw` (see Listing 17-10.) For `update`, the function needs to add in the effects of gravity on the exploding particles and then step each particle using forward Euler. The `draw` function does something a little more interesting. In the preceding initialization function, you created a 3-pixel by 3-pixel `imageData` object for use by the `draw` function. You need to fill up that 9-pixel `imageData` object with the color of each particle and then draw it to the Canvas by using the `Canvas putImageData` method (see `www.w3.org/TR/2dcontext/#pixel-manipulation`).

LISTING 17-10: Updating and drawing the explosion particles

```
step: function(dt) {
  for(var i =0,len=this.particles.length;i<len;i++) {
    var v = this.particles[i];
    if(v.lifetime > 0) {
      v.vy += 20 * dt;
      v.x += dt * v.vx;
      v.y += dt * v.vy;
      v.lifetime -= dt
    }
    if(v.lifetime <= 0) { Q.stageScene('level'); return; }

  }

},
draw: function(ctx) {
  for(var i=0,len=this.particles.length;i<len;i++) {
    var v = this.particles[i];

    if(v.lifetime > 0) {
      for(var l=0;l<36;l+=4) {
        this.drawPixel[l+0] = v.r;
        this.drawPixel[l+1] = v.g;
        this.drawPixel[l+2] = v.b;
        this.drawPixel[l+3] = v.a;
      }

      ctx.putImageData(this.pixelData,v.x,v.y);
    }
  }

}
});
```

To fill in the 9-pixel `imageData` object, you need to loop over each of the 9 pixels. Because `imageData.data` is a one-dimensional array, you can use a single loop to copy the data in. You can optimize the loop in the draw function by incrementing i by 4 instead of by 1 for each 4 elements of pixel data to prevent the need for multiplications in the loop.

putImageData is an interesting method because it literally does a blit from the image data onto the Canvas—in other words each pixel is copied bit-for-bit ignoring any transparencies. This means it's not generally a great tool for composition, but in this case because you're just drawing opaque squares, it serves its purpose quite nicely, with the added advantage of being *fast*. If you want to use multiple layers of straight pixel data, you need to use putImageData to place the data onto an off-screen canvas and use drawImage to draw the image onto the active buffer with globalAlpha set to a number less than 1.

Calling createImageData is actually a (relatively) slow process, so reusing the 3-by-3 square for each of the particles results in a performance boost.

Is this the only way to do it? Definitely not; there are at least a couple of other methods you could use. One option is to simply draw a 3-pixel rectangle of the correct color on the page. Another is to use the original image and draw individual pixel squares of the image instead. This method is just shown as an example of how you could use putImageData.

To get the particles working, you'll need to modify Ship to create a new explosion object when the it blows up. Modify the highlighted code below, inside of the ship's step method:

```
var col;
if(col = this.checkCollision()) {
  if(col == 1 && Math.abs(p.vy) < 30) {
    if(p.vy > 0) {
      p.vy = 0;
    }
  } else {
    this.parent.insert(
      new Q.Explosion(p.x,p.y,p.vx,p.vy,this.imageData)
    );
    this.parent.remove(this);
    this.dead=true;
  }
}
```

Adding Particle Wall Collisions

For your purposes this *Lander* game is almost done, with one missing enhancement to the explosions. Although the explosions give you the wanted effect, they aren't interacting with the background. Because you already have access to the pixel data, there's no reason you can't do a quick per-pixel check to get pixel-perfect particle collisions. Using a simpler version than what you did checking the lander for collisions, as shown in Listing 17-11, you can update the Explosion.update method to take those walls into consideration. Pretend each of the particles is only 1-pixel large to simplify the collision detection because moving all these particles at once can cause a slowdown, especially on mobile browsers.

LISTING 17-11: Letting the particles interact with the walls

```
step: function(dt) {

  var bgData = Q.backgroundPixels;
  var pixels = bgData.data;

  for(var i =0,len=this.particles.length;i<len;i++) {
    var v = this.particles[i];
    if(v.lifetime > 0) {

      var oldx = v.x,  oldy = v.y;
      v.vy += 20 * dt;
      v.x += dt * v.vx;
      v.y += dt * v.vy;
      var loc = Math.floor(v.x)*4 + Math.floor(v.y) * bgData.width * 4;
      if(pixels[loc + 3]) {
        v.x = oldx;
        v.y = oldy;
        v.vy *= -0.2;
        v.vx *= -0.2;
      }
      v.lifetime-=dt;
    }
    if(v.lifetime <= 0) { Q.stageScene('level'); return; }

  }

},
```

To determine the offset location (stored in the `loc` variable) into the pixels array, you need to use the `Math.floor` method. The reason for this is that the particle's position is represented by floating point numbers that won't fall on integer boundaries. To index into the array, those numbers need to be converted to integers. `Math.floor` does that by taking an arbitrary floating-point number and chopping off any decimals to return an integer.

If you run the game, or run `lander_explosion.html` from the chapter code, you should now have a ship that blows up into a number of different particles when it dies.

SUMMARY

Canvas makes it possible to play around with pixel data directly. Although this is a feature that isn't used often, it can be useful for a number of different circumstances in which you need pixel-perfect collisions or Canvas post-processing. However, be careful with how much per-pixel processing you use because many mobile devices are lighter on CPU horsepower than their desktop cousins, and you must be careful not to overload them.

18

Creating a 2-D Platformer

WHAT'S IN THIS CHAPTER?

➤ Creating a tile layer

➤ Optimizing tile rendering

➤ Adding 2-D platformer collision detection

➤ Building a platformer game

WROX.COM CODE DOWNLOADS FOR THIS CHAPTER

You can find the `wrox.com` code downloads for this chapter at `www.wrox.com/remtitle`
`.cgi?isbn=9781118301326` on the Download Code tab. The code is in the Chapter 18
download and individually named according to the names throughout the chapter.

INTRODUCTION

The 2-D platformer will always have a special place in the hearts of developers who grew up
in the era of the Nintendo Entertainment system (and who, like me, can and often do hum the
opening 8-bit chords of Super Mario Brothers in their heads). The 2-D platformer remains
a popular genre for mobile games because it has simple controls that match nicely to an
onscreen keypad and is easy to pick up. This chapter builds the basic elements of a simple 2-D
platformer, using the animation tools from Chapter 16, "Getting Animated," and adding some
platformer-specific tiles and collisions.

CREATING A TILE LAYER

The naive collision detection scheme used so far suffers from one major flaw: The collisions don't scale as the number of items to collide with grows. If you remember the way collisions have been done to this point in Quintus (except the use of Box2D), it's been to compare each sprite against every other sprite on the stage.

Although this is fine for stages in which there are a limited number of sprites and potential collisions, for a platformer—where there might be sprawling levels with potentially thousands of tiles in the level for sprites to collide with—this would get quickly out of hand. To get around this, the engine needs to support the idea of a collision layer. Determining which tile a sprite interacts with at any given point is simple, given that tiles don't move between frames and are located at fixed points.

Because levels can get big, you also need to draw only the pieces of the level visible on the page, so optimizing what's drawn will be another duty of the tile layer.

Writing the TileLayer Class

To add platformer support to the engine, add in another Quintus module: `Quintus.Platformer`. This module adds in the `Q.TileLayer` class with a `2d` component and a special stage optimized to work the `Q.TileLayer`. The initial unoptimized `TileLayer` is straightforward. Its job is to load the tiles and draw all the tiles on each frame.

Create a new JavaScript file called **quintus_platformer.js**, and add the code from Listing 18-1.

LISTING 18-1: The basic TileLayer class

```
Quintus.Platformer = function(Q) {

  Q.TileLayer = Q.Sprite.extend({
    init: function(props) {
      this._super(_(props).defaults({
        tileW: 32,
        tileH: 32,
        blockTileW: 10,
        blockTileH: 10,
        type: 1
      }));
      if(this.p.dataAsset) {
        this.load(this.p.dataAsset);
      }
      this.blocks = [];
      this.p.blockW = this.p.tileW * this.p.blockTileW;
      this.p.blockH = this.p.tileH * this.p.blockTileH;
      this.colBounds = {};
      this.directions = [ 'top','left','right','bottom'];
    },

    load: function(dataAsset) {
      var data = _.isString(dataAsset) ?  Q.asset(dataAsset) : dataAsset;
```

```
        this.p.tiles = data;
        this.p.rows = data.length;
        this.p.cols = data[0].length;
        this.p.w = this.p.rows * this.p.tileH;
        this.p.h = this.p.cols * this.p.tileW;
      },

    setTile: function(x,y,tile) {
      var p = this.p,
          blockX = Math.floor(x/p.blockTileW),
          blockY = Math.floor(y/p.blockTileH);

      if(blockX >= 0 && blockY >= 0 &&
         blockX < this.p.cols &&
         blockY <  this.p.cols) {
        this.p.tiles[y][x] = tile;
        if(this.blocks[blockY]) {
          this.blocks[blockY][blockX] = null;
        }
      }
    },

    draw: function(ctx) {
      var p = this.p,
          tiles = p.tiles,
          sheet = this.sheet();
      for(var y=0;y < p.rows;y++) {
        if(tiles[y]) {
          for(var x =0;x < p.cols;x++) {
            if(tiles[y][x]) {
              sheet.draw(ctx,
                         x*p.tileW + p.x,
                         y*p.tileH + p.y,
                         tiles[y][x]);
            }
          }
        }
      }
    }
  });
};
```

The TileLayer sprite doesn't do much yet. The init method sets up a couple of properties as usual and calls the load method if a dataAsset is passed in. It also sets up some properties that will be used in the next section.

The setTile method will be used to modify the tile at a certain location on the map after the fact. It has code that will clear out prerendered blocks; this code will make sense after the next section adds in prerendering.

To limit the number of tiles that the game has to draw each frame, the TileLayer is optimized to prerender blocks of tiles to off-screen Canvas elements. The additional initialization code at the top of the init method sets that up for the code you add later in this chapter in the section "Optimizing the Drawing," precalculating the size (in pixels) of each block.

The `load` method just loads in an array of arrays that defines the frame of the spritesheet for the tiles at each position and calculates the size of the `TileLayer` from that.

Finally, the `draw` method overloads the default `Sprite draw` method and loops over each row of tiles and draws those tiles that have a nonzero value at that position.

Exercising the TileLayer Code

To test out this code, you need the standard HTML bootstrap file. Create a new file called **platform.html** and enter in the code in Listing 18-2.

LISTING 18-2: The platform.html bootstrap

```html
<!DOCTYPE HTML>
<html lang="en">
  <head>
    <meta charset="UTF-8">
    <meta name="viewport" content="width=device-width, ➡
 user-scalable=0, minimum-scale=1.0, maximum-scale=1.0"/>
    <title>Platformer</title>
    <script src='js/jquery.min.js'></script>
    <script src='js/underscore.js'></script>
    <script src='js/quintus.js'></script>
    <script src='js/quintus_input.js'></script>
    <script src='js/quintus_sprites.js'></script>
    <script src='js/quintus_scenes.js'></script>
    <script src='js/quintus_anim.js'></script>
    <script src='js/quintus_platformer.js'></script>
    <script src='platform.js'></script>
    <style>
      * { padding:0px; margin:0px; }
    </style>
  </head>
  <body>
  </body>
</html>
```

This is the standard Quintus code, pulling in the required dependencies and previously written modules along with the new `quintus_platformer.js` module you started to write.

Next, create the **platform.js** file mentioned in the preceding file, and enter the start of the platformer that will be built in the rest of this chapter. Note that it contains some additional loading and animation code that won't be used right away. The initial code for `platform.js` is shown in Listing 18-3.

LISTING 18-3: The initial platformer code

```javascript
$(function() {
  var Q = window.Q = Quintus()
                     .include('Input,Sprites,Scenes,Anim,Platformer')
                     .setup('quintus', { maximize: true })
```

```
                          .controls();

    Q.scene('level',new Q.Scene(function(stage) {

      Q.compileSheets('sprites.png','sprites.json');

      stage.insert(new Q.Repeater({ asset: 'background-wall.png',
                                    speedX: 0.50, y:-225, z:0 }));
      var tiles = stage.insert(new Q.TileLayer({ sheet: 'block',
                                                 x: -100, y: -100,
                                                 tileW: 32,
                                                 tileH: 32,
                                                 blockTileW: 10,
                                                 blockTileH: 10,
                                                 dataAsset: 'level.json',
                                                 z:1 }));
      stage.add('viewport');
      stage.centerOn(0,0);
      Q.input.bind('right',function() {
        stage.viewport.centerOn(stage.viewport.centerX + 64,
                                stage.viewport.centerY)
      });
      Q.input.bind('left',function() {
        stage.viewport.centerOn(stage.viewport.centerX - 64,
                                stage.viewport.centerY)
      });
    }, { sort: true }));

    Q.load(['background-wall.png','sprites.png',
            'sprites.json','level.json'],function() {

      Q.stageScene("level");
    });
  });
```

This code should look similar to the code from Chapter 15, but with some additional animations and loaded assets. You need to grab the assets from the chapter code for the example to work, making sure to put the image files in the images/ directory and the .json files in the data/ directory.

In this code, the stage binds the left and right actions to allow you to move the viewport around, so you should scroll the background around on your desktop browser with the arrow keys or with the keypad on a mobile device.

Optimizing the Drawing

With small tiles and large levels, the number of tiles that need to be drawn for each frame would quickly bog down performance. One quick optimization would be to draw only the tiles that are actually on the screen, but even then the 150 32 × 32 tiles that would be needed to fill up an iPhone's 480 × 320 screen is still too many to draw for each frame. A better solution is to prerender blocks of tiles (the tiles aren't changing each frame after all) and then draw a smaller number of blocks at the correct position.

To add this code into the `TileLayer` class, replace the `draw` method in that class with the code from Listing 18-4.

LISTING 18-4: Tile prerendering

```
prerenderBlock: function(blockX,blockY) {
  var p = this.p,
      tiles = p.tiles,
      sheet = this.sheet(),
      blockOffsetX = blockX*p.blockTileW,
      blockOffsetY = blockY*p.blockTileH;

  if(blockOffsetX < 0 || blockOffsetX >= this.p.cols ||
     blockOffsetY < 0 || blockOffsetY >= this.p.rows) {
       return;
  }

  var canvas = document.createElement('canvas'),
      ctx = canvas.getContext('2d');

  canvas.width = p.blockW;
  canvas.height= p.blockH;
  this.blocks[blockY] = this.blocks[blockY] || {};
  this.blocks[blockY][blockX] = canvas;

  for(var y=0;y<p.blockTileH;y++) {
    if(tiles[y+blockOffsetY]) {
      for(var x=0;x<p.blockTileW;x++) {
        if(tiles[y+blockOffsetY][x+blockOffsetX]) {
          sheet.draw(ctx,
                     x*p.tileW,
                     y*p.tileH,
                     tiles[y+blockOffsetY][x+blockOffsetX]);
        }
      }
    }
  }
},

drawBlock: function(ctx, blockX, blockY) {
  var p = this.p,
      startX = Math.floor(blockX * p.blockW + p.x),
      startY = Math.floor(blockY * p.blockH + p.y);

  if(!this.blocks[blockY] || !this.blocks[blockY][blockX]) {
    this.prerenderBlock(blockX,blockY);
  }

  if(this.blocks[blockY]  && this.blocks[blockY][blockX]) {
    ctx.drawImage(this.blocks[blockY][blockX],startX,startY);
  }
},

draw: function(ctx) {
```

```
    var p = this.p,
        viewport = this.parent.viewport,
        viewW = Q.width / viewport.scale,
        viewH = Q.height / viewport.scale,
        startBlockX = Math.floor((viewport.x - p.x) / p.blockW),
        startBlockY = Math.floor((viewport.y - p.y) / p.blockH),
        endBlockX = Math.floor((viewport.x + viewW - p.x) / p.blockW),
        endBlockY = Math.floor((viewport.y + viewH - p.y) / p.blockH);

    for(var y=startBlockY;y<=endBlockY;y++) {
      for(var x=startBlockX;x<=endBlockX;x++) {
        this.drawBlock(ctx,x,y);
      }
    }
  }
```

The rendering code has been broken down into three separate methods. The `draw` method from the first version is replaced with one that calculates the starting and ending block in each direction and then calls the `drawBlock` helper method for each block.

The `drawBlock` method takes in the block position and converts it into a pixel position to calculate the `startX` and `startY` variables. It then checks if an off-screen Canvas has already been created; if not, it calls the `prerenderBlock` method to create it. The `drawBlock` method then draws the off-screen Canvas onto the screen using the standard Canvas `drawImage` method, which accepts a Canvas element as a first parameter (in addition to the standard image object).

Finally, the `prerenderBlock` method creates an off-screen Canvas sized to the dimensions of the block and then draws each of the tiles in the block. It then saves the Canvas in the `this.blocks` property for later reuse.

HANDLING PLATFORMER COLLISIONS

As mentioned earlier, collision detection in a platformer needs some special attention. The first issue, as described already, is that, given the size of levels, collisions between sprites and tiles need to be highly optimized. A second requirement is that the collision detection should be stable and reasonably accurate. Because sprites spend most of their time hanging out on, well, platforms, the engine should be optimized for this case. Sprites will also be running around jumping and generally causing a ruckus. As the sprites run into things, they need to get feedback based on the direction of the impact.

Building a physics engine that does realistic collision calculations and responses to collisions is both difficult and processor-intensive. A simpler solution is to build a simplified model of how a sprite should react to collisions that is easier to implement and less work on the processor.

Taking a hint from the old-school platformers of yesteryear, sprites can be treated as a rigid collection of points that represent the extents of the object. If each point is also given a position label like `top`, `left`, `right`, or `bottom`, and if that point collides with something, it's easy to determine the reaction the sprite should have. If the top of the sprite collides with an object, the engine can just move the sprite down until it's no longer in contact. The same applies for each of the other directions. See Figure 18-1.

Using this algorithm, collision detection between arbitrarily shaped sprites and the world's tiles has been reduced to checking points against squares, an extremely inexpensive calculation.

Adding the 2-D Component

The first step to add in platformer collisions is to create a component that sprites can add to implement 2-D collision detection as described earlier. This component will be called, not surprisingly "2d." Its job is to allow the setting of collision points. It can also steal the basic physics code from the last chapter to allow the sprite to react to gravity and velocity.

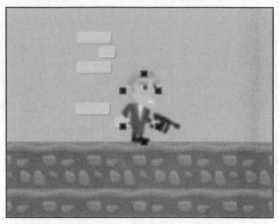

FIGURE 18-1: Collision detection.

Add the code for the 2-D component in Listing 18-5 to the bottom of `quintus_platformer.js` before the final closing brace.

LISTING 18-5: The 2-D component

```
Q.gravityY = 9.8*100;
Q.gravityX = 0;
Q.dx = 0.05;

Q.register('2d',{
  added: function() {
    var entity = this.entity;
    _(entity.p).defaults({
      vx: 0,
      vy: 0,
      ax: 0,
      ay: 0,
      gravity: 1,
      collisionMask: 1
    });
    entity.bind('step',this,"step");
    if(Q.debug) {
      entity.bind('draw',this,'debugDraw');
    }
  },

  extend: {
    collisionPoints: function(points) {
      var p = this.p, w = p.w, h = p.h;
      if(!points) {
        p.col = {
          top:  [ [w/2, 0]],
          left: [ [0, h/3], [0, 2*h/3]],
```

```
          bottom:[ [w/2, h]],
          right: [ [w, h/3], [w, 2*h/3]]
        }
      } else {
        p.col = points;
      }
    }
  },

  step: function(dt) {
    var p = this.entity.p,
        dtStep = dt;

    while(dtStep > 0) {
      dt = Math.min(1/30,dtStep);
      // Updated based on the velocity and acceleration
      p.vx += p.ax * dt + Q.gravityX * dt * p.gravity;
      p.vy += p.ay * dt + Q.gravityY * dt * p.gravity;
      p.x += p.vx * dt;
      p.y += p.vy * dt;
      this.entity.parent.collide(this.entity);
      dtStep -= 1/30;
    }
  },
  debugDraw: function(ctx) {
    var p = this.entity.p;
    ctx.save();
    ctx.fillStyle - "black";
    if(p.col) {
      _.each(p.col,function(points,dir) {
        for(var i=0;i<points.length;i++) {
          ctx.fillRect(p.x + points[i][0] - 2,
                       p.y + points[i][1] - 2,
                       4,4);
        }
      });
    }
    ctx.restore();
  }
});
```

The added method of the component adds on some velocity and acceleration properties and a multi-plier to indicate how strongly the sprite reacts to gravity. It also sets a collision mask that can deter-mine which objects the sprite should actively collide with. It then binds to the step event to update the sprite on each step. As a convenience it adds an optional binding to the draw event if a Q.debug property is turned on.

The 2d component adds the collisionPoints method directly onto the sprite to let it set the colli-sion points as a hash of arrays of points. If no points are passed in, the method creates some default ones that size to the bounding box of sprite.

The step method uses the familiar equations from the last chapter for updating the position of the sprite based on the acceleration and velocity. It then calls the collide method of the parent stage, which is responsible for keeping the sprite out of tile objects and sending callbacks whenever it collides with something.

One thing that's different about this step method, though, is that it puts an upper bound of 1/30th of a second on the dt so that it moves each call and loops over these smaller steps to prevent any sprite from moving too far. The reason for this is that the collision mechanism relies on sprites not being embedded too far into objects because that would trigger the wrong collision point—because HTML5 games can still suffer from the occasional stutter due to garbage collection.

Lastly, the debugDraw method, if turned on in added, draws a small rectangle at the position of each collision point for debugging after each frame.

Calculating Platformer Collisions

The job to calculate collisions with a sprite's collision points falls upon the TileLayer class from the last section. Its duty is to check each of the sprite's points against potential tile collisions and return the information about the collision and how to correct.

How it calculates collisions is simple: Divide the position of each point by the size of each tile; look at the array of tiles to see if a tile is present; and if it is, use the type of the point to figure out which way to push the sprite to keep it from continuing to collide.

Add the three methods in Listing 18-6 to the Q.TileLayer class in quintus_platformer.js. You can put it before the prerenderBlock method, making sure you have your method-ending commas lined up correctly.

LISTING 18-6: Collision points checking in TileLayer

```
checkBounds: function(pos,col,start) {
  start = start || 0;
  for(var i=0;i<4;i++) {
    var dir = this.directions[(i+start)%4];
    var result = this.checkPoints(pos,col[dir],dir);
    if(result) {
      result.start = i+1;
      return result;
    }
  }
  return false;
},

checkPoints: function(pos,pts,which) {
  for(var i=0,len=pts.length;i<len;i++) {
    var result = this.checkPoint(pos.x+pts[i][0],
                                 pos.y+pts[i][1],which);
    if(result) {
      result.point = pts[i];
      return result;
    }
  }
  return false;
```

```
      },

    checkPoint: function(x,y,which) {
      var p = this.p,
          tileX = Math.floor((x - p.x) / p.tileW),
          tileY = Math.floor((y - p.y) / p.tileH);

      if(p.tiles[tileY] && p.tiles[tileY][tileX] > 0) {
        this.colBounds.tile = p.tiles[tileY][tileX];
        this.colBounds.direction = which;
        switch(which) {
          case 'top':
            this.colBounds.destX = x;
            this.colBounds.destY = (tileY+1)*p.tileH + p.y + Q.dx;
            break;
          case 'bottom':
            this.colBounds.destX = x;
            this.colBounds.destY = tileY*p.tileH + p.y - Q.dx;
            break;
          case 'left':
            this.colBounds.destX = (tileX+1)*p.tileW + p.x + Q.dx;
            this.colBounds.destY = y;
            break;
          case 'right':
            this.colBounds.destX = tileX*p.tileW + p.x - Q.dx;
            this.colBounds.destY = y;
            break;
        }
        return this.colBounds;
      }
      return false;
    },
```

The primary method, checkBounds, takes in a position object and a collision point's object and checks each of the points against its tiles by calling checkPoints, returning the first collision it finds, otherwise returning false. To prevent a situation in which a sprite gets caught in a corner and keeps inching through a wall, the start parameter cycles through the starting edge to check.

The checkPoints method checks one array of points. It does this by looping over the array and calling checkPoint (singular) and again returning the first result that causes a collision.

Finally, the workhorse checkPoint calculates the tile position of the point, and if a tile is at that position, it fills in the colBound object, which is an object reused from collision to collision to save garbage collection time. That method, because it knows the type of point that caused the collision, can move that point to the top, bottom, or sides of the tile as necessary to resolve the collision.

Stitching It Together with the PlatformStage

To connect the 2d component and the TileLayer, a specialized stage object needs to be created. Its job is to check the object for collisions against the TileLayer along with a more basic bounding box to check any other sprites, adjust the position of the sprite if it collides, and then call events on the objects as necessary based on the collision detected.

This Q.PlatformStage class has the task to handle these different pieces. This stage class, although it might have multiple tile layers on the screen, is allowed to have only a single tile layer used for collisions, called the collisionLayer. Sprites that have a matching collisionMask with the collisionLayer go through the tile collision process.

The stage also performs the normal bounding box check between sprites.

Add the code for Q.PlatformStage from Listing 18-7 to the bottom of quintus_platformer.js to finish that file's functionality.

LISTING 18-7: The PlatformStage Class

```
Q.PlatformStage = Q.Stage.extend({
  collisionLayer: function(layer) {
    this.collision = this.insert(layer);
  },

  _tileCollision: function(obj,start) {
    if(obj.p.col) {
      var result = this.collision.checkBounds(obj.p,obj.p.col,start);
      if(result) {
        return result;
      }
    }
    return false;
  },

  _hitTest: function(obj,collision) {
    if(obj != this && this != collision &&
       this.p.type && (this.p.type & obj.p.collisionMask )) {
      var col = Q.overlap(obj,this);
      return col ? this : false;
    }
    return false;
  },

  collide: function(obj) {
    var col;
    if(obj.p.collisionMask & this.collision.p.type) {
      while(col = this._tileCollision(obj,col ? col.start : 0)) {
        if(col) {
          var destX = col.destX - col.point[0],
              destY = col.destY - col.point[1];
          obj.p.x = destX;
          obj.p.y = destY;
          if(col.direction == 'top' || col.direction == 'bottom') {
            obj.p.vy = 0;
          } else {
            obj.p.vx = 0;
          }
          obj.trigger('hit',this.collision);
          obj.trigger('hit.tile',col);
        }
      }
    }
```

```
        col = this.detect(this._hitTest,obj,this.collision);
        if(col) {
          obj.trigger('hit',col);
          obj.trigger('hit.sprite',col);
        }
      }
    });
```

The `collisionLayer` setter method sets the `TileLayer` that should handle collisions.

Two helper methods—`_tileCollision` and `_hitTest`—check an object against the tile layer and against other sprites. `_tileCollision` calls the `checkBounds` method from the last section if the object in question has a collision point's property or just returns `false` if not. The `_hitTest` is only a slightly modified version of the standard stage method. The only addition is the collision parameter, which checks if the opposing sprite is the collision sprite, and if so, ignores it as the tile collisions are handled separately.

Finally, the `collide` method, which is called by each `2d` sprite in each step, does the bulk of the work. First, it checks if this sprite collides with the collision layer using a bitwise AND. If so, it loops over any potential tile collisions and adjusts the position of the sprite based on how the collision tells it to resolve based on the collision's returned `destX` and `destY` parameters (returned by the `checkPoint` method from `TileLayer`). The sprite also gets its velocity reset in whatever direction it collided (vertical or horizontal). Each collision also triggers a `hit` event on the sprite that passes the collision object (the `TileLayer`) along with a more specific `hit.tile` event that passes the collision information itself, which allows the sprite to react to the direction of its collision.

When the tile collisions are done, the sprite loops over any other sprites by calling `detect` with the aforementioned `_hitTest` method, triggering `hit` events if a collision arrives.

BUILDING THE GAME

With all the pieces in place, it's time to attack the game. The simple platformer built in this section uses a shrunken-down version of the man from Chapter 16 along with some blobs as enemies. The game will have only three sprites, the player, bullets, and blobs.

Boostrapping the Game

Start from the outside in and create the outline of the game before filling in the necessary sprite class. Open up `platform.js` and replace it with the code from Listing 18-8.

LISTING 18-8: The platformer code

```
$(function() {
  var Q = window.Q = Quintus()
                    .include('Input,Sprites,Scenes,Anim,Platformer')
                    .setup('quintus', { maximize: true })
                    .controls();

  Q.Enemy = Q.Sprite.extend({
```

continues

LISTING 18-8 *(continued)*

```
    // TODO
  });
  Q.Player = Q.Sprite.extend({
    // TODO
  });
  Q.Bullet = Q.Sprite.extend({
    // TODO
  });

  Q.scene('level',new Q.Scene(function(stage) {
    stage.insert(new Q.Repeater({ asset: 'background-wall.png',
                                  speedX: 0.50, y:-225, z:0 }));
    var tiles = stage.insert(new Q.TileLayer({ sheet: 'block',
                                        x: -100, y: -100,
                                        tileW: 32,
                                        tileH: 32,
                                        dataAsset: 'level.json',
                                        z:1 }));
    stage.collisionLayer(tiles);
    var player = stage.insert(new Q.Player({ x:100, y:0,
                                        z:3, sheet: 'man' }));

    stage.insert(new Q.Enemy({ x:400, y:0, z:3 }));
    stage.insert(new Q.Enemy({ x:600, y:0, z:3 }));
    stage.insert(new Q.Enemy({ x:1200, y:100, z:3 }));
    stage.insert(new Q.Enemy({ x:1600, y:0, z:3 }));

    stage.add('viewport');
    stage.follow(player);
  }, { sort: true }));

  Q.load(['sprites.png','sprites.json',
          'background-wall.png','level.json'],function() {
    Q.compileSheets('sprites.png','sprites.json');

    Q.animations('player', {
      run_right: { frames: _.range(7,-1,-1), rate: 1/15},
      run_left: { frames: _.range(19,11,-1), rate:1/15 },
      fire_right: { frames: [9,10,10], next: 'stand_right', rate: 1/30 },
      fire_left: { frames: [20,21,21], next: 'stand_left', rate: 1/30 },
      stand_right: { frames: [8], rate: 1/5 },
      stand_left: { frames: [20], rate: 1/5 },
      fall_right: { frames: [2], loop: false },
      fall_left: { frames: [14], loop: false }
    });

    Q.animations('blob', {
      run_right: { frames: _.range(0,2), rate: 1/5 },
      run_left: { frames: _.range(2,4), rate: 1/5 }
    });
    Q.stageScene("level",0,Q.PlatformStage);
  });
});
```

This code sets up the engine and the scene, and then it loads some assets and sets up some animations. All these setup pieces should look familiar from previous chapters and the example earlier in this chapter.

This time the player has a number of animations for each direction, and a second set of simple animations for the nefarious blob character are added as well.

The three sprites will be added in each of the following sections.

Creating the Enemy

The enemy sprite (aka "the blob") is just a sprite that moves back and forth on a platform and changes direction when it runs into a wall. To do this it needs to listen for `hit.tile` events and flip direction when it encounters that event. It also needs to damage the player whenever it runs into him, which it can do by listening for the `hit.sprite` event.

Replace the stub for the `Q.Enemy` class with the code in Listing 18-9.

LISTING 18-9: The Q.Enemy class

```
Q.Enemy = Q.Sprite.extend({
  init:function(props) {
    this._super(_(props).extend({
      sheet: 'blob',
      sprite: 'blob',
      rate: 1/15,
      type: 2,
      collisionMask: 5,
      health: 50,
      speed: 100,
      direction: 'left'
    }));
    this.bind('damage',this,'damage');
    this.bind('hit.tile',this,'changeDirection');
    this.bind('hit.sprite',this,'hurtPlayer');
    this.add('animation, 2d')
        .collisionPoints()
  },

  changeDirection: function(col) {
    if(col.direction == 'left') {
     this.p.direction = 'right';
    } else if(col.direction == 'right') {
      this.p.direction = 'left';
    }
  },

  hurtPlayer: function(col) {
    if(col.p.x < this.p.x) {
      col.p.x -= 10;
      col.damage(5);
    } else {
```

continues

LISTING 18-9 *(continued)*

```
            col.p.x += 10;
            col.damage(5);
        }
    },

    damage: function(amount) {
      this.p.health -= amount;
      if(this.p.health <= 0) {
        this.destroy();
      }
    },

    step: function(dt) {
      var p = this.p;
      if(p.direction == 'right') {
        this.play('run_right');
        p.vx = p.speed;
      } else {
        this.play('run_left');
        p.vx = -p.speed;
      }
      this._super(dt);
    }
  });
```

As usual the init method sets up properties and binds to events. It also adds the animation and 2d components to the sprite and uses the default collision points for the sprite. In this case the type and collisionMask are important because the type is set to 2—so bullets can differentiate it from the player—and the collisionMask is set to 5—so it can run into the player (type of 4) and tiles (type of 1).

The changeDirection method is called in response to the hit.tile event. The event is passed the details of the collision, which includes where the collision happened. The blob will move in the opposite direction from the collision.

hurtPlayer is called every time the blob runs into another sprite. Because the only other sprite around that matches the blob's collisionMask is the player, the blob knows to damage them. The reverse is true when a bullet runs into a blob, in which case it calls damage on the blob, and the blob reduces its health until it's less than 0 and then destroys itself.

Because the blob can move only left and right, the step method is simple. It checks the direction it's currently moving in, sets the velocity to the correct direction, and plays the proper animation.

Adding Bullets

To take down the blob, the player needs some firepower. Bullets are a simple sprite that doesn't even use a spritesheet to draw itself, but instead just draws a small rectangle.

Replace the stub for the bullet with the code from Listing 18-10.

LISTING 18-10: The bullet sprite

```
Q.Bullet = Q.Sprite.extend({
  init: function(props) {
    this._super(_(props).extend({ w:4, h:2,
                                  gravity:0, collisionMask:3  }));
    this.add('2d')
    this.collisionPoints();
    this.bind('hit.tile',this,'remove');
    this.bind('hit.sprite',this,'damage');
  },

  remove: function() {
    this.destroy();
  },

  damage: function(obj) {
    obj.trigger('damage',10);
    this.destroy();
  },

  draw: function(ctx) {
    var p = this.p;
    ctx.fillStyle = "#000";
    ctx.fillRect(p.x,p.y,p.w,p.h);
  }
});
```

There isn't much to the bullet class. It sets the `gravity` property to 0 to prevent gravity from affecting the bullet. It also destroys itself when it runs into a tile and damages any sprite it runs into. Finally, it overrides the `draw` method to just draw a small black rectangle to represent the bullet.

Again the `type` and `collisionMask` come into play so that the bullet collides only with sprites and enemies.

Creating the Player

Last up is the player. He has some added complexity because he needs to move, jump, and fire bullets.

One issue that always needs some attention is the issue of jumping. Characters should jump only when they are standing on solid ground, so the player needs to keep track of where that is. One way to do this is track the last time that a collision with the `bottom` point occurred and allow jumps only when the last bottom collision was in the past few frames. This is the technique used here.

To sync up the bullet firing animation with when a bullet is actually launched, the player can listen for events indicating that the bullet animation has finished before actually adding the bullet sprite on the stage.

Add the code from Listing 18-11 to finish the platformer and add in the player sprite.

LISTING 18-11: The player

```
Q.Player = Q.Sprite.extend({
  init:function(props) {
    this._super(_(props).extend({
      sheet: 'man',
      sprite: 'player',
      rate: 1/15,
      speed: 250,
      standing: 3,
      type: 4,
      health: 100,
      collisionMask: 1,
      direction: 'right'
    }));

  this.add('animation, 2d')
      .collisionPoints({
        top: [[ 20, 3]],
        left: [[ 5,15], [ 5,40]],
        bottom: [[ 20,51 ]],
        right: [[ 30,15], [ 30,40]]
      });

    this.bind('animEnd.fire_right',this,"launchBullet");
    this.bind('animEnd.fire_left',this,"launchBullet");
    this.bind('hit.tile',this,'tile');
    Q.input.bind('fire',this,"fire");
    Q.input.bind('action',this,"jump");
  },

  fire: function() {
    this.play('fire_' + this.p.direction,2);
  },

  damage: function(amount) {
    this.p.health -= amount;
    if(this.p.health < 0) {
      Q.stageScene("level",0,Q.PlatformStage);
    }
  },
  launchBullet: function() {
    var p = this.p,
        vx = p.direction == 'right' ? 500 : -500,
        x = p.direction == 'right' ? (p.x + p.w) : p.x;
    this.parent.insert(new Q.Bullet({ x: x, y: p.y + p.h/2, vx: vx }));
  },

  jump: function() {
    if(this.p.standing >= 0) {
      this.p.vy = -this.p.speed * 1.4;
      this.p.standing = -1;
    }
```

```
    },

    tile: function(collision) {
      if(collision.direction == 'bottom') {
        this.p.standing = 5;
      }
    },

    step: function(dt) {
      var p = this.p;
      if(p.animation == 'fire_right' || p.animation == 'fire_left') {
        if(this.p.standing > 0) {
          this.p.vx = 0;
        }
      } else {
        if(this.p.standing < 0) {
          if(p.vx) {
            p.direction = p.vx > 0 ? 'right' : 'left';
          }
          this.play('fall_' + p.direction,1);
        }
        if(Q.inputs['right']) {
          this.play('run_right');
          p.vx = p.speed;
          p.direction = 'right';
        } else if(Q.inputs['left']) {
          this.play('run_left');
          p.vx = -p.speed;
          p.direction = 'left';
        } else {
          p.vx = 0;
          this.play('stand_' + p.direction);
        }
        this.p.standing~DH;
      }
      this._super(dt);
    }
  });
```

The `Player` sprite has a lot more going on than the `Bullet` or the `Enemy`. The `init` method sets up a custom set of `collisionPoints` to allow better interaction with tiles. It also binds to events for collisions, jumping, and firing bullets.

The `fire` method, called when the player fires a bullet, plays the `fire_right` or `fire_left` animation at a higher priority level to prevent any other animation from overriding it. The `damage` callback is called whenever the blob hits the player. After the full fire animation plays, the animation engine triggers an event that lets the player know it's time to actually drop the `Bullet` sprite onto the Canvas.

The `tile` method is used to track collisions with tiles with the sole purpose to track whether the player is standing on a tile. The `standing` property it calculates is used with the `jump` method to launch the player into the air but only if he is currently standing on solid ground.

Finally, the most complicated method, `step`, has the responsibility to play the right animation and update the player's speed as he runs around the screen.

It has a few different states to consider: firing bullets, falling, running, or standing. The first is considered the most important and overrides the other animations. The falling animation is the second most important state because if the player is jumping, his feet shouldn't be walking on air. Next, the running animations in each direction are played if the player holds down right or left. If none of those conditions are true, the player stands stiffly, pointed in whatever direction the player left him.

You should now be able to walk, jump, and shoot bullets around the short level defined in `level.json`. You can see the final game running on an iPhone in Figure 18-2.

FIGURE 18-2: The final game.

The next chapter shows you how to build a more entertaining playground for the player using a level editor to edit the unruly .json files needed for creating levels.

SUMMARY

You have now tied together the Canvas and animation code along with some new tile and collision detection to build a simple platformer game. In a production game there are a number of places where you could continue to optimize and enhance the engine, including adding in polygon-to-polygon collisions to get more accurate sprite collisions and using a quadtree or a tile-based system to keep the calculations for sprite collisions to a minimum.

19

Building a Canvas Editor

WHAT'S IN THIS CHAPTER?

➤ Serving a game with Node.js

➤ Creating a touch-friendly editor

➤ Saving level data

WROX.COM CODE DOWNLOADS FOR THIS CHAPTER

You can find the wrox.com code downloads for this chapter at www.wrox.com/remtitle .cgi?isbn=9781118301326 on the Download Code tab. The code is in the Chapter 19 download and individually named according to the names throughout the chapter.

INTRODUCTION

Building off the last chapter, where you built a 2-D platformer, this chapter builds an editor that enables you to edit the level to modify the tile data that makes up the level and save those changed levels. To allow the level data to be saved, you need to wrap the game inside of a Node.js application that can handle writing out the saved game data.

SERVING THE GAME WITH NODE.JS

Before your app can handle requests to save level data, the game needs to be served from something besides a static web server. One solution for this would be to write a simple PHP script that takes in the data and saves the file to disk. Because this is a book about JavaScript, however, and you'll be using Node.js to build a multiplayer game in the next couple of chapters, it makes more sense to build the editor using Node to get more experience with it.

Creating the package.json File

Just like the spritesheet creator application from Chapter 8, "Running JavaScript on the Command Line," the editor needs a `package.json` file to let Node know some details about the application, including dependencies.

Create a new directory called **editor** for the editor, and create a file called `package.js` with the contents in Listing 19-1.

LISTING 19-1: The package.json file

```
{
    "name": "platformer-editor"
,   "version": "0.0.1"
,   "private": true
,   "dependencies": {
      "express": "2.5.8"
,     "jade": ">= 0.0.1"
,     "underscore": "1.3.3"
    }
}
```

This application has three dependencies, your good friend underscore.js; a Node.js application framework called Express; and its dependency, jade.

Setting Up Node to Serve Static Assets

Node.js provides a minimal baseline of functionality for processing web requests. To get it to do something such as serve static files, you need to pull in a module. There are a number of different modules you could use whose only purpose is to serve static files, including `node-static` and `node-paperboy`, but because this app is going to do more than just serve files, it makes sense to pull in a more full-featured framework that can handle static files in addition to other tasks. The framework you use for this is a Node module called Express: `http://expressjs.com/`.

Express provides a number of different features, including views, caching, routing, sessions, and static files. This chapter uses only a small subset of Express's features, but it still makes your life easier than trying to use Node.js without support. You'll install Express via `npm`, so don't worry about downloading it.

Create a file called **app.js** in the `editor` directory for your app that you just created and fill it with the contents of Listing 19-2, which is a basic boilerplate Express application.

LISTING 19-2: Express boilerplate application

```
var express = require('express'),
    fs = require('fs'),
```

```
    _ = require('underscore');

var app = module.exports = express.createServer();

// Configuration
app.configure(function(){
  app.use(express.bodyParser());
  app.use(express.static(__dirname + '/public'));
});
app.configure('development', function(){
  app.use(express.errorHandler({ dumpExceptions: true, showStack: true }));
});
app.configure('production', function(){
  app.use(express.errorHandler());
});

// Start the server on port 3000
app.listen(3000, function(){
  console.log("Express server listening on port %d in %s mode",
app.address().port, app.settings.env);
});
```

This application loads a few dependencies at the start, sets up the server to parse incoming POST messages using `express.bodyParser`, and sets up the public directory as the location to serve static assets using `express.static`. Next it sets up a couple of error handlers depending on whether the server is run in Development or Production mode. (The default is Development.) Finally, the app server is started on port 3000.

To try this, copy all the code and image, js, and data directories from the last chapter into a new subdirectory called **public** underneath the `app.js` file. Rename the file from `platform.html` to **index.html**.

You then need to run `npm` to install the necessary modules. From the command prompt in the same directory as your `package.json` and `app.js` file, run:

```
npm install
```

This creates the necessary `node_modules` directory and installs the dependencies.

You should run the application by running the following:

```
node app.js
```

This starts the server on port 3000 and allows you to play the platformer game from the last chapter by visiting `http://localhost:3000/` in a browser. If you determine your IP address, you can play the game from a mobile device on the same Wifi network as your computer as well.

CREATING THE EDITOR

The editor consists of a layer of editing tools that sits on top of the existing platformer code. By making use of as much of the existing platformer code as possible, the editor needs to add only the ability to move the view around and changes tiles.

Modifying the Platform Game

The changes needed to get the editor code into the existing `platform.js` file are minimal. Open up the `index.html` file in the `public/` directory and add the soon-to-be-created `quintus_editor.js` file, as shown in Listing 19-3.

LISTING 19-3: Modified index.html file

```
<!DOCTYPE HTML>
<html lang="en">
  <head>
    <meta charset="UTF-8">
    <meta name="viewport" content="width=device-width, user-scalable=0,
minimum-scale=1.0, maximum-scale=1.0"/>
    <title>Platformer</title>
    <script src='js/jquery.min.js'></script>
    <script src='js/underscore.js'></script>
    <script src='js/quintus.js'></script>
    <script src='js/quintus_input.js'></script>
    <script src='js/quintus_sprites.js'></script>
    <script src='js/quintus_scenes.js'></script>
    <script src='js/quintus_anim.js'></script>
    <script src='js/quintus_platformer.js'></script>
    <script src='js/quintus_editor.js'></script>
    <script src='platform.js'></script>
    <style>
      * { padding:0px; margin:0px; }
    </style>
  </head>
  <body>
  </body>
</html>
```

Next open up the `platform.js` file in the same directory; at the top of the file, add the Editor module and remove the controls call. (Controls will be enabled later by the editor.)

```
$(function() {
  var Q = window.Q
        = Quintus()
          .include('Input,Sprites,Scenes,Anim,Platformer,Editor')
          .setup('quintus', { maximize: true });
```

Next, to support loading the editor and different levels, the bottom of the same file needs to be modified with a regular expression to optionally load a different level file into the game and set up the editor into the game.

The lines of code that need to be changed are shown here (the first block should be added above the `Q.scene` call, and the remaining changes are inside the `Q.scene` callback):

```
var match = window.location.search.match(/level=([^\&]+)/),
    levelFile = 'level.json';
if(match) {
  levelFile = match[1] + '.json';
```

```
    }

    Q.scene('level',new Q.Scene(function(stage) {
      stage.insert(new Q.Repeater({ asset: 'background-wall.png',
                                    speedX: 0.50, y:-225, z:0 }));
      var tiles = stage.insert(new Q.TileLayer({ sheet: 'block',
                                                 x: -100, y: -100,
                                                 tileW: 32,
                                                 tileH: 32,
                                                 dataAsset: levelFile,
                                                 z:1 }));
      stage.collisionLayer(tiles);
      var player = stage.insert(new Q.Player({ x:100, y:0, z:3 }));
      stage.insert(new Q.Enemy({ x:400, y:0, z:3 }));
      stage.insert(new Q.Enemy({ x:600, y:0, z:3 }));
      stage.insert(new Q.Enemy({ x:1200, y:100, z:3 }));
      stage.insert(new Q.Enemy({ x:1600, y:0, z:3 }));
      stage.add('viewport');
      stage.follow(player);

      stage.add('editor');
      stage.editor.setFile(levelFile);
      stage.bind('reset',function() {
        Q.stageScene("level",0,Q.PlatformStage);
      });

    }, { sort: true }));
    Q.load(['sprites.png','sprites.json',
            'background-wall.png',levelFile],function() {

      Q.compileSheets('sprites.png','sprites.json');
      Q.animations('player', {
        run_right: { frames: _.range(7,-1,-1), rate: 1/15},
        run_left: { frames: _.range(19,11,-1), rate:1/15 },
        fire_right: { frames: [9,10,10], next: 'stand_right', rate: 1/30 },
        fire_left: { frames: [20,21,21], next: 'stand_left', rate: 1/30 },
        stand_right: { frames: [8], rate: 1/5 },
        stand_left: { frames: [20], rate: 1/5 },
        fall_right: { frames: [2], loop: false },
        fall_left: { frames: [14], loop: false }
      });
      Q.animations('blob', {
        run_right: { frames: _.range(0,2), rate: 1/5 },
        run_left: { frames: _.range(2,4), rate: 1/5 }
      });
      Q.stageScene("level",0,Q.PlatformStage);

    });
```

The primary change is the addition of the levelFile variable, which stores the name of the level file loaded into the editor. This can be changed by adding a parameter called level to the end of the URL, for example:

```
http://localhost:3000/?level=level2
```

This would attempt to load `data/level2.json` instead of the default file `data/level.json`.

The second change marked here is adding the `editor` component to the stage. This component isn't written yet, so running the code currently results in an error, but it will be written in the next section.

The code also binds to a new event on the stage called `reset`, which is used by the editor to tell the game to reset itself (which the game does by just reloading the required scene).

Creating the Editor Module

The `Quintus.Editor` module consists of just a single component, `editor`, which can be added to a Stage object. It creates a number of tool buttons to let the user move the game around, paint and erase tiles, select tiles, zoom in and out, and finally save the level back to the server.

The first version of the editor adds some buttons onto the screen and enables you to select between the various tools.

Create a **js/quintus_editor.js** and add the code in Listing 19-4 to get the editor up-and-running.

LISTING 19-4: The basic editor module

```
Quintus.Editor = function(Q) {

  Q.register('editor',{

    added: function() {
      var stage = this.entity;
      stage.pause();
      $("#quintus-editor").remove();
      this.controls = $("<div id='quintus-editor'>")
          .appendTo(Q.wrapper)
          .css({position:"absolute",top:0, zIndex: 100});
      _.bindAll(this);

      this.buttons = {
        move: this.button("move",this.move),
        paint: this.button("paint",this.paint),
        erase: this.button("erase",this.erase),
        select: this.button("tile",this.tile),
        play: this.button("play",this.play),
        out: this.button("-",this.out),
        in: this.button("+",this.in),
        save: this.button("save",this.save)
      };

      this.select('move');
      this.activeTile = 1;

      Q.el.on('touchstart mousedown',this.touch);
      Q.el.on('touchmove mousemove',this.drag);
      Q.el.on('touchend mouseup',this.release);
```

```
  },

  setFile: function(levelFile) {
    this.levelFile = levelFile;
  },

  button: function(text,callback) {
    var elem = $("<div>")
                  .text(text)
                  .css({float:'left',
                        margin: "10px 5px",
                        padding:"15px 5px",
                        backgroundColor:'#DDD',
                        width:35,
                        textAlign:'center',
                        fontSize: "14px",
                        cursor:'pointer',
                        fontFamily: 'Arial',
                        fontWeight:'bold',
                        boxShadow: "2px 2px 5px #999",
                        borderRadius: "5px",
                       color:"black"})
                  .appendTo(this.controls);

    elem.on('mousedown touchstart',callback);
    return elem;
  },

  select: function(button) {
    if(this.selected) {
      this.buttons[this.selected].css('backgroundColor','#DDD');
    }
    this.selected = button;
    if(this.buttons[this.selected]) {
      this.buttons[this.selected].css('backgroundColor','#FFF');
    }
  },

  move: function() {
    this.select('move');
  },

  paint: function() {
    this.select('paint');
  },

  erase: function() {
    this.select('erase');
  },

  play: function(e) {
    if(this.playing) {
      this.buttons['play'].text('Play');
      Q.input.disableTouchControls();
```

continues

LISTING 19-4 *(continued)*

```
            this.entity.trigger('reset');
            this.select();
        } else {
            Q.el.off('touchstart mousedown',this.touch);
            Q.el.off('touchmove mousemove',this.drag);
            Q.el.off('touchend mouseup',this.release);
            this.select('play');
            this.buttons['play'].text('reset');
            this.playing = true;
            this.entity.unpause();
            Q.controls();
        }
        e.preventDefault();
    },

    out: function() {
        this.entity.viewport.scale /= 1.5;
        this.entity.viewport.recenter();
    },

    in: function() {
        this.entity.viewport.scale *= 1.5;
        this.entity.viewport.recenter();
    },
    });
};
```

The added method, as you know, gets called immediately after a component is added to an object. The first thing the method does is pause the stage so that the step method is no longer called, freezing all sprites in place. Next, it sets up a container for the editor. It also removes any elements of the same ID, which is useful when the editor is reset. Then the editor calls the _.bindAll method. This binds every method in the object to the object itself, which prevents any confusion during jQuery event callbacks with the state of the this object. The method sets up a number of buttons, which are added onto the top of the screen. These all use the button method, which is defined a few methods down. Next, it preselects the move tool, sets the activeTile (the tile used to paint) to the first sprite, and binds some event handlers on touch events and their mouse equivalents.

The touch, drag, and release methods aren't added until the next section. jQuery won't cause an exception if you pass null into the on method as you do here.

The setFile method simply saves the name of the level file for later use.

The button method creates a rectangular DOM element with some styling to make it look like a button. It then appends that element to the container created in added. These buttons are used to control the editor and select the currently active tool.

The select button is used to highlight the currently active tool. Although some of the buttons just take an action when you click them, the first three buttons—move, paint, and erase—are used as tools to control what happens when the user clicks or touches the canvas. Each of the callback methods for those three buttons just has the job to call the select method to set the current tool.

You can use the `play` button to toggle between Editing mode and activating the game so that you can try out the level. The first time you press the button, the editor turns off all the bound events, selects the play button, and then unpauses the stage. The second time you press, it triggers the `reset` method, which the stage uses to reset the scene.

The last two methods—`out` and `in`—modify the viewport to zoom out and in.

If you have this code running correctly and pull the editor up in the browser, you should select between the first three tools and use the + and – buttons to zoom in and out and press Play to start the game. None of the tools do anything yet, but the next section remedies this.

Adding Touch and Mouse Events

To turn this into an editor, the three missing event methods—`touch`, `drag`, and `release`—need to be written to look at the current tool and take the appropriate action. The code for these three methods along with the code for two supporting methods, `tilePos` and `tool`, is shown in Listing 19-5 and should be added to the bottom of `quintus_editor.js` inside of the `editor` component definition.

LISTING 19-5: The Canvas event methods

```
touch: function(e) {
  var touch = e.originalEvent.changedTouches ?
                e.originalEvent.changedTouches[0] : e,
      stage = this.entity;
  this.start = { pageX: touch.pageX, pageY: touch.pageY };
  this.viewportX = stage.viewport.centerX;
  this.viewportY = stage.viewport.centerY;
  this.tool(touch);
  e.preventDefault();
},

drag: function(e) {
  var touch = e.originalEvent.changedTouches ?
                e.originalEvent.changedTouches[0] : e,
      stage = this.entity;
  if(this.start) {
    this.tool(touch);
  }
  e.preventDefault();
},

release: function(e) {
  this.start= null;
},

tilePos: function(x,y) {
  var canvasPos = $(Q.el).offset(),
      canvasX = (x - canvasPos.left) / Q.el.width() * Q.width,
      canvasY = (y - canvasPos.top) / Q.el.height() * Q.height,
      viewport = this.entity.viewport,
```

continues

LISTING 19-5 *(continued)*

```
            tileLayer = this.entity.collision,
            tileX = Math.floor( (canvasX / viewport.scale +
                                viewport.x - tileLayer.p.x)
                               / tileLayer.p.tileW),
            tileY = Math.floor( (canvasY / viewport.scale +
                                viewport.y - tileLayer.p.y)
                               / tileLayer.p.tileH);
        return { x: tileX, y: tileY };
    },

    tool: function(touch) {
      var stage = this.entity,
          viewport = stage.viewport;
      switch(this.selected) {
        case 'move':
          stage.centerOn(this.viewportX +
                        (this.start.pageX - touch.pageX)
                        / viewport.scale,
                      this.viewportY +
                        (this.start.pageY - touch.pageY)
                        / viewport.scale);
          break;
        case 'paint':
          var tile = this.tilePos(touch.pageX, touch.pageY);
          stage.collision.setTile(tile.x,tile.y,this.activeTile);
          break;
        case 'erase':
          var tile = this.tilePos(touch.pageX, touch.pageY);
          stage.collision.setTile(tile.x,tile.y,0);
          break;
      }
    },
```

The touch method, called on touchstart or mousedown, grabs either the mouse event data or the data for the first changed touch and stores the start position of the event as well as the original viewport center location. It then calls the tool method, which does the actual work based on the currently-selected tool.

The drag method, called on touchmove or mousemove, first checks that there is a current action that the editor is tracking, and if so it just calls the tool method to take whatever action is necessary.

Finally, the release method just sets the start property to null. Because that property is used by drag to determine if it should be doing something, it effectively stops the tool.

The tilePos method has the somewhat involved task to figure out the exact tile location based on an *x* and *y* location on the page. It determines this by first determining the pixel position on the Canvas element (stored in canvasX and canvasY) and then calculates the tile position (in tileX and tileY) by determining an accurate offset position for the viewport scale, the viewport location, and the tile layer offset and divides all those by the size of each tile.

The tool method looks at the currently active tool. If move is selected, the stage is recentered based on how far the user has dragged his finger or moved the mouse. If paint is selected, it sets the tile at that location to the active tile. If erase is selected, that tile is cleared.

If you load the editor in your browser or on a mobile device, you should move around and paint and erase tiles. Figure 19-1 shows how the editor looks on an iPhone in Landscape mode.

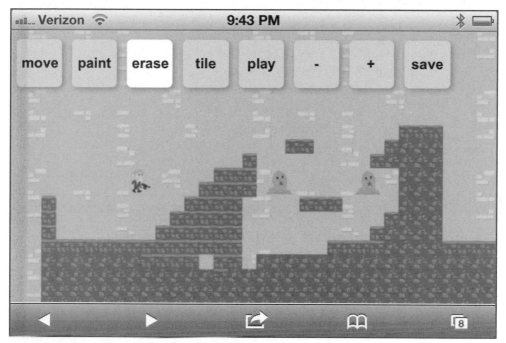

FIGURE 19-1: The editor on an iPhone.

Selecting Tiles

Only two pieces of functionality remain: the ability to select which tile to paint and the code to save levels back to the server. This section adds the first piece: the tile selection. The mechanism for selecting tiles enables the `tile` button to pop up an image of all the tiles in the spritesheet and lets the user select the tile to draw. To do this a Canvas element is created to hold the images, and then the events on that Canvas are converted to a tile selection.

To add the tile functionality, add in the code in Listing 19-6 to the bottom of the component definition in `quintus_editor.js`.

LISTING 19-6: The tile functionality

```
tile: function() {
  if(!this.tiles) this.setupTiles();
  $(this.tiles).show();
},

setupTiles: function() {
  var sheet = this.entity.collision.sheet();
  this.tiles = document.createElement("canvas");
  this.tiles.width = Q.el.width();
```

continues

LISTING 19-6 *(continued)*

```
        this.tiles.height = Q.el.height();
        var x = 0, y = 0, ctx = this.tiles.getContext('2d');
        for(var i=0;i<sheet.frames;i++) {
          sheet.draw(ctx, x, y, i);
          x += sheet.tilew;
          if(x >= this.tiles.width) {
            x = 0;
            y += sheet.tileh;
          }
        }
        $(this.tiles)
          .prependTo(Q.wrapper)
          .css({position:'absolute',
               top:60,
               zIndex: 200,
               backgroundColor:'white',
               width: Q.el.width(),
               height: Q.el.height()
             })
          .on('touchstart mousedown',this.selectTile);
      },

      selectTile: function(e) {
        var touch = e.originalEvent.changedTouches ?
                       e.originalEvent.changedTouches[0] : e,
            canvasPos = $(this.tiles).offset(),
            canvasX = (touch.pageX - canvasPos.left),
            canvasY = (touch.pageY - canvasPos.top),
            tileLayer = this.entity.collision,
            sheet = tileLayer.sheet(),
            tileX = Math.floor(canvasX / sheet.tilew),
            tileY = Math.floor(canvasY / sheet.tileh),
            frame = tileX + tileY *
                       Math.floor(this.tiles.width / sheet.tilew);
        $(this.tiles).hide();
        if(frame <= sheet.frames) {
          this.activeTile = frame;
        }
        e.preventDefault();
      },
```

The primary tool method, `tile`, has the job to first check if the tile Canvas has been set up, and if not, calls the `setupTiles` method to generate it. It then just shows that element, which blocks the rest of the screen and waits for an event on the element to select a tile.

The `setupTiles` method creates a Canvas element, draws each tile in the tile map's spritesheet, and then adds that element into the editor `controls` DOM element. It then adds an event handler to let the user select a tile by clicking or touching it.

Finally, the `selectTile` method grabs the wanted tile frame by doing a little bit of math to calculate the frame based on the size of the tiles and the size of the Canvas. It then checks that the frame is a valid frame and if so sets the `activeTile`.

Running the editor in the browser should now allow you to choose different tiles that make up elements on the page.

ADDING LEVEL-SAVING SUPPORT

The last task of the editor is to support the ability to save the level you've modified back to the server. On the client side, the code for doing this, as shown in Listing 19-7, is straightforward. This code should go in the same spot as usual at the bottom of the component definition in `quintus_editor.js`.

LISTING 19-7: The editor save method

```
save: function() {
  var levelName = prompt("Level Name?",this.levelFile);
  if(levelName) {
    $.post('/save',{ tiles: this.entity.collision.p.tiles,
                     level: levelName });
  }
}
```

This code pops up the browser prompt dialog to ask the user for a filename and then posts that filename back to the server using `$.post` to send along the tiles data directly from the collision layer `tile` property.

On the server side, things are almost as easy. Using Express's syntax for adding routes to the server, add the code in Listing 19-8 to the bottom of `app.js`.

LISTING 19-8: The server save method

```
app.post('/save', function(req, res){
  var data = _(req.body.tiles).map(function(row) {
    return _(row).map(function(tile) { return Number(tile); });
  });
  fs.writeFile("public/data/" + req.body.level,
               JSON.stringify(data));
  res.send(201);
});
```

This code simply defines a route at `/save` that grabs the data that was posted in, transforms the `tiles` data into numbers, and then writes out a file. By default the posted tile data comes in correctly as an array of arrays, but each element in the array is a string, so it needs to be converted into a number.

Writing the file is as simple as calling `fs.writeFile` and passing the filename and the level data converted to a JSON string using `JSON.stringify`.

SECURITY WARNING

This code is not something you would want to deploy to a public web server but would be something you might use internally to develop levels. Because the code lets the user write to an arbitrarily-named file, it could be used to overwrite data files or operating system files. A production end-user-friendly editor would check the validity of the passed in filename or save the data to a database instead of the filesystem.

If you restart the server and reload the editor, you should now have a working editor that you can use to create and edit level tile data. This chapter doesn't cover the details to add and manipulate sprites, such as the location of the player and the blobs, in addition to the tile data. This is something that would be game-dependent, but the basic idea is the same: Add an interface to add and manipulate elements, and then provide a serialization method to save that data back to the server.

SUMMARY

This chapter went through the steps to add an interactive game tile editor to the platformer game from the last chapter. The chapter showed you how to add a tool system and let the user select, paint, and erase tiles. It also added support for saving the level data back to the server, which makes it easier to create and edit levels than trying to edit JSON data files by hand. You'll continue with Node.js in the next chapters to build some more complicated functionality for multiplayer gaming.

PART VI
Multiplayer Gaming

20

Building for Online and Social

WHAT'S IN THIS CHAPTER?

➤ Understanding HTTP-base multiplayer

➤ Building a simple social game with Node.js

➤ Integrating with Facebook

➤ Connecting to a NoSQL database

➤ Deploying your game

WROX.COM CODE DOWNLOADS FOR THIS CHAPTER

You can find the wrox.com code downloads for this chapter at www.wrox.com/remtitle .cgi?isbn=9781118301326 on the Download Code tab. The code is in the Chapter 20 download and individually named according to the names throughout the chapter.

INTRODUCTION

The games built so far in this book have been single-player experiences, but it doesn't need to be that way: With the Internet easily accessible from any HTML5-powered device at almost any time, you can connect your game to a central database and make it playable from within Facebook on both desktop and mobile. This chapter creates a simple game playable from within Facebook.

UNDERSTANDING HTTP-BASED MULTIPLAYER GAMES

The most basic type of a multiplayer game you can build is the one in which the client does full-page or AJAX requests to update itself. This type of game relies on the client sending information to and requesting information from the server. If this sounds like a typical web page, you're correct. The downside is that the server has no capability to reverse the equation and instantly notify the client when something happens. The upside is that you can use a standard web architecture and server to build and scale your game.

Most small-scale websites share a similar architecture: server code written in a scripting language (be it PHP, Ruby, Python, or JavaScript) that writes and reads data to and from a persistence layer, such as a database. No information is shared between requests except a small amount of session data; instead everything is stored in the database (or other persistence layer such as a key-value store such as Redis). Keeping the architecture simple means that you can continue to add web servers to handle an increased load, and the only area in which you need to worry about having a scaling problem is at the database layer.

This type of architecture has served the web well for the past couple of decades and can be a suitable architecture for building multiplayer games provided it's used appropriately. It's not a great architecture for games that need to have a lot of direct interactions between different players because the server can't immediately notify one player of something another player does.

This act of periodically requesting information from the server is called *polling* because the client periodically polls the server for new information. Doing AJAX polling frequently can give the appearance of a pseudo-real-time multiplayer in which things happen even when the player isn't explicitly taking an action.

The best types of multiplayer games for polling are ones in which the actions of each player are mostly autonomous and the multiplayer aspect of the game doesn't involve players interacting too much with each other. These include games where players play primarily by themselves, but a central server keeps players honest by running a lot of the game logic on the server. Games in the older generation of social games, such as *Mob Wars*, are a good fit for this.

The other option, discussed in Chapter 21, "Going Real Time," is to use a socket-based technology, such as Websockets, Flash sockets, or a pseudo-socket workaround such as long-polling to allow the server to initiate requests. Chapter 21 explains these terms and concepts in depth.

PLANNING A SIMPLE SOCIAL GAME

The best way to understand how to create an HTTP-based multiplayer game is to build one. You could build lots of complicated social games, but building a simple game that serves as an example of how the various pieces of a multiplayer game connect should be enough to get you started on something more involved.

The game that you build is a simple game based on Ian Bogost's social game parody *Cow Clicker*. The point of *Cow Clicker* is, as you may have guessed, to click your cow at regular intervals and get points for doing so. The game built in this chapter builds a similar game but with an exciting twist: You click a blob instead of a cow. The blob in question is the enemy blob from the platformer game built in Chapter 18, "Creating a 2-D Platformer."

Although the game is quite simple, it requires all the pieces of a typical HTTP-based multiplayer game: a server to run the game, an authentication system to log in users, a database to store the user's progress, and game logic that resides on the server to control the actions a player can take.

The server used is a simple Node.js application running the Express framework. Being a social game, it uses Facebook as an authentication system to allow users to log in without entering their e-mail address or creating a password. To store progress, the game connects to a NoSQL database named MongoDB. The server will be set up to allow only the players to click on their blob at some specified interval to prevent them from accumulating points too quickly.

INTEGRATING WITH FACEBOOK

To create a game that uses Facebook for authentication, you need to create a Facebook application to generate an Application ID and App secret.

Generating the Facebook Application

To create the application, make sure you are logged in to Facebook, and then go to `https://developers.facebook.com`. Click the Apps button on the top of the page, and then the + Create New App button. Enter the name **Blob Clicker** as the name of the Application, as shown in Figure 20-1, leaving the app namespace blank.

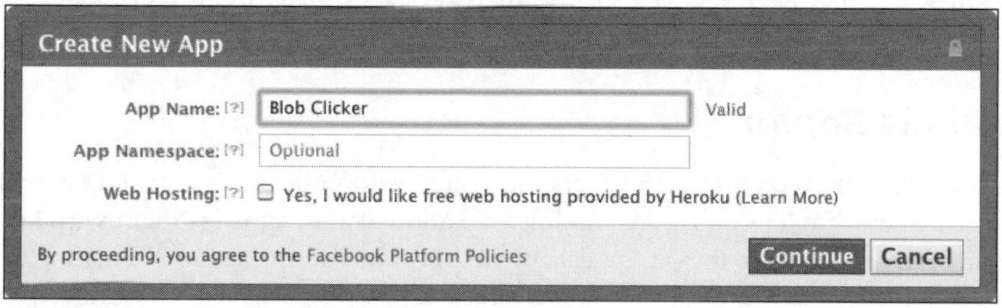

Create New App	
App Name: [?]	Blob Clicker Valid
App Namespace: [?]	Optional
Web Hosting: [?]	☐ Yes, I would like free web hosting provided by Heroku (Learn More)
By proceeding, you agree to the Facebook Platform Policies	Continue Cancel

FIGURE 20-1: Creating a new app.

If you haven't yet verified your account, you'll need to go through a security check as well.

Next, you are presented with your App ID, App Secret, and a screen of options to configure the Application. To start, the Application runs off of `localhost` for testing purposes. To set this up, fill in the domain name **localhost** in the App Domains field. Next, further down the page, click the section Website with Facebook Login, and type the URL **http://localhost:3000/** (don't forget the final forward slash "/") into the Site URL field. Figure 20-2 shows how this screen should look.

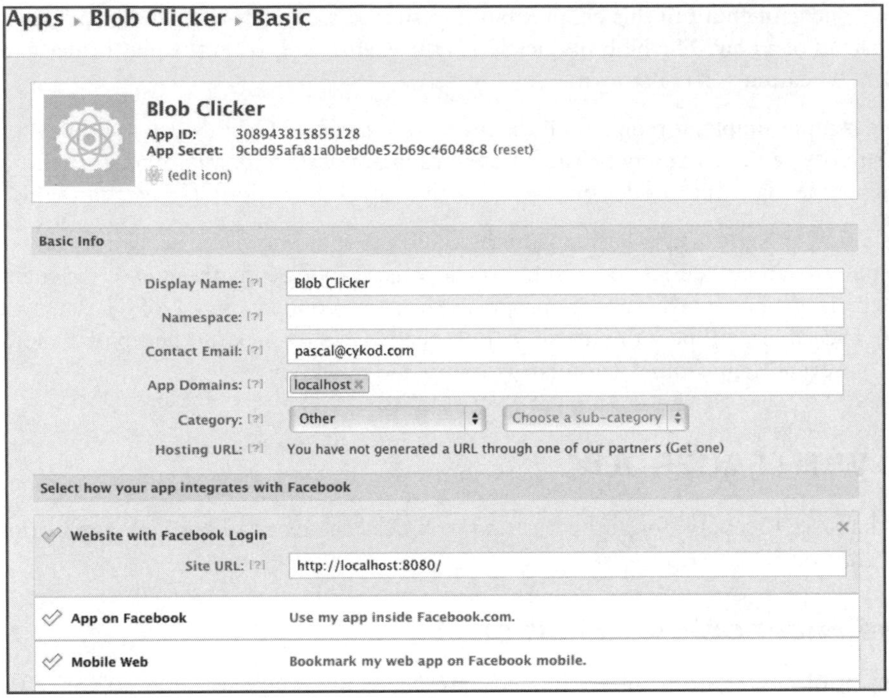

FIGURE 20-2: Basic app information.

At the bottom of the page, click the Save Changes button. Don't share your App Secret with anyone else. (The secret in Figure 20-2 has been reset.) The App ID is public information used to identify your application.

Creating the Node.js Server

To create a Node.js server that can integrate with Facebook, you'll use a node module called Faceplate, created by the web hosting company Heroku. This module will allow you to let users login with Facebook and read and write Facebook data via the Facebook API. Later in the section "Pushing to a Hosting Service," you will generate a hosting URL on Heroku to allow others to play the game.

As usual, the first step to create a Node.js application is to create a `package.json` file that describes the dependencies of the application. Because this application is hosted on Heroku, you also need to add an "engines" section that indicates the version of Node.js that is required.

Create a new directory called **blob_clicker** and in that directory create a new **package.json** file with the contents of Listing 20-1.

LISTING 20-1: Blob Clicker package.json

```
{
  "name": "blob-clicker",
  "version": "0.0.1",
```

```
    "private": true,
    "engines": {
      "node": "0.6.11",
      "npm":  "1.1.1"
    },
    "dependencies": {
      "express": "2.5.8",
      "ejs":         "0.4.3",
      "faceplate": "0.0.4",
      "mongodb": "1.0.2"
    }
  }
```

The dependencies for this game are Express, the aforementioned Faceplate, and a module called ejs (embedded JavaScript), which is a simple templating system that enables you to create views with server-side JavaScript embedded directly in them. Finally, mongodb is a module that connects to the MongoDB database later in this chapter.

Next, create a **web.js** file that can hold the basic stub of the server and enter the code in Listing 20-2.

LISTING 20-2: web.js application stub

```
var express = require('express');

var fbId = process.env.FACEBOOK_APP_ID || "YOUR FACEBOOK APP ID",
    fbSecret = process.env.FACEBOOK_SECRET || "YOUR FACEBOOK SECRET",
    sessionSecret = process.env.SESSION_SECRET || "A RANDOM STRING",
    port = process.env.PORT || 3000;

var app = express.createServer(
  express.logger(),
  express.static(__dirname + '/public'),
  express.bodyParser(),
  express.cookieParser(),
  express.session({ secret: sessionSecret }),
  require('faceplate').middleware({
    app_id: fbId,
    secret: fbSecret,
    scope:  'email'
  })
);

app.listen(port);

function login_page(req,res) {
  if(req.facebook.token) {
    req.facebook.me(function(user) {
      req.session.user_id = user.id;
      req.session.user_name = user.name;
      res.redirect('/game');
    });
```

continues

LISTING 20-2 *(continued)*

```
      } else {
        req.facebook.app(function(app) {
          res.render('login.ejs', {
            layout:    false,
            req:       req,
            app:       app
          });
        });
      }
    }

    app.get('/',login_page);
    app.post('/',login_page);

    function authenticated(method) {
      return function(req,res) {
        if (req.session.user_id) {
          method(req,res);
        } else {
          res.redirect('/');
        }
      }
    }
    app.get('/game',authenticated(function(req,res) {
      res.end("You are: " + req.session.user_name );
    }));
```

The server has three main parts. The first part sets up defaults along with app as an express-powered server. The second part deals with the home page, which allows Facebook login. Lastly, the authenticated method and the /game page is used by the game to verify you are logged in to actually play the game.

The top of the file needs to be modified with your Facebook App ID, your Facebook App Secret, and a random string used to encode the session. You should change the random string to prevent users from modifying their session data, but you can also leave it as is until you deploy. The boolean OR || is used to check environment variables for a corresponding value first. Heroku uses environment variables to store configuration data to make it easier to use different values for development and production.

The express app is created. It sets up the various pieces of the server needed, including logging, a public directory for serving files, the body and cookie parsers, a session for tracking who is logged in, and the faceplate middleware used for Facebook authentication using OAuth2. The app is told to listen on the specified port, which either defaults to 3000 or the port set up by the hosting server.

The login_page method is used as the homepage of the application. Its job is to check if the user has a valid session token from Facebook and if so save the user's Facebook ID and name in the session and redirect to the /game page. If not it renders the login.ejs page, which shows the login button to allow players to log in.

login_page is bound to both GET and POST methods. The GET method is used by default when you hit the page, but the POST method is used to send the data about the user back to the server.

In canvas applications, Facebook connects directly to the canvas URL of the application with the signed request if the user is already logged in.

The `authenticated` method is a meta-method that takes in a method and wraps it in a check to see if the user is logged in. If not, the user is redirected back to the home page to log in.

Finally, the `/game` path, which uses the `authenticated` method, displays a message to the users with their name. It's just a stub to verify that authentication works correctly and is filled out with the game logic in the section "Finishing Blob Clicker."

Adding the Login View

The basic Facebook integration is almost done; all that's still needed is to add the `login.ejs` view file and a special file called `channel.html`, which helps Facebook deal with cross-domain issues in Internet Explorer.

Create a new directory inside of your `blob_clicker` directory called **views**, and add the code in Listing 20-3 to a file in that directory called `login.ejs`.

LISTING 20-3: The login.ejs view file

```
<!DOCTYPE html>
<html>
  <head>
    <title>Login to Blob Clicker</title>
    <script src="//code.jquery.com/jquery-1.7.2.min.js"></script>
    <meta name="viewport" content="width=device-width,➡
user-scalable=0, minimum-scale=1.0, maximum-scale=1.0"/>
    <link href='/style.css' rel='stylesheet' type='text/css' />
  </head>
  <body>
    <div id="fb-root"></div>
    <script type="text/javascript">
      window.fbAsyncInit = function() {
        FB.init({
          appId      : '<%= app.id %>',
          channelUrl : '//<%= req.headers['host'] %>/channel.html',
          status     : true,
          xfbml      : true
        });

        FB.Event.subscribe('auth.login', function(response) {
          $("#login").hide();
          $("#signed_request").val(response.authResponse.signedRequest);
          $("#signed_form").submit();
        });
        FB.Canvas.setAutoGrow();
      };

      $(function() {
        window.scrollTo(0,10);
```

continues

LISTING 20-3 *(continued)*

```
        $("html").on("touchmove",function(e) { e.preventDefault(); });
    });

    // Load the SDK Asynchronously
    (function(d, s, id) {
      var js, fjs = d.getElementsByTagName(s)[0];
      if (d.getElementById(id)) return;
      js = d.createElement(s); js.id = id;
      js.src = "//connect.facebook.net/en_US/all.js";
      fjs.parentNode.insertBefore(js, fjs);
    }(document, 'script', 'facebook-jssdk'));
  </script>

  <form action='/' id='signed_form' method='post'>
    <input type='hidden' name='signed_request'
          id='signed_request' value=''/>
  </form>
  <div id='title-screen'>
    <div id='login'>
      <div class="fb-login-button" data-scope="email"></div>
    </div>
  </div>
  </body>
</html>
```

This view file consists of nothing more than a little bit of JavaScript to set up the Facebook JavaScript SDK, display a login button, and submit the signed_request to the page when the user is logged in.

The file references a style.css file that you can find in the code for the chapter along with three images: blog.png, title.png, and interior.png. Place the style.css file into a new public/ directory underneath the blob_clicker directory, and place the images into public/images/. If you don't use the files, the app is still playable; however, it appears just as unstyled text. The login screen with the images and styles loaded is shown in Figure 20-3.

Facebook calls a method called fbAsyncInit when it has finished loading and initializing its JavaScript. This means that after you're inside of fbAsyncInit, you know that the Facebook SDK is available to use. To get the SDK set up, first you need to call FB.init with the App ID you created, which is passed automatically using the ejs tag <%= app.id %>. Then FB.init also needs to be passed the URL of a special channel.html file. This is complicated by the fact that this needs to be an absolute URL, which is generated using the host header.

FIGURE 20-3: Blob Clicker login screen.

Next, the application subscribes to the auth.login event on the Facebook SDK. This event is triggered when the user logs in or is logged in. To pass the signed-request to the server, the code uses a form with a hidden field that it POSTs to. The server picks up the parameter `signed_request` and performs the necessary logic to log the user in.

The `FB.init` method also accepts a `cookie` option, which sets a session cookie with the signed request. This cookie would automatically pass the signed request data to the server. Unfortunately, the `faceplate` middleware parses this signed request on each HTTP request, which results in a separate server-side HTTP request to the Facebook API that slows down your game. By setting the signed request only on login, the game can be much snappier.

Next, the code that Facebook provides to load the Facebook JavaScript SDK asynchronously is included.

Finally, a Facebook login button is added onto the page by including a `<div>` tag with the correct class:

```
<div class="fb-login-button" data-scope="email"></div>
```

The last piece needed is to create the `channel.html` for browsers that don't support cross-domain communication. Create a directory under your application called **public/** and enter the code in Listing 20-4 into a file called `channel.html` in that public directory.

LISTING 20-4: channel.html

```
<script src="http://connect.facebook.net/en_US/all.js"></script>
```

As mentioned, this file is required for Internet Explorer and some older browsers, so if it's not set up correctly, you may not notice until the bug reports start coming in.

Testing the Facebook Authentication

With all the pieces in place, you should now test the Facebook authentication. You can run your Node.js application by typing **node web.js**. This starts the server on port 3000. You should now visit the server in your desktop browser by visiting `http://localhost:3000`.

If everything runs correctly, you should see the title screen and a small Facebook login button that you can click. Clicking the button pops up an OAuth login screen, as shown in Figure 20-4.

FIGURE 20-4: Blob Clicker OAuth login.

Clicking on the Log in with Facebook button takes you back to your application, which redirects to the `/game` screen and displays the name from your Facebook account.

CONNECTING TO A DATABASE

To track how many times the users click their blob and prevent them from clicking too frequently, you need a storage mechanism. As mentioned earlier, the mechanism used is the popular NoSQL database MongoDB.

Installing MongoDB on Windows

To install MongoDB you can download a recent version from its website at `www.mongodb.org/downloads`.

This is the recommended installation method for Windows. You need to download the correct version for the version of Windows you run, either 32 bit or 64 bit. After you have the file downloaded, unzip the folder to some location. (`C:\Program Files\` is a good spot.) You probably want to rename the resulting folder from mongo-xxxxxxx (where xxxxxxx is the version number you downloaded) to just **mongo**.

When you have the folder downloaded, you need to create a data directory. Mongo uses the directory `C:\data\db` by default, but it won't create those directories for you. Create the directories in Explorer or by launching the CMD terminal window and running the following:

```
C:\> mkdir \data
C:\> mkdir \data\db
```

After you create that folder, you can `CD` to the `mongo\bin` directory:

```
C:\> cd \Program Files\mongo\bin
```

From there you can run the `mongod` command to start the database server:

```
C:\Program Files\mongo> mongod
```

This launches the server. (You need to keep the window open.) For up-to-date installation instructions, see the Windows Quickstart tutorial on the Mongodb website at `www.mongodb.org/display/DOCS/Quickstart+Windows`.

You'll probably get tired of running Mongo from the command line, so to set it up to run as a service, you can see further instructions at `www.mongodb.org/display/DOCS/Windows+Service`.

Installing MongoDB on OS X

On OS X, if you followed the instructions in Chapter 8, "Running JavaScript on the Command Line," you can use Homebrew to install MongoDB:

```
$ brew install mongo
```

This should install MongoDB and start the server for you. If you don't have Homebrew installed, you need to download the software and follow the Quickstart instructions on the website.

Installing MongoDB on Linux

On Linux, you can use your package manager to install a recent version. On Ubuntu or Debian this means running the following:

```
$ apt-get install mongodb
```

This should install MongoDB and start the server for you as well.

Connecting to MongoDB from the Command Line

If everything goes according to plan, you can load the interactive shell by running `mongo` from any directory on OS X and Linux. On Windows, you need to run the command `mongo.exe` from the `bin/` directory inside of the directory where you unzipped it.

You should be presented with the interactive shell, which should enable you to type mongo commands at the > prompt. The MongoDB shell is a JavaScript-based shell, which makes it a good fit for everything you've been doing in this book so far. (MongoDB also supports a JavaScript-based map-reduce query language for complicated queries, but that's more complicated than what is covered in this chapter.)

MongoDB is a document-oriented storage database. What this means is that you can store arbitrary documents and data in it without needing to explicitly craft a database schema, as you would with a traditional relational database system (RDBMS) such as MySQL, PostgreSQL, or SQL Server.

A sample session with the interactive shell is shown following this paragraph; you can follow along by entering the commands after the prompt (>). The session shows how to switch databases, and insert and query data. Like an RDBMS, MongoDB supports having multiple different databases on a single installation. Instead of tables, however, MongoDB calls its equivalent structure *collections*. The following session switches to a database called `blob` and then inserts a couple of records into a collection called `clicks` and queries those records back out. At no point do you need to actually define the database `blob` or the collection `clicks`; you can start using them, and MongoDB creates them if necessary.

```
> use blob
switched to db blob
> db.clicks.save({ user: "Tester", clicks: 5 })
> db.clicks.save({ user: "Tester 2", clicks: 15 })
> db.clicks.save({ user: "Tester 3", clicks: 10 })
> db.clicks.find()
{ "_id" : ObjectId("4fb945ec8137643c2ae4085e"), ➡
"user" : "Tester", "clicks" : 5 }
{ "_id" : ObjectId("4fb945f28137643c2ae4085f"), ➡
"user" : "Tester 2", "clicks" : 15 }
{ "_id" : ObjectId("4fb946508137643c2ae40860"), ➡
"user" : "Tester 3", "clicks" : 10 }
>
> db.clicks.find({user:"Tester"})
{ "_id" : ObjectId("4fb945ec8137643c2ae4085e"), ➡
"user" : "Tester", "clicks" : 5 }
>
> db.clicks.findOne({user:"Tester 2"})
```

```
{
        "_id" : ObjectId("4fb945f28137643c2ae4085f"),
        "user" : "Tester 2",
        "clicks" : 15
}
>
> db.clicks.find().sort({ clicks: -1 }).limit(2)
{ "_id" : ObjectId("4fb945f28137643c2ae4085f"), ➡
"user" : "Tester 2", "clicks" : 15 }
{ "_id" : ObjectId("4fb946508137643c2ae40860"), ➡
"user" : "Tester 3", "clicks" : 10 }
> db.clicks.drop();
true
> exit
bye
```

Creating records in MongoDB is as easy as calling `db.collectionName.save({..})` with the model data in a JavaScript object.

Querying the collection is done by calling `db.collectionName.find()` either by itself to return all the objects or with the properties that you want to match in a JavaScript object. For example, to find all users with the `user` property set to "Tester," the command used earlier is

```
db.clicks.find({user:"Tester"})
```

If you are looking for a single object, you can use `db.collectionName.findOne({..})`. As you might expect, you can also order and limit the results by calling `sort` and `limit`. Finally `db .collectionName.drop()` can destroy the entire collection.

> **NOTE** *This scratches only the surface of what you can do with MongoDB. You can find more information about MongoDB in the official MongoDB manual at http://docs.mongodb.org/manual/.*

MongoDB provides a rich interface to query documents (including querying deep into nested documents), but the basics shown here are all that you need for the *Blob Clicker* game in this chapter.

Integrating MongoDB into the Game

Because Node.js works in an asynchronous manner, interacting with any external resources such as a database tends to be callback-heavy and results in heavy nesting that can make it hard to follow the application logic.

In a larger app, the solution to this would be to use something such as the promise pattern, which was discussed in Chapter 8. In the case of *Blob Clicker*, another solution is to separate the database code from the rest of the code so that it's easier to follow the flow of the actual pages.

To add database support into the game, replace the dummy `app.get("/game"...)` command at the end of the `web.js` file with the code in Listing 20-5. This code sets up three database methods— `fetchUser`, `clickUser`, and `topTen`—that are then used by the application's routes.

LISTING 20-5: Blob Clicker DB and Routes code

```
var clickTime = 5000,
    dbMethods = {};

require("mongodb").connect(process.env.MONGOHQ_URL ||
                           "mongodb://localhost/blob_clicker",
                           {}, function(error,db) {
  db.collection('users', function(err, collection){
    dbMethods.fetchUser = function(session,callback) {
      collection.findOne({ user_id: session.user_id },
                         function(error,user) {
        if(!user) {
          user = {
            user_id: session.user_id,
            name: session.user_name,
            clicks: 0,
            next_click: new Date().getTime()
          }
        }
        callback(user);
      });
    };

    dbMethods.clickUser = function(user, callback) {
      var now = new Date().getTime();
      if(user.next_click <= now) {
        user.clicks += 1;
        user.next_click = now + clickTime;
        collection.save(user, function() { callback(user); });
      } else {
        callback(false);
      }
    };

    dbMethods.topTen = function(callback) {
      collection.find().sort({ clicks: -1 })
                       .limit(10)
                       .toArray(function(error,results) {
        var output = [];
        for(var i in results) {
          output.push([ results[i].name, results[i].clicks ]);
        }
        callback(output);
      });
    };
  });
});

app.get('/game',authenticated(function(req,res) {
  dbMethods.fetchUser(req.session,function(user) {
```

continues

LISTING 20-5 *(continued)*

```
        var now = new Date().getTime(),
            nextClick = (user.next_click - now)/1000;
        res.render('game.ejs', {
            layout:   false,
            req:      req,
            user:     user,
            nextClick: nextClick
          });
    });
 }));

 app.post("/click",authenticated(function(req,res) {
   dbMethods.fetchUser(req.session,function(user) {
     dbMethods.clickUser(user,function(clicked) {
       if(clicked) {
         var now = new Date().getTime(),
             nextClick = (user.next_click - now)/1000;
         res.json({ clicked: true, user: clicked, nextClick: nextClick });
       } else {
         res.json({ clicked: false })
       }
     });
   });
 }));

 app.get('/top-ten',authenticated(function(req,res) {
   dbMethods.topTen(function(results) {
     res.json({ users: results });
   });
 }));
```

The top var declaration sets up the clickTime variable, which controls how long a player needs to wait to click, and a dbMethods object, which will be filled with the database methods.

Next, the application pulls in the mongodb driver and connects to the database. Again, an environment variable is used if it exists; otherwise, the local database blob_clicker is used.

Next, the system connects to the users collection and defines the three database methods: fetchUser, clickUser, and topTen. The first uses collection.findOne to look up a user by her Facebook ID, and if one is found it returns that. Otherwise it sets up a new object that can be used instead. The user object is then passed to the callback. The system relies on the user's Facebook ID as the unique identifier by which to look up users.

The second method, clickUser, takes in the user object and sees if that object is ready to be clicked again. If so, it updates the click count and the next click and saves the object, returning true to the callback after the object is saved. If not, it calls the callback with false.

The third method, topTen, uses the find, sort, and limit methods to return a list of the top-ten clickers, sorted by the clicks field in descending order. The MongoDB collection method supports chaining multiple query methods together, with a final call to toArray returning the array of results.

> ### DON'T FORGET YOUR INDEXES
>
> The code presented earlier doesn't create any structures known as indexes on the collection. Although this works passably well when you have a small number of users, it means that MongoDB needs to look through every document of the collection to find users by their ID. To speed up this and other queries, you need to tell MongoDB how to create indexes for its collections much in the same way you would in an RDBMS. From the `mongo` shell, you can run the following:
>
> ```
> db.users.ensureIndex({user_id:1});
> ```
>
> This ensures there is an index on the `user_id` field in the `users` collection. See `www.mongodb.org/display/DOCS/Indexes` for more details.

After the database methods, the three routes for the game are defined. The first route, `/game`, ensures that the user is authenticated by wrapping the response in the aforementioned `authenticated` call. It then grabs the user's object from the database, calculates the time to the next click, and renders the `game.ejs` view.

The `click` method, which is where the application POSTs clicks by the user, first grabs the user object from the database and then tries to click the user. If the click succeeds, it returns `clicked:true`, the updated user object (which contains the click count), and the newly calculated next click time; otherwise, it returns `clicked:false`. The method uses Express's `res.json` method to return JSON back to the client, which can be easily parsed and processed by jQuery.

Finally, the `top-ten` method simply returns the JSON for the top 10 clickers as JSON.

FINISHING BLOB CLICKER

To finish the Blob Clicker game, the last piece needed is the `game.ejs` file, which contains the code for the game. Because the game in this case is extremely simple, rather than pull in the Quintus engine, the code just uses a few jQuery calls to update the page.

Add the code in Listing 20-6 to a new file in the `views/` directory called **game.ejs**.

LISTING 20-6: The view/games.ejs file

```
<!DOCTYPE html>
<html>
  <head>
    <title>Blob Clicker</title>
    <script src="//code.jquery.com/jquery-1.7.2.min.js"></script>
    <link href='/style.css' rel='stylesheet' type='text/css' />
    <meta name="viewport" content="width=device-width, ➥
user-scalable=0, minimum-scale=1.0, maximum-scale=1.0"/>
```

continues

LISTING 20-6 *(continued)*

```
    </head>
    <body>
      <div id="fb-root"></div>
      <div id="main-screen">
        <h1><%= user.name %></h1>
        <div id='blob'>Click Me</div>
        <div id='clicks'><%= user.clicks %></div>
        <div id='show-top-ten'>See Top Ten</div>
        <div id='hide-top-ten'>Back to game</div>
        <ol id='top-ten'></ol>
      </div>
      <script>
        $(function() {
          var nextClick = <%= nextClick %>,
              clickTimer = null;

          function updateNextClick() {
            $("#blob").text(nextClick >= 0 ?
                              Math.ceil(nextClick) + " seconds" :
                              "Click Now");
          }

          function setClickTimer() {
            clearInterval(clickTimer);
            clickTimer = setInterval(function() {
              nextClick--;
              updateNextClick();
            },1000);
          }

          updateNextClick();
          setClickTimer();

        $("#blob").on("click",function() {
  $.post("/click",function(data) {
            if(data.clicked) {
              $("#clicks").text(data.user.clicks);
              nextClick = data.nextClick;
              updateNextClick();
              setClickTimer();
            }
          });
        });

        $("#show-top-ten").on("click",function() {
          $("#show-top-ten,#blob").hide();
          $.get("/top-ten",function(data) {
            $("#hide-top-ten,#top-ten").show();
            $("#top-ten").empty();
            $(data.users).each(function(idx) {
              $("#top-ten").append("<li> " + this[0] + ": " + this[1]);
            });
```

```
      });
    });

    $("#hide-top-ten").on("click",function() {
      $("#show-top-ten, #blob").show();
      $("#hide-top-ten, #top-ten").hide();
    });

    window.scrollTo(0,10);
    $("html").on("touchmove",function(e) { e.preventDefault(); });
  });

</script>
</body>
</html>
```

For conciseness, this 80-line file contains all the pieces of the client side of the game (except the styles). A larger game would be broken into multiple separate JS files, as you've seen previously.

The file first sets up a number of HTML elements that contain the visual pieces of the game. Again, if you have the styles and images loaded in, you get something nicer looking; otherwise, you just see text. Figure 20-5 shows the final game in action.

The first portion of the game defines the methods for updating the countdown timer to let the users know when they can make the next click on the blob. It uses setInterval, which, although bad for animation, is great for a countdown timer because it triggers automatically each second.

Next, the click handler for the actual blob click sends off a POST to /click, which either responds with a { clicked: false } JSON object if the user were clicking preemptively or with the details about the total clicks and the next click if the user clicks appropriately.

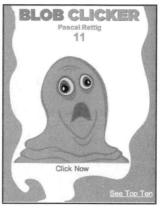

FIGURE 20-5: The final Blob Clicker game.

Clicking the top-ten link in the bottom of the page pulls the JSON for the top-ten list of users and creates a number of list items to display in the list.

Finally, hiding the top-ten list swaps what's visible on the page between the blob and the fetched top-ten list.

With game.ejs built, you can run the application locally, log in, and click the blob.

PUSHING TO A HOSTING SERVICE

Playing a Facebook game by yourself isn't much fun, so to let other players use the game, you want to push to a hosting service. Luckily, Facebook makes it extremely simple to deploy your game to a hosted service.

To start, go to the Basic settings page of your Facebook Application, and click the Get One link in the Hosting URL line, as shown in Figure 20-6.

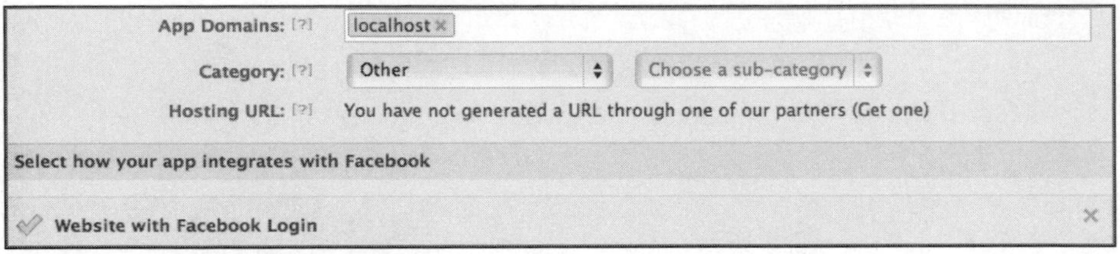

FIGURE 20-6: Setting a hosting URL.

Clicking this enables you to create an app on the Heroku hosting service. Click Next; then choose Node.js for the environment, and click Create. If you don't have a Heroku hosting account, you need to follow the prompts to set one up.

To tell Heroku what to run, you need to create a file called `Procfile` that tells the platform what to run to start your web server. Create the **Procfile** file in your main game directory, and put the following single line into it:

```
web: node web.js
```

This tells Heroku to run the command `node web.js` to run your web server when it deploys.

To use Heroku, install the Heroku Toolbelt, which is a command-line interface that enables you to push your app to Heroku using Git (which is also installed with the toolbelt). To install the toolbelt, go to `https://toolbelt.herokuapp.com/`. Download the package appropriate for your platform (which should be preselected) and install it.

After you have the toolbelt installed, you need to log in to Heroku. Open up a shell prompt and run the following:

```
heroku login
```

Enter the Heroku login e-mail and password. You may also be prompted to create a new SSH key if you don't have one. (If you don't know what an SSH key is, don't worry about it and just follow the prompts.)

After you log in, you need to create a new Git repository, commit your app, add a remote repository, add support for MongoDB, and then push to that repository. Although this sounds complicated, it is accomplished quickly with a single command for each step.

The only information you need to do this is the name of the application you just created, which will be something that resembles `severe-mountain-1301` (Heroku creates names in the form of adjective-noun-number).

Replacing the `severe-mountain-1301` with the name of the application Heroku created for you (which is in your Heroku account), enter the commands at the following command line from your game's directory:

```
git init
git commit . -m "Initial Commit"
git remote add heroku git@heroku.com:severe-mountain-1301.git
heroku addons:add mongohq:free
git push -f heroku master
```

The final command takes a few moments because it sends your game up into the cloud for deployment. The -f flag, which stands for *force*, is used because Facebook creates a default application that you want to overwrite; in most cases you never want to use the -f flag from this point forward.

> **ABOUT GIT VERSION CONTROL**
>
> Git is an extremely popular open-source version control system. If you haven't used Git yet, the best place to start is at `http://git-scm.com/book`. You have probably come across `http//github.com`, which is a Git hosting service that is free for open-source projects. Heroku uses Git to handle deployment, which can make it easy to integrate into your workflow but can be confusing for newcomers to Git.

Next, you must update the details of your Facebook application to match the URL of your Hosted app. Return to your Facebook application Basic settings to modify the App Domains and Site URL to match your application. Click to turn on App on Facebook and Mobile Web, which should have the hosting UR: prefilled in, as shown in Figure 20-7.

FIGURE 20-7: Hosting URLs set up in the Facebook application.

With the application deployed and the Facebook application updated, you can now play *Blob Clicker* in all its glory directly on the Site URL and inside of a Facebook canvas. To find the Facebook canvas URL, click the Apps link on the top of the page to return to your Applications summary page and locate the Canvas Page URL to play inside of Facebook.

SUMMARY

This chapter showed you how to create a simple social game and deploy it to the web. Although the game—*Blob Clicker*—isn't revolutionary, you can use the pieces needed to implement it, using Facebook Authentication, connecting to a database, and deploying to the web, to build a full-featured social game.

21

Going Real Time

WHAT'S IN THIS CHAPTER?

➤ Understanding WebSockets

➤ Creating a WebSocket-enabled server with Socket.io

➤ Building a real-time multiplayer game

WROX.COM CODE DOWNLOADS FOR THIS CHAPTER

You can find the wrox.com code downloads for this chapter at www.wrox.com/remtitle
.cgi?isbn=9781118301326 on the Download Code tab. The code is in the Chapter 21
download and individually named according to the names throughout the chapter.

INTRODUCTION

As shown in the preceding chapter, you can use a standard HTTP architecture to build multiplayer social games. There are some limits, however, to what type of game you can build without
resorting to various hacks if you want the server to push data to the client. WebSockets provides a
solution to this problem by bringing a socket-based, real-time, two-way conversation mechanism
natively to the browser. This chapter examines building real-time games using a Node.js library
named Socket.io, which supports WebSockets and a number of fallback mechanisms.

UNDERSTANDING WEBSOCKETS

WebSockets provide a browser-native API that enables the creation of a socket connection to
a server that provides a real-time, bidirectional channel with which to pass messages in both
directions: client to server and server to client.

TCP sockets are a familiar concept in network programming; all HTTP traffic over the web is transported via sockets. The problem from an HTML5 gaming perspective is that the browser opens a socket to the server, makes an HTTP request for a resource, waits for it to finish downloading, and then closes the socket. After the socket closes, sending any additional data requires opening a new socket. Furthermore, if the server has something to tell the client, it needs to wait until the client requests a new resource before it can send data.

Prior to WebSockets, one solution that saw a fair amount of usage is long polling. *Long polling* means that the client opens a request to the server that the server cannot write data to and instead remains open until it has something to tell the client. After it has data for the client, it writes data to the socket and then closes it, treating it like a normal request. The client processes the data sent from the server and then opens a new request immediately to wait for more data. This mechanism enables the server to send data to the client; however, the overhead associated with creating a new socket for each piece of data pushed in either direction means that performance suffers.

Flash had socket support for a long time, so another workaround was to use a Flash socket via a loaded SWF that has an interface exposed over a Flash-to-JavaScript. One problem with Flash sockets, however, is that to also serve normal HTTP requests on the same server, they need to exist on other ports than the normal HTTP port 80 and HTTPS port 443; so the Internet infrastructure that was built up around those specific ports (firewalls, proxies, and so on) needed updating to allow all web browsers and servers, many of which might be behind a household or corporate firewall that limits access to nonstandard ports.

In 2009, the WebSocket specification (`www.w3.org/TR/websockets`) was proposed as a solution to the lack of permanent sockets in the browser and the port problem. The idea behind WebSockets is to upgrade a standard HTTP socket into a WebSocket using a handshake technique that both the server and client need to understand. That socket is then kept open and allows bidirectional, full-duplex communication between the client and server.

The capability to use WebSockets in HTML5 applications was a bit slow in coming. The primary reason for this is that there has been an evolution of the specification, which means that different browsers support different versions of the spec, and some security issues related to cache positioning of proxies caused WebSocket support to be removed from Firefox until the issue was fixed.

The good news is that the issue has now been fixed, and all current-generation browsers except IE9 have some version of WebSockets turned on. The bad news is that because of proxies, caches, and IE9, you can't use standard WebSockets without support for some fallback. For this reason, in lieu of using straight WebSockets, this chapter spends the most time covering a Node.js library called Socket.io that provides a consistent client and server API regardless of whether native WebSockets or one of the supported fallback mechanisms are supported.

USING NATIVE WEBSOCKETS IN THE BROWSER

The native WebSocket API available in supported browsers is quite small and clean, but it doesn't do a lot other than send text to and from the server, so the addition of compatibility and fallback issues make it a chore to work with directly.

Assuming you have a server that supports WebSockets, you can open a connection using a new WebSocket object from the browser with the following:

```
var socket = new WebSocket("ws://servername.com/socket-resource");
```

The WebSocket equivalent of the `http://` URL prefix is `ws://`. Secure WebSockets, the equivalent of `https://`, has a `wss://` prefix.

That socket object has four callbacks used to listen for events on the socket:

```
socket.onopen = function(){
   // Socket has been opened
};
socket.onmessage = function(event) {
   // Message data in event.data
};
socket.onclose = function() {
   // WebSocket has been closed
};
socket.onerror = function(event) {
   // Error triggered
};
```

To send data on the socket, call `socket.send`:

```
socket.send(message);
```

This sends the message string to the server. One thing to remember with WebSockets is that all the data sent back and forth is in the form of a string, so it's up to you to encode and decode those strings with some mechanism. (JSON is an obvious and popular choice.)

Rather than set up a server simply to test out native WebSockets, the `websocket.org` website provides an echo server you can use to test writing the client-side WebSocket code.

Create a new file called **echo.html** and add the code in Listing 21-1 to it.

LISTING 21-1: A simple echo-server client

```
<!DOCTYPE HTML>
<html lang="en">
<head>
  <meta charset="UTF-8">
  <script src="http://ajax.googleapis.com/➡
ajax/libs/jquery/1.7.2/jquery.min.js" ></script>
  <title>WebSocket Test</title>
</head>
<body>
<script>
  var echoURI = "ws://echo.websocket.org/";
  var socket;

  $(function() {
    socket = new WebSocket(echoURI);
```

continues

LISTING 21-1 *(continued)*

```
        socket.onopen = function() {
          $("#output").append("<div>WebSocket Opened</div>");
        };

        socket.onclose = function() {
          $("#output").append("<div>WebSocket Opened</div>");
        };

        socket.onmessage = function(event) {
          $("#output").append("<div>WebSocket Message:" +
                                      event.data + "</div>");
        };

        socket.onerror = function() {
          $("#output").append("<div>WebSocket Error</div>");
        }
        $("#send").on("click",function() {
          var value = $("#message").val();
          $("#output").append("<div>Sending: " + value + "</div>");
          socket.send(value);
          $("#message").val("");
        });
      });

  </script>
  <input type='text' id='message'/>
  <button id='send'>Send</button>
  <div id="output"></div>
  </body>
  </html>
```

Load up this file in a WebSocket-enabled browser, and you can send messages to the server, which it will promptly echo back to you.

This code sets up a basic socket with the URI of the echo server and then adds callbacks that simply add a message to a <div> with an ID of output whenever one of the four basic events is triggered.

It also adds a click handler to the Send button to send whatever message is typed. Because the server it connects to is an echo server, any message sent should trigger a return message.

The preceding code covers using WebSockets on the client; on the server side you need a library that can handle long-lived requests. This means that using a standard PHP or Ruby on Rails framework won't work. Luckily your good friend Node works well with handling lots of concurrent connections.

As mentioned in the introduction, this chapter covers an abstraction on top of WebSockets called Socket.io on the server side. If you want to use straight WebSockets, you can take a look at the Node ws module, available on Github at https://github.com/einaros/ws.

This module enables you to create a WebSocket server in Node.js in a few lines of code and has syntax similar to the browser WebSocket API.

USING SOCKET.IO: WEBSOCKETS WITH FALLBACKS

If you want to create a real-time game without the hassles of worrying about browser compatibility and fallbacks, a number of libraries are available that can help, but one of the most popular and simplest to use is Socket.io, available at `http://socket.io`.

Socket.io is a Node library that abstracts WebSockets and multiple supported fallbacks on both the client and the server side. It also provides the capability to transparently send JSON data over sockets and adds support for any number of custom events. Socket.io also integrates nicely into Express, which means you can use a single app to serve your HTTP methods, your WebSockets, and your static files. Add in support for heartbeats, timeouts, and disconnection support, and you see why using a library over straight WebSockets makes your life easier.

To become familiar with Socket.io before building a game using the library, you'll build a simple multiuser scribble application that enables people to scribble over each other's drawings in real time.

Creating the Scribble Server

On the server side, Socket.io works by listening for `connection` events. These events trigger a callback with a `socket` object. You can then attach additional listeners for both standard events, such as `disconnect` and custom named events.

To send data you can call `socket.emit` with a name for the event and any data that needs to be passed along. You can send events to all sockets except the `socket` itself by calling `socket.broadcast.emit`.

To create the scribbler, first create a `package.json` file for the dependencies. Create a new project directory called **scribble**, and add the `package.json` file in Listing 21-2 to it.

LISTING 21-2: Scribbler package.json

```
{
    "name": "scribbler"
, "version": "0.0.1"
, "private": true
, "dependencies": {
    "express": "2.5.8",
    "socket.io": "0.9.6"
  }
}
```

Now run `npm install` from the command line in that directory to grab the dependencies—Socket.io has a few.

Next, create your `app.js` file, and add the code from Listing 21-3 to it.

LISTING 21-3: The Scribbler app.js

```
var express = require('express'),
    app = express.createServer(),
    io = require('socket.io').listen(app);

app.configure(function(){
  app.use(express.static(__dirname + '/public'));
});

app.listen(3000);

// Clear the board every 60 seconds
setInterval(function() {
  io.sockets.emit('clear');
},60000);

io.sockets.on('connection', function (socket) {
  socket.on('paint',function(data) {
    socket.broadcast.emit('paint', data);
  });
  socket.on('disconnect', function () {
   console.log("Someone disconnected");
  });
});
```

As Listing 20-3 shows, the code necessary to get the Socket.io server up and running is minimal. After creating an express server, to attach Socket.io to it, you simply call `listen`:

```
io = require('socket.io').listen(app);
```

The remaining code to set up Express, configure a static directory, and bind to a port is the same as you've seen previously.

Because the scribbles of a bunch of random users can most likely get messy, the server unceremoniously clears the board every 60 seconds by sending a `clear` message that tells the clients to clear their scribble areas. To target all sockets, you can call `io.sockets.emit`, which takes an event name and an optional data object.

To respond when a new socket connects, you need to bind to the `connection` event on the list of sockets, `io.sockets`. It triggers its callback with the `socket` object for the individual client connection.

You can store that socket object for later reference and bind additional events onto it. In this case, a `paint` event bound to the client triggers whenever it draws a line. The server responds by calling `socket.broadcast.emit`, which works like `io.sockets.emit` except it skips that socket it is called on.

Adding the Scribble Client

To round out the scribble app, add the client side of the app. This app uses Quintus primarily to save the steps of setting up and maximizing the Canvas. Create a **public/** subfolder underneath your app, and create an **index.html** with the content of Listing 21-4.

LISTING 21-4: The scribble index.html file

```
<!DOCTYPE HTML>
<html lang="en">
  <head>
    <meta charset="UTF-8">
    <meta name="viewport" content="width=device-width, user-scalable=0, ➡
minimum-scale=1.0, maximum-scale=1.0"/>
    <title>Scribble</title>
    <script src='js/jquery.min.js'></script>
    <script src='js/underscore.js'></script>
    <script src='js/quintus.js'></script>
    <script src='scribble.js'></script>
    <script src="/socket.io/socket.io.js"></script>
    <style>
      * { padding:0px; margin:0px; }
    </style>
  </head>
  <body>
  </body>
</html>
```

You need to create a `public/js/` subdirectory underneath `public/` that contains the three dependencies listed earlier: `jquery.min.js`, `underscore.js`, and `quintus.js`. You can pull these from the chapter code.

Notice one special script tag at the end:

```
<script src="/socket.io/socket.io.js"></script>
```

This is a path created by Socket.io that provides a number of conveniences. First, it sets the default WebSocket path and server to match the requested file to make connecting easier and prevent any issues determining the correct address between development and production environments. It also automatically determines which transport mechanism to use: straight WebSockets or one of the fallbacks.

Next, create the **scribble.js** file mentioned in Listing 21-4 in the `public/` directory. Add the code in Listing 21-5.

LISTING 21-5: scribble.js

```
$(function() {
  var Q = Quintus().setup('quintus', { maximize: true }),
```

continues

LISTING 21-5 *(continued)*

```
      socket = io.connect(),
      start = {},
      move = {};
  function getTouch(e) {
    var touch = e.originalEvent.changedTouches ?
                e.originalEvent.changedTouches[0] : e,
        canvasPos = Q.el.offset(),
        canvasX = (touch.pageX - canvasPos.left) / Q.el.width() * Q.width,
        canvasY = (touch.pageY - canvasPos.top) / Q.el.height() * Q.height;
    e.preventDefault();
    return { x: canvasX, y: canvasY };
  }

  function drawLine(from,to) {
    Q.ctx.strokeStyle= "#000";
    Q.ctx.beginPath();
    Q.ctx.moveTo(from.x,from.y);
    Q.ctx.lineTo(to.x,to.y);
    Q.ctx.stroke();
  }

  Q.el.on('touchstart mousedown',function(e) {
    start = getTouch(e);
  });

  Q.el.on('touchmove mousemove',function(e) {
    if(!start.x) return;
    move = getTouch(e);
    drawLine(start,move);
    socket.emit("paint",{ start: start, move: move });
    start = move;
  });

  Q.el.on('touchend mouseup mouseleave',function(e) {
    start.x = null;
  });

  socket.on("connect",function() {
    console.log("Connected");
  });

  socket.on("paint",function(data) {
    drawLine(data.start,data.move);
  });

  socket.on("clear",function(data) {
    Q.ctx.clearRect(0,0,Q.width,Q.height);
  });

});
```

As you can see, this code uses Quintus, but to set up only the Canvas, resize it, and make it available in the `Q.ctx` property.

Creating the socket connection to the server is as easy as calling

```
socket = io.connect();
```

Because the `socket.io.js` file was pulled to the same server as the socket is being connected to, you don't need to provide a URI or port to connect to. (You can provide these if necessary to connect to a different server.)

Next are two helper methods, `getTouch` and `drawLine`. `getTouch` grabs a Canvas pixel position from an event location. `drawLine` draws a new line on the Canvas between two points.

Scribbler next defines three event handlers that track touches, moves, and releases. On a touch or a mouse click, the app marks the start of the line. When you move your mouse or move your finger after that initial touch, the app simply draws a straight line from the start to the current location.

To let other users of the app see the line you have drawn, in addition to drawing the line, it also calls `socket.emit` to send a `paint` event back to the server. As you can see, the client API is similar to the one on the server.

Finally, if you release your finger or the mouse, the application stops drawing. The last three listeners bind to the socket. The first, `connect`, simply logs that the socket is connected to the console. It's there to show you that built-in events and custom events are treated the same way.

The first custom event `paint` draws a line based on data passed from the server. If you remember, the server simply repeats any `paint` events it receives and sends them to all the other clients.

The `clear` event, which is sent every 60 seconds by the server, tells the app to clear its entire Canvas.

This introduction should be enough to get you started with Socket.io, but the next section shows you how to build a simple pong game where two players can bounce a ball back and forth between each other.

BUILDING A MULTIPLAYER PONG GAME USING SOCKET.IO

Using a WebSocket-based technology opens up a lot of different possibilities for multiplayer game play, including real-time action games. To see this in action, you build a two-player pong game where players bat a ball back and forth across the screen.

In the game, both players simulate the entire game on each device; however, one player acts as the "master," and one acts as the "slave." The master controls the true location of the ball and sends updates periodically to the slave, who updates the location of the ball to reflect the true game state.

Dealing with Latency

One of the problems with multiplayer, real-time gaming is the issue of latency. Depending on the speed of the network and the distance between the server and players, latencies of more than 100ms and dropped packets are common on mobile. This means that to keep the action going you need to do some predictive modeling that takes latency into account.

Your pong game deals with this by calculating a "delay," which is the time it takes to get a packet from one player to another. It uses that delay to calculate how much farther the ball or other player should have moved from the time the data left one player to the time it arrived at another.

Because both games simulate the path of the ball, each player should see the ball updating smoothly while the slave player occasionally sees a blip course correction if the ball on one device is out of sync with the other device.

As you can see when playing the game, this works to varying levels of success depending on the browser and connection. As of this writing, mobile devices still have a way to go with WebSocket support, so a semi-real-time game might be a better option than a multiplayer action game.

Combating Cheating

There's only one way to combat cheating in a multiplayer HTML5 game: Never trust anything the client tells you except for user input. This means that the server needs to simulate the entire game and take user input only to update the state of the game.

Rather than, for example, a client saying, "My paddle is at x location 200," the client tells the server, "I want to move my paddle to the right," and the server updates the position of the paddle appropriately, responding to all the clients with the updated paddle position. Doing this means that the client can never tell the server to do something that's not physically possible in the game because the server is going to calculate the only game simulation that matters.

For example, in a game of pong, the player can't suddenly move from the left side of the screen to the right side of the screen. If the server just accepts the player's paddle position as fact, though, this could happen.

The downside to processing on the server is that it means you have a lot more processor load than you would if the clients handled all the simulation responsibilities.

The pong game in this chapter will not simulate everything on the server to keeps things simple, but because it's JavaScript all the way down, there's no reason you couldn't have the same game code run on the clients and authoritatively on the server.

Deploying Real-Time Apps

The hosting server used in the last chapter, Heroku, unfortunately doesn't support WebSockets because they don't make it through Heroku's various caching and proxying layers. Because WebSockets are only slowly starting to filter out into the web at large, you'll come across the same problem in some of the other managed hosting platforms. Nodejitsu is a Node.js hosting platform that supports native WebSockets.

If you want to work around this and force the use of long polling instead of WebSockets (at a hit to performance), you can modify your server code to force long polling and limit the transports used with (a max duration of 10 seconds is also required to prevent Heroku from timing out) the following code:

```
io.configure(function () {
  io.set("transports", ["xhr-polling"]);
  io.set("polling duration", 10);
});
```

Your other option is to deploy Node.js on your server or VPS. Although going through the steps to do this is outside of the scope of this book, with Amazon micro-instances running $14 month, it's not out of reach from a budget perspective.

Creating an Auto-Matching Server

One big part of a two-player multiplayer game is that you need two players to play the game. This provides a matching challenge: How do you pair players?

As you may have experienced, player matching in multiplayer games can become involved, with lobbies that show stats and images from games in progress and ones that match players up by skill level or other characteristics. Instead of building a lobby that requires a front end and UI, your pong game tries to create as many games with two players as possible. This means that the first player to hit the site will wait until the second one arrives. If a player leaves, the next player to join will rejoin the game with one player.

The other main task of the server is simply to pass messages back and forth between the players to keep the game in sync. In addition the server bounces a `delay` message from one client to the other client and back again to try to track the timing delay between clients.

Create a new directory called **pong**, and start with a `package.json` file similar to the one from the Scribble example in that directory, as shown in Listing 21-6.

LISTING 21-6: Pong package.json file

```
{
    "name": "multi-player-pong"
,   "version": "0.0.1"
,   "private": true
,   "dependencies": {
      "express": "2.5.8"
    , "socket.io": "0.9.6"
  }
}
```

Next, create the **app.js** file in the same directory with the contents of Listing 21-7. Per usual, the code sets up an Express server. As in the paint example, it connects Socket.io to the app to listen for socket connections.

LISTING 21-7: Pong app.js server code

```
var express = require('express'),
    app = module.exports = express.createServer(),
    io = require('socket.io').listen(app);
app.configure(function(){
  app.use(express.bodyParser());
  app.use(express.static(__dirname + '/public'));
```

continues

LISTING 21-7 *(continued)*

```
});

app.listen(3000);

var games = [];

io.sockets.on('connection',function(socket) {
  var game = null;
  for(var i=0;i<games.length;i++) {
    if(games[i].length < 2) {
      game = i;
    }
  }
  if(game === null) {
    games.push([])
    game = games.length-1;
  }
  games[game].push(socket);
  socket.set('game',game);
  if(games[game].length == 2) {
    games[game][0].set('partner',socket);
    games[game][1].set('partner',games[game][0]);
    games[game][0].emit('master');
    games[game][1].emit('slave');
  }

  socket.on('delay',function(data) {
    socket.get('partner',function(err,partner) {
      if(partner) {
        data.steps += 1;
        partner.emit('delay',data);
      }
    });
  });

  socket.on('move',function(data) {
    socket.get('partner',function(err,partner) {
      if(partner) {
        partner.volatile.emit('move',data);
      }
    });
  });

  socket.on('ball',function(data) {
    socket.get('partner',function(err,partner) {
      if(partner) {
        partner.volatile.emit('ball',data);
      }
    });
  });

  socket.on('disconnect',function() {

    socket.get('partner',function(err,partner) {
```

```
      if(partner) {
        partner.emit('end');
        partner.set("partner",null);
      }
    });

    socket.get('game',function(err,game) {
      var idx = games[game].indexOf(socket);
      if(idx!=-1) games[game].splice(idx, 1);
    });
  });
});
```

Now run `npm install` from the command line in that directory to grab the dependencies.

On new connections the server finds the first entry in the `games` array that has less than two entries. This array keeps sets of players who are playing together paired. If it can't find an entry that has fewer than two players, it adds a new entry to the array for the new game. In both cases it keeps the index in the games array to keep track of the game a socket is associated with.

The game uses Socket.io's capability to associate extra data with a socket via `socket.set` and `socket.get`.

If after adding the socket to the current game there are two players for the current game, the server sets one to be the master (the client that controls the canonical simulation of the ball) and one to be the slave. It also adds an item of data called `partner` to each socket that maps to its paired socket.

If you were to take this example to a more complete lobby-style game, you could create an object for each game that keeps a list of players in that game and makes it easy to send messages to all players in that game.

When the server receives a `delay` event, which is used to time the round-trip time for a packet, it passes it to the partner of the socket, incrementing the number of steps. When a socket receives a `delay` event with 3 hops, it knows that that packet has made a full round-trip, so an estimation of the time from one client to the other is one half the total delay time.

The primary data events, `move` and `ball`, simply pass data from one socket to the partner. Both are emitted as *volatile*, which means that the data is time dependent and in the case of a client doing long-polling, they may be skipped if the client is between requests. This is done as the data is passed along often enough; it's better to drop packets than to have the ball "fast-forward" when a player receives a bunch of packets in a row.

Finally, when a socket disconnects, it emits an event to its partner and removes itself from the game list. This means the next player to join will get matched if the player is still hanging around.

Building the Pong Front End

The front end to two-player pong consists of the basic HTML file in the `public/` directory that loads all the necessary dependencies, a `js/` directory with the dependencies and the Quintus engine, and a `pong.js` file for the game.

The basic HTML file is shown in Listing 21-8; it doesn't hold many surprises other than the addition of a black border to mark the Canvas on the desktop.

LISTING 21-8: pong index.html

```
<!DOCTYPE HTML>
<html lang="en">
  <head>
    <meta charset="UTF-8">
    <meta name="viewport" content="width=device-width, user-scalable=0, ➥
minimum-scale=1.0, maximum-scale=1.0"/>
    <title>Pong</title>
    <script src='js/jquery.min.js'></script>
    <script src='js/underscore.js'></script>
    <script src='js/quintus.js'></script>
    <script src='js/quintus_input.js'></script>
    <script src='js/quintus_sprites.js'></script>
    <script src='js/quintus_scenes.js'></script>
    <script src='pong.js'></script>
    <script src="/socket.io/socket.io.js"></script>
    <style>
      * { padding:0px; margin:0px; }
      canvas { border:1px solid black; }
    </style>
  </head>
  <body>
  </body>
</html>
```

Make sure you have jQuery, underscore, and all the necessary quintus*.js files in the public/js file; otherwise, the game won't run.

Next is the game in the pong.js file, as shown in Listing 21-9. Much of this should look familiar from the Block Break game from Chapter 10, "Bootstrapping the Quintus Engine, Part II." The pieces of the code that deal with Socket.io are highlighted as follows (the rest of the code is substantially different than blockbreak.js, however, so don't just add the highlighted pieces to the previous file):

LISTING 21-9: pong.js

```
$(function() {
  var Q = window.Q = Quintus()
                     .include('Input,Sprites,Scenes')
                     .setup('quintus');
  var socket = io.connect();
  Q.input.keyboardControls()
  Q.input.touchControls({
          controls: [ ['left','<' ],[],[],[],['right','>' ]]
        });
  var gameType = null, delay = 0;
  Q.Paddle = Q.Sprite.extend({
    init: function(props) {
      this._super(_(props).defaults({
        w: 60, h: 20,
        speed: 200,
        direction: null
```

```
      }));
    },
    step: function(dt) {
      dt += this.p.paddleDelay / 1000;
      this.p.paddleDelay = 0;
      if(this.p.direction == 'left') {
        this.p.x -= this.p.speed * dt;
      } else if(this.p.direction == 'right') {
        this.p.x += this.p.speed * dt;
      }
      if(this.p.x < 0) { this.p.x = 0; }
      if(this.p.x > Q.width - this.p.w) { this.p.x = Q.width - this.p.w; }
    },
    draw: function(ctx) {
      ctx.fillStyle = "black";
      ctx.fillRect(Math.floor(this.p.x),
                   Math.floor(this.p.y),
                   this.p.w,this.p.h);
    }
});

Q.PlayerPaddle = Q.Paddle.extend({
  step: function(dt) {
    var lastDirection = this.p.direction;
    this.p.direction = null;
    if(Q.inputs['left']) {
      this.p.direction = 'left';
    } else if(Q.inputs['right']) {
      this.p.direction = 'right';
    }
    this._super(dt);
    if(lastDirection != this.p.direction) {
      socket.emit("move",[this.p.direction,this.p.x]);
    }
  }
});

Q.EnemyPaddle = Q.Paddle.extend({
  init: function(props) {
    this._super(props);
    var self = this, p = this.p;
    socket.on("move",function(data) {
      p.direction = data[0];
      p.x = data[1];
      self.step(delay/1000);
    });
  }
});

Q.Ball = Q.Sprite.extend({
  init: function(props) {
    this._super(_(props||{}).defaults({
      x: 200, y: 100,
      w: 10,  h: 10,
```

continues

LISTING 21-9 *(continued)*

```
          dx: -1, dy: -1,
          speed: 100,
          ballRate: 0.5,
          ballSend: 0.5
        }));
      var self = this, p = this.p;
      if(gameType == 'slave') {
        socket.on("ball",function(pos) {
          p.x = pos.x;
          p.y = pos.y;
          p.dx = pos.dx;
          p.dy = pos.dy;
          self.step(delay/1000);
        });
      }
    },
    step: function(dt) {
      var p = this.p;
      var hit = Q.stage().collide(this);
      if(hit) {
        p.dy = hit.p.y < 100 ? 1 : -1;
      }
      p.x += p.dx * p.speed * dt;
      p.y += p.dy * p.speed * dt;
      var maxX = Q.width - p.w;
      if(p.x < 0) { p.x = 0; p.dx = 1; }
      else if(p.x > maxX) { p.dx = -1; p.x = maxX; }

      if(p.y < 0 || p.y > Q.height) {
        p.x = 200; p.y = 100;
        p.dy *= -1;
      }
      if(gameType == 'master') {
        p.ballSend -= dt;
        if(p.ballSend < 0) {
          socket.emit("ball", { x: p.x, y: p.y, dx: p.dx, dy: p.dy });
          p.ballSend += p.ballRate;
        }
      }
    },
    draw: function(ctx) {
      ctx.fillStyle = "black";
      ctx.beginPath();
      ctx.arc(this.p.x + this.p.w/2,
              this.p.y + this.p.h/2,
              this.p.w/2,0,Math.PI*2);
      ctx.fill();
    }
  });

Q.scene('game',new Q.Scene(function(stage) {
  if(gameType == 'master') {
```

```
      stage.insert(new Q.PlayerPaddle({ x:0, y: 40}));
      stage.insert(new Q.EnemyPaddle({ x:0, y: Q.height - 100}));
    } else if(gameType == 'slave') {
      stage.insert(new Q.EnemyPaddle({ x:0, y: 40}));
      stage.insert(new Q.PlayerPaddle({ x:0, y: Q.height - 100}));
    }
    stage.insert(new Q.Ball());
  }));

  socket.on("master",function() {
    gameType = 'master';
    Q.stageScene("game");
  });

  socket.on("slave",function() {
    gameType = 'slave';
    Q.stageScene("game");
  });

  socket.on("end",function() {
    Q.clearStage(0);
  });

  socket.on('delay',function(data) {
    if(data.steps == 3) {
      // delay 1/2 of the round trip time
      delay = (new Date().getTime() - data.timer)/2;
      if(delay > 50) {
        delay = 50;
      }
    } else {
      data.steps += 1;
      socket.emit('delay',data);
    }
  });

  setInterval(function() {
    socket.emit('delay',{ steps: 0, timer: new Date().getTime() });
  },2000);
});
```

Figure 21-1 shows the final game played on two adjacent desktop browsers.

As mentioned, although this is a lot of code to look at in one pass, the majority of it should look familiar from Block Break. After the initial engine set-up code, the game defines three paddle classes.

The first, Q.Paddle, simply defines a paddle that moves left or right depending on its direction attribute. The draw method is also overridden to draw a simple black rectangle.

The second paddle class inherits from Q.Paddle and defines the player's paddle: Q.PlayerPaddle. Its only job is to override the step method to control the direction property based on player input. It also emits a move event to the server that includes its direction and current x position every time its direction changes.

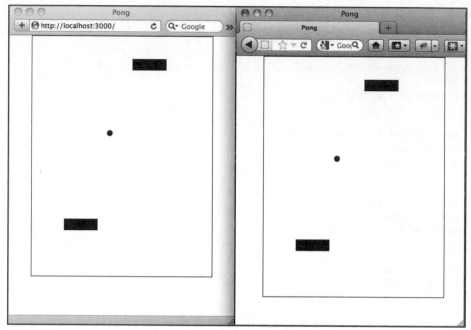

FIGURE 21-1: A game of pong between Safari and Firefox.

The third paddle class, Q.EnemyPaddle, represents the opposing paddle when the player is playing. Its only override from the base Q.Paddle class is to bind to the socket to set the paddle's direction and position. This is the move message passed from the Q.PlayerPaddle passed through by the app server.

The Q.Ball class used to represent the ball bears a lot of similarities to the ball from Block Break. The primary difference is that properties of the ball here either are updated occasionally by the server or periodically sent to the server to pass to the other player.

Even though both games are simulating the game at theoretically the same speed, differences in clocks, network delays, and graphics capabilities mean that the two clients would slowly fall out of sync with each other. To combat this, the full position and direction of the ball is passed from client to the server at a rate of ballRate, which is set to half of a second in the example.

When the slave receives the ball message indicating an updated ball position, callback updates the position and direction of the ball and then manually calls the step method to advance the ball by whatever the length of the network delay is between the two clients.

With the sprites defined, there is the additional complexity of setting up the scene according to whether the player is the master of the slave. It does this by looking at the gameType global variable to put the player on top and the enemy on the bottom if this client is the master or vice versa if it's the slave. Then it just inserts a ball and lets it fly.

The last chunks of code are the socket events. The slave and master events, if you remember how the server was set up, kick off the game by indicating the player is either the master or the slave and then stage the game scene. The end event, called when the other player disconnects, simply stops the game by clearing the stage.

More complicated is the delay event. This event is sent every two seconds via the final setInterval call at the end of the code, which sends a message with a steps variable and the current time in milliseconds. As you saw in the server code, this message is bounced from one client back to the originating client as a way to measure the delay in sending packets end to end. The client looks at the step variable and if it's equal to 3, it knows the message has made a complete trip.

When the originating server receives the message back, it grabs the updated time in milliseconds and calculates the round-trip delay by subtracting the current time from the time it sent the message originally. Dividing that number in half gets the time it takes to send a message from one client to another via the server.

Pulling it all together, you now have a game where two players can play directly against each other using a simple form of client-side prediction to try to keep the players in sync with each other.

SUMMARY

This chapter examined how to use WebSockets and a library called Socket.io to build real-time games where multiple players can interact directly with each other. It showed how to take code that is similar to a single-player game from earlier in the book and change it into a multiplayer game that passes messages through a central server. Using the code presented here you should be able to build both real-time and semi-real-time games that have near-instant interaction between multiple players.

22

Building Nontraditional Games

WHAT'S IN THIS CHAPTER?

➤   Creating a Twitter application

➤   Connecting to the Twitter API

➤   Building a game on the Twitter API

WROX.COM CODE DOWNLOADS FOR THIS CHAPTER

You can find the wrox.com code downloads for this chapter at www.wrox.com/remtitle .cgi?isbn=9781118301326 on the Download Code tab. The code is in the Chapter 22 download and individually named according to the names throughout the chapter.

INTRODUCTION

HTML5 game developers have the opportunity to take web games out of their customary confines in hard-edged Adobe Flash boxes and open them up to the rest of the page and the rest of the web. Beyond simple gamification, HTML5 games have the opportunity to diverge from the standard game genres into other areas and mediums. One way you can do this is by using other services and websites as the medium on which to play your game. This chapter uses Twitter, which has a mobile-friendly website and client, as a medium for a collaborative version of the word-guessing game *Hangman*.

CREATING A TWITTER APPLICATION

To interact with Twitter, you need to create a Twitter application. In this case you most likely also want to create a new Twitter account if you already have one to prevent testing the Twitter API and annoying your followers.

You can sign up for a Twitter account and pick a new, unique name at `https://twitter.com/signup`. The game you build in this chapter is a simple *Hangman* game. After you complete the signup and confirm your account, go to: `https://dev.twitter.com`. This is the Twitter developer site where you can find documentation and create Twitter applications. You need to log in again with the account that you just created.

When logged in, mouse over your account name in the top right and click My Applications. On the applications page, click Create New Application (see Figure 22-1).

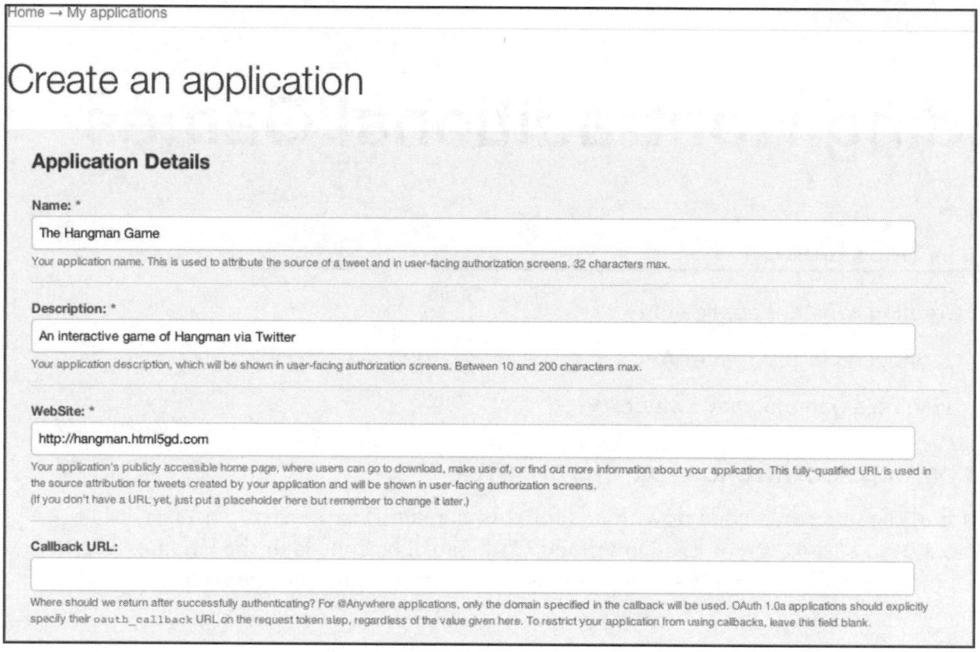

Home → My applications

Create an application

Application Details

Name: *

The Hangman Game

Your application name. This is used to attribute the source of a tweet and in user-facing authorization screens. 32 characters max.

Description: *

An interactive game of Hangman via Twitter

Your application description, which will be shown in user-facing authorization screens. Between 10 and 200 characters max.

WebSite: *

http://hangman.html5gd.com

Your application's publicly accessible home page, where users can go to download, make use of, or find out more information about your application. This fully-qualified URL is used in the source attribution for tweets created by your application and will be shown in user-facing authorization screens.
(If you don't have a URL yet, just put a placeholder here but remember to change it later.)

Callback URL:

Where should we return after successfully authenticating? For @Anywhere applications, only the domain specified in the callback will be used. OAuth 1.0a applications should explicitly specify their `oauth_callback` URL on the request token step, regardless of the value given here. To restrict your application from using callbacks, leave this field blank.

FIGURE 22-1: The Application setup screen.

Fill in the first three required fields: Name, Description, and WebSite. (You may need to get a little creative to come up with a unique name.) Accept the terms of use, fill in the captcha, and submit the form. Your application's settings screen displays.

Because the game is going to tweet, you need to change the permissions for the app. Click the Settings tab and then scroll down the page to Application Type. Change the type from Read Only to Read and Write and click Update.

To make it easier to start with the API without going through the normal OAuth process (which you saw in Chapter 21, "Going Real Time"), Twitter provides a mechanism to grab an access token. To get the access token, click the Details tab, scroll down to the bottom, and click Create My Access Token. This generates an access token you can use directly. (You may need to reload the page because Twitter can be a little slow occasionally to update the information on the page.)

Keep this page open because you need the following four pieces of information from it in the next section: Consumer Key, Consumer Secret, Access Token Key, and Access Token Secret.

CONNECTING A NODE APP TO TWITTER

To connect to Twitter from Node, use the wonderful module called `ntwitter` (which was forked from `node-twitter`, which was inspired by `twitter-node`). The `ntwitter` module makes it easy to interact with Twitter but, more importantly, it has support for Twitter's stream API, which means that you can get tweets sent to you in real time as opposed to polling Twitter on a regular basis.

Sending Your First Tweet

While you install the module via NPM, for reference the source code for the ntwitter module is up on GitHub at `https://github.com/AvianFlu/ntwitter`.

To start, create a new directory called **hangman** for the application and put the customary `package.json` file in it to pull in `ntwitter` as a dependency (see Listing 22-1).

LISTING 22-1: Package.json

```
{
    "name": "twitter-hangman"
,   "version": "0.0.1"
,   "private": true
,   "dependencies": {
      "ntwitter": "0.3.0"
    }
}
```

Run `npm install` to install the `ntwitter` dependency.

Next, try out tweeting via the API; open a new **app.js** file and fill in the code from Listing 22-2. You need to replace the configuration values for the keys and secrets in uppercase with the values from the previous section. Run the code by running `node app.js` from the command line.

LISTING 22-2: App.js sending your first tweet

```
var twitter = require("ntwitter");
var client = new twitter({
  consumer_key: "YOUR_CONSUMER_KEY",
  consumer_secret: "YOUR_CONSUMER_SECRET",
  access_token_key: "YOUR_ACCESS_TOKEN_KEY",
  access_token_secret: "YOUR_ACCESS_TOKEN_SECRET"
});

client.verifyCredentials(function (err, data) {
  if(err) {
    console.log("Unable to connect to twitter, please verify config");
  } else {
    client.updateStatus("Hello Twitter!", function (err, data) {
      if(!err) {
        console.log(data);
```

continues

LISTING 22-2 *(continued)*

```
      } else {
        console.log(err);
      }
    });
  }
});
```

This code requires the `ntwitter` module and then creates a new `client` with the credentials you created when you set up the app. If this were an app that could connect to multiple users, you would need to go through the OAuth authentication process to get the Access Token information for the user, but in this case Twitter enables you to generate those from the web interface.

Next it calls `verifyCredentials` to make sure you entered the configuration variables correctly. This check isn't necessary but can help you debug problems or invalid keys.

Finally, it calls `updateStatus` to send a tweet. Twitter responds with the full data details of the tweet.

If everything goes according to plan, you should see your tweet in the Timeline. If you click the expand link, you see the source is your app, as shown in Figure 22-2.

FIGURE 22-2: Your first tweet.

If you try to run the program again, Twitter returns an error message as it prevents the exact same tweet from being sent more than once.

Listening to the User Stream

Sending tweets is only half of the job. To respond to people playing the game, you need to listen for incoming messages.

Twitter provides two APIs for listening to incoming messages: a REST API that relies on polling and a stream API that pushes messages in real time. For a game such as *Hangman* where users might be tweeting at the user to play the game, better performance can be achieved via the stream API.

The documentation for the Twitter stream API is available at `https://dev.twitter.com/docs/streaming-apis/streams/user`.

To listen to tweets associated with a specific username via the stream API, you can use the `client` `.stream` method in `ntwitter`. Because the *Hangman* game will be playing with people it may not be following, it needs to also listen to the replies from people it is not following. To achieve this, the `replies:all` option must be passed as an option.

Replace the bottom of your `app.js` file with the highlighted content in Listing 22-3 to listen for tweets directed at your account. You need to replace the value of the `accountName` property with the name of the account you created.

LISTING 22-3: Reading from the user stream

```
var twitter = require("ntwitter");
var client = new twitter({
  consumer_key: "YOUR_CONSUMER_KEY",
  consumer_secret: "YOUR_CONSUMER_SECRET",
  access_token_key: "YOUR_ACCESS_TOKEN_KEY",
  access_token_secret: "YOUR_ACCESS_TOKEN_SECRET"
});

var accountName = 'hangmangame';
client.stream('user', { track:accountName ,replies:'all' }, function(stream) {
  stream.on('data', function (data) {
    console.log("****************");
    console.log(data);
    console.log("****************");
  });
  stream.on('end', function (response) {
    // Need to reconnect
  });
  stream.on('destroy', function (response) {
    // Need to reconnect
  });
});
```

If you run this file via `node app.js`, you should first see a list of friend account IDs for the account populated, and then the interface should sit and wait for activity on the user (your development account may not have anyone followed or following yet).

If you tweet at the account (@hangmangame in the example) or from the account itself, those tweets log to the console.

GENERATING RANDOM WORDS

To play a game of *Hangman*, the app needs access to a list of words to play. Luckily lists of words are available in a number of places on the web. One of the best spots to grab a list is at `http://wordlist.sourceforge.net/`. Of the myriad lists available there, the best list for the purposes of *Hangman* is the 12dicts list, which contains a list approximating the common core of the vocabulary of American English.

You can download the original 12dicts source files from `http://downloads.sourceforge.net/wordlist/12dicts-5.0.zip`, but the chapter code has a file called `words.txt` that is a single list of the most common words, which has been slightly modified to adjust the line endings. The 12dicts file uses the Automatically Generated Inflection Database (AGID) list as a source, so the license for the AGID is included in the chapter download. It can be used freely but must include the copyright notice if distributed.

To indicate words that are somehow peculiar, the `words.txt` has some files marked with punctuation at the end; the code to generate a random word will be set up to ignore these words.

The basic mechanism to generate a random word is to load the `words.txt` file into a large array and then pick a random item out of the array until one is found that consists only of alphabetical characters.

This code will be incorporated into the main game later in this chapter, but to play around with generating random words, you can create a file called `word.js` using the code in Listing 22-4, which logs 10 random words to the console.

LISTING 22-4: Generating 10 random words

```
var fs = require('fs'),
    words = fs.readFileSync('words.txt').toString().split("\n");

function randomWord() {
  var word;
  do {
    word = words[Math.floor(Math.random()*words.length)];
  } while(!word.match(/^\w+$/) || word.length < 5)
  return word;
}

for(var i=0;i<10;i++) {
  console.log(randomWord());
}
```

You can see the first thing the code does is load up the `words.txt` file and split it by new lines. The `randomWord` method then just picks a random word out of the list of words and checks using a regular expression that it contains only word characters (`\w`) and has at least five letters.

Running this file with `node word.js` should log 10 random words to the console every time it is run. The `words.txt` file has more than 32,000 words in it, so there should be plenty of variety.

CREATING TWITTER HANGMAN

With the libraries in place to create the game, it's time to dig in to the actual code for the game. The main idea is to post a tweet with the blanks for a game of *Hangman* and respond to tweets from users guessing the missing letters. The application responds to any user that sends tweets at it with the number of times that letter appears and tweets the updated board state.

The complete code for the game appears in Listing 22-5. Replace any code you have in `app.js` with the code in Listing 22-5. You need to replace the `accountName` and Twitter configuration variables as you did earlier.

LISTING 22-5: Twitter Hangman

```
var twitter = require("ntwitter"),
    fs = require('fs'),
    words = fs.readFileSync('words.txt').toString().split("\n");

var client = new twitter({
  consumer_key: "YOUR_CONSUMER_KEY",
  consumer_secret: "YOUR_CONSUMER_SECRET",
  access_token_key: "YOUR_ACCESS_TOKEN_KEY",
  access_token_secret: "YOUR_ACCESS_TOKEN_SECRET"
});
var accountName = "hangmanword";
function randomWord() {
  var word;
  do {
    word = words[Math.floor(Math.random()*words.length)];
  } while(!word.match(/^\w+$/) || word.length < 5)
  return word;
}
var Hangman = function(accountName,client) {
  var self = this;
  this.gameNumber = 0;
  var hangman =  "__U-[-<";
  this.newWord = function() {
    this.word = randomWord();
    this.currentWord = this.word.split("");
    this.currentGuesses = [];
    this.guesses = [];
    this.lettersRemaining = this.currentWord.length;
    this.guessesRemaining = 5;
    this.gameNumber++;
    this.sendGameUpdate();
    console.log("\n");
    console.log("New Word:" + this.word);
  };
  this.sendTweet = function(status) {
    client.updateStatus(status,function(err,data) {
      if(!err) {
        console.log("Sent Tweet:" + status);
      } else {
        console.log("Error Sending Tweet:" + status +
                  "\nError:" + err);
      }
    });
  };
  this.sendGameUpdate = function() {
    var status = "Game " + this.gameNumber + ": " +
```

continues

LISTING 22-5 *(continued)*

```
                hangman.substring(0,hangman.length - this.guessesRemaining ) +
                " Word:";
    for(var i=0;i<this.currentWord.length;i++) {
      if(this.currentGuesses[i]) {
        status += " " + this.currentWord[i];
      } else {
        status += " _"
      }
    }
    this.sendTweet(status);
  };
  this.sendExistingGuess = function(tweeter,guess) {
    this.sendTweet("@" + tweeter + ' Sorry someone has already guessed "' +
                  guess + '"');
  };
  this.sendIncorrect = function(tweeter,guess) {
    var extra = this.guessesRemaining <= 0 ?
                " - Game Over (Word was " + this.word + ")" : ""
    this.sendTweet("@" + tweeter + ' sorry there are no ' +
                  guess + "'s in game " + this.gameNumber + extra);
  };
  this.sendCorrect = function(tweeter,guess,correct) {
    var extra = this.lettersRemaining == 0 ?
                " - Congratulations you win!" : ""
    this.sendTweet("@" + tweeter + ' yes, ' + guess + " appears " +
                  correct + (correct > 1 ? " times" : " time") +
                  " in game " + this.gameNumber + extra);
  };
  this.handleGuess = function(tweet) {
    if(!tweet.text) return;
    var guess = tweet.text.replace(/[^a-z]/gi,""),
        tweeter = tweet.user.screen_name,
        correct = 0;
    try {
      if(tweet.text.indexOf("@" + accountName) === 0) {
        guess = guess[guess.length-1].toLowerCase();
        if(this.guesses.indexOf(guess) != -1) {
          return this.sendExistingGuess(tweeter,guess);
        }
        this.guesses.push(guess);
        for(var letter=0;letter < this.currentWord.length;letter++) {
          if(this.currentWord[letter].toLowerCase() == guess) {
            correct++;
            this.lettersRemaining~DH;
            this.currentGuesses[letter] = true;
          }
        }
        if(correct > 0) {
          this.sendCorrect(tweeter,guess,correct);
          if(this.lettersRemaining == 0) {
            this.newWord();
          } else {
```

```
              this.sendGameUpdate();
          }
      } else {
          this.guessesRemaining~DH;
          this.sendIncorrect(tweeter,guess);
          if(this.guessesRemaining > 0) {
            this.sendGameUpdate();
          } else {
            setTimeout(function() { self.newWord(); }, 2000);
          }
        }
      }
    } catch(e) {
      console.log("Error:" + e.toString());
    }
  };

  this.connect = function() {
    client.stream('user',
                  { track:accountName ,replies:'all' },
                  function(stream) {
      stream.on('data', function (data) {
        setTimeout(function() {
          self.handleGuess(data);
        },1);
      });

      stream.on('end', function (response) {
        self.connect();
      });

      stream.on('error', function (response) {
        console.log("Error");
      });

      stream.on('destroy', function (response) {
        self.connect();
      });
    });
  };
  this.newWord();
  this.connect();
};
var hangman = new Hangman(accountName,client);
```

The main game is contained in the *Hangman* object, which keeps track of the state of the current game. To start a new game, the newWord method is called, which grabs a random word and then initializes the guesses and posts the game to Twitter. Next, the sendTweet method simply calls updateStatus on the client to send a tweet, capturing the tweet sent or any errors to the console.

The sendGameUpdate method outputs a tweet of the form:

```
Game 1: __O-[- Word: _ _ _ m _ _ _
```

This shows the current game number, how far along the man is from being hanged (in a poor ASCII rendering), and the letters that have been found.

The next three methods are used to respond to the person who was trying to play with a message directed at him letting him know how his last guess did.

The main meat of the game is in the `handleGuess` method, which takes in a tweet, checks to make sure it's a tweet directed at the account name, and then grabs the last alphabetic character of the tweet and uses that as the guess character.

This allows users to tweet messages such as the following:

```
@hangmangame is there an a?
@hangmangame how about a b?
@hangmangame c
```

All the preceding examples should work. Allowing a little creativity in messaging is necessary because Twitter won't let you post the same tweet in succession.

After it extracts the guess, the game checks if the guess has already been tried. If so, it lets the player know. If it's not a repeat guess, the game then checks for the number of occurrences and the number of letters remaining and then sends a tweet to the user based on whether the user correctly guessed the word.

If the player guessed the word or has run out of guesses, the game lets him know and then sends out a new word. Figure 22-3 shows a sample game.

FIGURE 22-3: A sample game.

SUMMARY

This chapter showed you how to build a game on top of the Twitter API. Combined with the push notifications Twitter provides, you have an asynchronous game of *Hangman* that players can play from their mobile phone. Rather than just build games on top of Twitter, you can instead expand your horizons on what pieces of the web you can use to build games. There is a tremendous number of web and mobile-accessible interaction media available, including SMS, Photo APIs, search APIs, and more, all of which you can creatively combine and remix to create innovative games.

PART VII
Mobile Enhancements

23

Locating via Geolocation

WHAT'S IN THIS CHAPTER?

➤ Locating users with geolocation

➤ Drawing static maps

➤ Drawing interactive maps

WROX.COM CODE DOWNLOADS FOR THIS CHAPTER

You can find the wrox.com code downloads for this chapter at www.wrox.com/remtitle
.cgi?isbn=9781118301326 on the Download Code tab. The code is in the Chapter 23
download and individually named according to the names throughout the chapter.

INTRODUCTION

Up to this point this book has treated the word *mobile* as referring primarily to a form factor
(small screen) and an input mechanism (touchscreen). A third major aspect to mobile devices
is that they are portable, and thus the user's location can be made into an interesting aspect
of game play. This chapter examines the support to determine a device's location, known as
geolocation, which is available in one of the HTML5 families of specifications, and discusses
how you can use it in games.

GETTING STARTED WITH GEOLOCATION

Geolocation support is technically not part of HTML5 but resides in a separate geolocation
API specification. The latest published version of the specification lives on the W3 website at
www.w3.org/TR/geolocation-API/.

Although this book discusses geolocation from the perspective of mobile devices, the API is also available in desktop browsers. Desktop browsers that support the API (IE9+ and recent versions of all other browsers) use a less-accurate IP-address reverse lookup mechanism.

The API defines two mechanisms for grabbing the position: one time and watches. The first type is used when you just need the position once. The second works like `setInterval` in that it calls the callback repeatedly as the device moves.

Because getting the user's position via a web page involves privacy concerns, both mechanisms provide a notification to users giving them the power to allow or deny the request to grab the location.

GETTING A ONE-TIME POSITION

Getting the position of the user is simple enough; just call `navigator.geolocation` `.getCurrentPosition` with a callback. This triggers a notification at the top of the browser, as shown in Figure 23-1, giving the user the power to allow or deny the request. If you supply a second callback, that callback is called if the browser couldn't get the location due to a denied request or other error.

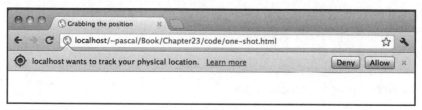

FIGURE 23-1 The geolocation permission dialog.

To see the data in the console that's returned from a request, you can enter the code in Listing 23-1 into a file called `position.html`, load the page in a desktop browser, and open up the JavaScript console.

LISTING 23-1: Getting a one-time position

```html
<!DOCTYPE HTML>
<html lang="en">
<head>
  <meta charset="UTF-8">
  <title>Grabbing the position</title>
</head>
<body>
  <script>
    function logPosition(position) {
      console.log(position);
    }
    function positionError(error) {
      console.log(error);
    }
    navigator.geolocation.getCurrentPosition(logPosition,positionError);
  </script>
</body>
</html>
```

Examining the console shows you the result of the request. If you denied the request or the system couldn't look up your location, the `positionError` method is called with a `PositionError` object. If you run this from a `file://` URL, Chrome will give you an error by default so you'll want to run it from `localhost`.

If the geolocation was successful, the `logPosition` callback is called with a `Position` object, which is logged to the console, as shown in Figure 23-2.

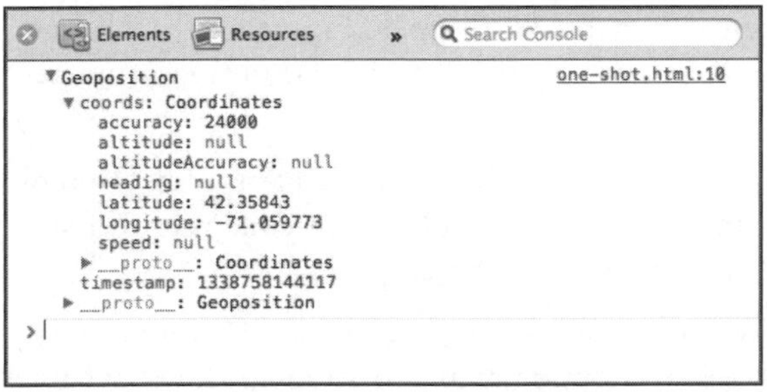

FIGURE 23-2 A sample returned position.

Most of the details are in a `coords` subobject that contains at minimum the latitude, longitude, and accuracy in meters. It might also contain additional data.

The full fields available in the position object follow:

➤ `Latitude`: The best guess latitude as a number

➤ `Longitude`: The best guess longitude as a number

➤ `Altitude`: An altitude estimate or `null` if there is no estimate

➤ `Accuracy`: The accuracy of latitude and longitude in meters

➤ `altitudeAccuracy`: The accuracy of the altitude in meters or `null`

➤ `heading`: If speed is greater than zero, the direction in degrees, otherwise `NaN`

➤ `speed`: The speed in meters per second

As mentioned, only the longitude, latitude, and accuracy are guaranteed to be present.

`getCurrentPosition` also accepts a third parameter that is an options object. The three options available as of this writing follow:

➤ `enableHighAccuracy`: Provides a hint that accuracy is important. This may require longer to generate a position and uses more battery, but the results will be more accurate if possible.

➤ `Timeout`: How long in milliseconds to wait for a position before timing out.

➤ `maximumAge`: The maximum age in milliseconds of the position. If greater than zero the method may return a cached position.

By default `enableHighAccuracy` is set to `false`; `timeout` is set to 0, which means never to time-out; and `maximumAge` is set to 0 as well, which means don't use cached data. If you want a position quickly, set `maximumAge` to a number greater than zero.

PLOTTING A LOCATION ON A MAP

The latitude and longitude don't tell you a whole lot, so one of the first things you must do is plot the location on a map. To do this you need access to a map API. Google Maps is one of the most popular map APIs and provides two different APIs: a static map API and the traditional interactive map you are probably familiar with.

Generating static maps is easy. All it involves is sending a properly formed request in the form of an `<img>` tag `src` to Google, which returns an image to you. The API for static maps is available at `https://developers.google.com/maps/documentation/staticmaps/`.

If you want a map with a marker at a specific location, you need to generate a URL with the size of the output image, the marker, and a value for the sensor option, which lets Google know whether this application uses a sensor to determine the position. (This field is required.) You also need to pass a zoom value to control how zoomed in the resultant image is.

Markers are defined by a number of attributes separated by pipe characters (|), for example:

```
markers=color:red||label:A|lat,long
```

Because this needs to be encoded into a URL, the pipe character is URL encoded into the string `%7C`.

Listing 23-2 shows the first example modified to output a static map at your location. Desktop browsers have wildly varying levels of accuracy, so it may show a location that's only a rough approximation of your actual location.

LISTING 23-2: Static map

```
<!DOCTYPE HTML>
<html lang="en">
<head>
  <meta charset="UTF-8">
  <title>Grabbing the position</title>
  <script src='js/jquery.min.js'></script>
</head>
<body>
  <script>
    function logPosition(position) {
      var url = "http://maps.googleapis.com/maps/api/staticmap?" +
                "zoom=13&size=320x420&" +
                "markers=color:blue%7Clabel:S%7C" +
                position.coords.latitude + "," +
                position.coords.longitude + "&sensor=true";
    $("<img>").attr("src",url)
              .appendTo("body");
    }
```

```
      function positionError(error) {
        console.log(error);
      }
      navigator.geolocation.getCurrentPosition(logPosition,positionError,{
        enableHighAccuracy: true
      });
    </script>
  </body>
</html>
```

This example uses jQuery for DOM manipulation, and `enableHighAccuracy` is set to `true` to get as accurate a position as possible.

WATCHING THE POSITION CHANGE OVER TIME

The geolocation API provides a second method called `watchPosition` that takes in the same parameters as `getCurrentPosition`. It works like `setInterval` in that it returns an ID that can be used to clear the watch at a later time with `clearWatch`.

If you want to walk around a bit, run the code in Listing 23-3, which uses `watchPosition` to log the latitude and longitude to a `<div>` on a mobile browser and see how the numbers change.

LISTING 23-3: Watching the position change

```
<!DOCTYPE HTML>
<html lang-"en">
<head>
  <meta charset="UTF-8">
  <title>Watching the position</title>
  <script src='js/jquery.min.js'></script>
</head>
<body>
  <script>
    function logPosition(position) {
      $("#logs").prepend(position.coords.latitude + "," +
                         position.coords.latitude + "<br/>");
    }
    function positionError(error) {
      console.log(error);
    }
    var watchID = navigator.geolocation.watchPosition(
                               logPosition,positionError,{
                                   enableHighAccuracy: true
                               });
    setTimeout(function() {
      navigator.geolocation.clearWatch(watchID);
    },30000);
  </script>
  <div id='logs'></div>
</body>
</html>
```

You can see that after 30 seconds the watch is cleared to prevent the system from continuing to update the position.

> **NOTE** *Activating the GPS on a mobile device (which is what you are effectively requesting by turning on* `enableHighAccuracy`*) drains the battery, so be courteous to your users and use watches only when you must update the position.*

DRAWING AN INTERACTIVE MAP

To draw an interactive map, you need to use the interactive Google Maps API. Previous versions required an API key, but the current version, v3, doesn't require one. If you want to make money from the API or track your usage, however, you must get one from `https://code.google.com/apis/console`.

The full Maps v3 API documentation is available on the Google website at `https://developers.google.com/maps/documentation/javascript/reference`.

Although the API is extensive, it's well documented and you use only a small subset of the objects available: `Map`, `Marker`, and `LatLng`. The `Map` object represents the entire map. The `Marker` object is a marker that you can drop on the page as you did in the static map. Use `LatLng` to store a single position.

To create a map, you need to create a new map object and pass it a DOM element to fill, and the three required options are the center, the initial zoom level, and the `mapTypeId`.

The center is a `LatLng` object, which you can create by passing in two floats to represent a latitude and longitude. Zoom level is a number between 1 and 18 and controls how zoomed in the map is. Some areas don't go up to 18. (This is usually rural areas in the United States and other parts of the world.) The `mapTypeId` object is one of four constants on the `google.maps.MapTypeId` class, each representing a different type of map supported by Google Maps: `HYBRID`, `ROADMAP`, `SATELLITE`, and `TERRAIN`.

If you are still up for walking around, run the code in Listing 23-4 to create an interactive map that can follow you with a pin that updates itself as you move.

LISTING 23-4: An auto-updating interactive map

```
<!DOCTYPE HTML>
<html lang="en">
<head>
  <meta charset="UTF-8">
  <title>Interactive Map</title>
  <script src='js/jquery.min.js'></script>
  <meta name="viewport" content="width=device-width, user-scalable=0,
minimum-scale=1.0, maximum-scale=1.0"/>
```

```
  <script type="text/javascript"
src="https://maps.googleapis.com/maps/api/js?sensor=true"></script>
  <style> body { padding:0px; margin:0px; }. </style>
</head>
<body>
  <script>
  $(function() {
    var map = null,
        marker = null;
    function createMap(latlng) {
      var mapOptions = {
        zoom: 18,
        center: latlng,
        mapTypeId: google.maps.MapTypeId.TERRAIN
      };
      var div = $("<div>").css({ width: "100%",
                                 height:"100%",
                                 position:"absolute"})
                          .appendTo("body")[0];

      map = new google.maps.Map(div, mapOptions);
      marker = new google.maps.Marker({
        position: latlng,
        map: map,
        title: "Me"
      });
    }
    function updateMap(pos) {
      var latlng = new google.maps.LatLng(pos.coords.latitude,
                                          pos.coords.longitude);
      if(!map) {
        createMap(latlng);
      } else {
        marker.setPosition(latlng);
      }
    }
    function positionError(error) {
      alert("Error tracking your position");
      navigator.geolocation.clearWatch(watchID);
    }
    var watchID = navigator.geolocation.watchPosition(
                              updateMap,positionError,{
                                enableHighAccuracy: true
                              });
  });
  </script>
</body>
</html>
```

The event loop starts by calling watchPosition to trigger a call to updateMap every time the position changes. updateMap creates a new LatLng object and then determines if the map has been drawn before. If not it calls createMap to generate the initial map. If the map has already been drawn, it calls the marker's setPosition command to update the marker to the new position.

CALCULATING THE POSITION BETWEEN TWO POINTS

When you start building games with geolocation, one of the first difficulties you'll face is the problem to calculate the distance between two latitudes and longitudes. Whether this is to detect the proximity between players or distance to a goal, this is something that you definitely must do.

On the client side, Google's Map v3 API provides a static method under `google.maps.geometry` `.spherical` called `computeDistanceBetween`, which takes two `LatLng` objects and returns the distance in meters.

If you don't have an API readily handy to do the calculation for you, your can use the Haversine distance formula (`http://en.wikipedia.org/wiki/Haversine_formula`) to calculate the distance on a sphere between two points.

There are a number of resources for this formula in JavaScript, but one of the best available on the web is at `www.movable-type.co.uk/scripts/latlong.html`. It provides a succinct Haversine formula in JavaScript that takes in `lat1`, `lon1` `lat2`, and `lon2` and outputs the distance between the two in kilometers:

```
var R = 6371; // km
var dLat = (lat2-lat1).toRad();
var dLon = (lon2-lon1).toRad();
var lat1 = lat1.toRad();
var lat2 = lat2.toRad();

var a = Math.sin(dLat/2) * Math.sin(dLat/2) +
        Math.sin(dLon/2) * Math.sin(dLon/2) * Math.cos(lat1) * Math.cos(lat2);
var c = 2 * Math.atan2(Math.sqrt(a), Math.sqrt(1-a));
var d = R * c;
```

You can plug this formula directly into a method in your code to calculate the distance between two points.

SUMMARY

This chapter showed you how to use geolocation in the browser to generate a position that can be used to display an interactive map. With the ability to track a position and display and update interactive maps, a number of augmented-reality games can be built in the browser. This includes scavenger hunts, geocaching, proximity-based games, and more. The hope is that putting geolocation tools in your arsenal can open up a new world of HTML5 games that breaks gaming outside of its normal confines.

24

Querying Device Orientation and Acceleration

WHAT'S IN THIS CHAPTER?

- ➤ Learning about screen orientation
- ➤ Understanding the device orientation API
- ➤ Playing with device orientation
- ➤ Combatting device rotation

WROX.COM CODE DOWNLOADS FOR THIS CHAPTER

The wrox.com code downloads for this chapter are found at www.wrox.com/remtitle .cgi?isbn=9781118301326 on the Download Code tab. The code is in the Chapter 24 download and individually named according to the names throughout the chapter.

INTRODUCTION

Using the orientation of your mobile device to control a game was one of the first "wow" moments of the smartphone gaming era. With the support for device orientation and acceleration in the browser, that capability is now within your reach as an HTML5 game developer. This chapter examines the DeviceOrientation event API, which has two useful events: device orientation and device motion. A third event, compass, is also available, but unless you have a long-running application that needs precise direction details, you can safely ignore this event.

LOOKING AT A DEVICE ORIENTATION

Before examining the DeviceOrientation Event API, it's worth a brief look at the `window` `.orientation` property. This property won't tell you the exact angle you hold your device at, but it can tell you an angle that indicates which way—portrait or landscape—your device's screen is oriented.

You can also listen for `orientationchange` events to detect when the device is rotated to a different configuration. To try this, add the following to any page that has jQuery loaded on it:

```
$(window).on("orientationchange",function(e) {
  alert(window.orientation);
});
```

Depending on your device, as you rotate your device every time the screen rotates, you should see values in increments of 90 that tell you what angle the device is at. Although it seems like it should be easy to decode this value, it's not that simple.

Phones, specifically the iPhone and the Galaxy Nexus, treat the normal portrait position as a `window.orientation` value of 0. Neither supports an upside-down portrait, so there is no 180 value. The iPhone has two landscape orientations: 90 and –90, whereas the Galaxy Nexus treats landscape direction as having a `window.orientation` of 90.

For tablets it's more confusing. The Kindle Fire and iPad both treat normal portrait mode as having an orientation of 0, but they also support an inverted portrait mode with an orientation of 180 that is not supported on phones. Other tablets, such as the Android ASUS Transformer, treat landscape mode as an orientation of 0, and everything else is rotated off this.

These different values are not, however, out of line with the specification; for the ASUS tablet, an orientation of 0 is given to landscape mode because landscape is defined as the tablet's "standard orientation."

The idea of a "standard orientation" is an important concept for a device because the `deviceorientation` events are also all relative to the standard orientation and assume that standard orientation is always portrait mode.

GETTING STARTED WITH DEVICE ORIENTATION EVENTS

When you want more information than just the screen portrait or landscape orientation, it's time to dive into the `deviceorientation` event, which gives you three angular values indicating precisely how the device is held in 3-D space and is triggered at a high rate as the device is adjusted.

The specification associated with device orientation is the DeviceOrientation Event Specification; the latest version is available at: `www.w3.org/TR/orientation-event/`. The most important event is `deviceorientation`, which you can use to determine the angle at which you are holding your device.

Although this event is useful in mobile devices, desktop browsers have also started supporting the event (MacBooks started including an accelerometer a couple of years ago), and it's available in Chrome. Firefox also has support for it, but at least in OS X, Firefox doesn't trigger the event. Desktop IE, Safari, and Opera don't have support as of this writing.

Detecting and Using the Event

To see if your browser supports the event, you can check for the existence of the event object on the window:

```
if (window.DeviceOrientationEvent) {
    // Device orientation supported
}
```

Firefox pre-version 6 had support for a nonstandard `OrientationEvent`, but since version 6 it has supported the standard event.

Next, to listen for the event, as usual you can either use `addEventListener` or jQuery. The only caveat is that if you use jQuery you need to pull out the original event object to access the event properties you care about because jQuery doesn't copy over the properties of the `deviceorientation` event into its universal event object.

```
// Use either method
window.addEventListener("deviceorientation",function(eventData) {
  // Handle event
});

$(window).on("deviceorientation",function(e) {
 var eventData = e.originalEvent;
 // Handle event
});
```

In both cases the `eventData` object holds the properties you care about.

Understanding the Event Data

The `deviceorientation` event triggers its callback with an object containing three different properties; each property has a different axis of rotation: alpha, beta, and gamma.

➤ `alpha` - [0–360]: The heading of the device (think North, South, East, West). You can determine the compass heading by subtracting alpha from 360.

➤ `beta` - [–180–180]: The amount you tilt the device front to back. A beta of 0 means the device is lying flat. A beta of 90 means it is held vertically, straight up.

➤ `gamma` - [–90–90]: The amount you tilt the device left to right. A gamma of 0 means the device is lying flat. A beta of –90 means the device is tilted vertically to the left.

Because `alpha` is dependent on the direction the user faces, you generally use only `beta` and `gamma` in your games because those can be used no matter what direction players are sitting in.

`alpha` is primarily useful in augmented reality-type settings, such as on Android devices. (However, the alpha value is not particularly accurate in the author's experience, so your mileage may vary.)

TRYING OUT DEVICE ORIENTATION

To try out the device orientation events, you can build a quick demonstration using the SVG and physics code from Chapter 14, "Building Games with SVG and Physics." Figure 24-1 shows the end result.

FIGURE 24-1: The final device orientation example.

The demonstration consists of a set of static walls enclosing a set of balls that can react to gravity. Gravity always stays consistent with reality, but as you rotate the device, gravity changes relative to it, which will cause the balls to fly around the screen.

Creating a Ball Playground

To start, create a new HTML file called **orient.html** with the contents of Listing 24-1. You need a number of quintus files and the engine's dependencies along with Box2dWeb-2.1.a.3.js from Chapter 14.

LISTING 24-1: The orientation example HTML file

```
<!DOCTYPE HTML>
<html lang="en">
  <head>
```

```
    <meta charset="UTF-8">
    <meta name="viewport" content="width=device-width, user-scalable=0,
minimum-scale=1.0, maximum-scale=1.0"/>
    <title>DeviceOrientation</title>
    <script src='js/jquery.min.js'></script>
    <script src='js/underscore.js'></script>
    <script src='js/Box2dWeb-2.1.a.3.js'></script>
    <script src='js/quintus.js'></script>
    <script src='js/quintus_input.js'></script>
    <script src='js/quintus_sprites.js'></script>
    <script src='js/quintus_scenes.js'></script>
    <script src='js/quintus_physics.js'></script>
    <script src='js/quintus_svg.js'></script>
    <script src='orient.js'></script>
    <style>
      * { padding:0px; margin:0px; }
    </style>
  </head>
  <body>
  </body>
</html>
```

Next, create the **orient.js** file referenced in Listing 24-1 and fill it with the contents of Listing 24-2.

LISTING 24-2: orient.js

```
$(function() {
  var Q = window.Q = Quintus()
                     .include('Input,Sprites,Scenes,SVG,Physics')
                     .svgOnly()
                     .setup('quintus',{ maximize: true });
  Q.Ball = Q.Sprite.extend({
    init: function(props) {
      this._super(_(props).defaults({
        shape: 'circle',
        color: 'red',
        r: 25,
        restitution: 0.9,
        density: 4,
        seconds: 5
      }));
      this.add('physics');
    }
  });

  Q.scene('level',new Q.Scene(function(stage) {

    stage.add("world");

    // Create the walls
    stage.insert(new Q.Sprite({ x: 5, y: 300, w: 10, h: 600 }));
    stage.insert(new Q.Sprite({ x: 395, y: 300, w: 10, h: 600 }));
    stage.insert(new Q.Sprite({ x: 200, y: 5, w: 400, h: 10 }));
```

continues

LISTING 24-2 *(continued)*

```
    stage.insert(new Q.Sprite({ x: 200, y: 595, w: 400, h: 10 }));

    // Add the center object
    var center = stage.insert(new Q.Sprite({
      x: 200, y: 300, w: 100, h: 200
    }));

    stage.each(function() {
      this.p.type = 'static';
      this.add("physics");
    });

    // Add the balls
    stage.insert(new Q.Ball({ x: 100, y: 50, color:"blue" }));
    stage.insert(new Q.Ball({ x: 200, y: 50, color:"pink" }));
    stage.insert(new Q.Ball({ x: 300, y: 50, color:"black" }));
    stage.insert(new Q.Ball({ x: 100, y: 150, color:"green" }));
    stage.insert(new Q.Ball({ x: 200, y: 150, color:"teal" }));
    stage.insert(new Q.Ball({ x: 300, y: 150, color:"orange" }));
    stage.viewport(400,600);
    stage.centerOn(200,300);

  }));

  Q.stageScene("level");
});
```

At this point in the book, the code in Listing 24-2 should look familiar.

The code defines only a single reusable sprite: Q.Ball. This defines the shape, size, and physical properties of the ball and adds the physics component to make the balls react to gravity and other objects.

The wall sprites are created as normal Q.Sprite objects. (Remember these are Q.SVGSprite objects, but calling svgOnly() during setup copies them to Q.Sprite.) Then their type is set to static to make them nonmoving objects, and the physics component is added to them.

Next, six balls of different colors are added to the stage.

If you load this code in the browser, you should see six balls that fall vertically straight down.

Adding Orientation Control

To add in support for adjusting gravity relative to the device, add a deviceorientation event handler that grabs the rotation data and adjusts the gravity vector in the Box2D world as necessary.

Because a beta and a gamma of 0 means that the device is laid flat and thus the ball shouldn't be moving, the easiest way to adjust gravity is to multiply some constant by the sine of beta to get the *y* component of gravity and by the sine of alpha to get the *x* component of gravity (from the perspective of the balls).

To add more excitement to the experience, the center block, stored in the center variable, is also rotated to always face north (or alpha 0).

To try this, add the highlighted code in Listing 24-3, as shown near the bottom of the `orient.js` file.

LISTING 24-3: The orientation event handler

```
stage.viewport(400,600);
stage.centerOn(200,300);

if (window.DeviceOrientationEvent) {
  $(window).on("deviceorientation",function(e) {
    var eventData = e.originalEvent
        tiltLR = eventData.gamma,
        tiltFB = eventData.beta,
        direction = eventData.alpha;

    center.physics._body.SetAngle(direction * Math.PI / 180);

    var leanAngle = tiltLR * Math.PI / 180,
        tiltAngle = tiltFB * Math.PI /180,
        gravityX = 20 * Math.sin(leanAngle),
        gravityY = 20 * Math.sin(tiltAngle);
    stage.world._world.m_gravity.x = gravityX;
    stage.world._world.m_gravity.y = gravityY;
  });
}

}));
```

If you run the example again in your browser on a supported mobile device or on Chrome in a recent MacBook, you can play with the balls and adjust their movement by slightly rotating the device. (Up to the point where the orientation flips, then all bets are off; the balls no longer follow gravity.)

Dealing with Browser Rotation

Turning your device past the point where it changes orientation brings to the forefront a major problem with device orientation in HTML5 games: As a web developer you currently have no way to lock the display to prevent rotation. If the users angle their phones too much, they end up swapping between landscape and portrait mode or vice versa. There is no complete way around this except to build your game in such a way as to discourage the users from turning the device too much.

The good news is that there is a specification for a Screen Orientation API that includes the capability to lock the screen: www.w3.org/TR/screen-orientation/. The bad news is this specification has been implemented only in Firefox Mobile, as of this writing.

Until the Screen Orientation API becomes more commonplace, a partial solution is to examine the `window.orientation` value whenever there is an `orientationchange` event. `window.orientation` contains the value in degrees of the orientation from the default position that the device is held. This is actually a little more complicated than you might think because the `window.orientation` value is not consistent across devices or platforms as you saw in the section "Looking at a Device Orientation."

For handling devices other than Android phones, which currently appear to, unfortunately, treat landscape mode in either direction as having a `window.orientation` of 90, you can add the code in Listing 24-4 before the `Q.Scene` code in `orient.js` to transform the container based on the value of `window.orientation`.

LISTING 24-4: Handling window rotation

```
function rotateContainer() {
  $("#quintus_container")[0].style.webkitTransform =
                  "rotate(" + -1*window.orientation + "deg)";
}
rotateContainer();
$(window).on("orientationchange",rotateContainer);

Q.scene('level',new Q.Scene(function(stage) {
```

The `rotateContainer` method is WebKit vendor prefix specific, but it can be extended to other browsers by handling the various prefixes for rotation. It gives a value for `window.orientation` and rotates the container element back in the other direction so that the container's angle is unchanged.

As mentioned earlier, because Android phones, as of this writing, give only an orientation value of 90 (never –90), this fix won't work for those phones when the device is rotated –90 degrees.

NEED MORE CONTROL?

The DeviceOrientation event specification provides a more complex event called `devicemotion` that gives even finer-grain control over device motion. It provides an `acceleration` and an `accelerationIncludingGravity` child object that have raw x, y, and z acceleration values. It also has a `rotationRate` object that provides `alpha`, `beta`, and `gamma` values for the rotation of the device over a given period of time. `devicemotion` is a little more difficult to work with and in most situations doesn't provide a lot of additional value, but if you need finer-grained control, check out the details in the specification linked earlier.

SUMMARY

This chapter provided an introduction to the `window.orientation` value along with the details of using the `deviceorientation` event to enable the addition of accelerometer-based gameplay into your HTML5 games. This capability, however, comes with the caveat that rotations that cause the device screen orientation to change don't play nice with HTML5 gaming. By opening up the device orientation to the browser, HTML5 game developers now have more tools in their tool belt to build games that use creative input mechanisms.

25

Playing Sounds, the Mobile Achilles Heel

WHAT'S IN THIS CHAPTER?

➤ Learning the <audio> tag

➤ Creating a desktop sound engine

➤ Creating a mobile sound engine

WROX.COM CODE DOWNLOADS FOR THIS CHAPTER

You can find the wrox.com code downloads for this chapter at www.wrox.com/remtitle .cgi?isbn=9781118301326 on the Download Code tab. The code is in the Chapter 25 download and individually named according to the names throughout the chapter.

INTRODUCTION

Along with its many other enhancements to browser capabilities, HTML5 finally brought with it the promise of sound as a first-class citizen. Despite its limitations, the basic <audio> tag can be used in desktop HTML5 games for music and sound effects with a little coaxing. Unfortunately, HTML5 audio on mobile has been somewhat neglected. This chapter examines the current limitations of HTML5 audio on mobile and some possible workarounds for those limitations.

WORKING WITH THE AUDIO TAG

As mentioned, HTML5 defines an <audio> tag as part of the core HTML5 specification. It's designed primarily for in-page sound playback, but the flexibility of the tag means that game developers have repurposed it for game audio as well.

Using the Audio Tag for Basic Playback

The `<audio>` tag can be used to create an on-page audio player with a single tag:

```
<audio src="music.mp3" controls/>
```

More interesting from a game development perspective, however, is that the `<audio>` tag can also be created entirely separate from a visual component using the `Audio` object as you saw briefly in Chapter 10, "Bootstrapping the Quintus Engine: Part II."

```
var snd = new Audio();
snd.src = "music.mp3";
snd.addEventListener("canplaythrough",function() {
  snd.play();
});
snd.load();
```

The preceding example creates a new audio object, sets the source to the file `music.mp3`, and then starts the music playing as soon as the `canplaythrough` event triggers. `canplaythrough` means that the audio file has loaded enough that it can start playing, and if it keeps loading at the current rate, it will finish loading before the playback reaches the end of the file.

Dealing with Different Supported Formats

Also as mentioned in Chapter 10, different browsers support different audio formats, with no single format supported by all browsers currently. To cover the widest range of browsers, you need to support at least two formats: either .mp3 and .ogg or .mp3 and .wav. Because .ogg is lossy compressed comparable to .mp3's small file size, it's a better choice than .wav.

If you want to support this from a markup perspective, you can use separate source tags and count on browsers to pick the first one that they support:

```
<audio controls>
  <source src="music.mp3" type="audio/mp3" />
  <source src="music.ogg" type="audio/ogg" />
</audio>
```

If you use JavaScript to load the file, you can use the `canPlayType` method on the `Audio` object to check for support to decide which element to load:

```
var snd = new Audio();

if(snd.canPlayType('audio/mpeg')) {
  snd.src = "music.mp3";
} else if(snd.canPlayType('audio/ogg; codecs="vorbis"')) {
  snd.src = "music.ogg";
}

// ... load and play the sound
```

Because the `audio/ogg` mime type is a container that can support multiple different codecs, you need to check for the specific code (generally "vorbis" for audio) to use.

> ### WHY NOT SUPPORT A SINGLE FORMAT?
>
> As a web developer, it's unimaginably frustrating that no single audio (or video for that matter) format is supported in all browsers. The primary reason for this is patents. Encoding and decoding audio data to and from the MP3 audio format, by far the most popular format, is a process protected by patented technology owned by the Fraunhofer Institute. For this reason the open-source Firefox browser has chosen not to support the MP3 file format in its browser, but instead support the open OGG file format for audio.
>
> Other browsers such as Internet Explorer and Safari unfortunately don't support OGG. The reason for this is fuzzy; some people guess it's because Microsoft and Apple don't want the open-source format, which some claim is less performant from a technical perspective, to "win." The assumption on everyone's part is that the first file format supported in all browsers will win the format battle because developers will be happy to have only one format to support.

Understanding the Limitations of Mobile Audio

With the basics of the HTML5 audio tag covered, there's good news and there's bad news. The good news is that the `<audio>` tag is supported by current versions of iOS and Android. The bad news is that support is severely crippled in several instances.

The first issue is that iOS has the limitation to require sounds to be loaded and played only from a user-initiated action. Furthermore iOS plays only a single channel of HTML5 audio at a time. On Androids newer versions than 2.3, the limitations aren't as severe, but the latency associated with loading and swapping audio files means effectively the same limitations as iOS applies.

As you can imagine, this severely limits the sound capabilities of mobile devices for games: You must play sound effects whenever they are appropriate (such as when a missile hits an enemy) and not just in response to a user action.

The workarounds to still allow some audio playback are quite limited, but you can get some amount of audio playback on mobile from a game perspective using the concept of audio sprites, as shown in the section "Using Sound Sprites."

All this changes in iOS 6, which will have support for some implementation of Audio Data API. Android will also support the Audio Data API at some point in the future, but currently sound sprites are the best you can use as of this writing.

BUILDING A SIMPLE DESKTOP SOUND ENGINE

Before delving into the contortions necessary to get audio playing on a mobile device, it's worth taking a look at what's involved in playing sound effects via the `<audio>` tag on the desktop.

Using Audio Tags for Game Audio

One of the problems with Audio objects from a game perspective is that each object can play only one sound at a time. This means that if you want to play the same sound effect twice at almost the exact same time (because, for example, two missiles just blew up) you can't if you use a single audio element.

As a workaround to this limitation, HTML5 game developers quickly discovered that after a sound had been loaded, if you assigned its source to another, different audio element, the sound effect wouldn't be downloaded again but would start playing almost immediately. This led to a design of game audio systems that had a number of pre-created Audio objects that were used as channels to play sound effects.

To make this work, it would be the audio system's job to keep track of which of the channels were still playing audio and add any new sound effects only to channels that weren't in the middle of playing.

Adding a Simple Sound System

In Chapter 10 the asset loader code has some functionality for loading sound files based on supported formats. This means that the loading side of things is already built. The only piece of code needed is setting up the channels and playing back audio where appropriate.

This example adds sound to the Block Break example from Chapter 11, "Bootstrapping the Quintus Engine: Part III." To start, create a new file called **quintus_audio.js** in the same directory as `blockbreak.html` and add the code from Listing 25-1.

LISTING 25-1: The desktop quintus audio system

```
Quintus.Audio = function(Q) {
  Q.audio = {
    channels: [],
    channelMax:  Q.options.channelMax || 10,
    active: {}
  };
  // Dummy methods
  Q.play = function() {};
  Q.audioSprites = function() {};

  Q.enableSound = function() {
    var hasTouch =  !!('ontouchstart' in window);
    if(!hasTouch) {
      Q.audio.enableDesktopSound();
    } else {
      Q.audio.enableMobileSound();
    }
    return Q;
  };

  Q.audio.enableDesktopSound = function() {
    for (var i=0;i<Q.audio.channelMax;i++) {
Q.audio.channels[i] = {};
      Q.audio.channels[i]['channel'] = new Audio();
```

```
              Q.audio.channels[i]['finished'] = -1;
        }
        Q.play = function(s,debounce) {
          if(Q.audio.active[s]) return;
          if(debounce) {
            Q.audio.active[s] = true
            setTimeout(function() {
              delete Q.audio.active[s];
            },debounce);
          };

          for (var i=0;i<Q.audio.channels.length;i++) {
            var now = new Date();
            if (Q.audio.channels[i]['finished'] < now.getTime()) {
      Q.audio.channels[i]['finished'] = now.getTime() +
                                        Q.asset(s).duration*1000;
              Q.audio.channels[i]['channel'].src = Q.asset(s).src;
              Q.audio.channels[i]['channel'].load();
              Q.audio.channels[i]['channel'].play();
              break;
            }
          }
        }
      }

      Q.audio.enableMobileSound = function() {
        // TODO: Add mobile support
      }
    };
```

As you can see, the audio system code, at least for the desktop is fairly short and consists primarily of a few configuration variables and dummy methods followed by the enableSound method, which checks if this is a touch device and determines which sound system to load. If it's a desktop browser, the code calls enableDesktopSound, which sets up the audio channels and adds the real play method (one that actually plays sounds) onto Q. The dummy play and audioSprites methods are present so that games can still call those methods even if the audio system isn't enabled.

Setting up the audio channels consists of creating an array of sound objects paired with a finished property that indicates the time that the sound will finish playing. Because no sounds are playing to start with, the property is initialized to –1 for all channels.

Next up is the real play method, which has the main job to find an open channel; in other words, one that has a finished time less than the current time, grabbing the src for a preloaded audio file from Q.asset, loading, and playing it. To make it slightly more useful, the method takes a second parameter that is a debounce time, which prevents the same sound from being played for approximately that number of milliseconds. This is useful for situations in which play might be called repeatedly in a short period of time, but it should trigger only a single sound effect.

Adding Sound Effects to Block Break

To add the sound effects to Block Break, you need to add the quintus_audio.js file to blockbreak.html and make three small changes to blockbreak.js.

First, open `blockbreak.html` and add the required `<script>` tag:

```
<script src='quintus.js'></script>
<script src='quintus_input.js'></script>
<script src='quintus_sprites.js'></script>
<script src='quintus_scenes.js'></script>
<script src='quintus_audio.js'></script>
<script src='blockbreak.js'></script>
```

Next, open `blockbreak.js` and add the `Audio` module to the top of the file and call `enableSound()` to enable the sound system.

```
$(function() {
   var Q = window.Q = Quintus()
                   .include('Input,Sprites,Scenes,Audio')
                   .setup()
                   .enableSound();
```

Next, modify the `step` method in `Q.Ball` to play `paddle.mp3` when the ball hits a paddle and `block.mp3` when the ball hits a block.

```
Q.Ball = Q.Sprite.extend({
    init: function() {
        this._super({
            sheet: 'ball',
            speed: 200,
            dx: 1,
            dy: -1,
        });
        this.p.y = Q.height / 2 - this.p.h;
        this.p.x = Q.width / 2 + this.p.w / 2;
    },
    step: function(dt) {
     var p = this.p;
     var hit = Q.stage().collide(this);
     if(hit) {
       if(hit instanceof Q.Paddle) {
         Q.play('paddle.mp3',500);
         p.dy = -1;
       } else {
         Q.play('block.mp3');
         hit.trigger('collision',this);
       }
     }
   }
```

The `paddle.mp3` playback is debounced to occur only every 500 milliseconds. This is because the ball may overlap the paddle for multiple frames, so the sound playback needs to be debounced to prevent the game from trying to play a new sound every frame. The `block.mp3` file, on the other hand, doesn't need to be debounced because the block is removed after a collision.

Finally, modify the `Q.load` call to load `paddle.mp3` and `block.mp3`:

```
Q.load(['blockbreak.png','blockbreak.json',
        'paddle.mp3','block.mp3'], function() {
   Q.compileSheets('blockbreak.png','blockbreak.json');
```

```
Q.scene('game',new Q.Scene(function(stage) {
  stage.insert(new Q.Paddle());
  stage.insert(new Q.Ball());
```

Next, make sure you have the necessary files: .mp3 and .ogg files in `audio/`. Although the load method mentions files ending in .mp3, the engine will automatically substitute the extension based on what's supported on the platform you are on.

If you fire up the game in a desktop browser, you should now have basic sound effects for when the ball hits blocks and the paddle.

As mentioned in the last section, for mobile devices, this simple, straightforward mechanism isn't going to work. You'll add sound for mobile in the next section.

BUILDING A SOUND SYSTEM FOR MOBILE

I would like nothing better than for the code in this section to become obsolete; it's hackish and does things no game should have to do just to play some simple sound effects. Unfortunately, it's also the only option that's currently available to HTML5 game developers building mobile games. It's not a great solution: Sound effects on iOS aren't synced-up well on iOS, and preloading sounds isn't allowed. Android has similar restrictions. Until the Web Audio API is available for mobile devices, sound support on mobile will be limited.

Using Sound Sprites

So what's the solution? Sound sprites. Much like image spritesheets, audio sprites work by putting multiple sounds into a single audio file, separated by gaps of silence.

If you want a standalone library for doing this, there is the Zynga jukebox library, on GitHub at `https://github.com/zynga/jukebox`. It is a library for playing sounds on mobile devices and works in the same way as the code you add to Quintus does. Jukebox is designed to play on the widest range of devices possible, has been tested all the way back to Android 1.6, and includes a Flash fallback for older Android devices. The code in Listing 25-2 is targeted only at recent iOS and Android devices.

To make audio sprites work, on the first user interaction with the game (such as a touch of the title screen) the sound system starts preloading a single sound. When the sound is playable, the engine starts playing the sound at an initial position in the sound file, which contains only silence. The system then sets a timer to keep looping over the initial silence portion of the sound.

The reason it keeps looping over the sound is that iOS enables automated chaining of sounds: When one sound ends, you can start the next one without user interaction. However, it doesn't enable you to arbitrarily start playing a sound when there are no other sounds playing.

This means the single audio sprite sound file needs to always be playing, even if what it's playing is just silence.

To actually trigger a sound effect, the system fast forwards to the spot in the audio file where the effect is positioned and then sets a timer to go back to playing silence as soon as that sound has finished playing. Because this is not an exact science, it's important that there are delays of at least 1 second between effects to ensure one effect doesn't accidentally start playing the sound after it.

To see how the code that does this looks, fill in the stub of the enableMobileSound method in quintus_audio.js with the code in Listing 25-2.

LISTING 25-2: The enableMobileSound method

```
Q.audio.enableMobileSound = function() {

  var isiOS = navigator.userAgent.match(/iPad|iPod|iPhone/i) != null;

  Q.audioSprites = function(asset) {
    if(_.isString(asset)) asset = Q.asset(asset);
    Q.audio.spriteFile = asset['resources'][0].replace(/\.[a-z]+$/,"");
    Q.audio.sprites = asset['spritemap'];
    Q.el.on("touchstart",Q.audio.start);
  }

  // Turn off normal sound loading and processing
  Q.options.sound = false;

  Q.audio.timer = function() {
    Q.audio.sheet.currentTime = 0;
    Q.audio.sheet.play();
    Q.audio.silenceTimer = setTimeout(Q.audio.timer,500);
  };

  Q.audio.start = function() {
    Q.audio.sheet = new Audio();
    Q.audio.sheet.preload = true;
    Q.audio.sheet.addEventListener("canplaythrough", function() {
      Q.audio.sheet.play();
      Q.audio.silenceTimer = setTimeout(Q.audio.timer,500);
    });

    var spriteFilename = Q.options.audioPath + Q.audio.spriteFile;
    if(isiOS) {
      Q.audio.sheet.src = spriteFilename + ".caf";
    } else {
      Q.audio.sheet.src = spriteFilename + ".mp3";
    }

    Q.audio.sheet.load();
    Q.el.off("touchstart",Q.audio.start);
  };

  Q.play = function(sound,debounce) {
    if(!Q.audio.sheet || !Q.audio.silenceTimer) return;
    if(Q.audio.activeSound) return;
    if(debounce) {
      Q.activeSound = true
      setTimeout(function() {
        Q.audio.activeSound = null;
      },debounce);
```

```
        }

        sound = sound.replace(/\.[a-z0-9]+$/,"");
        if(Q.audio.sprites && Q.audio.sprites[sound]) {
          var startTime = Q.audio.sprites[sound].start - 0.05,
              endDelay = Q.audio.sprites[sound].end - startTime;
          Q.audio.sheet.currentTime = startTime;
          Q.audio.sheet.play();
          clearTimeout(Q.audio.silenceTimer);
          Q.audio.silenceTimer = setTimeout(Q.audio.timer,
                                            endDelay*1000 + 500);
        }
      };
    };
```

This method first checks if the device is an iOS device using userAgent matching. This is not an ideal method (user agent matching never is) but it's the only way to put in a specific file-type work-around for iOS.

Next is the Q.audioSprites method, which is used to pass in the JSON data asset that provides position and length information about the sprites. It stores the filename to load and the sprites inside of the Q.audio object. It also binds to the first touch event on Q.el (the Canvas element) to start the audio system. This is the trick that allows the system to start playing the sprite sound.

Next, it sets Q.options.sound to false, which has the effect of telling the loading system in Quintus not to try to load any sound files in the normal Q.load process. This needs to be done to prevent the engine from trying to load sound files because these files will never trigger their canplaythrough callbacks due to mobile preloading restrictions.

The Q.audio.timer method is the default callback that ensures that when no other sounds are playing, the audio element continues to loop over the first 500 milliseconds of the sprite, which are known to be silent.

The Q.audio.start method is called on the first touch event. Because it's triggered by a user event, it can set up and load a sound file. When the canplaythrough event triggers, it calls play and starts the silence timer.

Next, the system loads the sound file into the audio spritesheet at Q.audio.sheet. On iOS devices, although mobile Safari has support for a number of different sound formats, only the .caf file format (when encoded with the IMA-ADPCM codec) can be played natively without using iTunes to do the actual playing. Using iTunes to play sounds causes a noticeable delay and stutter inside of mobile Safari.

Finally, Q.audio.start turns off the touchstart callback to prevent it from being called twice.

After handling debouncing much in the same way as on the desktop, the Q.play method itself has the job to find the sprite in the Q.audio.sprites object. It first removes any file extensions off the sound name (the sprite names don't include the filenames in them, compared to the assets, which generally do); it then checks that the sound is present.

With the sound found, the game can calculate the start time for the sound and how long it should play for. It then simply scrubs the audio sheet to the point in the file where the sound starts and calls play on the audio file again to force it to continue playing. The start time is set back slightly by 0.05 seconds because otherwise short effects or effects that start right away can be skipped by both Android and iOS. Finally, it clears out the silence timer timeout and resets it to trigger after the sound has finished playing.

Generating the Sprite File

In order to generate the combined sound file necessary for the game and the accompanying JSON data file, you could open an audio editing program and manually place the sound effects with the proper silence gaps and then manually create a JSON file. As things progress, however, this could become a maintenance nightmare.

Luckily, there is a tool that has been written to generate the combined files and output JSON for Zynga's jukebox. Because the Quintus code you added earlier uses a subset of the features in jukebox, you can use that tool, available at https://github.com/tonistiigi/audiosprite.

The library relies on the ffmpeg tool, which you need to install separately. It is available via the ffmpeg website at http://ffmpeg.org/ or can be installed via Homebrew on OS X (brew install ffmpeg) or via your package manager on Linux. Windows users need to download and run the installer.

After you have ffmpeg installed, to install audiosprite, use NPM and install it globally via the following:

```
npm installl -g audiosprite
```

This installs a command called audiosprite that generates the combined audio sprite files. To combine the block.wav and paddle.wav files into the output file called audiosprites, you can run

```
audiosprite --silence 1 ~DHoutput audiosprites block.wav paddle.wav
```

This generates audiosprites.caf, audiosprites.mp3, and audiosprites.json (along with .ogg and .m4a files). The audiosprites.json file looks something like Listing 25-3.

LISTING 25-3: The audiosprites.json file

```json
{
  "resources": [
    "audiosprites.caf",
    "audiosprites.ac3",
    "audiosprites.mp3",
    "audiosprites.m4a",
    "audiosprites.ogg"
  ],
  "spritemap": {
    "silence": {
      "start": 0,
      "end": 1,
      "loop": true
    },
    "block": {
      "start": 2,
      "end": 2.03,
      "loop": false
    },
    "paddle": {
      "start": 4,
```

```
      "end": 4.04,
      "loop": false
    }
  },
  "autoplay": "silence"
}
```

Because the audiosprite tool just takes a list of files and generates both the combined file and the JSON, it's an easy tool to include in your build process to make generating sound sprite files slightly less painful.

Adding Sound Sprites to the Game

To get sound sprites into the *Block Break* game, you need to make only a couple of minor changes to the loading code to load the audiosprites.json file and tell the engine to use that JSON file as the audio sprites. Modify the highlighted code in the Q.load callback in blockbreak.js to read:

```
Q.load(['blockbreak.png','blockbreak.json','audiosprites.json',
         'paddle.mp3','block.mp3'], function() {
  Q.compileSheets('blockbreak.png','blockbreak.json');
  Q.audioSprites("audiosprites.json");

  Q.scene('game',new Q.Scene(function(stage) {
```

If you run this game on a mobile iOS or Android device, you should now have sound. On iOS the sound will be a little choppy and not particularly well synced, but it's unfortunately the best that can be done within the limitations of the medium.

LOOKING TO THE FUTURE OF HTML5 SOUND

Although HTML5 audio on mobile devices is in a particularly bad state, the situation on the desktop isn't that much better. Of the current generation browsers, IE9 actually has the best performing <audio> tag support. Other browsers (Chrome in particular) actually regressed during 2011 and added new issues with <audio> tag playback. These are slowly being fixed, and the long-term outlook for game audio on HTML5 is bright.

In particular, the Web Audio API is particularly impressive. (See the spec at www.w3.org/TR/webaudio/ for more details.) However, because the Web Audio API is only available in Chrome and Safari on the desktop at this time, it will be a while before there is a performant, low-level sound API that is cross-browser supported, so it may still be for a while yet that the <audio> tag is the game engine building block of choice.

SUMMARY

This chapter looked at one of the few less-than-bright spots in mobile HTML5 gaming: audio. It looked at some of the basics of using the HTML5 <audio> tag and then jumped into adding a simple sound engine for both desktop and mobile into the Quintus engine. While sound in mobile browsers is limited, you make use of it provided you are aware of the limitations and use it to augment the game experience rather than rely on it as a core feature of your mobile game.

PART VIII
Game Engines and App Stores

26

Using an HTML5 Game Engine

INTRODUCTION

The ease to start with HTML5 game development combined with the growing popularity of
HTML5 as a medium to build games quickly has led to a proliferation of game engines, both
open-source and commercial. This chapter examines some of the most popular engines available.

LOOKING AT THE HISTORY OF HTML5 ENGINES

Although the canvas element has been around in some form since it was introduced by Apple
to power OS X Dashboard components in 2004, it has been only in the past few years that
people began to take HTML5 seriously as a platform for game development. There are a
myriad of reasons for this, but the performance limitations of JavaScript and the lack of high-
performance rendering kept JavaScript from being considered for serious game development by
most sane individuals.

That began to change in 2008. In response to the processing requirements of the increasingly massive amounts of JavaScript that were beginning to appear in Ajax-heavy applications, such as Google's GMail JavaScript, performance began to be taken seriously by browser makers.

To help speed up its own applications, Google released the Chrome browser powered by the V8 JavaScript engine, and Safari and Firefox both launched new JavaScript engines that boosted performance immensely. The JavaScript arms race was on in full force, and people slowly began to look at JavaScript more and more like a real language that could be used for larger-scale application development.

Developers have an uncontrollable impulse to program games in whatever medium they work in, and JavaScript was no different. Simple games in JavaScript have been around since its inception, but in 2008 things began to change as some brave souls, such as the developers behind GameQuery (http://gamequeryjs.com/) began putting together larger, more sophisticated game frameworks.

As the canvas element started to appear in more and more browsers, developers turned their attention to it as a potential game development tool. Early tools such as gameJS (http://gamejs.org/), based on the popular Python PyGame library, tended to provide a thin wrapper on top of canvas.

Into this mix a game engine called Akihabara (www.kesiev.com/akihabara/) appeared in early 2010. More a loose collection of tools than a full game engine, the magic of Akihabara was that it ran on just about anything that supported the canvas tag. This included the iPhone, iPad, Android, and newer desktop browsers as well as the Internet Channel inside of the Nintendo Wii.

As the Italian creator of Akihabara wrote:

> *The Akihabara which you can download here is my personal dream too. It is a set of libraries, tools and presets to create pixelated indie-style 8/16-bit era games in JavaScript that runs in your browser without any Flash plugin, making use of a small small small subset of the HTML5 features, that are actually available on many modern browsers.*

By targeting classic pixelated indie-style games at lower resolutions, Akihabara hit a performance sweet spot but also provided a glimmer of what could be when browsers and devices caught up with the needs of HTML5 game developers and provided a speedy, stable platform for games.

Since then a large number of engines have appeared on the scene, both commercial and open-source, each with its own philosophy and supported platforms and technologies (Canvas, DOM, and WebGL).

The JavaScript Wiki has a page dedicated to HTML5 game engines that is updated on a regular basis: http://jswiki.org/game-engines.html.

Every engine has a target market and target developer demographic, so picking an engine that matches your requirements and needs is important.

USING A COMMERCIAL ENGINE

Although there might seem to be a little incongruity to the idea of using a commercial engine on a platform all about standards and openness, there are significant benefits to using a commercial engine over an open-source one: a dedicated team working on the engine and better and more up-to-date documentation and tutorials (in general).

The most obvious downside to commercial engines is that they cost money; however, the currently popular HTML5 engines are relatively inexpensive (the cost of 1–2 console games if you want to put it in perspective) or will take a percentage of revenue once your game is making money, so cost shouldn't be the largest concern you have.

The primary downsides of commercial engines revolve around the restrictions placed on development and distribution. Most of the HTML5 engines are licensed per developer, which means that anyone who helps you on your game needs to have a license as well. Second, although the nature of HTML5 means that you always have some sort of source code for the engine you could theoretically modify, for engines that rely on an IDE to build and export games, you may not have code that can easily be modified. Instead you need to work within the limits of the functionality baked into the engine.

Impact.js

One of the most popular commercial HTML5 engines out there, Impact is the product of a single developer, Dominic Szablewski, and was one of the earliest commercial HTML5 game engines to gain wide appeal. The engine is $99 per developer and is available at `http://impactjs.com`.

Impact comes with a powerful level editor called Weltmeister that enables you to easily create layered, parallax scrolling tile maps and place and edit entities (game objects). Figure 26-1 shows the Weltmeister in action with the jumpnrun demo provided with the engine.

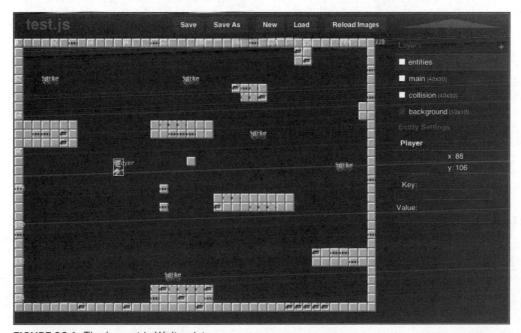

FIGURE 26-1: The Impact.js Weltmeister.

Impact is a programmer game engine, and although the Weltmeister is a great tool to create levels, most of your game will be built in your code editor writing code and creating entities. Impact is designed around a classical inheritance model and a module system that makes it easy to manage dependency loading among objects. When you are ready to release your game, Impact provides a system for packaging your game into a single JavaScript file for release, a process Impact calls *baking*.

As you would expect from an HTML5 game engine, Impact is designed to play on mobile devices. Szablewski even went so far as creating a way to build and package your game in iOS and have the graphics run using hardware-accelerated OpenGL instead of the mobile Safari canvas. This is called iOSImpact and enables you to publish Impact games in the Apple App Store written entirely in HTML5. The mobile HTML5 company AppMobi has used this technology to build its DirectCanvas open-source project, which is discussed in the next chapter, to allow other game engines to publish natively on iOS.

As a game engine, Impact is optimized primarily for 2-D scrolling platformers, but any type of game can theoretically be built with the engine. Using it for other genres simply means that you end up writing more code. As long as you keep within the confines of image-based sprites, Impact can nicely abstract away from the details of HTML5 specific rendering issues provided you keep to the basic image sprites and tile maps it supports.

Spaceport.io

Spaceport.io (`http://spaceport.io`) is a hybrid engine that supports vector graphics running on HTML5 (as well as Flash and native iOS and Android apps). It's JavaScript-based but has a Flash-inspired API and loads vector assets from .SWF files that are run through a converter.

If you have existing ActionScript 3.0 games, you can run them through a converter to get you most of the way into JavaScript, but some additional manual changes are required.

The big selling point for Spaceport.io is its similarity to Flash's API, which can help a lot of Flash-based game developers make the leap, and its support for Flash and vector graphics in its asset development pipeline. One of the major drawbacks for HTML5 game development in its current state is that animations are generally handled by spritesheets of bitmapped graphics, leading to single-layer, canned animations.

From a licensing standpoint, Spaceport.io is free to start developing in, but after you publish your game commercially, the engine requires a 10% revenue share.

IDE Engines

In addition to the two commercial engines previously described, there are also two IDE-based engines (GameMaker HTML5 and Scirra's Construct 2) that can output mobile-playable HTML5 games. These are both applications that you need to download and install and then build your game inside of.

GameMaker has a custom scripting language called GameMaker Language (GML) used for scripting elements, whereas Construct 2 prides itself on enabling users to build games without programming using mostly drag-and-drop. Both engines support 2-D scrolling action games best, but again, they can be used to build just about any type of game you like.

USING AN OPEN-SOURCE ENGINE

On the open-source side of things, HTML5 engines have proliferated as well. Although there are too many to cover in a single book (let alone in a single chapter), there are a few worth mentioning because of their popularity and their support for mobile HTML5 gaming.

Crafty.js

Crafty.js (`http://craftyjs.com`) is a lightweight HTML5 engine based entirely around the idea of components and entities. At under 90k Minified and Gzipped with no dependencies, it has a small footprint.

Instead of defining classes, you simply create entities and add components onto them. Components, as you've seen in Quintus, can add additional functionality as well as trigger and respond to events.

The main Crafty object also acts like the jQuery object in that it can be used to query for objects that have a specific component or combination of components:

```
Crafty("Enemy");
// will return all entities with the Enemy component
```

Crafty ships with a number of useful components, including basic physics; polygon-based collision detection; two-way (platformer), four-way (top-down) and touch controls; and sound support.

You can create new components by calling `Crafty.c` and passing in an `init` method and any additional methods that should be added onto the entity.

A separate site for components has been set up: `http://craftycomponents.com`. This site enables users to submit components and makes it easy to load components directly from the web.

To get a sense of what working with Crafty looks like, look at the code in Listing 26-1. It creates a white box for the play area and adds in gravity and two-way controls that enable you to run around and jump. Below the player a blue floor object is created that enables the player to run around on top of it.

LISTING 26-1: A simple example in Crafty

```
<html>
<head>
 <script src="jquery.min.js"></script><script src="crafty-min.js"></script>
</head>
<body>
<script type="text/javascript">
$(function() {

  Crafty.init(640,480).canvas.init();
  Crafty.background("black");

  // Create the player object with some initial components
```

continues

LISTING 26-1 *(continued)*

```
    var player = Crafty.e("2D, Canvas, Color, Player, Physics")
        .color("white")
        .attr({w:50, h:50, x:126, y:0});

    // You can also add additional components after the fact
    player.addComponent('Gravity').gravity("Floor");
    player.addComponent("Twoway").twoway(5,50);
    player.addComponent("Collision");

    var floor = Crafty.e("2D, Canvas, Color, Collision, Floor")
                .color("blue")
                  .attr({h:30, w:400, x:0, y:380 })
});
</script>

</body>
</html>
```

As you can see, Crafty gets its work done without needing to create a complicated class hierarchy. To run the example you just need to place it inside of an HTML file that has the `crafy.js` library loaded.

Because of the flexibility of using a component-entity system, Crafty is a versatile engine that can be adapted to most genres. Using the built-in components, it works best for anything except 2-D platformers, for which it needs some additional code to handle correct interaction with platforms. Because it provides an advanced collision-detection system based on convex polygons, it works well with top-down games such as 2-D RPGs that need more than just simple tile-based gameplay.

For more on Crafty, visit the website at `http://craftyjs.com/`. Crafty is dual-licensed under the MIT and GPL licenses, which means you can build any type of both commercial or open-source game using the engine.

LimeJS

LimeJS is an engine that explicitly describes itself as an "HTML5 game framework for building fast, native-experience games for all modern touchscreens and desktop browsers." LimeJS is a more full-featured framework than Crafty (this is both a good and a bad thing) that uses Google's closure library (`http://closure-library.googlecode.com/`) for dependency resolution and its event system. It also comes with Google's closure compiler, a Closure-optimized version of Box2d JS and Closure Templates.

As you would expect from a framework of this size, using LimeJS is a little more involved to start with than Crafty, which involves only a single file.

LimeJS has a main object called a `Director` that acts as the main coordinating object and runs the main timing loop. Each separate level or screen of your game is called a `Scene`, and a `Scene` can have many `Layer` objects, each of which can contain any number of `Node` objects. Classes that inherit from `Node`, such as `Sprite`, `Circle`, `Label`, and `Polygon`, are the actual objects you place on the screen.

Although a four-level hierarchy to get an object displayed on the screen might seem complex, each of these layers provides a useful abstraction as you build a game.

To get a sense of what a simple example in LimeJS might look like, look at Listing 26-2. This example drops a circle on the screen wherever you touch, has that circle follow your touch or mouse around, and then fades in and gets larger when you release.

LimeJS handles multitouch just fine without any extra code, so you can touch and drag with multiple fingers at a time.

LISTING 26-2: A Lime.js example

```
goog.provide('movingballs');

goog.require('lime.Director');
goog.require('lime.Scene');
goog.require('lime.Circle');
goog.require('lime.animation.Spawn');
goog.require('lime.animation.FadeTo');
goog.require('lime.animation.ScaleTo');
goog.require('lime.animation.MoveTo');

movingballs.start = function(){
  var director = new lime.Director(document.body,1024,768),
      scene = new lime.Scene();
  director.makeMobileWebAppCapable();
  goog.events.listen(scene,['mousedown','touchstart'],function(e){
    var circle = new lime.Circle()
                        .setSize(50,50)
                        .setFill(Math.floor(Math.random()*255),
                                 Math.floor(Math.random()*255),
                                 Math.floor(Math.random()*255));
    scene.appendChild(circle);
    circle.setPosition(e.position.x,e.position.y)
          .setOpacity(0.5);

    e.swallow(['mousemove','touchmove'],function(e) {
      circle.runAction(
        new lime.animation.MoveTo(e.position)
                          .setEasing(lime.animation.Easing.LINEAR)
      );
    });

    e.swallow(['mouseup','touchend'],function(e){
      circle.runAction(new lime.animation.Spawn(
        new lime.animation.FadeTo(1),
        new lime.animation.ScaleTo(1.5)
      ));
    });
  });
  director.replaceScene(scene);
};
```

This example is a modified version of the helloworld example you can generate from the command line with `bin/lime.py create helloworld`. Getting the example up and running is more involved than using Crafty because you need to download LimeJS, run the `bin/lime.py init` command to download the dependencies, and then create the project directory.

As you can see, everything is a little more verbose because of the heavy namespacing that the Google Closure library uses, but because of the power of the library, the code still manages to stay fairly compact.

A couple of nice things that LimeJS does are worth mentioning. The first is the mechanism it uses to track touches. The `e.swallow` code intelligently applies only to the same touch that initiated the original event. It can track the touch identifier for you internally, so you don't need to worry about it.

The animation system that LimeJS provides makes it easy to set up fire-and-forget animations (much like jQuery). It also enables you to combine those animations to run concurrently via `lime.animations.Spawn`.

LimeJS is licensed under the Apache License, which enables you to use it for any purpose personal or commercial, as long as proper attribution is provided. To learn more about LimeJS and download the engine, visit `www.limejs.com`.

EaselJS

EaselJS is a framework created during building of the Microsoft-sponsored game Pirates Love Daises (`www.pirateslovedaisies.com`). EaselJS is an interesting position because it's not actually a game engine, but rather a framework to make canvas easier to work with. It provides a scene graph, some base classes, and a number of utility methods that make working with canvas simpler and more productive.

If you think the goal of EaselJS is to create a similar scripting environment as Flash, you wouldn't be far off from the mark. It provides a `Stage` object that acts much like the Flash stage, a `Shape` object that behaves a lot like a Flash graphic, and a `MovieClip` that keeps track of animation frames much like the Flash equivalent.

Just like Flash, EaselJS doesn't come with a lot of game-specific functionality, so things such as tile maps, object physics, and the like all need to be added by you. But because the framework has such a small, focused API, EaselJS is easy to start with and to use.

Because it's packaged into a single JavaScript library and CDN-hosted, you can easily pull EaselJS into your project simply by adding a `<script>` tag to your HTML:

```
<script src="http://code.createjs.com/easeljs-0.4.1.min.js"></script>
```

To get a sense of what some EaselJS code looks like, see Listing 26-3. This example adds a rotating, bouncing ball that scales up and down on the screen. When you click or touch that ball, it will be flung in a new, random direction.

Although it might not seem like EaselJS provides that much functionality in this example, it's actually doing a fair amount. It handles pixel-perfect hit-detection on the ball shape, which was drawn with an arbitrary `Graphics` object. It handles scaling and rotation of the object. It also handles running the main loop at a specific wanted FPS using the `Ticker` object.

LISTING 26-3: EaselJS example

```html
<!DOCTYPE HTML>
<html lang="en">
<head>
  <meta charset="UTF-8">
  <title></title>
  <script src="http://code.createjs.com/easeljs-0.4.1.min.js"></script>
  <meta name='viewport' content='width=device-width, user-scalable=no'>
</head>
<body>
  <canvas id='canvas' width='320' height='480'></canvas>
  <script>
    var canvas, stage, graphic, ball;

    canvas = document.getElementById("canvas");
    stage = new Stage(canvas);
    Touch.enable(stage);

    graphic = new Graphics();
    graphic.setStrokeStyle(1);
    graphic.beginStroke(Graphics.getRGB(0,0,0));
    graphic.beginFill(Graphics.getRGB(255,0,0));
    graphic.drawCircle(0,0,25);
    graphic.lineTo(0,0,0,25);

    ball = new Shape(graphic);
    ball.x = 50;
    ball.y = 50;
    ball.vx = 100;
    ball.vy = 1000;
    ball.pulse = 0;

    ball.onPress = function() {
      var direction = Math.random()*Math.PI*2;
      ball.vx = Math.cos(direction) * 200;
      ball.vy = Math.sin(direction) * 200;
    }

    stage.addChild(ball);
    window.tick = function(dt) {
      var seconds  = dt / 1000;

      ball.vy += 50 * seconds; // Add some gravity
      ball.x += ball.vx * seconds;
      ball.y += ball.vy * seconds;
      ball.pulse += seconds;
      ball.scaleX = 1 + Math.sin(ball.pulse)/2;
      ball.scaleY = 1 + Math.sin(ball.pulse)/2;
      ball.rotation += ball.vx * seconds;

      if(ball.x + 25 > canvas.width) {
        ball.vx = -Math.abs(ball.vx);
```

continues

LISTING 26-3 *(continued)*

```
    } else if(ball.x - 25 < 0) {
      ball.vx = Math.abs(ball.vx);
    }

    if(ball.y + 25 > canvas.height) {
      ball.vy = -Math.abs(ball.vy);
    } else if(ball.y - 25 < 0) {
      ball.vy = Math.abs(ball.vy);
    }

    stage.update();
  }
  Ticker.setFPS(60)
  Ticker.addListener(window);
  </script>
</body>
</html>
```

Because the library can be loaded via a CDN, the entire example is shown in the listing.

You can set up the stage object by passing in a canvas element and then calling `Touch.enable` on the stage to let it handle touch events.

The `Graphics` object, which enables you to create objects that have arbitrary vector artwork, is created first. Next, that graphic is added to a `Shape` called `ball`.

Because `ball` is a JavaScript object, you can add additional properties on to the object. In this case the *x* and *y* properties are built into EaselJS, whereas the `vx`, `vy`, and `pulse` properties are custom.

The `ball` can have event handlers such as `onPress`, which is called whenever the object is clicked or touched. In this case the `onPress` method just generates a random direction and adjusts the ball's velocity to point in that direction.

The actual logic for the ball bouncing around is in a `tick` method on the window object. You can add arbitrary listeners to the `Ticker` object, which is the object EaselJS uses for the game loop. The object must just respond to the `tick` method, which is called each frame with the number of milliseconds that have elapsed since the last call.

The `tick` method moves the ball using the simple Newtonian physics you saw in Chapter 17, "Playing with Pixels," but also pulses the size of the ball up and down.

EaselJS is released under the MIT license and can be used for any commercial or open-source project without restriction. It's part of a suite of JavaScript libraries available at `http://createjs.com` that provides additional functionality that is useful in games: TweenJS, which provides tweening and animation support; SoundJS, which simplifies working with sounds from JavaScript; PreloadJS, which makes it easy to load and play sounds; and Zoe, a tool that exports spritesheets from Flash SWF files.

SUMMARY

This chapter introduced some of the most popular commercial and open-source HTML5 game engines that support mobile. The goal of the chapter was to give you a taste of what developing in a few of the popular open-source libraries looks like from a philosophy and coding standpoint. There are many more engines and libraries to choose from, each with their own philosophy and game target. The HTML5 game framework space is still in its early days, and there are lots of exciting developments in the space happening daily.

SUMMARY

27

Targeting App Stores

INTRODUCTION

Just because your game is developed for the web using HTML5 doesn't mean that's where it has to stay. There are a number of ways you can package your game so that it's playable in the various app stores. For the desktop version of your game, this chapter shows you how to publish your game in the Chrome Web Store. For packaging mobile versions of your app, you examine two technologies: Ludei's CocoonJS and AppMobi's DirectCanvas. Both of these technologies enable you to take a Canvas HTML5 game and package it into a native app that replaces the normal Canvas rendering calls with hardware-accelerated OpenGL ES calls, greatly boosting the graphical performance of your HTML5 games with only a few code changes. The generated apps can then be distributed in the various mobile app stores, including the Apple App Store and Google Play.

PACKAGING YOUR APP FOR THE GOOGLE CHROME WEB STORE

The Google Chrome Web Store is an online marketplace for both free and paid web applications and is available at `https://chrome.google.com/webstore/`.

The applications in the Google Chrome Web Store are what Google calls "installable web apps." Put simply, they are just normal web apps that have been configured to work as Chrome extensions and that can be installed via the Chrome Web Store.

The Web Store supports two different types of apps: hosted apps and packaged apps. *Hosted apps* are just normal web apps that have been submitted to the Web Store with a little bit of additional meta data. *Packaged apps*, on the other hand, are downloaded to the user's computer and can be used offline without any additional work. Hosted apps can also be used offline if they are configured to properly use an application cache manifest.

Creating a Hosted App

Creating a hosted app for the Chrome browser for testing purposes is as simple as creating a directory with the required manifest and icon and then loading it as an unpackaged extension from within Chrome.

To walk through the required steps, you turn the *Alien Invasion* game, hosted on github pages at `http://cykod.github.com/AlienInvasion/`, into a hosted app.

First, create a new folder called **invasion-app**. Next, create a **manifest.json** file in that directory with the contents of Listing 27-1.

LISTING 27-1: Invasion app manifest.json

```
{
  "name": "Alien Invasion",
  "description": "Save the world, you know the drill...",
  "version": "1.0.0",
  "app": {
    "urls": [
      "*://cykod.github.com/AlienInvasion/"
    ],
    "launch": {
      "web_url": "http://cykod.github.com/AlienInvasion/"
    }
  },
  "icons": {
    "128": "invasion_128.png"
  },
  "offline_enabled": true,
  "permissions": [
  ]
}
```

This manifest file has a few important parts. The first are the basic information fields: name, description, and version. These all appear in the extensions screen and provide information to the user. Next is the app information that lets Chrome know what urls should be allowed in the permissions listed at the bottom of the manifest. (In this case, no additional permissions are needed.) The app information also includes the launch information. Because this is a hosted app, you need to include a web_url from where to launch the app.

For icons, you need to specify only a 128 x 128 pixel icon. To match the size of other icons, it should fill up only approximately a 96-pixel box and have a 16-pixel transparent border on each side (see Google's image guidelines for more details: https://developers.google.com/chrome/web-store/docs/images.

Next, if your app supports application cache, you can set the offline_enabled key to true, and the icon for your game won't be grayed-out in the launch screen when the browser is offline.

Finally, there are additional permissions you can request that your app receives by default without needing to ask the user each time your app loads. The available permissions are background, clipboardRead, clipboardWrite, geolocation, notifications, and unlimitedStorage. With the exception of background, these should be self-explanatory.

The background permission is something special that enables you to continue to run code in the background even if the app isn't active or hasn't even been launched. This might be useful for multiplayer games to notify users of actions occurring in the game world even if the user isn't actively playing the game. You can read more in-depth documentation on the background feature at https://developers.google.com/chrome/apps/docs/background.

Now copy the icon invasion_128.png into the same directory as the manifest file and you're done!

You can test out the hosted app by loading it as an unpackaged extension. Click the Chrome Wrench menu; then select the Tools menu and click Extensions.

If you're not already in Developer Mode, click the Developer Mode check box in the top right of the page. Next, click the Load Unpacked Extension button and find the folder you just created. Click Select. (You are selecting a folder, not a file, so just single-click the folder and click Select.)

If everything went according to plan, you should see the *Alien Invasion* extension at the top of the extensions page with its icon, as shown in Figure 27-1.

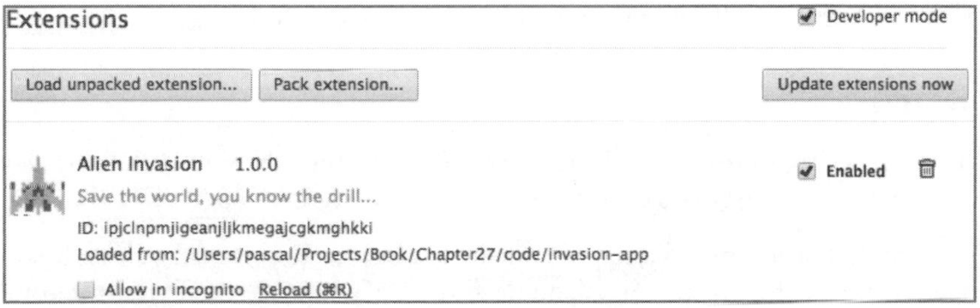

FIGURE 27-1: The *Alien Invasion* extension.

If you create a new tab, you should see the *Alien Invasion* icon in your app screen and you can jump right to the game by clicking it.

Creating a Packaged App

The difference between a hosted app and a packaged app is simply that the packaged app includes all the files necessary to run the game in the app directory and points to a local file rather than a `web_url`.

To create a packaged app from *Alien Invasion*, you need to create a new directory and copy all the files for *Alien Invasion* inside of it.

Next, create a **manifest.json** file, as shown in Listing 27-2, and copy the same `invasion_128.png` icon into the directory along with an `invasion_16.png` that serves as the favicon for the app.

LISTING 27-2: manifest.json for a packaged app

```
{
  "name": "Alien Invasion Packaged",
  "description": "Save the world, you know the drill...",
  "version": "1.0.0",
  "app": {
    "launch": {
      "local_path": "index.html"
    }
  },
  "icons": {
    "128": "invasion_128.png",
    "16" : "invasion_16.png"
  }
}
```

As you can see, this file looks similar to the one for the hosted app, with the primary difference in the `launch` section, which has a `local_path` instead of a `web_url`. The only other difference is the 16×16 pixel icon used for the app tabs that serves as a favicon. (Hosted apps used the website's favicon, so this image wasn't necessary.)

You can load the app the same way by clicking Load Unpacked Extension from the Chrome extensions page and can play it from the launch screen when you create a new tab.

Publishing Your App

To publish your app, you need to log in to a Google account and go to the Chrome Web Store developer dashboard: `https://chrome.google.com/webstore/developer/dashboard`.

Then click the Add New Item link and upload a .zip file of the extension directory. You can upload both hosted and packaged apps, but for hosted apps you need to verify you are the owner of any domains listed in the URLs section of your manifest by using Google Webmaster tools.

After you upload the zip file, you have the opportunity to enter a detailed description, upload an icon and promotional image, and select categories and regions and hook in Google Analytics.

To publish your first app, you also need to pay a $5.00 one-time fee that Google uses to prevent SPAM accounts. After that your app will be published in the Chrome store and easily available to the millions of Chrome users around the world.

USING COCOONJS TO ACCELERATE YOUR APP

CocoonJS is a native wrapper created by Ludei that enables you to create native iOS and Android apps from your HTML5 games. Its claimed value proposition is particularly attractive: Without making any changes to your game, you can package it into a native app and get performance increases of several orders of magnitude.

The fine print is that Cocoon supports a limited subset of HTML and primarily works by exposing an API in JavaScript that mimics the Canvas API. The full list of features that CocoonJS supports is available on the Wiki at `http://wiki.ludei.com/cocoonjs:featurelist`.

As of this writing, the DOM support is limited to elements that are useful for games: Canvas, image, and sound elements.

Getting a Game Ready to Load into CocoonJS

Despite Ludei's claim, depending on how your HTML5 game is written, you may need to make some modifications for the game to load in CocoonJS. The primary consideration is how you put a Canvas onto the page. CocoonJS parses your `index.html` file, but only to load the JavaScript files mentioned therein. This means that you need to make sure you generate your `<canvas>` element via JavaScript and not via a `<canvas>` tag in your HTML.

The CocoonJS `<canvas>` tag also supports a special option you can apply to make the `<canvas>` element scale up to fill the size of the screen while still maintaining its aspect ratio.

To modify the *Alien Invasion* game from Chapter 3, "Finishing Up and Going Mobile," to work with CocoonJS, modify the `Game.initialize` method in `engine.js` to read as shown in Listing 27-3.

LISTING 27-3: A modified Game.initialize method

```
// Game Initialization
this.initialize = function(canvasElementId,sprite_data,callback) {

    this.canvas= document.createElement("canvas");
    // CocoonJS extension
    this.canvas.style.cssText="idtkscale:ScaleAspectFit;";
    this.canvas.width = 320;
    this.canvas.height = 480;
    document.body.appendChild(this.canvas);

    this.playerOffset = 10;
    this.canvasMultiplier= 1;
```

continues

LISTING 27-3 *(continued)*

```
    this.mobile = true;

    this.width = this.canvas.width;
    this.height= this.canvas.height;

    this.loop();
    if(this.mobile) {
      this.setBoard(4,new TouchControls());
    }
    SpriteSheet.load(sprite_data,callback);
  };
```

The method ignores the passed-in `canvasElementId` and just creates a new Canvas element that it calls `appendChild` on to make visible.

It also sets the special `idtkscale` property to `ScaleAspectFit` to make sure the Canvas element scales up as wanted.

Next, the mobile setup method is removed and just replaced with a `this.mobile = true` statement because the Canvas element doesn't need to get resized anymore. Other than that *Alien Invasion* is ready to be wrapped inside of CocoonJS.

The other thing you want to check is to make sure you use `requestAnimationFrame` to handle the animation, specifically the `webkitRequestAnimationFrame` vendor-prefixed version because that's the one supported by CocoonJS.

To add this to *Alien Invasion*, modify the `Game.loop` method in `engine.js` to read as shown in Listing 27-4.

LISTING 27-4: A modified Game.loop

```
  var lastTime = new Date().getTime();
  var maxTime = 1/30;

  // Game Loop
  this.loop = function() {

    var curTime = new Date().getTime();
    webkitRequestAnimationFrame(Game.loop);
    var dt = (curTime - lastTime)/1000;
    if(dt > maxTime) { dt = maxTime; }

    for(var i=0,len = boards.length;i<len;i++) {
      if(boards[i]) {
        boards[i].step(dt);
        boards[i].draw(Game.ctx);
      }
    }

    lastTime = curTime;
  };
```

Doing so ensures that your app refreshes at the maximum rate the device can support to give you the smoothest animation.

Testing CocoonJS on Android

CocoonJS has an application in the Google Play marketplace called the CocoonJS Launcher.

If you open this app, you are presented with two options: The first is to view some of the pre-created demos, and the second is to launch your own app. To launch your app, you need to first get a registration code. You can get that code by clicking the Register button, filling out the form, and confirming your e-mail.

Next, you need to package the files for the game into a .zip file. In creating the .zip file, make sure you don't zip the directory but instead just zip up all the files because CocoonJS needs to find an index.html file in the top level of your zip.

Now place that .zip file somewhere where you can access it from a URL on your device. If you run a web server on your development machine, that works just fine as long as the Android device is on the same Wi-Fi network; otherwise, just upload the file to a web host.

From the Android Launcher app, enter the URL for the .zip file in the Zip URL field and click Launch Current. After a few moments to download the file and boot it up, you should have *Alien Invasion* running at an elevated frame rate on your phone. In addition, Ludei supports Android all the way back to 2.2, so phones that might not run your HTML5 game can still be targeted.

In the case of the Galaxy Nexus, the frame rate on the game rose from the mid-teens to approximately 200 FPS using CocoonJS, so there are significant performance benefits.

To restart your app or load a new version, you need to explicitly restart the app by removing it from the running app list and then run it again.

> ### TESTING COCOONJS IN IPHONE
>
> As of this writing, Ludei had just released its iOS SDK, and the Launcher App was not yet approved in the Apple App Store. To test your app on iOS, you need to run through an involved process that requires you to modify the downloaded file's Bundle ID, generate an add-hoc provisioning profile on developer.apple.com, and use XCode to create an .ipa file. Rather than detail a process that will hopefully be obsolete by the time this goes to print, you should check the latest details on the Ludei wiki at http://wiki.ludei.com/cocoonjs:launcherios for how to get the launcher up and running for iOS.

Building Your App in the Cloud

As of this writing, Ludei has not yet opened up its cloud service for building apps in the cloud for public consumption. When it does, you can build native apps without having to download XCode or have the Android SDK installed on your machine.

For iOS development, you still need to create an account on `developer.apple.com` and join the $99-per-year iOS Developer Program at `https://developer.apple.com/programs/ios/`. This enables you to create and distribute apps in the Apple App Store.

BUILDING APPS WITH THE APPMOBI XDK AND DIRECTCANVAS

AppMobi is an alternative to CocoonJS for packaging up HTML5 apps as native apps on iOS and Android. AppMobi built its technology on top of the open-source PhoneGap project, which uses a native web-browser component augmented with native device APIs, such as audio and video recording and access to contacts stored on the device.

As mentioned in the last chapter, work done during Impact.js development to create iOSImpact was used to develop the initial version of AppMobi's DirectCanvas, which replaces the standard `<canvas>` object with a custom, OpenGL ES accelerated implementation.

Understanding DirectCanvas

DirectCanvas works a little differently from CocoonJS in that it requires that you split your game into two parts. The first part is an initial HTML file that connects to the primary PhoneGap web view, which has a normal DOM and can accept user input. The second component is JavaScript only and consists of the main portion of your game that draws to the hardware-accelerated Canvas. This second component cannot bind any listeners to get touch input however, so you need to pass that information manually from the first piece to the second using a bridge that DirectCanvas provides.

Installing the XDK

The AppMobi XDK is a powerful Java application and Chrome browser extension that enables you to build and test your application in an emulator and then send it to be built in the cloud, all without requiring you to install local copies of development tools to build iOS and Android Apps. You can learn more from the AppMobi website at `www.appmobi.com/?q=node/154`.

To install the XDK, go to the Chrome Web Store at `https://chrome.google.com/webstore` and search for AppMobi XDK. Ignore the other results and install the AppMobi HTML5 XDK. Follow the prompts to complete adding the extension to Chrome.

Launching the XDK requires you to log in with an AppMobi account or create a new account by following the onscreen instructions.

After you make it into the main XDK, you should see a screen that looks something like Figure 27-2, depending on the example running and the device selected.

The XDK enables you to test the form factors of different devices in both Portrait and Landscape mode as well as test geolocation and device acceleration. A word of warning, however: The browser engine used to run all the examples is still the Chrome JavaScript engine and WebKit renderer, so the emulation is more for general behavior and form factor rather than actually emulating device characteristics or performance.

You can try the various demos that ship with the XDK by clicking the green drop-down arrow to pick a different demo.

FIGURE 27-2: The AppMobi XDK.

Creating the App

To create a new app, click the big Plus button to the left of the project selector drop-down. At the next screen, choose Client-Side as the project type and click Next. Give the project a name like **alieninvasion** and click Next. Click Next again to skip the API injection screen because you won't need any of those services for this app. Finally, click Finish to complete the app and load it in the XDK.

Next, click the open project folder icon at the top of the page to open the location where AppMobi wants you to put your game's files. Copy the final *Alien Invasion* code from Chapter 3 into the new folder for your project and then click the Reload App button near the top left of the XDK. (It looks like a recycle symbol.) The App pops up a warning because you removed the code that loads the XDK, but if you click OK, the game should still load.

Modifying *Alien Invasion* to Use DirectCanvas

For *Alien Invasion* to use DirectCanvas, you need to separate the user input from the main game.

To start this process, replace the `index.html` file for the game with the code in Listing 27-5, which is a modified version of the boilerplate `index.html` AppMobi provides.

LISTING 27-5: The DirectCanvas index.html

```
<!DOCTYPE html>
<html>
<head>
<title>Alien Invasion</title>
<meta http-equiv="Content-type" content="text/html; charset=utf-8">
<style type="text/css">
    /* Prevent copy paste for all elements except text fields */
    *   { -webkit-user-select:none;
          -webkit-tap-highlight-color:rgba(255, 255, 255, 0); }
    input, textarea  { -webkit-user-select:text; }

    /* Set up the page with a default background image */
    body {
        background-color:#fff;
        color:#000;
        font-family:Arial;
        font-size:48pt;
        margin:0px;padding:0px;
        background-image:url('images/background.jpg');
    }
</style>
<script type="text/javascript" charset="utf-8" ➥
src="http://localhost:58888/_appMobi/appmobi.js"></script>
<script type="text/javascript" charset="utf-8" ➥
src="http://localhost:58888/_appMobi/xhr.js"></script>
<script type="text/javascript">

/* This code is used to run as soon as appMobi activates */
var onDeviceReady=function(){

    // Size the display to 320px by 480px
    AppMobi.display.useViewport(320,480)

    // hide splash screen
    AppMobi.device.hideSplashScreen();

    // Load files for Direct Canvas
    AppMobi.canvas.load("index.js");

    var keys = {}
    var trackTouch = function(e) {
      var touch, x;
      var gutterWidth = 10;
      var unitWidth = 320/5;
      var blockWidth = unitWidth-gutterWidth;
      e.preventDefault();
      keys['left'] = false;
      keys['right'] = false;
      for(var i=0;i<e.touches.length;i++) {
       touch = e.touches[i];
       x = touch.pageX;
       if(x < unitWidth) {
```

```
        keys['left'] = true;
      }
      if(x > unitWidth && x < 2*unitWidth) {
        keys['right'] = true;
      }
    }
    if(e.type == 'touchstart' || e.type == 'touchend') {
      for(i=0;i<e.changedTouches.length;i++) {
        touch = e.changedTouches[i];
        x = touch.pageX;
        if(x > 4 * unitWidth) {
          keys['fire'] = (e.type == 'touchstart');
        }
      }
    }
    AppMobi.canvas.execute('Game.setKeys('+ keys["left"] + ","
                           + keys["right"] + ","
                           + keys["fire"] + ")");
  };
  document.addEventListener('touchstart',trackTouch,false);
  document.addEventListener('touchmove',trackTouch,false);
  document.addEventListener('touchend',trackTouch,false);
  document.addEventListener('touchcancel',trackTouch,false);
};

document.addEventListener("appMobi.device.ready",onDeviceReady,false);

</script>
</head>
<body>
</body>
</html>
```

All the code before the `onDeviceReady` method is the standard AppMobi boilerplate that sets up some default styles and loads the AppMobi JavaScript.

The application sets up a proper-sized viewport, hides the splash screen, and loads the `index.js` file into DirectCanvas. Because DirectCanvas is a completely different execution environment than the `index.html`, no variables or methods leak across, so you need to explicitly execute code to run in the other context to shuttle information back and forth.

The `touch` method from the main game has been moved into `index.html` from `engine.js`. This is because all the input needs to be gathered in the `index.html` file because the DirectCanvas context can't receive any user input.

At the end of the touch method, you can see the call used to transfer data to the Canvas context:

```
AppMobi.canvas.execute('Game.setKeys(' + keys["left"] + ","
                       + keys["right"] + ","
                       + keys["fire"] + ")");
```

The `setKeys` method is new and needs to be added to `engine.js`.

Next, create the **index.js** file referenced in the Listing 27-5. This file just has two lines, shown in Listing 27-6, that tell it to load the `engine.js` and `game.js` files into the context.

LISTING 27-6: The index.js file

```
AppMobi.context.include( 'engine.js' );
AppMobi.context.include( 'game.js' );
```

All that's left is to modify the `engine.js` to use the AppMobi DirectCanvas and pull input values from the `setKeys` method rather than from bound events. You also want to modify the loop method to again use `requestAnimationFrame`. Finally, after everything has been drawn, you need to explicitly call `context.present()` to draw it on the screen.

Modify the top of `engine.js` as shown in the highlighted code in Listing 27-7, adding in the `requestAnimationFrame` shim along with changes to the initialize method and the new `setKeys` method.

LISTING 27-7: Changes to engine.js for DirectCanvas

```
(function() {
    var lastTime = 0;
    var vendors = ['ms', 'moz', 'webkit', 'o'];
    for(var x = 0;
        x < vendors.length && !window.requestAnimationFrame;
        ++x) {
        window.requestAnimationFrame =
                    window[vendors[x]+'RequestAnimationFrame'];
        window.cancelAnimationFrame =
          window[vendors[x]+'CancelAnimationFrame'] ||
                    window[vendors[x]+'CancelRequestAnimationFrame'];
    }

    if (!window.requestAnimationFrame)
        window.requestAnimationFrame = function(callback, element) {
            var currTime = new Date().getTime();
            var timeToCall = Math.max(0, 16 - (currTime - lastTime));
            var id = window.setTimeout(function() {
                            callback(currTime + timeToCall);
                    }, timeToCall);
            lastTime = currTime + timeToCall;
            return id;
        };

    if (!window.cancelAnimationFrame)
        window.cancelAnimationFrame = function(id) {
            clearTimeout(id);
        };
}());

var Game = new function() {
  var boards = [];
  // Game Initialization
```

```
this.initialize = function(canvasElementId,sprite_data,callback) {

  var ctx = this.ctx = AppMobi.canvas.getContext("2d");

  this.ctx.width = 320;
  this.ctx.height = 480;

  this.playerOffset = 10;
  this.canvasMultiplier= 1;
  this.mobile = true;

  this.width = 320;
  this.height = 480;
  this.loop();
  this.setBoard(4,new TouchControls());

  SpriteSheet.load(sprite_data,callback);
};

this.keys = {};
this.setKeys = function(l,r,fire) {
  Game.keys['left'] = l;
  Game.keys['right'] = r;
  Game.keys['fire'] = fire;
};

var lastTime = new Date().getTime();
var maxTime = 1/30;
// Game Loop
this.loop = function() {
  var curTime = new Date().getTime();
  requestAnimationFrame(Game.loop);
  var dt = (curTime - lastTime)/1000;
  if(dt > maxTime) { dt = maxTime; }

  for(var i=0,len = boards.length;i<len;i++) {
    if(boards[i]) {
      boards[i].step(dt);
      boards[i].draw(Game.ctx);
    }
  }
  Game.ctx.present();
  lastTime = curTime;
};
```

The requestAnimationFrame shim is the same as what you saw in Chapter 9, "Bootstrapping the Quintus Engine: Part I."

In the Game.initialize method, in lieu of creating a Canvas element, with DirectCanvas you need to grab the context from the AppMobi.canvas element. The context can also be resized directly—something you normally can do only to the canvas element. The remainder of the initialize method just defaults to mobile and hardcodes a width and height into the game.

The setKeys method replaces the input handlers that were there before and explicitly sets the keys that are active based on what index.html is sending over.

The last important change is that the loop explicitly calls Game.ctx.present() to render to the screen.

Testing Your App on a Device

AppMobi makes it easy to test your game live on a device. It provides the AppLab app for both iOS and Android that you can download from the respective app stores for each. After you install this on your device, start it up. AppLab enables you to run your apps (click the small My Apps button in the top right) that have been synced to the cloud.

To sync an app to the cloud, click the Test Anywhere button in the top bar of the XDK. After the app syncs, you should run the active version on your device. (Be careful because as of this writing the Android version of DirectCanvas is still in beta and has a number of visual defects. These will hopefully be fixed by the time this book is in print.)

BUILDING YOUR APP IN THE CLOUD

When you have your app running properly in the AppLab, it's time to push it out to production. To do this you can click the Build for App Store button on the top of the XDK bar. The process to build your app for either iOS or Android involves a number of steps that AppMobi guides you through quite nicely.

Building for iOS in particular is a painful process that involves creating and downloading certificates and provisioning profiles from the app developer portal developer.apple.com. You need a $99/year membership to join the iOS developer program at https://developer.apple.com/programs/ios/ to complete the process. When you're done, you have either an .ipa file for iOS or an .apk file for Android that you can install on your device to test the final app.

SUMMARY

This chapter showed you how to package your HTML5 game in different ways to get it deployed in the various app stores. It discussed creating both Hosted and Packaged Chrome Web Store apps and looked at two platforms to create native mobile games out of your HTML5 app: CocoonJS and AppMobi. Mobile HTML5 games are no longer just for the browser but can be deployed natively to almost any iOS or Android device. As you'll see in the next chapter, there are a lot of cool new things coming down the pipeline, but native performance and features will always be at least slightly ahead of what's in the browser, so packaging HTML5 games into app stores is something that will only become more prevalent.

28

Seeking Out What's Next

WHAT'S IN THIS CHAPTER?

➤ Looking at 3-D in the browser with WebGL

➤ Previewing upcoming APIs

➤ Looking to the future of native support with WebAPI

INTRODUCTION

This book has covered a lot of ground, but the HTML5 space moves quickly, and a number of cutting-edge specifications for technologies that are not yet available for general use in mobile browsers are worth considering because they will expand the type of mobile HTML5 games you can develop. This includes direct access to hardware-accelerated 3-D in the browser via OpenGL ES, access to better sound support via Web Audio API, and access to additional native hardware features. This chapter describes these cutting-edge specifications.

GOING 3-D WITH WEBGL

One of the biggest drawbacks to canvas-based gaming is that it's stuck in two-dimensional flatland. Sure, you could build your own 3-D rendering and rasterization engine in JavaScript on top of 2-D canvas, but the performance would not be suitable.

Luckily there is help coming down the pipeline. *WebGL*, which is a web-based version of OpenGL ES, is a specification that enables hardware-accelerated 3-D in the browser. *OpenGL ES*, which is short for OpenGL for Embedded System, is the smaller, more power-consumption-friendly cousin of the desktop OpenGL standard that has powered various types of 3-D software (including games) for the past two decades.

OpenGL ES has been available via native APIs on iOS and Android and powers the 3-D games you see in the app stores. Exposing a JavaScript-based API via WebGL means that HTML5 apps can create detailed 3-D scenes and games in the browser without plug-ins. To access a WebGL canvas in a supported browser, you simply need to create a standard canvas element and then request a webgl context instead of the standard 2-D context.

> **NOTE** *WebGL is a standard proposed by the Khronos group, and you can find up-to-date details on the Khronos.org website:* `www.khronos.org/webgl/`.

WebGL provides a low-level API for generating 3-D scenes, relying on shader programs written in a specialized shader language called WebGL Shader Language (GLSL) that is based on C. Unless you have experience writing GPU shaders, working with WebGL can be a little daunting to get started.

Luckily, a popular library called Three.js provides a high-level abstraction that enables you to start building 3-D in the browser without needing to worry about shaders. You can get Three.js and view a large number of examples at `http://mrdoob.github.com/three.js/`.

Although Three.js makes working with WebGL easier, 3-D programming can still be fairly complex. Some projects exist to make developing with Three.js even easier. One of the most popular is tQuery: `http://jeromeetienne.github.com/tquery/`.

tQuery aims to provide a jQuery-like interface on top of Three.js to make it easier to start and work with 3-D in the browser. Three.js also supports 3-D renderers other than WebGL, so some simple examples may run on mobile devices, but more complicated examples require the WebGL renderer be used.

The main sticking point from a mobile standpoint is that only one mobile browser, Opera 12, has WebGL enabled for general use. On the desktop every current-version browser except Internet Explorer has WebGL support, including Firefox, Chrome, Safari, and Opera. Microsoft has unfortunately not committed to providing support for WebGL at any point in the future, but given WebGL's popularity with developers, it seems a little like browser-suicide for Microsoft to continue that position.

Although WebGL is not yet available in mobile Safari, it is already turned on in iAds, so support is built in but disabled. If you have a jail-broken iPad, you can find resources to turn WebGL support back on. On Android, WebGL pops up on various places, such as the Xperia smartphone and demos of the Xoom tablet, but there's currently no timeline for support in Chrome for Android.

GETTING BETTER ACCESS TO SOUND WITH THE WEB AUDIO API

As you saw in Chapter 25, "Playing Sounds, the Mobile Achilles' Heel," sound in HTML5 on mobile devices is not well supported. The good news is that an extremely rich Audio API called the Web Audio API has made its way into the desktop versions of Chrome and Safari. The API can be a little daunting because it's low level but feature rich and is something a game developer would be used to rather than a web developer. The most recent published specification is available at `www.w3.org/TR/webaudio`.

If it gains wider browser support, the Web Audio API can provide a powerful audio layer for HTML5 games, enabling real-time creation and mixing of effects and music via JavaScript.

As of this writing Apple has announced that iOS 6 will have support for the audio API, but what level of support this will be and what restrictions will be placed on playing audio are yet to be determined. Because the Web Audio API is a project that Google first implemented in Chrome, it appears likely that the API will make its way into Chrome for Android in the near future.

As of this writing neither Microsoft, Mozilla, or Opera have announced any intention to support the API.

MAKING YOUR GAME BIGGER WITH THE FULL-SCREEN API

With the smaller screens available on mobile devices, anything you can do to maximize the screen real estate available to your game can benefit playability.

On the desktop, Firefox, Chrome, and Safari have added support for a full-screen API that enables you to indicate a single DOM element that should be shown full screen. The specification for this API is still in flux. A working draft is available at `http://dvcs.w3.org/hg/fullscreen/raw-file/tip/Overview.html`.

The API is currently available only with vendor prefixes in desktop browsers. No announcement of support has been made for mobile browsers, although Apple has announced that iOS 6 will have a full-screen landscape mode. This mode is different from a full-screen API but should still provide game developers with some extra screen space.

LOCKING YOUR DEVICE SCREEN WITH THE SCREEN ORIENTATION API

Some of the fun that game developers could have with the Device Orientation API, which you saw in Chapter 24, "Querying Device Orientation and Acceleration," was mitigated because the screen would rotate when you got past a certain point.

The good news is that there is a W3C specification that can enable web developers to both more accurately capture the current state of the screen orientation and lock the screen to a specific orientation. The working draft of this specification is available at `www.w3.org/TR/screen-orientation/`.

The only implementation available on devices as of this writing is in the Mozilla Android browser Fennec, but hopefully Chrome for Android and Mobile Safari will get this API in the future.

ADDING REAL-TIME COMMUNICATIONS WITH WEBRTC

The WebRTC project is an open project that aims to add real-time communications capabilities to web browsers via a JavaScript API. This includes the ability to make voice and video calls through both a centralized server and via peer-to-peer. This technology would be a great addition to two-player games to allow players to play against each other while staying in communication (among a myriad of other users).

The project has a website located at `www.webrtc.org` to go along with a draft specification available at `www.w3.org/TR/webrtc/`.

No current desktop browsers have support for WebRTC, but you can try out a version by using the Chrome development channel. See the WebRTC website for more details.

TRACKING OTHER UPCOMING NATIVE FEATURES

The Mozilla WebAPI project, on the web at `https://wiki.mozilla.org/WebAPI`, has links to other device-native features that are slowly being exposed via JavaScript APIs. Although the majority of these are only tangentially interesting to game developers, some, such as the Vibration API (`www.w3.org/TR/vibration/`), could be used for interesting game feedback.

Mozilla also has a project called AreWeFunYet (on the web at `www.arewefunyet.com`) that is set up to track how the Gecko is doing as a platform for gaming. Although a lot of the details are Mozilla-specific, the project is worth looking at.

The W3C also has a Games Community Group, on the web at `www.w3.org/community/games/`, dedicated to "improve the quality of open web standards that game developers rely on to create games." If you are interested in the future of HTML5 game development, this is a group worth joining.

SUMMARY

This chapter took a look at exciting APIs that, although currently out of reach for mobile HTML5 game developers, should be coming down the pipeline and into mobile browsers sometime in the near future. These APIs will give HTML5 game developers some of the same tools native app developers have to craft engaging experiences, in a cross-browser, multiplatform way.

With a look at what features are on the horizon, this book's journey through the world of HTML5 Mobile game development has come to an end. This book took you from the basics of putting together a simple Canvas-based game to building a full mobile-centric HTML5 game engine from the ground up. That engine was used to build a number of different games and demos using CSS, SVG, and, most importantly, Canvas. Along the way you were introduced to using libraries like Underscore.js and jQuery for game development and running JavaScript on the server with Node.js. You saw how to make your game available offline, connect it up to a NoSQL database, let players play against each other using Socket.io, and push it to the Internet at large using a hosting platform.

HTML5 is the technology that will give you access to an unprecedented number of potential players, any of which can access your game at any time from a supported mobile device or desktop browser. Now it's time to take what you've learned and build the next great game—one that will engage and entertain people around the globe and one that can spread as quickly as a link can travel across the data pipes of the Internet.

APPENDIX

Resources

This appendix contains a variety of highly recommended resources for further exploration of HTML5 and JavaScript.

BOOKS ON HTML5 AND JAVASCRIPT

For more information on HTML5 and JavaScript, the following books are recommended:

➤ *JavaScript: The Good Parts* by Douglas Crockford (O'Reilly, 2008): The seminal work that helped put JavaScript on the map as a "real language" and pushed a set of best practices for developers. Required reading for JavaScript developers.

➤ *JavaScript Patterns* by Stoyan Stefanov (O'Reilly, 2010): A great second book on JavaScript that pushes the language further and provides a number of different ways to bend JavaScript to your will.

➤ *Introducing HTML5 Game Development* by Jesse Freeman (O'Reilly, 2012): One of the first books on a single HTML5 game engine. An in-depth (but compact) guide to Impact.js.

➤ *Foundation HTML5 Canvas: For Games and Entertainment* by Robert Hawkes (friendsofED, 2011): A gentler yet thorough introduction to HTML5 canvas suitable for less experienced developers.

➤ *Foundation HTML5 Animation with JavaScript* by Billy Lamberta and Keith Peters (friendsofED, 2011): A book making things move in an interesting way using HTML5 Canvas.

➤ *HTML5 Games Most Wanted: Build the Best HTML5 Games* by Egor Kuryanovich, et al (friendsofED, 2012): An HTML5 cookbook including articles from a number of different authors on different HTML5 game development techniques.

➤ *Making Isometric Social Real-Time Games with HTML5, CSS3, and JavaScript* by Mario Andres Pagella (O'Reilly, 2011): A short book that focuses on a single genre of games and covers it quite well, providing the code needed to build the generation of social Facebook games.

WEB RESOURCES

For more information on HTML5 and JavaScript, the following web resources are recommended:

➤ `www.html5gamedevelopment.org`: A website run by the author tracking the latest trends in HTML5 game development.

➤ `www.html5gamedevs.com`: An active aggregator site that posts on the newest HTML5 games and game development news.

➤ `www.badassjs.com`: In-depth first-party posts on cutting edge JavaScript.

➤ `www.creativejs.com`: In-depth first-party posts on cool new stuff in JavaScript.

➤ `buildnewgames.com`: A Microsoft sponsored site with in-depth articles on various HTML5 game development topics.

➤ `javascriptweekly.com`: Not a website but a once-weekly newsletter that rounds up what's new in JavaScript that week. A must read for JavaScript developers.

➤ `www.html5rocks.com`: One of the most authoritative resources on HTML5 on the web. When a new API comes out, HTML5 Rocks usually is the first to post an in-depth article on it.

➤ `developer.mozilla.org`: In competition with the html5rocks site as the best resource for learning the newest HTML5 techniques.

➤ `www.lostdecadegames.com/lostcast`: A bi-weekly podcast by HTML5 game development company Lost Decade Games, often with special guests active in the HTML5 game development community.

➤ `www.chromeexperiments.com`: If it's cool and it's in JavaScript, you'll probably find it as a Chrome experiment. Visit here if you want to see how far you can push the browser.

INDEX

P

Q

X–Y–Z

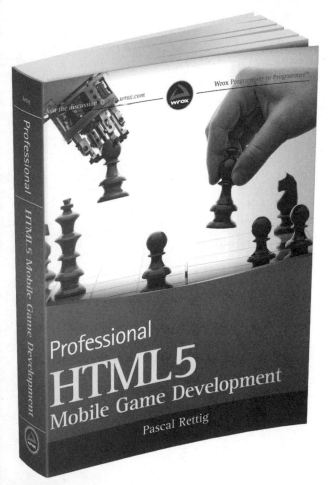